Bioarchaeology of Marginalized People

Bioarchaeology of Marginalized People

Edited by

Madeleine L. Mant
Memorial University, St. John's, NL, Canada

Alyson Jaagumägi Holland
McMaster University, Hamilton, ON, Canada

ELSEVIER

ACADEMIC PRESS
An imprint of Elsevier

Academic Press is an imprint of Elsevier
125 London Wall, London EC2Y 5AS, United Kingdom
525 B Street, Suite 1650, San Diego, CA 92101, United States
50 Hampshire Street, 5th Floor, Cambridge, MA 02139, United States
The Boulevard, Langford Lane, Kidlington, Oxford OX5 1GB, United Kingdom

British Library Cataloguing-in-Publication Data
A catalogue record for this book is available from the British Library

Library of Congress Cataloging-in-Publication Data
A catalog record for this book is available from the Library of Congress

ISBN: 978-0-12-815224-9

For Information on all Academic Press publications
visit our website at https://www.elsevier.com/books-and-journals

Publisher: Stacy Masucci
Acquisition Editor: Elizabeth Brown
Editorial Project Manager: Carlos Rodriguez
Production Project Manager: Bharatwaj Varatharajan
Cover Designer: Mark Rogers

Typeset by MPS Limited, Chennai, India

Dedication

This volume is dedicated to the memory of
Dr. Antonio de la Cova.

Contents

List of Contributors

Juanita Bascu Saskatchewan Population Health and Evaluation Research Unit

Heather T. Battles Anthropology, School of Social Sciences, University of Auckland, Auckland, New Zealand

Matthew Betts Eastern Archaeology Research, Canadian Museum of History, Gatineau, QC, Canada

Terence Clark Department of Archaeology & Anthropology, University of Saskatchewan, Saskatoon, SK, Canada

Gary Coupland Department of Anthropology, University of Toronto, Toronto, ON, Canada

Jerome S. Cybulski Research Division, Canadian Museum of History, Gatineau, QC, Canada; Department of Anthropology, University of Western Ontario, London, ON, Canada; Department of Archaeology, Simon Fraser University, Burnaby, BC, Canada

Carlina de la Cova Department of Anthropology, University of South Carolina, Columbia, SC, United States

Shelby L. Doubek Department of Anthropology, Loyola University, Chicago, IL, United States; Department of Anthropology, Field Museum of Natural History, Chicago, IL, United States

Steven Feschuk Department of Culture, shíshálh Nation, Sechelt, BC, Canada

Philippe Froesch Forensic Art 3D, Visualforensic, Paris, France

Rebecca Gowland Department of Archaeology, Durham University, Durham, United Kingdom

Anne Grauer Department of Anthropology, Loyola University, Chicago, IL, United States

Paul Hackett Saskatchewan Population Health and Evaluation Research Unit; Department of Geography and Planning, University of Saskatchewan, Saskatoon, SK, Canada

Joseph T. Hefner Department of Anthropology, Michigan State University, East Lansing, MI, United States

Alyson Jaagumagi Holland Department of Anthropology, McMaster University, Hamilton, ON, Canada

Bonnie Jeffery Saskatchewan Population Health and Evaluation Research Unit; School of Social Work, University of Regina, Prince Albert, SK, Canada

Raquel Joe Tems Swiya Museum, shíshálh Nation, Sechelt, BC, Canada

Nancy C. Lovell Department of Anthropology, University of Alberta, Edmonton, AB, Canada

Natalie C. Ludlow Department of Geography and Planning, University of Saskatchewan, Saskatoon, SK, Canada

Madeleine L. Mant Department of Archaeology, Memorial University of Newfoundland, St. John's, NL, Canada

Debra L. Martin Department of Anthropology, University of Nevada, Las Vegas, NV, United States

Tom McIntosh Saskatchewan Population Health and Evaluation Research Unit; Department of Politics and International Studies, University of Regina, Regina, SK, Canada

Nazeem Muhajarine Saskatchewan Population Health and Evaluation Research Unit; Department of Community Health and Epidemiology, University of Saskatchewan, Saskatoon, SK, Canada

Andrew J. Nelson Department of Anthropology, The University of Western Ontario, London, ON, Canada

Kimberley E. Palichuk Department of Anthropology, University of Alberta, Edmonton, AB, Canada

Jasmine Paul Stewardship and Territorial Lands Management Division, shíshálh Nation, Sechelt, BC, Canada

Rebecca Redfern Centre for Human Bioarchaeology, Museum of London, London, United Kingdom

Brittney K. Shields Wilford NAGPRA Division, Southeast Archeological Center, National Park Service, Tallahassee, FL, United States; Department of Archaeology, Durham University, Durham, United Kingdom

Gretchen Williams Canadian Museum of History, Gatineau, QC, Canada

Foreword

Do we see [human disparity] as a human predicament—an inescapable result of frailty of our existence? That would be correct had these sufferings been really inescapable, but they are far from that. Preventable diseases can indeed be prevented, curable ailments can certainly be cured, and controllable maladies call out for control. Rather than lamenting the adversity of nature, we have to look for a better comprehension of the social causes of horror and also of our tolerance of societal abominations

—Paul Farmer (2004, p. xii). *Pathologies of power: Health, human rights and the new war on the poor.*

For at least the last 40,000 years the archaeological record demonstrates varying forms of social inequality—surfacing first in nascent symbolic expressions of difference or distinction, perhaps most clearly in hunter–gatherer mortuary patterns. Then, some 10,000 years ago, various human populations made collective decisions to transition from foraging to farming economies and sedentary lifeways. Our species was forever and irreversibly transformed. Inequality bloomed almost everywhere, from Mesopotamia to the Americas. The forms, mode, and tempo of such developments varied remarkably. Yet, inequality seems to have been a near-inevitable component of how complex societies have organized themselves for some 400 generations and counting.

Institutionalized inequality can take many forms, such as perceived and enacted differences in virtue, intellect, sexuality, knowledge, ability, gender, access to resources, or whatever else humans contrive. Marginalization is one such form of inequality, often intertwined with socioeconomic hierarchies. Materialist concepts of top-down power envision one segment of society possessing and transferring commodities or controlling resources in a way that excludes another group. It may also involve the coercive power of one social collective over another, forcing the subordinate group into actions they might not normally do or that might not be in their best interest. Marginalization nearly always involves embedded, normalized structural inequalities that produce measurably greater expressions of segregation, suffering, stigmatization, morbidity, and mortality among the marginalized, hence Paul Farmer's "pathologies of power."

Bioarchaeology is uniquely positioned to explore intersections between inequality, marginalization, biological plasticity, and the social determinants of health across time and space. Concepts from social epidemiology help explain such phenomena where the nature of cultural environments generates socially constituted patterns of behaviors that are deeply (and often messily) dialectically intertwined with our biological states. We embody within us the biological productions of our social lives from our biochemistry to our bones—biological manifestations of stress hormones, aberrant DNA methylation patterns, immunocompetence, nutrition, growth, parasite load, violence, disease exposure, labor, and so forth. Along these lines, inequality and marginalization are subjects that represent some of the largest-scale and most important questions anthropologists can explore regarding the human condition. This topic also helps uncover some of the deepest, most profound, and fundamental biocultural mechanisms that shape our lives and the potential near-term biocultural trajectories of humanity.

The editors of this book have assembled a compelling series of papers that productively build upon past bodies of scholarship, represent multiple developing advances in bioarchaeological praxis and theory-building, and point the way toward future horizons, particularly though confrontation with very difficult and painful truths.

This edited volume achieves its goals on many levels. As bioarchaeologists and paleopathologists, we often must work from "known" to "unknown" involving many different kinds and layers of analogies drawn from the living. Along these lines, explorations of the social determinants of health, historical epidemiology, and skeletal evidence are seen in various chapters. These are the most compelling and jarring parts of the volume, demonstrating the vulnerabilities of the marginalized, such as children, victims of disease, the poor, and "the other," such as Africans in Medieval London. Marginalization also impacts so-called "dead body politics," and can extend to the treatment of human remains centuries beyond death.

The editors and authors open many doors that reveal new horizons. Many chapters set the stage for a next step involving fuller bioarchaeological perspectives on personhood, and how and why human societies construct and deconstruct the value(s) of human life. These works also indicate the importance of incorporating more elements from health theory, life history theory, structural violence theory, the political economy of biocultural inequality, and applicable concepts from the bodies of work by Paul Farmer, Nancy Krieger, Phillipe Bourgois, Clarence Gravlee, and others. That is, I see a bioarchaeology of marginalization as a canvas upon which new theoretical syntheses await to coalesce. There is also the rather daunting challenge of properly articulating developmental biology and epigenetics with bioarchaeology. Phenomena such as the in utero programming of the adult health immune response and the insidious effects of health marginalization vis-à-vis intergenerational epigenetic inertia are just two examples. Such phenomena were certainly operating in the past and shaped the biological expressions of marginalization manifested in skeletal samples. We cannot observe them directly since these are longitudinal phenomena, and skeletal samples are cross-sectional snapshots. A careful, long-term, and multidisciplinary synthesis between the two is perhaps possible, but we are not there yet.

Another axis of this book revolves around deeply disquieting themes that require direct confrontation. That is, anthropologists have long been a tool of marginalization, perpetuating inequality, racism, injustice, and the status quo since the days of Samuel Morton, Nott and Glidden, Carlton Coon, and other 19th- and 20th-century practitioners. Several authors draw sharp attention to the fact that the modern investigator can be an agent of marginalization, and an uncritical and nonreflexive anthropology is a mirror upon our own deeply held biases and structural inequities. Martin's chapter is a particularly refreshing up-ending of typological thinking and exposure of our own bias. de la Cova's contribution is a powerful work that perhaps should be required reading for all students of anthropology. Indeed, it is a moving indictment against the very foundations of physical anthropology and bioarchaeology—which are built upon the bones of the most marginalized, powerless, and dispossessed members of our own society. Many of the 19th- and 20th-century skeletal collections used to establish standards of age estimation, sex estimation, metric variation, ancestry, and skeletal pathology were those of people who never consented to such use of their mortal remains because they did not have the ability to do so. The founders of our discipline took advantage of inherently structurally violent relationships, either consciously or unconsciously. This reality should cut us to our very core.

So where do we go from here? Much of bioarchaeology is grounded in empirical science. Yet, when exploring a social phenomenon such as marginalization, we are confronted with its reality today and presence in our own lives. As we strive and sometimes struggle to be ethical, moral, and just human beings, there are clearly actions to undertake that constructively address marginalization within anthropology and beyond. In this volume, Nelson's study of identity and personhood of a Roman Period Egyptian mummy considers a return of some degree of agency to the long dead. Clark et al.'s work describes a community-based partnership with members of the shíshálh Nation. They explore ways of returning humanity to the remains of once vital, living human beings who had become nothing more than accession numbers and museum "specimens" simply because their humanity counted less in the eyes of those who colonized the Western Hemisphere.

We bear the anthropological capacity and the ethical imperative to understand the distrust of the marginalized. We must listen. We must also realize that our authority and our privilege are far from immutable, and we must perhaps cede control over research questions, sampling, data, and publishing. Instead of historically extractive approaches, intense, mutually constitutive community engagements and lifelong relationships must be built. Mentoring and training students from marginalized populations are vital, but are also a top-down approach. These issues resonate particularly with Wade's (2018) recent look at the complex and painful relationships between indigenous peoples and anthropological geneticists. The SING (Summer Internship for Indigenous Peoples in Genomics) program funded jointly by the NIH and NSF trains indigenous scientists in genomics to both introduce genetic tools to their communities as well as bring their long-needed perspective and concerns to scholarly research—supporting indigenous sovereignty rather than undermining it. Savannah Martin, a doctoral student in biological anthropology at Washington University in St. Louis and a member of the Confederated Tribes of Siletz Indians in Oregon, put it this way: at SING, "you can exist as your authentic self, as both Indigenous and as a scientist, without having to code-switch all the time. It's like coming up for air" (Wade, 2018, p. 1305).

This book, with its strong reflexive qualities, brings forth calls for social justice. Bioarchaeologies of advocacy and activism will find much to reflect upon here as we add our collective and distinctly powerful voices to the growing chorus seeking social change, decolonization, empowerment of the dispossessed, and biologically healthier societies where the potential of all people can be more fully realized. This is going to be a hard, multigenerational task. Taking several steps back to consider the larger picture, we live in a world today witnessing progressive erosion of liberal democratic institutions, the rise of largely unchallenged authoritarians and powerful oligarchs, wholly negative forms of anthropogenic climate change, and unsustainable imbalances of wealth and socioeconomic capital in the hands of a very few. Antiintellectualism is increasingly celebrated as science is mocked. The marginalized grow in number as I write these words.

Given the predictive power that can come from cross-cultural and diachronic anthropological studies of human societies, it is safe to say that such conditions are a formula for egregious human suffering and societal self-destruction. Following Paul Farmer, work contained in books such as this helps us to understand the causes and tolerances of social horrors, but what we should choose to do with such knowledge draws me to one of Sagan's (1980) reflections on the near-term human future. He argued that the present moment represents the unfolding of a branch point of human history. We can choose a path of least resistance, of dystopia and of self-destruction. Far more difficult, it would seem, is the only possible alternative: to purposefully harness our capacities of creativity, compassion, wealth, and technology to make more abundant and meaningful lives for every inhabitant of this planet. No one else is going to do this *for* us. It is in our hands alone.

Haagen D. Klaus
Department of Sociology and Anthropology, George Mason University, Fairfax, VR, United States

References

Farmer, P. (2004). *Pathologies of power: Health, human rights and the new war on the poor.* Oakland, CA: University of California Press.

Sagan, C., Druyan, A., Soter, S., Malone, A., Weidlinger, T., Haines-Stiles, G., ... Gibson, K. (1980). *Cosmos: a personal voyage.* Studio City, CA: Cosmos Studios.

Wade, L. (2018). Bridging the gap. *Science, 361*(6409), 1304–1307.

Acknowledgments

Our deepest thanks go to Elsevier's Elizabeth Brown, who worked with us on *Beyond the Bones* in 2016 and queried if we had any more ideas—there are always ideas, but it takes the support of individuals like Liz to turn them into tangible results. Thank you also to Carlos Rodriguez, who graciously answered our many questions and made the editorial and production processes a real joy, and to Dr. Rachel Ives for her enthusiasm for this project and for livening up several London Tube trips with discussions of marginalization in the past. Many thanks to all of our contributors, who accepted our invitation and provided such thoughtful manuscripts. We are grateful for the team of reviewers who provided generous and constructive commentary on these varied chapters. Thank you also to Dr. Haagen Klaus for writing the foreword, and to our families for their continued support.

Chapter 1

Introduction

Madeleine L. Mant[1] and Alyson Jaagumagi Holland[2]
[1]*Department of Archaeology, Memorial University of Newfoundland, St. John's, NL, Canada,*
[2]*Department of Anthropology, McMaster University, Hamilton, ON, Canada*

Chapter Outline

Scholars in many disciplines have wrestled with topics surrounding the marginalization of individuals in past and contemporary populations. Marginalization can take many forms; while commonly viewed as a social process, whereby members perceived to be part of a specific group are treated differently than others in a society, marginalization can also be physical, cultural, economic, or political. Social theorists and clinicians have engaged with the topic of marginalization largely by examining the processes by which people become peripheralized in society and how these resulting "positions of ambiguity" (Lynam & Cowley, 2007, p. 141) come to affect health and resilience. The notion of marginalization as being ambiguous recognizes the liminal social space that the marginalized occupy. They are viewed as similar to the rest of their society, but also set apart as something "other." This liminality affects access; being part of a dominant social network is a major mechanism by which people gain access to resources, and a lack of belonging (and therefore resources) can manifest as differential changes to health status. While the mechanisms through which marginalization occurs are broad, Hall (2016) identifies a suite of marginalizing dynamics in the clinical sphere, including scapegoating, stigmatization, bullying, exclusion, incarceration, deprivation of basic resources, control, symbolic violence, microaggressions, implicit biases, and toxic environmental exposures. These methods share a common endpoint and emphasize that "marginalization is central to the nexus of person-health-environment" (Hall, 2016, p. 200). These processes are painfully universal and diachronic, which make marginalization such an important area of study. Through differential access to resources and the resulting emotional, physical, and cognitive stress, the act of being marginalized has potential chronic effects upon individuals' physical and mental health that may be underreported and underrecognized. In bioarchaeology,

Bioarchaeology of Marginalized People. DOI: https://doi.org/10.1016/B978-0-12-815224-9.00001-4

marginalization offers a route to explore not just diseased states, but the underlying forces that drive health and disease.

The embodiment of a marginalized state, which is the epidemiological concept of the synthesis of the environment into one's physical body, is of interest to bioarchaeologists. Social epidemiologists have explored this theme, defining embodiment as the "cumulative interplay between exposure, susceptibility and resistance" (Krieger, 2001, p. 672). Krieger (2005, p. 350) goes farther to emphasize that embodiment is literal, that bodies tell important stories about "spatial, temporal, and multilevel processes," a concept that is central to bioarchaeology where these stories are quite literally read from the bones. Skeletal remains are examined for markers of stress and inequality; biological markers of slowed growth and long-term infections alongside evidence of interpersonal violence are placed within their cultural contexts to provide interpretations of complex topics such as structural violence (e.g., Klaus, 2012; Martin, Harrod, & Fields, 2010) and slavery (e.g., Dent, 2017; Martin & Osterholtz, 2016; Shuler, 2011).

Through embodiment the adult skeleton is a record of lived experience "in both its strength and frailty" (Agarwal & Beauchesne, 2011, p. 314). Bone is both a lasting record of human lives and a living tissue with incredible plasticity that allows the body to remain "contextually dependent" (Sofaer, 2006, p. 161) as it changes in response to an individual's environment. Bioarchaeologists are tasked with the challenge of retrospectively identifying these events using only the final alterations made to bone. Theoretical approaches that borrow from the clinical literature present useful frameworks for attempting to uncover the sequences of events that led to observed skeletal alterations. The Developmental Origins of Health and Disease hypothesis, which views lifetime health changes as the product of exposures during key development periods, provides a useful lens into how the effects of this plasticity can be seen over the life course, and how it can extend beyond the individual to their parents and offspring. In the context of bioarchaeology, it has the potential to help disentangle the intergenerational effects of various health risks, though there is much to be learned about the relationship of epigenetics to skeletal manifestations of disease (Gowland, 2015). Bioarchaeological attention to the Barker hypothesis—stressful events in an individual's early life history have negative health consequences in adulthood—contributes to a deeper understanding of the role of frailty and the synergistic complications of stresses such as infectious diseases and chronic undernutrition (Armelagos, Goodman, Harper, & Blakey, 2009).

Socioeconomic status (SES) is an important mechanism by which differential health risks emerge. Marginalization and health are intimately tied to SES as it is the complex interplay between social standing and economic worth that determines access to resources. Studies that aim to elicit SES are critical for questions of marginalization since the distinctions between groups in the past, just as today, were not always clear and discrete. People's fortunes may change throughout their life courses, scrambling the signals that may be read from their bones. Reflecting upon the nexus of factors, including neighborhood conditions, working conditions, education, income, race, and stress, in addition to children's early experiences, is critical in understanding the mosaic of factors that may affect an individual's position in society. The relationship of SES and biological frailty has been investigated (DeWitte, Hughes-Morey, Bekvalac, & Karsten, 2016), revealing SES to be a strong predictor of mortality. Frailty is not equal across populations, however, and social theorists engaging with the social determinants of health address questions concerning inequality and health and wellness outcomes. Marmot (2005), working with contemporary living populations, emphasizes the clear connections existing between the SES of households and excess mortality rates. Braveman, Egerter, and Williams (2011, p. 384) explore the "stepwise social gradients" present today, acknowledging that while the differences between those of high and low SES are extreme, individuals falling in the middle also appear to be less healthy than the richest and/or best educated.

Assessing intangible concepts such as SES require analysis beyond the skeleton, looking at the mortuary practices themselves. Unequal treatment of the dead, seen in differential burial practices and varied grave goods within a population, remind us that the dead do not bury themselves. Mortuary practices that suggest inequalities reflect most strongly how the living viewed the dead and their place within society, which can then be compared to the physical evidence gained from their bones to approach an understanding of an individual's embodied experience. Murphy's edited collection (2008, p. xii) explores deviant burials in the archaeological record, noting that some individuals such as "criminals, women who died during childbirth, unbaptised infants, people with disabilities, and supposed revenants" may appear in different burial contexts in relation to other members of a population. Recognizing nonnormative burial patterns and evidence of necrophobia allows for the interpretation of potential marginalization during life and after death. Quinn and Beck (2016) examine both the lived (osteological evidence) and performed (mortuary context) aspects of identity to explore the contributions of economic, ideological, and political factors to an individual's position in society. This study demonstrates the power of bioarchaeology to explore embodied inequalities both synchronically and diachronically. Other authors have discussed biocultural models of systemic stress and violence (e.g., Harrod, 2012; Klaus & Tam, 2009; Robbins Schug, Gray, Mushrif-Tripathy, & Sankhyan, 2012) through a combination of bioarchaeological and archaeological evidence, underlining the importance of context in shedding light on past lives. Stigma and blame relating to syphilis, a disease associated with sexual and moral dangers, often led to social exclusion in postmedieval societies; Zuckerman (2017) found in her study of four postmedieval cemeteries in London that there was no evidence of nonnormative burial of individuals with syphilis. This research emphasizes the care that must be taken when dealing with the complex factors and context surrounding marginalization: intense pressures to bury the dead quickly due to high mortality rates and the pressures of poverty may have outweighed the desire to separate the stigmatized. Mortuary communities then cannot be assumed to represent "the members of an actual lived, dynamic, and interacting community in the past" (Zuckerman, 2017, p. 98). Robbins Schug (2016) explores the archaeological and textual evidence relating to leprosy in South Asia, concluding that stigma has not been constant through time and that individuals with leprosy were not consistently treated as "others."

The process of becoming marginalized is not limited to an individual's lifespan; contemporary understandings or representations of past peoples can contribute to marginalization. There is the potential for past and present human groups to be "forgotten" or ignored, leading to underrepresentation or erasure of their experiences. In this sense, marginalization may be considered "a sense of being overlooked, categorized or misrepresented" (Lynam & Cowley, 2007, p. 146). Cultural representation of Indigenous groups in museums is a key example that has come to the fore in museum studies (e.g., Kirshenblatt-Gimblett, 1998; Tuhiwai Smith, 2010; Unruh, 2015), with emphasis that Indigenous peoples should be provided the space to speak for themselves rather than continuing to be potentially misrepresented by other, colonizing powers. Power and influence emerge as important themes in how the marginalized come to be represented, especially with reference to memorialization and collective social remembrance. Fanning writes that "institutionalized social memories are created by the privileged" (2010, p. 127) in reference to the seemingly forgotten 1918 influenza pandemic, which has only relatively recently received attention by scholars (Phillips, 2014). When the dominant historical narratives are taken at face value, there is a risk of missing groups of stakeholders and of continuing to advance historical misremembering and marginalization. The relative roles of disease victims, the survivors, and the wider society must be considered when examining potential lacunae in collective remembering and memorialization.

Interest in topics relating to identity and marginalization in bioarchaeology has resulted in the recent publication of several excellent volumes. Stodder and Palkovich's (2012) *The Bioarchaeology of Individuals* and Knudson and Stojanowski's (2009) *Bioarchaeology and Identity in the Americas* use osteobiographies and a focus on the individualized experiences of people in the past to demonstrate the depth of understanding that may be drawn from a contextualized skeleton. These works respond to a need to identify and celebrate the individuals that make up past populations, resisting the top-down approach of previous explorations of the past and focusing on the individual actors within a skeletal cohort. Volumes such as *Bioarchaeology of Impairment and Disability* (Eds. Byrnes & Muller, 2017), *The Bioarchaeology of Dissection and Autopsy in the United States*

(Ed. Nystrom, 2017), *The Bioarchaeology of Violence* (Eds. Martin, Harrod, & Pérez, 2012), and *Broken Bones, Broken Bodies: Bioarchaeological and Forensic Approaches for Accumulative Trauma and Violence* (Eds. Tegtmeyer & Martin, 2017) demonstrate the profound interest in the interpretation of lives affected by potential marginalizing factors such as nonnormative bodies, postmortem dissection, and various forms of interpersonal violence.

It is our hope that *The Bioarchaeology of Marginalization* can add to this conversation through problematizing and challenging the breadth of the definition of marginalization. Through the papers in this volume, we showcase the varied approaches that are being used to identify groups who may have been marginalized during their lives and, in some cases, after their deaths using bioarchaeological and historical demographic methods. Borrowing from broader anthropological theory, this volume engages with those that have been "othered" in a broad range of ways—some were segregated, stigmatized, or forgotten, while others apparently separated themselves from larger groups with beneficial effects on their health.

Contributions

This volume aims to problematize the complex topic of marginalization by studying human bodies through time, highlighting individuals from disparate contexts.

Nelson (Chapter 2: Mummies, memories, and marginalization: the changing social roles of a mummy from ancient to modern times) and Lovell and Palichuk's (Chapter 3: Task activity and tooth wear in a woman of Ancient Egypt) contributions examine two Ancient Egyptian women through different lenses surrounding marginalization. Nelson explores the lived experiences and postmortem life of Lady Hudson, a Roman Period (30 BC to AD 395) mummy, whose remains took a journey from Egypt, eventually residing in the Department of Anthropology at Western University. He discusses four types of identity: personal, mortuary, curated, and bioarchaeological, showing that marginalization may occur at many stages of one's life and highlighting how bioarchaeological and historical studies of human remains may return some agency to an individual whose remains persist in the present. Lovell and Palichuk delve into the lived experience of an Ancient Egyptian woman through a detailed examination of her dentition. They draw attention to how the experiences of professional women in Ancient Egypt have been marginalized by the overall lack of evidence concerning the roles of women, and from what is known, prevailing depictions of quotidian activities that essentially eliminate women from craftsmanship positions. The distinctive patterning on this particular individual's teeth helps to shed light on one woman's occupation, bringing much needed attention to the diversity of women's work in this society.

Clark and colleagues (Chapter 4: Looking into the eyes of the Ancient Chiefs of Shíshálh: the osteology and facial reconstructions of a 4000-year-old high status family) highlight a successful example of a community-based partnership in which members of the shíshálh Nation and a team of archaeologists created an installation in the Canadian Museum of History celebrating the lives of shíshálh ancestors. In many unfortunate cases, Indigenous individuals have previously been reduced to marginalized "objects" of study in museums; this project demonstrates how powerful and ethical partnerships between Indigenous and academic groups can create mutually beneficial results.

Redfern and Hefner (Chapter 5: "Officially absent but actually present": bioarchaeological evidence for population diversity in London during the Black Death, AD 1348–50) integrate bioarchaeological and statistical techniques to interrogate the evidence for the presence of individuals with Black African ancestry in Medieval London, United Kingdom, using the Black Death skeletal population from East Smithfield. The 14th-century primary evidence for the presence of individuals with Black African ancestry or dual heritage was supported by the bioarchaeological evidence, providing a wealth of new information for a group whose history has been previously overlooked in bioarchaeological contexts, while also addressing the limitations of this type of data.

Martin (Chapter 6: Marginalized by choice—Kayenta Pueblo communities in the Southwest (AD 800–1500)) challenges the notion of marginalization as an inherently negative status. Her exploration of Kayenta Pueblo communities in the American Southwest (AD 800–1500) reveals a group of people living an environmentally marginalized existence. Martin concludes that the inward focus of the Kayenta likely reduced their risk of trauma, warfare, and nutritional and infectious diseases, suggesting that a population's marginal status may, under certain circumstances, have positive effects upon health.

de la Cova (Chapter 7: Marginalized bodies and the construction of American anatomical collections) challenges bioarchaeologists to examine the complex foundations of the Hamann-Todd, Robert J. Terry, and William Montague Cobb anatomical collections. Foundational studies of biological anthropological methods were conducted upon these collections, which were comprised of the bodies of marginalized individuals who did not provide their consent for their bodies to be donated to medicine. Demographic analyses of the Terry Collection reveal that it was the most vulnerable individuals of St. Louis, MO—those deemed socially deviant, destitute, or the unclaimed dead—that make up the majority of the collection. de la Cova draws our attention to the structural violence inherent in the creation of such a collection and the importance of anthropologists acknowledging their hand in perpetuating this continued marginalization of the vulnerable. She explores themes of bioethics and respect in regard to these collections as a reminder that the living can continue to marginalize the dead.

Ludlow and Hackett (Chapter 8: Health inequity and spatial divides: infant mortality during Hamilton, Ontario's industrial transition, 1880–12) and Battles (Chapter 9: In the shadow of war: the forgotten 1916 polio epidemic in New Zealand) focus on documentary sources to explore marginalized bodies for which no physical remains are available for study. They each tackle disparate issues using historical documents, revealing geographical gradients of risk for vulnerable infants during industrialization and the marginalization of certain pasts through explicit patterns of remembering and forgetting. Ludlow and Hackett use a historical epidemiological approach with an ecological lens to investigate infant mortality and the shifting social gradient of health in a rapidly industrializing city in early 20th-century Canada. Infants are particularly vulnerable to environmental stressors such as sanitation and housing quality. The authors use infant mortality from diarrheal and infectious respiratory diseases to reveal patterns of marginalization through time. Battles examines the history of epidemic poliomyelitis in New Zealand during the First World War. She illustrates that despite copious contemporary public health attention to the epidemic, the outbreak and its victims have seemingly been forgotten. This marginalization or "collective forgetting" of the disease and its effects in public memory speak to the complex issues surrounding memorialization and how epidemics linked with war may become lost in the overwhelming and emotional commemoration of these events.

Doubek and Grauer (Chapter 10: Exploring the effects of structural inequality in an individual from 19th-century Chicago) employ osteobiography to investigate the structural inequalities experienced by one marginalized individual during his life and after his death. They examine both his skeletal remains, curated at the Field Museum of Natural History, and the accession records concerning his inclusion in the Rush Medical College anatomical study collection. The authors conclude that those who experienced marginalization during life were more likely to experience discrimination postmortem and aim to provide both dignity and context to the life of this particular individual. Shields Wilford and Gowland (Chapter 11: Down and out in postmedieval London: changes in welfare ideology and the impact on the health of workhouse inmates) integrate bioarchaeological and historical datasets to explore how changes in welfare ideology, as represented by the New Poor Laws (AD 1834), may have affected individuals in English parish workhouses. Evaluation of workhouse menus reveals a deficit of calories, vitamins, and minerals in reference to the strenuous work required of workhouse inmates. Increased evidence of metabolic disease through time suggests that nutritional inadequacies were an issue, revealing how large-scale economic and political processes may become incorporated into individual bodies.

The final paper by Hackett and colleagues (Chapter 12: Innovation in population health intervention research: a historical perspective) draws attention to the effects of marginalization upon health inequalities faced by individuals living today through population health intervention research, drawing upon historical sources. This paper uses the example of the Saskatchewan

Population Health and Evaluation Research Unit to highlight the methodological innovations which aid in contextualizing the social determinants of health and predicting the potential outcomes of contemporary health interventions.

Engaging with a wealth of archaeological, bioarchaeological, and historical evidence, the authors "read" for marginalization in the bioarchaeological and historical record, expanding the potential definitions of marginalization and affording past individuals further agency in the present.

References

Agarwal, S. C., & Beauchesne, P. (2011). It is not carved in bone: Development and plasticity of the aged skeleton. In S. C. Agarwal, & B. A. Glencross (Eds.), *Social bioarchaeology* (pp. 312–332). Chichester: Wiley-Blackwell.

Armelagos, G. J., Goodman, A. H., Harper, K. N., & Blakey, M. L. (2009). Enamel hypoplasia and early mortality: Bioarchaeological support for the Barker hypothesis. *Evolutionary Anthropology*, *18*, 261–271.

Braveman, P., Egerter, S., & Williams, D. R. (2011). The social determinants of health: Coming of age. *Annual Review of Public Health*, *32*, 381–398.

Byrnes, J. F., & Muller, J. L. (Eds.), (2017). *Bioarchaeology of impairment and disability: Theoretical, ethnohistorical, and methodological perspectives*. Cham: Springer.

Dent, S. (2017). Individual differences in embodied marginalization: Osteological and stable isotope analyses of antebellum enslaved individuals. *American Journal of Human Biology*, *29*(4), e23021.

DeWitte, S. N., Hughes-Morey, S., Bekvalac, J., & Karsten, J. (2016). Wealth, health and frailty in industrial-era London. *Annals of Human Biology*, *43*(3), 241–254.

Fanning, P. J. (2010). *Influenza and inequality: One town's tragic response to the Great Epidemic of 1918*. Amherst and Boston, MA: University of Massachusetts Press.

Gowland, R. L. (2015). Entangled lives: Implications of the developmental origins of health and disease hypothesis for bioarchaeology and the life course. *American Journal of Physical Anthropology*, *158*, 530–540.

Hall, J. M. (2016). Marginalization: A revisitation with integration of scholarship on globalization, intersectionality, privilege, microaggressions, and implicit biases. *Advances in Nursing Science*, *39*(3), 200–215.

Harrod, R. P. (2012). Centers of control: Revealing elites among the Ancestral Pueblo during the "Chaco Phenomenon". *International Journal of Paleopathology*, *2*, 123–135.

Kirshenblatt-Gimblett, B. (1998). *Destination culture: Tourism, museums, and heritage*. Berkeley, CA: University of California Press.

Klaus, H. D. (2012). The bioarchaeology of structural violence: A theoretical model and a case study. In D. L. Martin, R. P. Harrod, & V. R. Pérez (Eds.), *The bioarchaeology of violence* (pp. 29–62). Gainesville, FL: University Press of Florida.

Klaus, H. D., & Tam, M. E. (2009). Contact in the Andes: Bioarchaeology of systemic stress in Colonial Mórrope, Peru. *American Journal of Physical Anthropology*, *138*, 356–368.

Knudson, K. J., & Stojanowski, C. M. (Eds.), (2009). *Bioarchaeology and identity in the Americas*. Gainesville, FL: University Press of Florida.

Krieger, N. (2001). Theories for social epidemiology in the 21st century: An ecosocial perspective. *International Epidemiological Association*, *30*, 668–677.

Krieger, N. (2005). Embodiment: A conceptual glossary for epidemiology. *Journal of Epidemiology and Community Health, 59*(5), 350–355.

Lynam, M. J., & Cowley, S. (2007). Understanding marginalization as a social determinant of health. *Critical Public Health, 17*(2), 137–149.

Marmot, M. (2005). Social determinants of health inequalities. *Lancet, 365*, 1099–1104.

Martin, D. L., Harrod, R. P., & Fields, M. (2010). Beaten down and worked to the bone: Bioarchaeological investigations of women and violence in the Ancient Southwest. *Landscape of Violence, 1*(1), Article 3.

Martin, D. L., Harrod, R. P., & Pérez, V. R. (Eds.), (2012). *The bioarchaeology of violence*. Gainesville, FL: University Press of Florida.

Martin, D. L., & Osterholtz, A. J. (2016). Broken bodies and broken bones: Biocultural approaches to ancient slavery and torture. In M. K. Zuckerman, & D. L. Martin (Eds.), *New directions in biocultural anthropology* (pp. 471–490). Hoboken, NJ: John Wiley & Sons.

Murphy, E. M. (Ed.), (2008). *Deviant burial in the archaeological record*. Oxford: Oxbow Books.

Nystrom, K. C. (Ed.), (2017). *The bioarchaeology of dissection and autopsy in the United States*. Cham: Springer.

Phillips, H. (2014). The recent wave of 'Spanish' flu historiography. *Social History of Medicine, 27*(4), 789–808.

Quinn, C. P., & Beck, J. (2016). Essential tensions: A framework for exploring inequality through mortuary archaeology and bioarchaeology. *Open Archaeology, 2*(1), 18–41.

Robbins Schug, G. (2016). Begotten of corruption? Bioarchaeology and "othering" of leprosy in South Asia. *International Journal of Palaeopathology, 15*, 1–9.

Robbins Schug, G., Gray, K., Mushrif-Tripathy, V., & Sankhyan, A. R. (2012). A peaceful realm? Trauma and social differentiation at Harappa. *International Journal of Paleopathology, 2*, 136–147.

Shuler, K. A. (2011). Life and death on a Barbadian sugar plantation: Historic and bioarchaeological view of infection and mortality at Newton Plantation. *International Journal of Osteoarchaeology, 21*, 66–81.

Sofaer, J. (2006). *The body as material culture: A theoretical osteoarchaeology*. Cambridge: Cambridge University Press.

Stodder, A. L. W., & Palkovich, A. M. (Eds.), (2012). *The bioarchaeology of individuals*. Gainesville, FL: University Press of Florida.

Tegtmeyer, C. E., & Martin, D. L. (Eds.), (2017). *Broken bones, broken bodies: Bioarchaeological and forensic approaches for accumulative trauma and violence*. Lanham: Lexington Books.

Tuhiwai Smith, L. (2010). *Decolonizing methodologies*. New York: St. Martin's Press.

Unruh, L. (2015). Dialogical curating: Towards Aboriginal self-representation in museums. *Curator: The Museum Journal, 58*(1), 77–89.

Zuckerman, M. K. (2017). The "poxed" and the "pure": A bioarchaeological investigation of community and marginalization relative to infection with acquired syphilis in post-medieval London. *Archeological Papers of the American Anthropological Association, 28*(1), 91–103.

Chapter 2

Mummies, memories, and marginalization: the changing social roles of a mummy from ancient to modern times

Andrew J. Nelson
Department of Anthropology, The University of Western Ontario, London, ON, Canada

Chapter Outline

Introduction

The subject of this contribution is a mummy from Ancient Egypt, affectionately referred to as "Lady Hudson." We do not know her real name; this mummy was named "Lady Hudson" in honor of the blanket in her coffin that is reminiscent of a Hudson's Bay blanket [actually a 19th-century trade blanket from France (H. Tichenor, Hudson's Bay Heritage Department, personal communication, 2004)]. Thus the name imperfectly reflects one small aspect of her identity. There are two goals for this contribution. The first is to examine Lady Hudson's identit*ies* and how she embodies her lived experiences, and the second is to examine the experiences she has had in her afterlife. In keeping with the theme of this volume, this examination will be undertaken using the lens of marginalization. Whether or not one is

Bioarchaeology of Marginalized People. DOI: https://doi.org/10.1016/B978-0-12-815224-9.00002-6

marginalized depends on one's identity and one's "associations, experiences and environments" (Hall, Stevens, & Meleis, 1994, p. 25). I will seek to demonstrate that Lady Hudson's identity has changed repeatedly over the past 2000 years, and so too has the nature and degree of her marginalization. This journey will take us into the deep past to follow, as best we can, "the physical and symbolic transformations bodies undergo as they pass through life, into death and beyond" (Geller & Suri, 2014, p. 509).

Some Preliminaries

Marginalization

Before getting into Lady Hudson's story, it is necessary to make it clear how I will use the term "marginalization." In addition, I will follow Buikstra and Scott's (2009, p. 43) advice that scholars should "define meaning explicitly at the outset of any publication," by briefly exploring some other relevant theoretical concepts.

The definition of the term "marginalization," as used here, can be traced back to the work of the sociologist Robert Park in the 1920s. Park (1928) was concerned with the effects of migration and racial relations, which brought individuals from one culture into the context of a second, majority culture. The migrant, who Park referred to as "The Marginal Man," was considered to be "a man of two cultures and two societies, which never completely interpenetrated and fused" (Park, 1928, p. 892). This concept was elaborated by Stonequist (1961), who emphasized that marginalization often led to cultural conflict, and Dickie-Clark (1966) who noted that the relationship between the two groups was necessarily hierarchical. Park (1928) argued that the resulting changes in both cultures led to the progress of civilization, but other authors (cf., Berry & Sam, 2003) have focused on the fact that the consequences for the individuals involved are often negative.

The negative aspects of marginalization have stimulated several detailed papers in the field of nursing (e.g., Hall, 1999; Hall et al., 1994; Vasas, 2005). As medical practitioners, nurses are concerned with identifying and effectively treating vulnerable (marginalized) people. Hall et al. (1994, pp. 24–25) suggested that "*margins* are defined as the peripheral, boundary determining aspects of persons, social networks, communities and environments" and "*marginalization* is defined as the process through which persons are peripheralized on the basis of their identities, associations, experiences and environments" (emphasis in original). The margins are defined with reference to a normative center and everyone who does not fit that center is therefore marginalized, or "othered." From the anthropological perspective, marginalization is "that complex and disputatious process by which means certain people and ideas are privileged over others at any given time" (Tucker, 1990, p. 19). Arnold (1995) argued, from the perspective of cultural evolution, that marginalization was the result of internal power differentiation in stratified societies that leads to some individuals having power (being at the center) and others not (being at the margins). Thus recent connotations of marginalization have moved beyond Park's binary racial context to more nuanced, multifaceted considerations of hierarchy and privilege.

For the purposes of this contribution, I will define marginalization as the identification and differentiation of individuals who are defined as other/peripheral, from those individuals who occupy a culturally defined normative, dominant center. This definition is placed within the context of specific social environments, which themselves may shift over time, changing the definitions of center and periphery. This concept of marginalization is multifactorial, dynamic, structural, relational, and socially constituted. As such, can a mummy, who is no longer capable of being socially relational, be said to be marginalized?

The question of whether a mummy can be marginalized can be addressed with reference to the recent discussions about whether dead bodies/bones have agency (see Crandall & Martin, 2014; Geller & Suri, 2014; Tung, 2014). Like marginalization, agency implies intentionality, where a willful act seeks to make a difference to the social order (Tung, 2014 citing Bourdieu, 1977 and Giddens, 1984), which would seem to negate the possibility that inanimate things can exercise agency. However, Robb (2004), following in the footsteps of art and museum theorists (e.g., Gell, 1998; Pearce, 1992), has argued that inanimate objects can have a kind of agency, depending on how social actors understand and feel about the object. Moreover, Crandall and Martin (2014) have argued that human remains, in the form of *memento mori*, saints' relics, skeletons, and mummies, have the power to shape social relations, behavior, and action because they embody the essence of humanity, they reflect our mortality, and they record the history in life and after death of the individual. Thus from the emic perspective, human remains have agency in a specific cultural context and understanding. This would be described from the etic perspective as secondary, or effective agency (following Gell, 1998 and Robb, 2004, respectively), where agency is projected by live actors onto the dead remains [in essence, giving them a soul (Pearce, 1992)]. In this sense a mummy is socially relational and capable of being marginalized precisely because she was once a live human being, and her mortal remains have agency and sociality because social actors give them those properties.

Identity

Whether one is identified as being marginalized depends on one's identity. Knudson and Stojanowski (2009, p. 1) defined identity as "people's perceptions of themselves and how they relate to larger social phenomena that characterize their existences." Identity can also be imposed externally, such as cranial modification undertaken at birth as a marker of ethnic identity (e.g., Torres-Rouff & Knudson, 2017), the manipulation of identity that happens in the mortuary context (e.g., Chesson, 2001), and indeed the construction of the identity of an individual from an archaeological site by a modern bioarchaeologist (examples in Stoddard & Palkovich, 2012).

In recent years, "identity" has become an increasingly important methodological, analytical, and theoretical focus for the field of bioarchaeology. Several authors have stressed the multidimensionality of identity, incorporating aspects of ethnicity, gender, and disease (e.g., Buikstra & Scott, 2009; Knudson & Stojanowski, 2008, 2009; Meskell, 1999). This bioarchaeological identity is typically based on an osteobiography (the story of her life as told through her bones and, in this case, mummified tissues, after Saul & Saul [1989]), supplemented with information about the archaeological context, and biogeochemical and other analytical information (cf., Torres-Rouff & Knudson, 2017). Discussions of bioarchaeological identity are often grounded in embodiment theory (Buikstra & Scott, 2009), which recognizes that bodies are simultaneously biological and social beings and they tell the stories of their lives, and in the case of human remains, their afterlives (Borić & Robb, 2008; Krieger, 2004).

For the purposes of this chapter, I will define four different kinds of identity: *personal identity*, *mortuary identity*, *curated identity*, and *bioarchaeological identity*, each reflecting a different mode of social production of the identity. *Personal identity* corresponds to the Knudson and Stojanowski (2009) definition earlier. This identity shapes the body, is dynamic, and will change throughout life. *Mortuary identity* is the identity expressed during the mortuary ritual, which reflects the personal identity to some extent, but is subject to manipulation by the kin and community. This identity can reshape the body to reflect larger social structures and rituals. *Curated identity* is that projected onto the mummy by a curator, collector, conservator, or museum visitor (note that curator*ial* identity refers to the identity of the curator rather than the curated; see Tatsi, 2011). This identity will vary greatly depending on the context and the understandings and beliefs of the observer, which will shape the effective agency that they project onto the human remains. Finally, *bioarchaeological identity* is the identity referred to earlier, reconstructed by a bioarchaeologist. The objective is to "read" the body to understand the personal identity embodied within it, but it must necessarily be an imperfect reconstruction of that lived identity.

Lady Hudson

Lady Hudson is an Ancient Egyptian mummy. She lived and died in the Roman Period [30 BC to AD 395 (Shaw, 2000)] based on the fine herringbone pattern of her wrappings and the individual wrapping of her limbs and fingers

FIGURE 2.1 Lady Hudson's mummy. This image shows the herringbone wrapping style and dark coloration that is typical of the Roman Period of Ancient Egypt [30 BC to AD 395 (Shaw, 2000)]. The black bars visible on the red (gray in print version) blanket led some to believe that she was lying on a Hudson's Bay Company blanket. *Photo credit: Wendy Palmer, UWO Photography Club.*

(Aufderheide, 2003; Hamilton-Paterson, 1978; Riggs, 2010) (see Fig. 2.1). However, her arm position (crossed-pectoral) is more typical of the preceding Ptolemaic Period (Gray, 1972). Her outer wrappings consisted of at least three kinds of fabric. The outermost wrappings are made of fine plain weave linen, there was a second less fine weave beneath, and then a coarse fabric against the body. The outer layers were heavily impregnated with resin (Marion-Bellemare, 2004; Williams, 2004).

Personal Identity

Unfortunately, we know almost nothing of Lady Hudson's personal identity, while a great deal is known about the personal identity of some Egyptian mummies. For instance the hieroglyph-rich cartonnage of Tayesmutengebtiu (a.k.a. Tamut), a mummy in the British Museum, gives us this mummy's name, her occupation ("Chantress of Amun"), her social position ("Lady of the House"), the natal place of her mother, and name and occupation of her father (Khonsumose, a priest of Amun). We also know where she was found (Thebes) and her date (22nd Dynasty) (Taylor & Antoine, 2014).

Lady Hudson does have a coffin (see Fig. 2.2), but its style and C-14 date (Beta Analytic Sample 131127; radiocarbon age: 2900 ± 80BP; calibrated age: 2870 ± 80BP) suggest that it dates to the 21st Dynasty [1069–945 BC (Shaw, 2000)], approximately 1000 years older than Lady Hudson. Furthermore, its beard (now broken) indicates that it was made for a male. It has no name glyph, but even it if did, it would clearly not be hers. Such mismatches are not uncommon and could have resulted from the reuse of an older coffin in antiquity, or by a match created by tomb robbers and antiquities dealers in the days of the mummy trade (Pawlowski, 2004; Sampsell, 2015). Since the focus here is on Lady Hudson herself, I will not discuss the coffin further in this chapter.

Unfortunately, we do not know where Lady Hudson came from. Knowledge of one's geographic origins and those of one's ancestors are an important part of personal identity, particularly in the social construction of ethnicity (Knudson & Stojanowski, 2009). The first we know of Lady Hudson is that she was acquired by a Canadian collector, George Bannister, from an auction house in Brussels in the early 1960s. That is probably where she acquired the 19th-century French trade blanket, but we do not know how or when she got there from Egypt.

European interest in Egyptian antiquities was piqued by Napoleon's military and scientific campaign to Egypt in 1798 (Aufderheide, 2003) and reached fever pitch in the context of Victorian Orientalism and the discovery of King Tutankhamun's tomb in 1922. During this time, antiquities traders were active, including the Cairo Museum, which had its own *salle de vente* (Hagen & Ryholt, 2016). Bannister family lore suggests that a married archaeologist couple got the mummy out of Egypt and that the final dealer had connections with Egypt's King Farouk (therefore between 1936 and 1952). Further, it is believed that the dealer retired to a castle in France upon his retirement. Unfortunately, we have no additional evidence to shed light on this part of Lady Hudson's journey. However, she got from Egypt to Europe, it is likely that Lady Hudson and her coffin were brought together to increase their combined value and were then swept up into the mummy trade during this time.

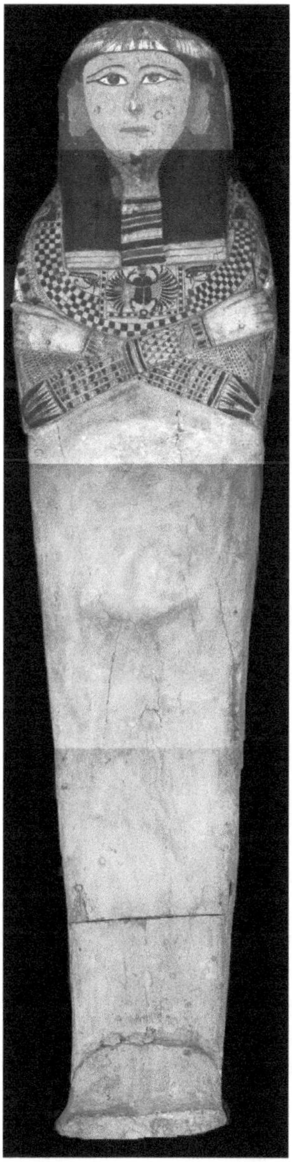

FIGURE 2.2 The coffin that accompanies Lady Hudson. The style and C-14 date are consistent with a 21st Dynasty date Dynasty [1069–945 BC (Shaw, 2000)]. *Photo credit: Andrew Nelson.*

Mortuary Identity

Fortunately, because of the rich archaeological and historical record that is available for Ancient Egypt, we can tell something about Lady Hudson's mortuary identity. Meskell has published extensively on the elements and meanings of the mortuary ritual of the New Kingdom Period of Egypt [1550–1069 BC (Shaw, 2000)] (e.g., Meskell, 2001) and many components of Roman Period mortuary rituals retained their dynastic character (Riggs, 2010). With colleague Andrew Wade, I have previously critiqued the monolithic application of the Herodotean "recipe" for mummification to the entire sweep of Ancient Egypt (e.g., Wade & Nelson, 2013a). However, Lady Hudson is close enough in time to the writings of the classical scholars that they can shed some light on the process of her mummification.

The Ancient Egyptians saw death as part of a cycle that included rebirth, where death was merely a transitory state during which the deceased person could continue to interact with the living (Meskell, 2001). A full afterlife required that the body be preserved, as the corporeal body and the spiritual soul were bound together (Meskell, 2001). There was a structure to the mortuary ritual that involved an extended period of separation (the length of which varies from source to source) for mourning, during which the body was desiccated in natron. In the Roman Period, the brain was commonly removed through the nose (more commonly than in earlier periods) rather than being left it in place or removed by other means (Wade, Nelson, & Garvin, 2011). The viscera were removed in this period, but the heart was rarely retained, despite the frequent claims of heart retention in the classical literature (Wade & Nelson, 2013b). Once the body was prepared, a public funeral took place that involved, among other things, the *opening of the mouth ceremony* that reanimated the body, allowing the individual to speak with their loved ones (Seiler & Rühli, 2015). Once interred, the family perpetuated the memory of the deceased through various commemorations, prayers, and festivals (Meskell, 2001).

While the Ancient Egyptians feared death, the deceased individual was not marginalized from society in the way that is common in Western society, and many other cultures, where the final stage of separation is much more complete. Rather, they continued to participate in the lives of their families and to have effective agency, as empowered by the living. Meskell (2001) has suggested that social memory could keep the deceased individual "alive" for one or two generations, at which point they would become completely socially marginalized by their loss from memory, effectively eliminating her agency and identity.

Curated Identity (I)—The Collector

In the personal identity section earlier, it was noted that we do not know Lady Hudson's original depositional context, nor do we know how she came to be in Brussels. The lack of a name and original context suggest that Lady Hudson is marginalized relative to some other Egyptian mummies, such as Tamut, referred to earlier, in terms of her archaeological/historical value. She still has the identity of an Egyptian mummy, but she is otherwise anonymous. Context, in archaeology, is crucial for the rich understanding of any artifact (Alderman, 2010), particularly a mummy for whom one is trying to build an identity.

This "value" is of course socially constructed in the archaeological/historical/academic context, which is different from the context in which she was presumably originally acquired by the Belgian collector or museum. In this context the mummy was probably more object than person, but for the same reason that it is easier to project agency onto human remains than onto a pot, a mummy-as-object is more than merely an ushabti (or shabti or shawabti—a small mummy-like figurine placed in the tomb to serve the deceased). To the collector or museum, the personal identity of the individual is less important than the "personification of Ancient Egypt" identity. Numerous internet sources attribute the quote "A museum without a mummy is not a museum" (e.g., Dawson, 2012) to Antoine-François Vivenel, a 19th-century entrepreneur/architect for whom a museum in Paris is named. A look at contemporary Egyptological exhibits suggests that the sentiment is still salient (see NBC News, 2014).

Lady Hudson was acquired by Mr. George Bannister of Ottawa, ON in 1963.[1] A Belgian judge declared the mummy and coffin to be an "ancient artifact" in order to satisfy Belgian export laws. For the next 21 years, she was part of the Bannister collection, which apparently included hundreds of mounted birds, mammals, and reptiles including a lion, an ostrich, and wild boars. A January 29, 1966 article in the Ottawa Journal tells us that George Bannister was a retired contractor and land surveyor who was an avid hunter. He collected trophies during six safaris to Africa and acquired taxidermy specimens and cultural objects from around the world. The Bannister collection was apparently extensive enough to require an addition to the family house. Unfortunately, we do not know why he chose to purchase the mummy. A black and white photograph shows the mummy next to a suit of armor and a series of firearms with what appears to be a sword lying across the coffin (see Fig. 2.3).

This characterization of Mr. Bannister and his collection is relevant to a consideration of his attitudes to these artifacts and the properties that he might have projected on them. The ruling by the Belgian judge and the juxtaposition of the mummy with mounted animals and weapons suggest that the mummy was viewed more as an object than as a person. There is a large body of literature that seeks to understand the psychology of collectors and their attitudes to the items they collect. Prentice (1987) grouped collectors

---

1. The information in this section is derived from interviews with George Bannister's daughter, Mrs. Dorothy Valliant, as well as from documents and correspondence with the MacSkimming Natural Science School Board, an anonymous and untitled article from the January 29, 1966 issue of the *Ottawa Journal* and other correspondence on file at the Department of Anthropology, The University of Western Ontario. All reports referred to are also on file with the Department.

FIGURE 2.3 Newspaper photograph from the Bannister family collection. The photo shows the mummy with some other items in the George Bannister collection. The article appeared in *The Ottawa Journal* on January 29, 1966. *Photo credit in the original article: Crombie McNeill, Jr.*

into two groups, those who collect symbolic or self-expressive objects, and those who collect instrumental objects. It would seem that Mr. Bannister would fall among the former group, particularly with the animal mounts reflecting his identity as a hunter. As Pearce (1992, p. 55) has observed, "in a very real sense, we and our collections are one." Pearce (1992) identified several motives for collecting, including the idea that many collectors amass large collections as a means of attaining immortality, as the collection would live on after they died. McIntosh and Schmeichel (2004) later added four more motives for collecting: passion, investment, pure enjoyment, and as a means of expressing self. Any of these motives may have driven Mr. Bannister's desire to collect things, but perhaps the acquisition of a mummy helped to ensure the immortality of the collection, while simultaneously reminding the collector and visitors of their mortality.

As discussed earlier, from the modern day archaeological/academic perspective, no matter the motivations of the collector, the collection of what are essentially looted cultural objects robs the material of context and damages the creator cultures and source nations (Alderman, 2010) leading to a loss of identity and marginalization. However, if agency and social properties are projected onto objects and mummies within a specific social context, then the collector projects his beliefs and identity onto them giving them effective agency and social properties. In this case the mummy is part of the core of the collection and cannot be said to be marginalized. I hasten to add that I do not make this argument to defend looting and collecting, but to highlight the importance of context in the social construction of identity of an object and its role in the process of marginalization, and to demonstrate that the same object-as-human can be simultaneously part of the collection and collector's core, and society/science's periphery.

Curated Identity (II)—Education

Mr. Bannister passed away in 1973, and in 1974 the Bannister family estate donated the collection of stuffed animals and the mummy to the MacSkimming Natural Science School in Ottawa, ON, which is part of the Ottawa-Carlton School Board. There, Lady Hudson was housed in a renovated barn in a plywood case with a glass lid. A report dated 1983 stated that in the 9 years that the collection was at the MacSkimming school, some 225,000 school children had viewed the mummy, then known as "The MacSkimming Mummy." This represents a shift in her identity as she started to play a role in educational programs. She was part of an "exotic species identification program" (although "early civilization" is listed as part of the social science curriculum), so one can assume that she was more of a curio and object-as-human than a representative of an exotic species.

In 1982 and following years the MacSkimming personnel began a series of consultations to learn more about their mummy. In particular, they noted that the mummy was only one of 12 Egyptian mummies in Canada and so had considerable cultural and monetary value. In 1982 The Canadian Conservation Institute noted that the mummy was in very fragile condition, that there was extensive damage to the chest and abdomen, and that she had no feet. They recommended the construction of a better case with silica gel to reduce the high ambient humidity. Receipts indicate that the case was constructed. In 1983 A.J. Spencer, Assistant Keeper of Egyptian Antiquities at the British Museum informed the school that the mummy was Roman Period in date, but he felt that the coffin was a modern imitation that incorporated 18th or 19th Dynasty design elements.

These actions indicate that cultural and monetary value and authenticity were now part of the MacSkimming Mummy's identity. Within the social context of an outdoor education school institution where she was being viewed by thousands of school children, she could be said to have been marginalized because of her peripheral fit with the dominant educational core of the school, but she would have been embraced (metaphorically) by the legions of students.

Curated Identity (III)—Museum Exhibit

In 1999 the Canadian Museum of Civilization (now the Canadian Museum of History; hereafter the CMC) reached out to the MacSkimming school to borrow their mummy to be part of a traveling exhibit entitled "Mysteries of Egypt." The rationale was (similarly to the Vivenel quote above regarding museums having to have a mummy) that an exhibit on Egypt just had to have a mummy! Preparation for the exhibit included 71.5 h of conservation work focusing on stabilization and consolidation of the coffin and the preparation of ethafoam inserts to replace the missing feet and the now largely missing chest and thorax. Between June 1, 1999 and March 11, 2001, the exhibit traveled to Cincinnati, Grand Rapids, Green Bay, Macon, and Calgary. Over the course of the tour, an estimated 500,000–750,000 people saw the installation, which included the mummy.

For these 2 years the mummy was firmly at the core of the exhibit and her identity shifted from being the curio at the margins of the MacSkimming mission to being the star of an exhibit on Ancient Egypt. Here the social context was the exhibit space and the interactions were with the visiting, interested public. The social properties that would have been projected on her were focused on her as the personification of Ancient Egypt, giving her the agency to affect how they understood and identified with this ancient culture.

Curated Identity (IV)—A Changing Role

At the completion of the exhibit tour the CMC sought to return the mummy to the MacSkimming school. However, at that time the exotic species identification program had lost its funding and she was deemed to be a poor fit with other programs, so an effort was started to find her a new home, ideally in Canada. The Mysteries of Egypt exhibit was a one-off program for the CMC, whose primary mission is Canadian heritage. Thus they started to look elsewhere for a new home contacting several museums and researchers across Canada. The Royal Ontario Museum (hereafter the ROM) was an obvious possibility, but she was initially rejected because of the mismatch between the mummy and coffin and because of her poor state of preservation, which in their eyes diminished her value for display or research. However, an advocacy effort by Gayle Gibson, an Egyptologist in the ROM's education department led to the mummy being shipped to the ROM to play a role in educational programming.

The mummy and coffin arrived at the ROM on October 30, 2001. However, upon arrival, registration staff noted that the ROM had a policy that they could not accept donations of human remains, so the registration department could not approve the accessioning of the mummy. At that point the mummy was housed in a store room with 19th-century armaments and a search began for a new home. For 18 months the search involved consultations with conservation programs, universities, and Egyptology associations. During this time the mummy could definitely be said to be marginalized. She held two identities simultaneously: a valued representative of Ancient Egypt who deserved a good home, and an unwanted, poorly preserved nuisance whose presence was a contravention of curatorial policy. The former social construction gave the mummy (now given the moniker "Our Lady of Hudson's Bay" or "Lady Hudson" for short) the agency to inspire a dedicated team, led by Gayle Gibson to find that new home.

Curated and Bioarchaeological Identity (V)—Research Subject

In March 2003, I received a phone call from Peter Sheldrick, a family doctor and avocational Egyptologist from Chatham, ON. Peter is a member of the Toronto Chapter of the Society for the Study of Egyptian Antiquities and was part of Gayle's dedicated team. Peter knew of my work with the Sulman Mummy, a Ptolemaic mummy housed at the Chatham-Kent Cultural Center. This work, which involved X-ray, CT, and the reconstruction of the osteobiography of the Sulman Mummy, was published in Gardner, Garvin, Nelson, Vascotto, and Conlogue (2004) and presented numerous times in public lectures to the Chatham community. Peter related Lady Hudson's saga to me and inquired if we could give her a home at the University of Western Ontario. Mummies were becoming an increasingly important part of my research program, so subject to the approval of my university's administration, I accepted. I received the enthusiastic approval and support of Paul Maxim, then Associate Dean of Research, Faculty of Social Science, made the connection with Gayle, and Lady Hudson arrived at her new home in London, ON, on May 3, 2003.

The fall semester of academic year 2003–04 marked the beginning of a new doctoral program in Bioarchaeology at the University of Western Ontario. Department colleague Ian Colquhoun and I created a special topics course for our first cohort of eight MA and PhD students entitled "Anthropology 503 A: Interdisciplinary Bioarchaeological Analysis of an Egyptian Mummy" that was composed of weekly seminars with experts on different aspects of Egyptology, imaging, paleopathology, Roman history, and other mummy-related topics. The focus was firmly on Lady Hudson, and the effort to reconstruct her osteobiography and as much of her cultural context as possible. The students each took on different parts of that effort and the initial results of our work were presented in a poster for the 2004 Canadian Association for Physical Anthropologists that had 30 coauthors (Nelson et al., 2004). The students' perspective on the exercise as a learning experience was presented in a second poster at the conference (Cross et al., 2004).

We discovered that Lady Hudson's mummy had suffered greatly over the past 50 years. An undated, but apparently early note in the collection of documents that accompanied the mummy suggests that she was "well preserved," but the Canadian Conservation Institute conservators noted damage from high humidity in the 1980s and condition reports in the 1990s document extensive destruction of her thorax and abdomen. Today the mummy consists of a number of disarticulated elements. The head is unwrapped but is relatively intact and is attached to the neck which extends to the sixth cervical vertebra. The rest of the spine is represented only by isolated fragments recovered from the coffin. The thoracic cage is represented only by fragments of ribs and sternum and the left clavicle (which is still attached to the left arm). The arms are largely intact and are still wrapped. Her pelvis is largely complete, although the pubic symphyses are broken away. The femora are unwrapped to just above the knees while the tibiae are still encased in original and intact wrapping. Her feet are missing.

While Lady Hudson's condition is unquestionably less than ideal, and it led to her initial rejection by the ROM, in some ways it also facilitates our particular program of research. My research emphasizes the nondestructive use of X-ray, CT, and micro-CT imaging and we have pursued that line of research with Lady Hudson in spades. The fact that her head can be moved without the rest of her body facilitates transport to places like the dentistry department for panoramic X-rays, to our micro-CT for high-resolution CT scans, and to the Lawson Research Institute for MRI scanning. The latter two scans would not be possible if the mummy was complete as the mummy would not fit into the scanner (micro-CT) or scanning coils (MRI). In addition, we have been able to mix nondestructive analytical techniques with selected minimally invasive techniques such as histology and isotopic analysis (see below) to increase the depth of our osteobiography. Thus while her state of preservation would marginalize her in many museum contexts, it has actually proved to be an advantage in the current context.

The remaining wrappings on Lady Hudson's arms and lower legs confirm that she is Roman Period in date (see Fig. 2.1). X-ray and CT scanning confirm that she was excerebrated through her nose, although in comparison to other mummies, the size of the defect created in her cribriform plate and sphenoid bone is quite large (Holler, Wright, Chhem, & Nelson, 2006; Nelson et al., 2007) (see Fig. 2.4). Approximately 1/3 of the posterior part of the cranial cavity is filled with hardened resin and a resin-impregnated tampon was used to plug the opening from the nose and into the vault. The mouth was packed with resin-impregnated linen, although no packing was used under the cheeks. A resin-impregnated mass of coarse linen that is preserved in the pelvic cavity demonstrates that she was eviscerated, but we cannot tell where the evisceration cut was, or whether or not her heart was left intact. The resin used in the embalming process has not yet been chemically analyzed, but it is dark in color and its odor is consistent with a bitumen containing compound (Williams, 2004), which would be consistent with mummification practice in the Roman Period (Buckley & Evershed, 2001).

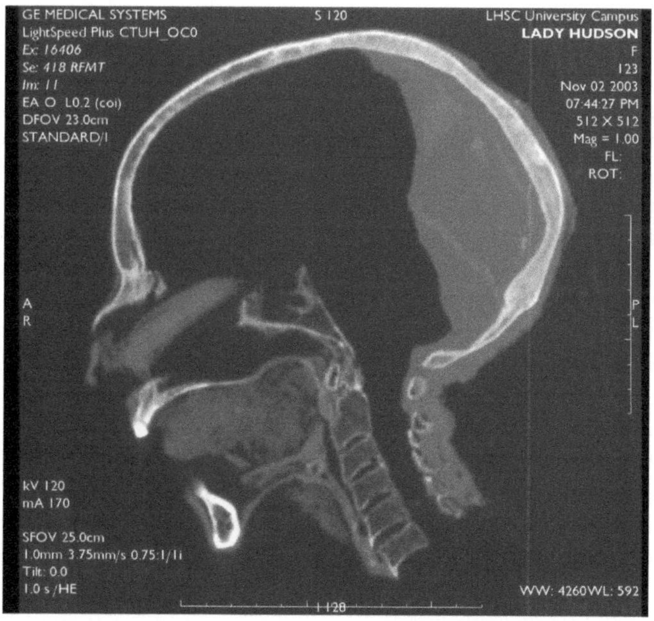

FIGURE 2.4 A coronal midsagittal CT slice, illustrating that the brain has been removed through the nose, and resin introduced into the cranial cavity. The black area in the cranial cavity is occupied by air, rather than brain matter. The dense material in the posterior 1/3 of the cavity is resin. The dense structure in the nose is a resin-soaked tampon that was used to plug the route of excerebration. The dense structure in the mouth is resin-soaked linen packing the oral cavity. *CT credit: London Health Sciences Centre & Andrew Nelson.*

Taken together, these observations are consistent with the body modifications that accompany the mortuary ritual of Roman Period Egypt.

Our ongoing analysis has allowed us to reconstruct many aspects of Lady Hudson's osteobiography. Her sex has been confirmed to be female, based on the form of her pelvis and gracile features of her skull. Her stature is estimated to have been 155 ± 4.25 cm in life, based on the length of her humeri measured on the CT images and the Trotter and Gleser (1958) estimation formulae for individuals of African descent (Cross, 2004). She is in extremely poor dental health. CT scans and a panoramic X-ray demonstrate that she has worn away most of the enamel crowns of her teeth, she is missing her lower central incisors, the lateral lower incisors are worn to the roots, she is missing several maxillary teeth, and she has at least three abscesses. Poor dental health is a common finding in Egyptian mummies, likely due to the omnipresent sand in the air and grit from the grain grinding process (Harris, Ponitz, & Ingalls, 1998). The grit would be baked into the bread, leading to high levels of dental attrition and the carbohydrates in the bread would have led to carious lesions. Lady Hudson demonstrates osteopenia and advanced osteonal remodeling, as assessed histologically (Beauchesne, 2004), as well as reduced cortical thickness throughout her skeleton, as assessed radiologically. In the absence of her pubic symphyses, we can use the last two observations to suggest that she was probably at least in her fourth decade of life when she died. A paucity of osteophyte formation and joint degeneration (Gardner, 2004) suggests that she was not of advanced age, so a consensus estimate would suggest that she was 30–40 years of age when she died. CT and micro-CT scanning have revealed atherosclerotic plaques in her carotid arteries, a condition normally associated with high fat diets. Atherosclerosis has also been observed in other Egyptian mummies by Allam et al. (2010) who have argued that the condition may be related to age, inflammation, or exposure to sooty fireplace smoke. Finally, carbon isotopic analysis (Beauchesne et al., 2008) suggests that Lady Hudson's diet was based on wheat, barley, fruits, and vegetables, a conclusion found in several other isotopic studies of Egyptian mummies (reviewed in Metcalfe, 2004). The analysis of her nitrogen isotopes shows a very high value that could indicate high protein (N) consumption. A comparison with mummies who have secure contexts along the Nile Valley or in desert oases suggests that she may have lived in an arid oasis environment, where the soils were enriched with nitrogen (Beauchesne et al., 2008).

Bioarchaeological Identity

With this new information on hand, we can begin to construct her bioarchaeological identity as the first approximation of her personal identity. She is clearly a Roman Period mummy, and her mortuary identity embodies the dominant practices of the time, although the cross-pectoral position of her arms is somewhat unusual for the period. We will never be certain where she lived and died, but we have been able to suggest that she lived in one of the desert oases. She lived into her thirties and demonstrated no evidence of trauma and scant evidence of degenerative joint disease. Her stature is well within the average ranges presented in Zakrzewski (2003) for Ancient Egyptian females, which, unfortunately, does not tell us much about her socioeconomic status. Her very poor dental health, while shared with many other Ancient Egyptian individuals, would have presented her with dental pain and some difficulty in processing tough foods. Further elaboration of her osteobiography will involve detailed comparisons with other Roman Period mummies, including those incorporated in the IMPACT database of radiological studies of mummies (Nelson & Wade, 2015).

Conclusions

Lady Hudson's new curated identity is multifaceted, reflecting her position as a research subject, a facilitator for student education and as a public ambassador for mummy research and the university. As a research subject, our efforts to construct her bioarchaeological identity are a step toward understanding her embodied personal identity and restoring her "personhood" (cf., Meskell, 1999). As a facilitator for education, the graduate student experience was discussed earlier, but she also been the high point of many high school outreach events and one second-year undergraduate course. She has played a role as an ambassador for mummy research in five television productions, and she is frequently a draw for the Department of Anthropology at University recruitment events. In all of these activities, we are mindful of, and ensure that any viewers also appreciate, the fact that these are the mortal remains of a woman who lived approximately 2000 years ago. We are guided by ethical guidelines, such as the Department for Culture, Media and Sport (2005) and Lohman and Goodnow (2006) who emphasize, among other things, that human remains should always be viewed and treated with respect. The details that we can provide of her personal identity (as approximated by her bioarchaeological identity), her mortuary identity, her multiple curated identities, and her new identities at Western help students and visitors to better understand her as a person and the narrative of her life and afterlife. That understanding shapes how they relate to her and what social qualities they project to her, giving her effective agency in shaping how they learn about Ancient Egypt and ensuring that she is no longer at the social or scientific margins. Rather, Lady Hudson lies at the core of an active research and teaching program, and she will contribute to both as her afterlife progresses.

Acknowledgments

The analysis of Lady Hudson has involved a wide interdisciplinary team of students, researchers, and other colleagues. Gayle Gibson (ROM) was the person who made this entire transfer possible. Peter Sheldrick (Dakhleh Oasis Project) made the crucial connection. Casey Kirkpatrick (UWO, Anthropology) deserves special mention for her work with the archival material housed at the University of Western Ontario.

Other collaborators include:

Ian Colquhoun, Christine White, Patrick Beauchesne, Alan Cross, Janet Gardner, Laura Marciano, Eileen Marion-Bellemare, Jessica Metcalfe, Andrew Pawlowski, Lisa Paulaharju, Sandra Wheeler, and Lana Williams (UWO Anthropology); Andrea Feilen, Julia Eckel (Ludwig Maximilian U., Munich), Rethy Chhem, Jill Friis, Karen Kennedy, Wendy MacIntyre, Cesare Romagnoli, and Gord Wood (London Health Sciences Centre); Liz Bishop, Stan Kogon, and Lesley Short (UWO Schulich Faculty of Medicine & Dentistry); Ron Martin (UWO Chemistry); Greg Garvin and Erin Wright (St. Joseph's Healthcare); Gian Vascotto (NRC); David Holdsworth and Louise Du (Robarts Research Institute); Anne and Jean Valliant (G. Bannister's granddaughters); Mummy Course participants Megan Cook (Dakhleh Oasis Project), Kelly Olson, and Paul Potter (UWO); Joan Murray (HBC Heritage Services) and Harold Tichenor (blanket expert); Corinna Robitaille (MacSkimming Centre); Tom Stone (Canadian Conservation Institute); Peter Sheldrick (Chatham, ON); Patrick Geyer (San Diego, CA); GE Medical Systems; Paul Maxim (Assoc. Dean, Social Science, UWO); Ross Davidson (Surface Science Western, UWO); Johannes von Kalckreuth (Welt der Wunder TV); Ellie Withers, Niall Murray, and Steve Kruithof (VETC, IMTI, National Research Council of Canada); John C. Posh (VP, InSight Health Corp.), Brian Luckman (UWO Geography), Fred Longstaffe (UWO, Earth Science); Andrew D. Wade (Anthropology, McMaster University); J.R. Butler, N. Gelman, and G. Moran (Lawson Research Institute); the Society for the Study of Egyptian Antiquities.

References

Alderman, K. (2010). The ethics of context: Exploring assumptions in discussions about the looting of archaeological sites. *Journal of Art Crime*, *4*, 93–94.

Allam, H., Nureldin, A., Adelmaksoub, G., Badr, I., Amer, H. A., Soliman, M. A., ... Wann, S. (2010). Something old, something new – computed tomography studies of the cardiovascular system of Ancient Egyptian mummies. *American Heart Hospital Journal*, *8*, 10–13.

Arnold, J. E. (1995). Social inequality, marginalization, and economic process. In T. D. Price, & G. M. Feinman (Eds.), *Foundations of social inequality* (pp. 87–103). New York: Plenum Press.

Aufderheide, A. C. (2003). *The scientific study of mummies*. Cambridge: Cambridge University Press.

Beauchesne, P. (2004). Paleohistological analysis of the Egyptian mummy, Lady Hudson. Manuscript on file, Department of Anthropology, The University of Western Ontario.

Beauchesne, P., Colquhoun, I., Cross, A., Longstaffe, F., Marciano, L., Metcalfe, J., ... Williams, L. (2008). The Lady Hudson project. In P. Atoche, C. Rodriguez, & M. A. Ramirez (Eds.), *Mummies and science. World mummies research*. Proceedings of the VI World Congress on Mummy Studies (pp. 637–640). Santa Cruz de Tenerife.

Berry, J. W., & Sam, D. L. (2003). Accuracy in scientific discourse. *Scandinavian Journal of Psychology, 44*, 65–68.

Borić, D., & Robb, J. (2008). Body theory in archaeology. In D. Borić, & J. Robb (Eds.), *Past bodies. Body-centered research in archaeology* (pp. 1–7). Oxford: Oxbow Books.

Bourdieu, P. (1977). *Outline of a theory of practice*. London: Cambridge University Press. (R. Nice, Trans.).

Buckley, S. A., & Evershed, R. P. (2001). Organic chemistry of embalming agents in Pharaonic and Graeco-Roman mummies. *Nature, 413*(6858), 837–841.

Buikstra, J. E., & Scott, R. E. (2009). Key concepts in identity studies. In K. J. Knudson, & C. M. Stojanowski (Eds.), *Bioarchaeology of identity in the Americas* (pp. 24–55). Gainesville, FL: University Press of Florida.

Chesson, M. S. (2001). Social memory, identity, and death: an introduction. In M. S. Chesson (Ed.), *Social memory, identity, and death: Anthropological perspectives on mortuary rituals*. Archaeological Papers of the American Anthropological Association (Vol. 10(1), pp. 1–10).

Crandall, J. J., & Martin, D. L. (2014). Special section: The bioarchaeology of post-mortem agency: Integrating archaeological theory with human skeletal remains. *Cambridge Archaeological Journal, 24*, 429–435.

Cross, A. (2004). 3-Dimensional analysis of Lady Hudson. Manuscript on file, Department of Anthropology, The University of Western Ontario.

Cross, A., Wheeler, S. M., Williams, L. J., Beauchesne, P., Marciano, L. D., Pawlowski, A., & Metcalfe, J. Z. (2004, October). The UWO Mummy Project: The students' perspective on multidisciplinary approaches to applied research. In *Poster presented to the Canadian Association for Physical Anthropology annual meeting*, London, ON.

Dawson, T. (2012). *A museum without a mummy*. Retrieved from https://archaeology-travel.com/history-of-archaeology/a-museum-without-a-mummy/.

Department for Culture, Media and Sport. (2005). *Guidance for the care of human remains in museums*. London: Department for Culture, Media and Sport.

Dickie-Clark, H. F. (1966). *The marginal situation. A sociological study of a coloured group*. London: Routledge & Keegan Paul.

Gardner, J. (2004). The radiological analysis of Lady Hudson. Manuscript on file, Department of Anthropology, The University of Western Ontario.

Gardner, J., Garvin, G., Nelson, A. J., Vascotto, G., & Conlogue, G. (2004). Paleoradiology in mummy studies: The Sulman Mummy Project. *Canadian Association of Radiologists Journal, 55*(4), 228–234.

Gell, A. (1998). *Art and agency. An anthropological theory*. Oxford: Clarendon Press.

Geller, P. L., & Suri, M. (2014). Relationality, corporeality and bioarchaeology: Bodies qua bodies, bodies in context. *Cambridge Archaeological Journal, 24*, 437–452.

Giddens, A. (1984). *The constitution of society: Outline of the theory of structuration*. Berkeley, CA: University of California Press.

Gray, P. H. K. (1972). Notes concerning the position of arms and hands of mummies with a view to possible dating of the specimen. *The Journal of Egyptian Archaeology, 58*, 200–204.

Hagen, F., & Ryholt, K. (2016). *The antiquities trade in Egypt 1880–1930*. The H.O. Lange papers. *Scientia Danica, Series H. Humanistica, 4* (Vol. 8). Copenhagen: The Royal Danish Academy of Science and Letters.

Hall, J. M. (1999). Marginalization revisited: Critical, postmodern, and liberation perspectives. *Advances in Nursing Science*, 22(2), 88–102.

Hall, J. M., Stevens, P. E., & Meleis, A. I. (1994). Marginalization: A guiding concept for valuing diversity in nursing knowledge development. *Advances in Nursing Science, 16*(4), 23–41.

Hamilton-Paterson, J. (1978). *Mummies: Death and life in Ancient Egypt*. London: William Collins Sons & Co Ltd.

Harris, J. E., Ponitz, P. V., & Ingalls, B. K. (1998). Dental health in Ancient Egypt. In A. Cockburn, E. Cockburn, & T. A. Reyman (Eds.), *Mummies, disease & ancient cultures* (pp. 59–68). Cambridge: Cambridge University Press.

Holler, T., Wright, E. D., Chhem, R., & Nelson, A. J. (2006, May). Lady Hudson: A case of transnasal craniotomy in Ancient Egypt. In *Paper presented at the Canadian Society of Otolaryngology-Head and Neck Surgery*, Kelowna, BC.

Knudson, K. J., & Stojanowski, C. M. (2008). New directions in bioarchaeology: Recent contributions to the study of human social identities. *Journal of Archaeological Research, 16*, 397–432.

Knudson, K. J., & Stojanowski, C. M. (2009). The bioarchaeology of identity. In K. J. Knudson, & C. M. Stojanowski (Eds.), *Bioarchaeology of identity in the Americas* (pp. 1–23). Gainesville, FL: University Press of Florida.

Krieger, N. (2004). Embodiment: A conceptual glossary for epidemiology. *Journal of Epidemiological Community Health, 59*, 350–355.

Lohman, J., & Goodnow, K. (Eds.), (2006). *Human remains and museum practice*. New York: Berghahn Books.

Marion-Bellemare, E. (2004). Mortuary treatment of a Roman Period mummy. Manuscript on file, Department of Anthropology, The University of Western Ontario.

McIntosh, W. D., & Schmeichel, B. (2004). Collectors and collecting: A social psychological perspective. *Leisure Sciences, 26*(1), 85–97.

Meskell, L. (1999). *Archaeologies of social life. Age, sex, class et cetera in Ancient Egypt*. Oxford: Blackwell Publishers.

Meskell, L. (2001). The Egyptian ways of death. In M. S. Chesson (Ed.), *Social memory, identity, and death: Anthropological perspectives on mortuary rituals*. Archaeological Papers of the American Anthropological Association (Vol. 10(1), pp. 27–40).

Metcalfe, J. (2004). Food and diet in Roman Egypt: Current knowledge and proposed investigation into the case of Lady Hudson. Manuscript on file, Department of Anthropology, The University of Western Ontario.

NBC News (2014, May). *King Tut's doppelganger tomb: The only thing missing is the mummy*. Retrieved from https://www.nbcnews.com/science/science-news/king-tuts-doppelganger-tomb-only-thing-missing-mummy-n94736.

Nelson, A. J., & Wade, A. D. (2015). IMPACT: Development of a radiological mummy database. *Anatomical Record, 298*, 941–948.

Nelson, A. J., Colquhoun, I., White, C. D., Beauchesne, P., Cross, A., Gardner, J., … Du, L. (2004, October). Lady Hudson and mummy studies at UWO. In *Poster presented to the Canadian Association for Physical Anthropology annual meeting*, London, ON.

Nelson, A. J., Conlogue, G., Beckett, R., Posh, J., Chhem, R., Wright, E., & Rogers, J. (2007, March). Multimodal analyses of variability in transnasal craniotomy lesions in Egyptian mummies. In *Poster presented to the North American Paleopathology Association annual meeting*, Durham, NC.

Park, R. (1928). Human migration and the Marginal Man. *American Journal of Sociology, 33*(6), 881–893.

Pawlowski, A. (2004). A bug, a match and wood: The life history of a 21st Dynasty Egyptian sarcophagus. Manuscript on file, Department of Anthropology, The University of Western Ontario.

Pearce, S. M. (1992). *Museums, objects, and collections: A cultural study*. Leicester: Leicester University Press.

Prentice, D. A. (1987). Psychological correspondence of possessions, attitudes, and values. *Journal of Personality and Social Psychology*, *53*(6), 993–1003.

Riggs, C. (2010). Funerary rituals (in Ptolemaic and Roman Periods). In J. Dieleman, & E. Wendrich (Eds.), *UCLA encyclopedia of egyptology* (pp. 1–7). UCLA. Available from http://digital2.library.ucla.edu/viewItem.do?ark = 21198/zz001nf66d.

Robb, J. (2004). The extended artifact and the monumental economy: a methodology for material agency. In E. DeMarrais, C. Godsen, & C. Renfrew (Eds.), *Rethinking materiality. The engagement of mind with the material world* (pp. 131–139). Cambridge: McDonald Institute Monographs, McDonald Institute for Archaeological Research.

Sampsell, B. M. (2015). Resolving a mummy mismatch. In S. Ikram, J. Kaiser, & R. Walker (Eds.), *Egyptian bioarchaeology. Humans, animals, and the environment* (pp. 119–130). Leiden: Sidestone Press.

Saul, F. P., & Saul, J. M. (1989). Osteobiography: A Maya example. In M. Y. İşcan, & K. A. R. Kennedy (Eds.), *Reconstruction of life from the skeleton* (pp. 287–302). New York: Alan R. Liss, Inc.

Seiler, R., & Rühli, F. (2015). "The Opening of the Mouth"—A new perspective for an Ancient Egyptian mummification procedure. *Anatomical Record*, *298*, 1208–1216.

Shaw, I. (2000). *Oxford history of Ancient Egypt*. Oxford: Oxford University Press.

Stoddard, A. L. W., & Palkovich, A. M. (Eds.), (2012). *The bioarchaeology of individuals*. Gainesville, FL: University Press of Florida.

Stonequist, E. V. (1961). *The marginal man. A study on personality and conflict*. New York: Russell and Russell Inc.

Tatsi, T. (2011). Identity struggles of museum professionals: Autonomous expertise and audience participation in exhibition production. *Journal of Ethnology and Folkloristics*, *5*(2), 65–80.

Taylor, J. H., & Antoine, D. (2014). *Ancient lives, new discoveries. Eight mummies, eight stories*. London: The British Museum Press.

Torres-Rouff, C., & Knudson, K. J. (2017). Integrating identities. An innovative bioarchaeological and biogeochemical approach to analyzing the multiplicity of identities in the mortuary record. *Current Anthropology*, *58*(3), 381–409.

Trotter, M., & Gleser, G. C. (1958). A re-evaluation of estimation of stature based on measurements of stature taken during life and of long bones after death. *American Journal of Physical Anthropology*, *16*(1), 79–123.

Tucker, M. (1990). Director's forward. In R. L. Ferguson (Ed.), *Out there: Marginalization and contemporary cultures* (pp. 19–38). Cambridge, MA: MIT Press.

Tung, T. (2014). Agency, 'til death do us part? Inquiring about the agency of dead bodies from the Ancient Andes. *Cambridge Archaeological Journal*, *24*, 437–452.

Vasas, E. B. (2005). Examining the margins. A concept analysis of marginalization. *Advances in Nursing Science*, *28*, 194–202.

Wade, A. D., & Nelson, A. J. (2013a). Evisceration and excerebration in the Egyptian mummification tradition. *Journal of Archaeological Science*, *40*, 4198–4206.

Wade, A. D., & Nelson, A. J. (2013b). Radiological evaluation of the evisceration tradition in ancient Egyptian mummies. *HOMO: Journal of Comparative Human Biology*, *64*(1), 1–28.

Wade, A. D., Nelson, A. J., & Garvin, G. (2011). A synthetic radiological study of brain treatment in ancient Egyptian mummies. *HOMO: Journal of Comparative Human Biology*, *62* (4), 249–269.

Williams, L. (2004). Organic chemistry of embalming materian from the late 'Lady Hudson' mummy using thermal desorption-gas chromatography-mass spectrometry and pyrolysis-gas-chromatography-mass spectrometry. Manuscript on file, Department of Anthropology, The University of Western Ontario.

Zakrzewski, S. R. (2003). Variation in Ancient Egyptian stature and body proportions. *American Journal of Physical Anthropology*, *121*, 219–220.

Chapter 3

Task activity and tooth wear in a woman of ancient Egypt

Nancy C. Lovell and Kimberley E. Palichuk
Department of Anthropology, University of Alberta, Edmonton, AB, Canada

Chapter Outline

Introduction

Social marginalization can be understood to refer to the treatment of individuals and/or groups as insignificant, unimportant, or peripheral to a community. While it has been a subject of investigation for many years in sociology and sociocultural anthropology, the bioarchaeological study of social marginalization is a relatively recent area of inquiry and interpretation. For more than 50 years, bioarchaeology's population-focused analyses aggregated individual osteobiographies, effectively homogenizing skeletal samples and neglecting biological and social diversity, and, hence, the realities of marginalization (Blom, 2017; Stodder & Palkovich, 2012). Within the last decade, however, examinations of the lived experiences of individuals have considered social identities and life histories, related to, for example, marginalization as a feature of immigration, craft specialization, impairment and disability, and the social stigma of disease (e.g., Byrnes & Muller, 2017; Juengst & Becker, 2017; Stodder & Palkovich, 2012). In this chapter, osteobiographical and archaeological data are used to socially contextualize the identity of a woman of ancient Egypt, and to explore how conventional depictions of daily life serve to marginalize women's work.

Teeth and jaws are usually the best-preserved parts of human skeletons found in archaeological contexts, and they play an important role in both individual and population studies of past peoples. For example, they can

Bioarchaeology of Marginalized People. DOI: https://doi.org/10.1016/B978-0-12-815224-9.00003-8

provide information on health status, biological affinities, aspects of diet, habitual activities, and esthetic, medical, or ritual practices. In this case, during routine data collection on the dentition from the Egyptian site of ancient Mendes (modern Tell er-Rub'a), two nonalimentary tooth wear patterns (i.e., tooth wear that is not associated with eating) were observed in an older adult woman. Dental disease and skeletal pathological conditions in the human remains from Mendes have been reported elsewhere (Lovell & Whyte, 1999; Mant, 2014; McConnan Borstad & Lovell, 2011–2012), but those studies present frequencies of lesions in the entire skeletal sample and discuss neither individualizing features nor nonalimentary tooth wear. This woman was the only individual in the skeletal sample to exhibit these wear patterns, and her burial was rich compared to all other nonelite burials at the site. Thus she appears to have been distinctive in her community yet rendered voiceless in previous reporting of pathological conditions at Mendes. Furthermore, she may also have been marginalized by systematic biases in ancient Egyptian accounts and depictions of the tasks and occupations undertaken by women.

Ancient Mendes is located in the eastern central delta of northern Egypt. Occupied continuously for approximately 5000 years, from the Predynastic until the Ptolemaic Period, it functioned variously as an administrative capital, hub for trade links, and religious cult center (de Meulenaere & Mackay, 1976; Redford, 2001, 2010). Sporadic excavations since the 1940s have uncovered residential, industrial, temple, and burial areas (Allen & Wilson, 1982; Brewer & Wenke, 1992; Hansen, 1967; Holz, Stieglitz, Hansen, & Ochsenschlager, 1980; Lovell, 1991–1992; Redford, 2001, 2004, 2009, 2010; Wilson, 1982). The burials uncovered at Mendes appear to be those of middle-class individuals, based on burial style, the nature of recovered grave goods, and their location near, or dug into, preexisting mudbrick tomb superstructures. Social differentiation was recognized at the site, however, and made manifest by variation in the quantity and quality of grave goods and in the size and nature of grave superstructures. Although her grave was not marked by a superstructure, this woman's burial was rich and elaborate compared to the others in the area of a similar date: her skeleton was in a wooden coffin that had been lined with reeds and deliberately placed on a bed of potsherds, while grave goods included alabaster vessels, a bronze mirror, cosmetics, and remnants of plaster-backed gold leaf (Allen & Wilson, 1982). Her burial dates to the First Intermediate Period, c.2181–2055 BCE, on the basis of recovered pottery and grave goods.

During field seasons in Egypt from 1976 to 1978, the New York University Institute of Fine Arts Expedition to Mendes excavated 68 burials. At the time of the excavations, the Egyptian antiquities department oversaw a "division of the finds" that permitted samples of nonroyal and nonmummified human remains and a selection of excavated artifacts to be distributed to the participating foreign institutions. Thus portions of the recovered human remains were exported to the United States, where they were stored until shipped to the University of Alberta for study. Some of the dentition is preserved for 26 individuals. The senior author also examined the dentitions of another 66 adults, dating to the Ptolemaic Period, that she and her team excavated at Mendes in the 1990s; those remains were not exported from Egypt, but serve to enlarge the dental dataset. Although the total sample from Mendes is therefore 92 adults, poor preservation and a high degree of fragmentation result in a sample of only 1070 teeth, which is about one-third of the total number of teeth that would be expected if all of the individuals possessed complete dentitions. Among all of these dental remains, the teeth of this woman (burial number 5MB12, a designation assigned in the field), show two patterns of wear, which are inconsistent with chewing food. The condition of her dentition is otherwise unremarkable although her occlusal wear is severe, ranging from stage 6 to stage 8 using Smith's illustrations and descriptions (Smith, 1984). Secondary dentin formed in the crowns and prevented exposure of the pulp chamber with one exception: the right mandibular first molar, retained in the alveolus, had an exposed pulp chamber and a periapical abscess had formed after invasion of the pulp by infectious bacteria. Her bony remains show no pathological lesions.

Although her skeletal remains were fragmentary, the woman was determined to be an older adult (estimated at greater than 50 years of age) at the time of her death on the basis of obliterated ectocranial sutures (Meindl & Lovejoy, 1985) and composite scores of morphological changes to the auricular surface of the ilium (Buckberry & Chamberlain, 2002). Sex was assessed on the basis of pelvic and cranial morphology, as outlined by Buikstra and Ubelaker (1994), and of features of the posterior distal humerus (Rogers, 1999). Other observed features consistent with female sex are the ratio of the width of the first sacral body to the alae, the vertical diameter of the humeral head (Bass, 1987), and the gracility of her bones. This last feature was assessed as suggested by White, Black, and Folkens (2012): the cranial and postcranial bones were compared to those of the entire skeletal sample, which was seriated using overall robusticity.

Assessment of Nonalimentary Tooth Wear

Teeth were cleaned with a soft brush and examined with the aid of a 10× hand lens. Twenty-four teeth in this woman's dentition had observable crowns, but 14 of these were isolated teeth. Preserved supporting bony structures were minimal: two maxillary fragments with four premolars in situ and portions of the left and right posterior mandible with two premolars and four molars in situ. Sixteen teeth show evidence of nonalimentary wear: the two central maxillary incisors show wedge-shape incisal wear and 14 teeth exhibit flat abrasions on the root, cemento-enamel junction (CEJ), or crown (Fig. 3.1). The left maxillary central incisor and the right maxillary lateral incisor were examined by scanning electron microscopy (SEM) in order to

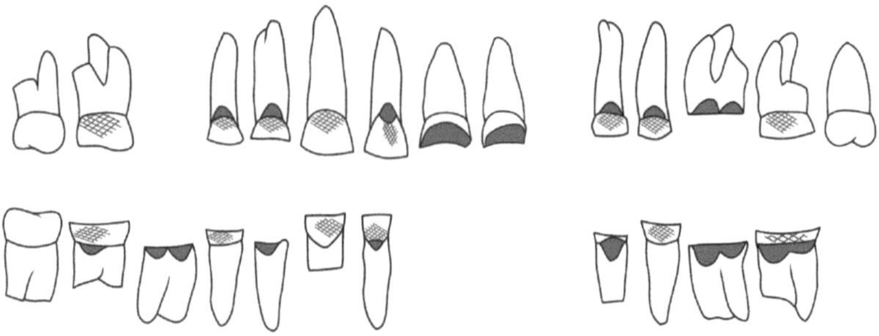

FIGURE 3.1 Illustration of dental preservation and nonalimentary wear across the arcades. Enamel polishing is indicated by cross-hatching; abrasion patches on dentin (underlying enamel and cementum) are drawn in solid black.

investigate possible causes of the abrasion features and the wedge-shaped wear. Although replication techniques are commonly used in dental microwear studies, the Mendes teeth were too fragile to be cast. The teeth were swabbed with an ethanol solution to remove any residual dirt and skin oil. In order to prevent cracking of the teeth from overheating, the teeth were coated with a thin layer of carbon to reduce the build-up of electric charge (Goldstein et al., 2018). Carbon coating also serves to increase the emission of low-energy secondary electrons, improving image contrast (Goldstein et al., 2018). Micrographs, ranging in magnification from 25 × for overall view to 570 × for detailed images, were taken in order to study the areas of interest. Each area was photographed at a standard orientation and then at a 90 degrees rotation to ensure the visibility of microwear features. Comparison and quantification of the features from both angles did not reveal an appreciable difference. The distinction between antemortem and postmortem microwear was recognized according to criteria outlined by Teaford (1988), including pattern, regularity, and distribution of wear. Any features that appeared to be isolated, extreme, or highly irregular as compared to the wear on the rest of the tooth were regarded as caused by postmortem wear or sample preparation and were disregarded.

The most unusual pattern of wear appears on the both the vestibular and oral surfaces of the maxillary central incisor crowns. Vestibular refers to the side of the tooth that is adjacent to the lips or cheeks; oral refers to the side of the tooth that is adjacent to the palate or tongue. The enamel on both these surfaces has been worn away, so that very little of the enamel remains on the tooth crown except for a few millimeters near the root; the underlying dentin is also severely worn (Fig. 3.2). The pattern is one of oblique wear on both vestibular and oral aspects, forming a blunt wedge that has its apex at the incisal edge (Fig. 3.3). The mesial and distal margins of the crown retain a vestige of the original vertical height; the greater degree of wear in the central portion of the incisal edge can be attributed to the softer nature of the

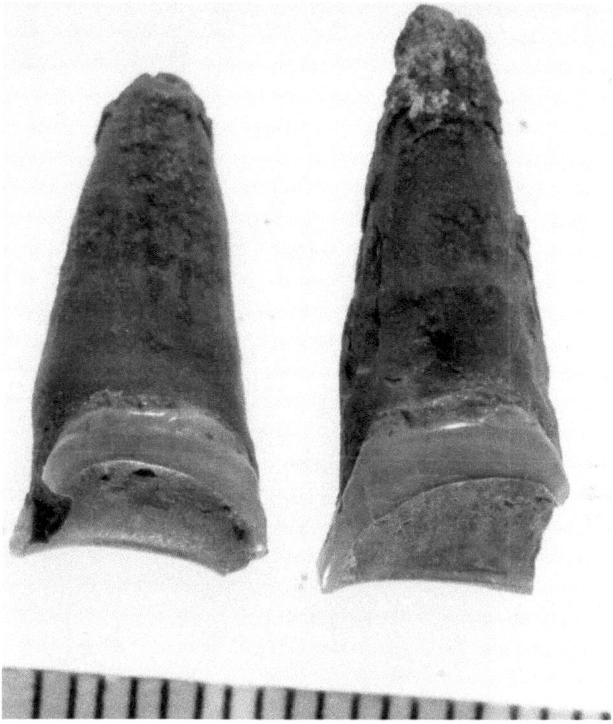

FIGURE 3.2 Maxillary incisor crowns, vestibular aspect. Most of the enamel on the crowns has been worn away, exposing the underlying dentin. Scale bar is in millimeters.

dentin and hence its somewhat faster rate of wear. The pulp chamber was not exposed in either tooth. The incisal edge of the left central incisor was examined using SEM; the striations of wear are clearly visible and appear vertically on the vestibular and oral surfaces of the crown, indicating that wear occurred over the incisal edge (Fig. 3.4). This direction of wear suggests that the incisal edge was used in the manner of a wedge. Unfortunately the crowns of the lower central incisors were not preserved and hence any associated wear on those teeth could not be assessed.

Both central incisors exhibit the same wear pattern. The adjacent maxillary right lateral incisor does not, but instead displays a quadrilateral shaped, flat abrasion patch on the vestibular surface that affects both the enamel and the cementum (Fig. 3.5). A low-power micrograph of the vestibular enamel directly adjacent to the wear facet reveals parallel horizontal striations of varying size and depth, with several large, deep scratches surrounded by numerous fine striations. This horizontal wear continues onto the area of the abrasion facet itself. The left maxillary lateral incisor was not preserved. The only other closely associated tooth that was recovered

FIGURE 3.3 Maxillary left central incisor, mesial aspect. Enamel wear has occurred on both vestibular and oral surfaces, producing a blunt wedge with its apex at the incisal edge. Scale bar is in millimeters.

was the mandibular right lateral incisor, which also shows vestibular abrasion.

The vestibular, but not oral, surface of this central incisor also exhibits horizontal microwear features, which appear to have been superimposed upon the vertical wear. There are also pits and multidirectional scratches on the dentin, which can be attributed in part to the normal chewing functions

FIGURE 3.4 SEM image of the incisal edge of the left maxillary central incisor. Scratches on the exposed dentin of the crown are vertically oriented and continuous over the incisal edge (arrow), connecting the vestibular and oral surfaces.

of teeth. The exposed dentin, for example, would come into contact with food of varying textures, including gritty substances (such as stone-ground bread) and softer substances (such as fruit). Field and laboratory studies of microwear among alloprimates have demonstrated that microwear features can change rapidly; in some cases, new features were created in a single day (Teaford & Oyen, 1989).

The observable anterior and posterior teeth in both jaws exhibit abrasion patches on the vestibular aspects of the root, CEJ, or crown. In most cases, these are clearly evident where the cementum has been abraded to expose the underlying dentin, which is also worn (Fig. 3.6). In some cases the abrasion has polished and thinned the enamel of the tooth crown, even serving to erase grooves attributable to linear enamel hypoplasia (Fig. 3.7). The abrasion patches are shallow and flat, and SEM imaging shows horizontal, not vertical, striations. Thus the patches would seem to be caused by a rubbing action that occurred horizontally at the gum line and would

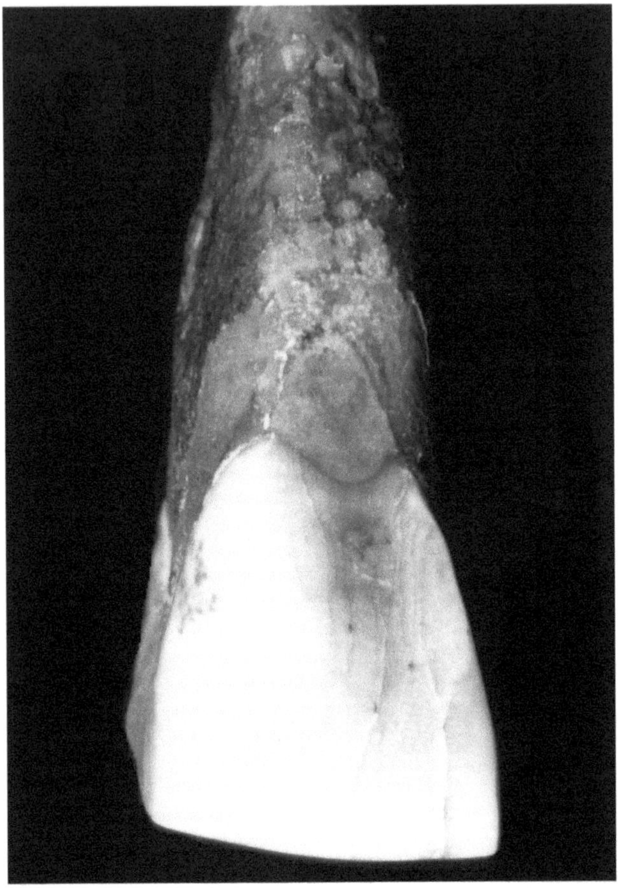

FIGURE 3.5 An abrasion patch of irregular quadrilateral shape on the vestibular aspect of a maxillary right lateral incisor at the CEJ on the cementum and the adjacent enamel.

have abraded the teeth subsequent to gingival recession or continued tooth eruption. Lukacs and Pastor (1988: Fig. 2) illustrate what appear to be identical abrasion patches on teeth from a prehistoric site in Pakistan although they could not identify the cause of these with any certainty. They also observed polishing of the vestibular surface of crowns that effectively erased evidence of linear enamel hypoplasia (Lukacs & Pastor, 1988: Fig. 10).

Interpretation of Nonalimentary Tooth Wear

A variety of nonalimentary modifications of teeth have been identified in past populations, some of which are intentional and some incidental (reviewed by Alt & Pichler, 1998; Milner & Larsen, 1991; Stojanowski,

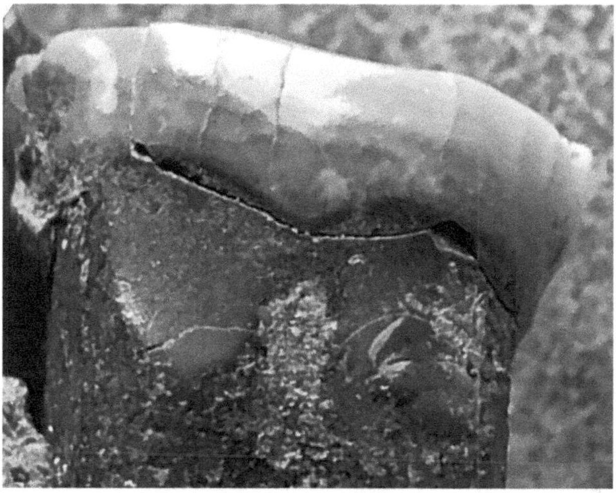

FIGURE 3.6 Abrasion patches at the CEJ on the left mandibular second molar.

Johnson, Paul, & Carver, 2016). Intentional modifications usually involve the anterior teeth and include inlays of semiprecious stones on vestibular crown surfaces, filing or notching of occlusal edges and vestibular crowns, and removal of the incisors. These intentional modifications are thought to be socially constrained and linked to ideas of beauty or group identity (Milner & Larsen, 1991; Romero, 1970; and see also Arcini, 2005). There being no evidence for intentional modification of teeth in ancient Egypt in texts, artistic depictions, or archaeologically recovered dental remains, the unusual wear this woman exhibits must have been acquired incidentally.

Incidental modifications are often by-products of the effects of cultural signifiers, therapeutic interventions, or the use of teeth as tools. An example of a cultural signifier that may leave evidence on teeth is the labret, or lip plug, which polishes the vestibular surface of anterior teeth (Torres-Rouff, 2003). Therapeutic effects include abrasion from habitual attempts to clean teeth or remove stains by rubbing with ash, sand, or the frayed ends of plant stems (Aubry, Mafart, Donat, & Brau, 2003; Sutton, 1978); interproximal grooving due to repeated probing between adjacent teeth to remove food particles, to relieve the pain associated with a carious tooth, or as a "toothpicking" habit (Berryman, Owsley, & Henderson, 1979; Lukacs & Pastor, 1988); and polishing of the vestibular surface of posterior tooth enamel due to the persistent use of a masticatory (a substance that is chewed but not usually swallowed) to mask mouth odor or to increase the flow of saliva. Task activities can cause pronounced modifications of teeth and have been the focus of many inquiries because of their significance for the interpretation of behaviors in the past. Prominent examples include

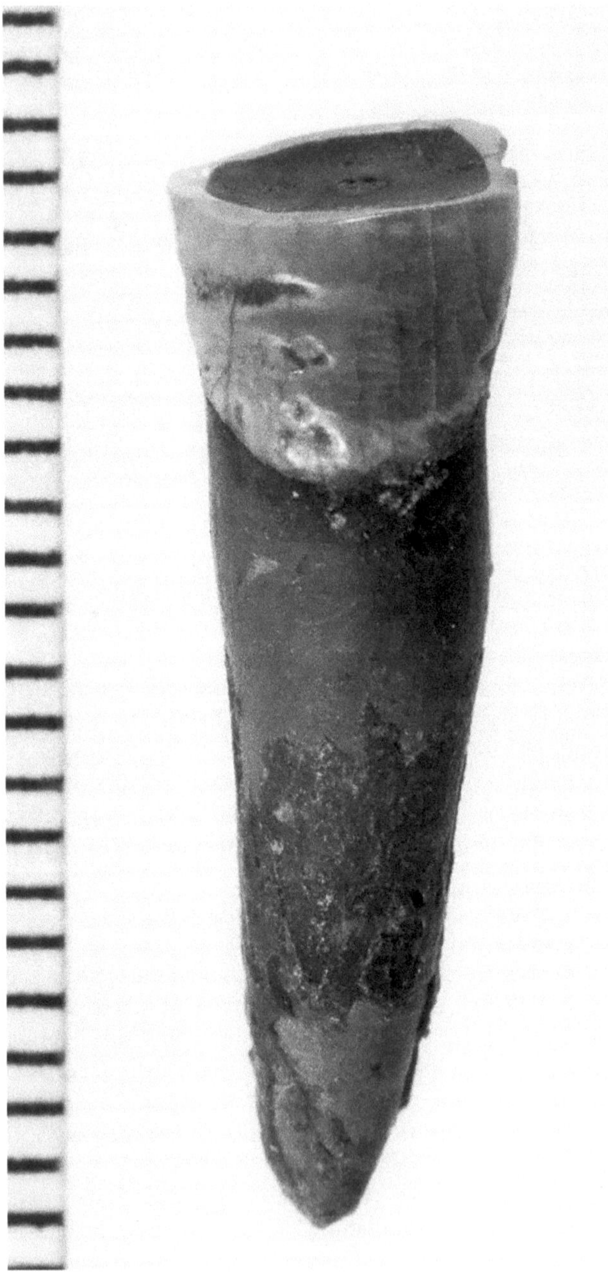

FIGURE 3.7 Enamel polish on the vestibular surface of the right mandibular canine, which has erased the mesiocentral portions of linear hypoplastic grooves. Scale bar is in millimeters.

grooving of the occlusal surfaces of teeth surfaces from working sinew, yarn, cordage, or basketry (Al-Shorman & Khalil, 2006; Boutin, 2012; Eshed, Gopher, & Hershkovitz, 2006; Lorkiewicz, 2011; Minozzi, Manzi, Ricci, di Lernia, & Borgognini Tarli, 2003; Molnar, 2008; Schulz, 1977; Scott & Jolie, 2008; Waters-Rist, Bazaliiskii, Weber, Goriunova, & Katzenberg, 2010); and abrasion caused by holding a bow-drill mouthpiece (Merbs, 1983). Tooth wear such as lingual surface attrition of maxillary anterior teeth (LSAMAT) is thought to be caused by shredding or peeling sugar cane or tubers held between the upper teeth and the tongue (Irish & Turner, 1997). Chipping of tooth edges can be caused by retouching stone tools (Gould, 1968), holding pins or nails between the teeth of needleworkers and shoemakers (Ronchese, 1948), and biting through thread by sewers (Prpić-Mehičić, Bunak-Kobler, Jukić, & Katunarić, 1998). Finally, interproximal notching of crowns in carpenters can be caused by holding nails between adjacent teeth (Turner & Anderson, 2003).

Wedge-Shaped Wear

Although the incisor wear exhibited by this woman does not include grooving and is not the same as the LSAMAT displayed by certain contemporary and archaeological populations, a number of ethnographic accounts record the use of the anterior teeth as aids in the preparation of vegetable fibers for basketry, cordage, and other products (e.g., Lous, 1970; Schulz, 1977). Well documented among indigenous people of Australia, for example, is the manufacture of a spindle bobbin by splitting a stick longitudinally with the teeth (Barrett, 1977). Both Micmac and Paiute women have used their teeth to initially split roots or stems (McBride, 1990; Wheat, 1967), and the Hadza are known to use their anterior teeth as tools to strip bark from branches to make twine and to puncture and peel tuber skins (Berbesque et al., 2012). Thus the wedge-shaped wear could have been caused by the splitting of vegetable material, such as reeds. Reeds were used extensively at Mendes; 74% of the individuals dated to the Old Kingdom or First Intermediate Period were buried in reed mats or coffins, according to the 1976–78 excavation records that are now archived at the Oriental Institute, University of Chicago. Ancient Egyptians used palm fibers and grass as well as reeds, but a strong case can be made that the plant was *Cyperus papyrus*, an aquatic sedge that grew abundantly in the delta. Papyrus stalks were used for firewood, to make boxes and baskets for storage and transport of goods, and to make sandals, curtains, and floor mats (Ammoun, 1991; Lewis, 1974; Pliny, trans. 1601; Stead, 1986). Usually the outer rind of the stalk was peeled off and used to make utilitarian objects, while the underlying pith was stripped longitudinally to make paper (Leach & Tait, 2000; Parkinson & Quirke, 1995; Wendrich, 2000). Aside from the abrasion expected from the oral processing of plant material, papyrus contains silica phytoliths, which are known for their hardness and ability to scour tooth enamel (Rabenold & Pearson, 2011); this could hasten tooth wear and contribute to the unusual incisal wear exhibited here.

Vestibular Abrasion Patches

It is clear from the SEM images that the vestibular abrasion was the result of a horizontal or side-to-side motion, and the similar appearance of wear on the crown, CEJ, and root suggest that they were caused by the same activity. The abrasion is flat and oriented perpendicular to the alveolar margin, and thus is not an extension of oblique occlusal wear. Further the abrasion occurs on the vestibular surface of maxillary crowns and hence cannot be attributed to the normal occlusal relationship between the maxillary and mandibular teeth, in which the upper teeth over-ride the lower. Similar wear patterns among a variety of contemporary, historic, and archaeological groups have led researchers to suggest a number of explanations. These can be discounted in the case of the woman from Mendes, however, because her anterior and posterior teeth are similarly abraded. For example, sinew or vegetable cordage can be threaded between the posterior teeth and then pulled back and forth at the front of the mouth, resulting in interproximal grooving on the posterior teeth, accompanied by vestibular abrasion near the CEJ but only on the posterior teeth (Lukacs & Pastor, 1988; Pedersen, 1979). Similarly the continuous contact and movement of reed blowpipes, used by metalworkers to fan the embers of charcoal-fired hearths (Scheel, 1989), could have caused vestibular abrasion on the anterior teeth, but not on the posterior teeth. Slippage of the mouthpiece of a bow drill, for which there is ample evidence in ancient Egypt (Montet, 1958; Stead, 1986), also could result in abrasion to the anchoring anterior teeth, but not posterior teeth. The continuous pressure against the teeth from a masticatory quid could cause abrasion. The use of masticatories was widespread in ancient Egypt and was practiced by individuals from both sexes and all social classes (Dixon, 1969; Kennedy, Plummer, & Chiment,1986). Specific mention of the practice among women is made in the Ebers Papyrus, which describes how women mixed resins and honey to form small pellets that they chewed to sweeten their breath (Dixon, 1969). But, because the polishing affects teeth in both dental arcades and anterior as well as posterior teeth in this woman, the wear cannot easily be attributed to the regular use of a masticatory, which is most often held preferentially in a buccal pouch on one side of the mouth and chewed on that side (Barrett, 1977).

The most parsimonious explanation for the abrasion patches lies in the habitual cleaning of the teeth. There is similarity between the back and forth action commonly used for brushing and the horizontal nature of the striations. The flat CEJ wear may be a precursor to notches in the neck region of anterior teeth among archaeological and contemporary populations, which are widely believed to be caused by excessive tooth brushing with an abrasive dentifrice (Barrett, 1977; Milner & Larsen, 1991; Pedersen, 1979). Modern toothbrushes are composed of synthetic bristles laid out in a regular pattern, whereas ancient people likely used a twig, softened and frayed at the end, which would have been gentler on the teeth and may not have caused notching. In some parts of the world, people may brush their teeth with a finger or twig combined with indigenous tooth powders (Pindborg, 1970). Attempts at dental hygiene such as this may have caused the vestibular abrasion observed in this woman, as dental practices were not wholly unknown in ancient Egypt. There is, however, some debate as to how extensive and practical the Egyptians' knowledge was. High frequencies of calculus, periodontal disease, and antemortem tooth loss among ancient Egyptians certainly suggest that habitual dental care was not widespread (Forshaw, 2009; Leek, 1966, 1967; Ruffer, 1920; Weeks, 1980). A rarity of tooth cleaning in ancient Egypt may help to explain why only one individual in the skeletal sample exhibited the abrasion patches; it may be the case that plant residues adhered to this woman's teeth as a result of her task activities, necessitating regular cleaning. A fine abrasive for this purpose would have been readily available. Sodium bicarbonate, a component of historical natron (sodium carbonate decahydrate), is used today by many people to clean teeth and is an ingredient in some toothpastes. Although the most well-known Egyptian source of historical natron is the Wadi el-Natrun (natron valley), which is home to a number of alkali lakes that supplied large amounts of natron for embalming purposes, natron can be harvested from the dry beds or shores of any salt or brackish water lake, such as Lake Manzala, now a brackish lagoon confined to the northeastern Nile delta but extending close to Mendes in the past.

Alternatively the abrasion patches may result from the regular application of an analgesic to sooth sore gums. Sodium bicarbonate is often used as an analgesic as well as a dentifrice. It seems unlikely that a medicinal substance was applied in order to alleviate acute pain from caries since only one tooth was infected in this way (and no others in the Mendes sample display vestibular abrasion patches although several suffered from caries and abscesses), but chronic dental pain may have plagued this woman if she persistently used her teeth in task activities. Although natural remedies, such as pastes made from ground cloves, garlic, or mint leaves, are known to soothe toothaches and gingiva inflamed from abscesses or "teething," these would tend to be localized and/or temporally limited in their application; hence, the most likely explanation is based on the habitual use of a compound that contained a naturally occurring salt, such as natron, to clean the teeth, which may have had the added value of possessing analgesic properties.

Women's Work in Ancient Egypt

This woman from ancient Mendes exhibits two patterns of wear that are unique in the dental sample from the site: abrasion patches on the vestibular aspects of teeth at the CEJ, root, and/or crown, and wedge-shaping of the maxillary central incisors, the latter also apparently unique in the bioarchaeological literature. The abrasion patches exhibit horizontal striations and may result from cleaning teeth or rubbing the gingiva with a compound such as natron salt. The wedge-shaped wear has been interpreted as resulting from the use of the teeth as tools, specifically to split reeds, enabling the parts of the stalks to be pulled apart more easily. The plant material may well have been papyrus, given its prevalence in the archaeological record of ancient Mendes. Since this woman was the only individual in the skeletal sample to exhibit these dental wear patterns, they likely indicate that this preparation of botanical material represents craft specialization rather than a domestic activity undertaken widely in the community.

This has important implications for our understanding of the professionalization of women in ancient Egypt. Based on tomb paintings and recovered texts, scholars assert that there were only seven professions open to women throughout ancient Egyptian culture history: as priestesses in temples dedicated to goddesses (for high status and well-connected women); as singers, musicians, and dancers (for women with skills and talent); as mourners; as weavers of cloth in the workshops of the aristocracy; and as midwives (Graves-Brown, 2010; Lesko, 1996; Robins, 1993; Strouhal, 1992; Tyldesley, 1994; Watterson, 1991). Reliefs and models that were placed in tombs to work for the deceased in the afterlife indicate that, other than in those seven professions, women were largely engaged in indoor domestic activities in their own homes or undertook the same work as servants in the households of others (Watterson, 1991). These depictions were commissioned and made by men, however, and represent an idealized and stereotyped world, conforming to the conventional view of daily life in which women do not work in anything other than domestic contexts (Tyldesley, 1994). Tomb scenes often depict workshops devoted to crafts such as carpentry, metal-working, leather-working, and jewelry-making, but only male figures are ever shown. It has been argued that women may have made coiled baskets for household use, but that products made by techniques other than simple coiling probably were made by part-time or full-time professionals (Wendrich, 2000). Regrettably, there appear to be no accounts of these professionals, whether male or female. The archaeological record sheds no greater light on the situation as it is difficult to distinguish on the basis of recovered artifacts between production for household use and specialized production for wages, sale, or barter.

Perhaps this woman, then, represents an example of the professionalization of women that is not registered in the documents and tomb scenes that are created by men and reflect male interests and biases. Scholars of women in ancient Egypt stress that women and men had equal legal status with respect to owning, purchasing, inheriting, or disposing of their property, and both could enter into contracts, take oaths, and witness statements (Graves-Brown, 2010; Lesko, 1996; Robins, 1993; Tyldesley, 1994; Watterson, 1991); in depictions of daily life, however, the implications are that women did not have equal access to professional opportunities. The bioarchaeological recognition of this woman as a craft specialist, a professional role for women that is not acknowledged by ancient Egyptian conventions, reveals how women were marginalized by the mainstream, male dominated, society. We therefore have, at present, an artificially constrained understanding of the full extent of women's professional activities. However, we can construct a richer representation of women's work in ancient Egypt by allowing individuals to tell their stories through their skeletons.

Acknowledgments

We thank Mike Wayman, Tina Barker, and Eileen Heidler for their assistance in obtaining the SEM images, and Chenée Merchant for creating the illustration used as Fig. 3.1. Macrophotographs were taken by Marnie Bartell and Nancy Lovell. The skeletal material excavated by the Institute of Fine Arts, New York University, and the associated field notes were made available through the courtesy of Bonnie Gustav Golub, Christine Lilyquist, and the late Donald Hansen. Excavations at Mendes, 1976–78, were sponsored by the Institute of Fine Arts of New York University, the Brooklyn Museum, and the American Research Center in Egypt, and were funded by the Smithsonian Institution. The University of Alberta and the Social Sciences and Engineering Research Council of Canada supported the research on the skeletal remains. We are very grateful to the editors and the anonymous reviewer, whose suggestions for revision served to improve the manuscript immeasurably.

References

Allen, S. J., & Wilson, K. L. (1982). *Excavations at Mendes, 1976–1979, . Colloques internationaux due CNRS No. 595 – L'Égyptologie en 1979. Axes prioritaires de recherches* (Vol. 1, pp. 139–151). Paris: Éditions du Centre National de la Recherche Scientifique.

Al-Shorman, A., & Khalil, L. (2006). The evidence of weaving at Khirbit Yajuz in Jordan using dental microwear. *International Journal of Dental Anthropology, 8*, 1–9.

Alt, K. W., & Pichler, S. L. (1998). Artificial modifications of human teeth. In K. W. Alt, F. W. Rösing, & M. Teschler-Nicola (Eds.), *Dental anthropology: Fundamentals, limits, and prospects* (pp. 387–415). New York: Springer Verlag.

Ammoun, D. (1991). *Crafts of Egypt*. Cairo: The American University in Cairo Press.

Arcini, C. (2005). The Vikings bare their filed teeth. *American Journal of Physical Anthropology, 128*, 727–733.

Aubry, M., Mafart, B., Donat, B., & Brau, J. J. (2003). Brief communication: Study of noncarious cervical tooth lesions in samples of prehistoric, historic, and modern populations from the south of France. *American Journal of Physical Anthropology, 121*, 10–14.

Barrett, M. J. (1977). Masticatory and non-masticatory uses of teeth. In R. V. S. Wright (Ed.), *Stone tools as cultural markers: Change, evolution and complexity* (pp. 18–23). Canberra: Australian Institute of Aboriginal Studies.

Bass, W. M. (1987). *Human osteology* (3rd ed.). Columbia: Missouri Archaeological Society, Special Publication No. 2.

Berbesque, J. C., Marlowe, F. W., Pawn, I., Thompson, P., Johnson, G., & Mabulla, A. (2012). Sex differences in Hadza dental wear patterns. *Human Nature*, *23*, 270–282.

Berryman, H. E., Owsley, D. W., & Henderson, A. M. (1979). Noncarious interproximal grooves in Arikara Indian dentitions. *American Journal of Physical Anthropology*, *50*, 209–212.

Blom, D. E. (2017). A bioarchaeological perspective on community and the tension between individual and population. In S. L. Juengst, & S. K. Becker (Eds.), *The bioarchaeology of community* (Vol. 28, pp. 104–111). Arlington: American Anthropological Association, Archaeological Papers.

Boutin, A. T. (2012). Written in stone, written in bone. In A. L. W. Stodder, & A. M. Palkovich (Eds.), *The bioarchaeology of individuals* (pp. 193–214). Gainesville, FL: University Press of Florida.

Brewer, D. J., & Wenke, R. J. (1992). Transitional Late Predynastic—Early Dynastic occupation at Mendes: A preliminary report. In E. C. M. van den Brink (Ed.), *Nile Delta in transition: 4th–3rd millennium BC* (pp. 191–197). Tel Aviv: E. C. M. van den Brink.

Buckberry, J. L., & Chamberlain, A. T. (2002). Age estimation from the auricular surface of the ilium: A revised method. *American Journal of Physical Anthropology*, *119*, 231–239.

Buikstra, J. E., & Ubelaker, D. H. (Eds.), (1994). *Standards for data collection from human skeletal remains*. Fayetteville, AR: Arkansas Archaeological Society, Research Series No. 44.

Byrnes, J. F., & Muller, J. L. (2017). *Bioarchaeology of impairment and disability*. Cham: Springer.

de Meulenaere, H., & Mackay, P. (1976). *Mendes II*. Warminster: Aris and Phillips.

Dixon, D. M. (1969). Masticatories in ancient Egypt. *Journal of Human Evolution*, *1*, 433–449.

Eshed, V., Gopher, V., & Hershkovitz, I. (2006). Tooth wear and dental pathology at the advent of agriculture: New evidence from the Levant. *American Journal of Physical Anthropology*, *130*, 145–159.

Forshaw, R. (2009). Dental health and disease in ancient Egypt. *British Dental Journal*, *206*, 421–424.

Goldstein, J. I., Newbury, D. E., Michael, J. R., Ritchie, N. W. M., Scott, J. H. J., & Joy, D. C. (2018). *Scanning electron microscopy and x-ray microanalysis* (4th ed.). New York: Springer.

Gould, R. A. (1968). Chipping stones in the outback. *Natural History*, *77*, 42–49.

Graves-Brown, C. (2010). *Dancing for Hathor: Women in ancient Egypt*. London: Continuum.

Hansen, D. P. (1967). Mendes 1965 and 1966. *Journal of the American Research Center in Egypt*, *6*, 5–51.

Holz, R. K., Stieglitz, D., Hansen, D. P., & Ochsenschlager, E. (1980). *Mendes I*. Cairo: American Research Center.

Irish, J. D., & Turner, C. G., II (1997). Brief communication: First evidence of LSAMAT in non-native Americans: Historic Senegalese from West Africa. *American Journal of Physical Anthropology*, *102*, 141–146.

Juengst, S. L., & Becker, S. K. (Eds.), (2017). *The bioarchaeology of community* (Vol. 28). Arlington, VA: American Anthropological Association, Archaeological Papers.

Kennedy, K. A. R., Plummer, T., & Chiment, J. (1986). Identification of the eminent dead: Penpi, a scribe of ancient Egypt. In K. J. Reichs (Ed.), *Forensic osteology* (pp. 290–307). Springfield: CC Thomas.

Leach, B., & Tait, J. (2000). Papyrus. In P. T. Nicholson, & I. Shaw (Eds.), *Ancient Egyptian materials and technology* (pp. 227–253). Cambridge: Cambridge University Press.

Leek, F. F. (1966). Observations on the dental pathology seen in ancient Egyptian skulls. *Journal of Egyptian Archaeology, 52*, 59–64.

Leek, F. F. (1967). The practice of dentistry in ancient Egypt. *Journal of Egyptian Archaeology, 53*, 51–58.

Lesko, B. S. (1996). *The remarkable women of Ancient Egypt* (3rd ed.). Providence: B. C. Scribe.

Lewis, N. (1974). *Papyrus in classical antiquity*. Oxford: Clarendon Press.

Lorkiewicz, W. (2011). Nonalimentary tooth use in the Neolithic population of the Lengyel culture in central Poland (4600–4000 BC). *American Journal of Physical Anthropology, 144*, 538–551.

Lous, I. (1970). The masticatory system used as a tool. *Tandlaegebladet, 74*, 1–10.

Lovell, N. C. (1991/1992). The 1992 excavations at Kom el-Adhem, Mendes. *Journal of the Society for the Study of Egyptian Antiquities, 21/22*, 20–36.

Lovell, N. C., & Whyte, I. (1999). Patterns of dental enamel defects at ancient Mendes, Egypt. *American Journal of Physical Anthropology, 110*, 69–80.

Lukacs, J. R., & Pastor, R. F. (1988). Activity-induced patterns of dental abrasion in prehistoric Pakistan: Evidence from Merhgarh and Harappa. *American Journal of Physical Anthropology, 76*, 377–398.

Mant, M. (2014). Paleopathology of human remains at ancient Mendes (Tell er-Rub'a), Egypt. *Bioarchaeology of the Near East, 8*, 1–27.

McBride, B. (1990). *Our lives in our hands: Micmac Indian basketmakers*. Halifax: Nimbus.

McConnan Borstad, C., & Lovell, N. C. (2011–2012). Dental disease at ancient Mendes (Tell er-Rub^{c}a), Egypt. *Journal of the Society for the Study of Egyptian Antiquities, 38*, 1–16.

Meindl, R. S., & Lovejoy, C. O. (1985). Ectocranial suture closure: A revised method for the determination of age at death based on the lateral–anterior sutures. *American Journal of Physical Anthropology, 68*, 57–66.

Merbs, C. (1983). *Patterns of activity-induced pathology in a Canadian Inuit population*. Ottawa: National Museums of Canada, Archaeological Survey of Canada, Paper 119.

Milner, G. R., & Larsen, C. S. (1991). Teeth as artifacts of human behavior: Intentional mutilation and accidental modification. In M. A. Kelley, & C. S. Larsen (Eds.), *Advances in dental anthropology* (pp. 357–378). New York: Wiley-Liss.

Minozzi, S., Manzi, G., Ricci, F., di Lernia, S., & Borgognini Tarli, S. M. (2003). Nonalimentary tooth use in prehistory: An example from early Holocene in central Sahara (Uan Muhuggiag, Tadrart Acacus, Libya). *American Journal of Physical Anthropology, 120*, 225–232.

Molnar, P. (2008). Dental wear and oral pathology: Possible evidence and consequences of habitual use of teeth in a Swedish Neolithic sample. *American Journal of Physical Anthropology, 136*, 423–431.

Montet, P. (1958). *Everyday life in ancient Egypt*. London: Edward Arnold.

Parkinson, R., & Quirke, S. (1995). *Papyrus*. London: British Museum Press.

Pedersen, P. O. (1979). The dentition of King Christian the third: Dental disease and oral hygiene of a sixteenth century King of Denmark and Norway. *OSSA, 6*, 229–241.

Pindborg, J. J. (1970). *Pathology of the dental hard tissues*. Philadelphia, PA: WB Saunders.

Pliny, the Elder. (1601). *The historie of the world, XIII: Booke of the historie of nature*, Chap. XI. Trans. (P. Holland, Trans.). London: Adam Islip.

Prpić-Mehičić, G., Bunak-Kobler, D., Jukić, S., & Katunarić, M. (1998). Occupational tooth-wear in clothing industry workers. *Collegium Anthropologicum*, *22*(Suppl), 241–249.

Rabenold, D., & Pearson, O. M. (2011). Abrasive, silica phytoliths and the evolution of thick molar enamel in primates, with implications for the diet of *Paranthropus boisei*. *PLoS One*, *6*(12), e28379.

Redford, D. B. (2001). Mendes. In D. B. Redford (Ed.), *The Oxford encyclopedia of ancient Egypt*. Oxford: Oxford University Press.

Redford, D. B. (2004). *Excavations at Mendes (Vol. 1): The royal necropolis*. Leiden: Brill.

Redford, D. B. (2009). *Delta reports, Vol. 1: Research in lower Egypt*. Oxford: Oxbow Books.

Redford, D. B. (2010). *City of the Ram-Man*. Princeton, NJ: Princeton University Press.

Robins, G. (1993). *Women in ancient Egypt*. Cambridge, MA: Harvard University Press.

Rogers, T. (1999). A visual method of determining the sex of skeletal remains using the distal humerus. *Journal of Forensic Sciences*, *44*, 57–60.

Romero, J. (1970). Dental mutilation, trephination, and cranial deformation. In R. Wauchope, & T. D. Stewart (Eds.), *Handbook of middle American Indians* (pp. 50–67). Austin, TX: University of Texas Press.

Ronchese, F. (1948). *Occupational marks and other physical signs: A guide to personal identification*. New York: Grune and Stratton.

Ruffer, M. A. (1920). Studies of abnormalities and pathology of ancient Egyptian teeth. *American Journal of Physical Anthropology*, *3*, 335–382.

Scheel, B. (1989). *Egyptian metalworking and tools*. Aylesbury: Shire.

Schulz, P. D. (1977). Task activity and anterior tooth grooving in prehistoric California Indians. *American Journal of Physical Anthropology*, *46*, 87–92.

Scott, G. R., & Jolie, R. B. (2008). Tooth-tool use and yarn production in Norse Greenland. *Alaska Journal of Anthropology*, *6*, 253–264.

Smith, B. H. (1984). Patterns of molar wear in hunter–gatherers and agriculturalists. *American Journal of Physical Anthropology*, *63*, 39–56.

Stead, M. (1986). *Egyptian life*. London: British Museum.

Stodder, A. L. W., & Palkovich, A. M. (2012). Osteoarchaeology and bioarchaeology. In A. L. W. Stodder, & A. M. Palkovich (Eds.), *The bioarchaeology of individuals* (pp. 1–8). Gainesville, FL: University Press of Florida.

Stojanowski, C. M., Johnson, K. M., Paul, K. S., & Carver, C. L. (2016). Indicators of idiosyncratic behavior in the dentition. In J. D. Irish, & G. R. Scott (Eds.), A companion to dental anthropology (pp. 377–395). Chichester: John Wiley and Sons.

Strouhal, E. (1992). *Life of the ancient Egyptians*. Norman: The University of Oklahoma Press.

Sutton, P. R. N. (1978). Unusual forms of abrasion of teeth: Unintentional 'filing' in Micronesians and Polynesians. *Archaeology and Physical Anthropology of Oceania*, *13*, 30–39.

Teaford, M. F. (1988). Scanning electron microscope diagnosis of wear patterns versus artifacts on fossil teeth. *Scanning Microscopy*, *2*, 1167–1175.

Teaford, M. F., & Oyen, D. (1989). In vivo and in vitro turnover in dental microwear. *American Journal of Physical Anthropology*, *80*, 447–460.

Torres-Rouff, C. (2003). Oral implications of labret use: A case from Pre-Columbian Chile. *International Journal of Osteoarchaeology*, *13*, 247–251.

Turner, G., & Anderson, T. (2003). Marked occupational dental abrasion from Medieval Kent. *International Journal of Osteoarchaeology*, *13*, 168–172.

Tyldesley, J. (1994). *Daughters of Isis: Women of ancient Egypt*. London: Penguin Viking.

Waters-Rist, A., Bazaliiskii, V. I., Weber, A., Goriunova, O. I., & Katzenberg, M. A. (2010). Activity-induced dental modification in Holocene Siberian hunter–fisher–gatherers. *American Journal of Physical Anthropology*, *143*, 266–278.

Watterson, B. (1991). *Women in ancient Egypt*. New York: St Martin's Press.

Weeks, K. R. (1980). Ancient Egyptian dentistry. In J. E. Harris, & E. F. Wente (Eds.), *An x-ray atlas of the royal mummies* (pp. 99–121). Chicago, IL: University of Chicago Press.

Wendrich, W. Z. (2000). Basketry. In P. T. Nicholson, & I. Shaw (Eds.), *Ancient Egyptian materials and technology* (pp. 254–267). Cambridge: Cambridge University Press.

Wheat, M. M. (1967). *Survival arts of the primitive Paiutes*. Reno: University of Nevada Press.

White, T. D., Black, M. T., & Folkens, P. A. (2012). *Human osteology* (2nd ed.). Amsterdam: Elsevier Academic Press.

Wilson, K. L. (1982). *Mendes: Preliminary report on the 1979 and 1980 seasons*. American Research Center in Egypt. Malibu: Undena.

Chapter 4

Looking into the eyes of the ancient chiefs of shíshálh: the osteology and facial reconstructions of a 4000-year-old high-status family

Terence Clark[1], Matthew Betts[7], Gary Coupland[2], Jerome S. Cybulski[3,4,5], Jasmine Paul[6], Philippe Froesch[8], Steven Feschuk[9], Raquel Joe[10] and Gretchen Williams[11]

[1]*Department of Archaeology & Anthropology, University of Saskatchewan, Saskatoon, SK, Canada,* [2]*Department of Anthropology, University of Toronto, Toronto, ON, Canada,* [3]*Research Division, Canadian Museum of History, Gatineau, QC, Canada,* [4]*Department of Anthropology, University of Western Ontario, London, ON, Canada,* [5]*Department of Archaeology, Simon Fraser University, Burnaby, BC, Canada,* [6]*Stewardship and Territorial Lands Management Division, shíshálh Nation, Sechelt, BC, Canada,* [7]*Eastern Archaeology Research, Canadian Museum of History, Gatineau, QC, Canada,* [8]*Forensic Art 3D, Visualforensic, Paris, France,* [9]*Department of Culture, shíshálh Nation, Sechelt, BC, Canada,* [10]*Tems Swiya Museum, shíshálh Nation, Sechelt, BC, Canada,* [11]*Canadian Museum of History, Gatineau, QC, Canada*

Chapter Outline

Introduction

Indigenous Peoples in Canada have a long history of marginalization driven by the economic, political, and social effects of decades of colonial rule.

Bioarchaeology of Marginalized People. DOI: https://doi.org/10.1016/B978-0-12-815224-9.00004-X

As the First Peoples on the land recognized as Canada, their interactions with the colonial government pushed them to the periphery of Canadian society, creating an environment of systemic oppression, dispossession, and discrimination that isolates and subjugates them socially, politically, and economically (Kenrick & Lewis, 2004). In recent years the increased attention paid to exposing the atrocities committed against Indigenous Peoples has led to both contemporary and retrospective examinations of how colonialism has shaped our understanding of Indigenous Peoples and their history. For archaeology, this approach has been twofold. On one hand, there has been a push to reassess existing archaeological collections and reevaluate the ethicality of their maintenance in non-Indigenous institutes (Kakaliouras, 2012). Movements toward repatriation and negotiating agreements for the curation and display of these collections are becoming the norm (see Canadian Museum of Civilization, 2011). On the other hand, the collection of archaeological data on Indigenous Peoples is moving toward community-based partnerships (CBPs), which place Indigenous Peoples as partners in research that involves their land, peoples, or material culture in a move to support ongoing Indigenous decolonization efforts (Atalay, 2012). CBP projects are designed to build an ethical archaeology that moves away from displaying Indigenous Peoples as "objects" within Canadian archaeological history and instead gives Indigenous Peoples an appropriate space in which to determine how their history is told.

The ideology of CBP is easier than the reality, as academics are often used to independently determining their research questions and how data should be collected and interpreted. Difficulties in striking these balances have led to a variety of levels of community engagement in CBP projects and raised questions as to what truly counts as a community partnership. If Indigenous community members are not involved in all stages of the project, then there is a danger of once again pushing Indigenous Peoples to the periphery, marginalizing the communities that these projects seek to empower, and manufacturing interpretations that cause strife between Indigenous groups (Supernant & Warrick, 2014). Within this danger is the labeling of Indigenous Peoples as objects of study, rather than as researchers and authors of their own heritage. However, amongst the doom and gloom of failed CBP projects, there are emerging examples that highlight the success of CBP in contemporary archaeology, such as the shíshálh Archaeological Research Project (sARP). sARP is a joint venture that grew out of a long-standing archaeological project in the Sechelt region and now includes the shíshálh Nation, the University of Toronto, the University of Saskatchewan, and previously the Canadian Museum of History (CMH). This chapter describes the role of sARP and the shíshálh Nation in the collaborative creation of an exhibit at the CMH in order to illustrate the empowering role that community partnerships with Indigenous Peoples can play in archaeology as a mechanism for combatting marginalization and aiding in ongoing decolonization efforts.

Kwenten Makw'ali and the Beginnings of a shíshálh Archaeological Research Project Partnership

In the spring of 2001, archaeologists from the shíshálh Nation discovered and recorded a new archaeological site on the shores of Skupa (Salmon Inlet), near Sechelt, BC (Fig. 4.1). The site, now known as Kwenten Makw'ali in shashishalhem, was recorded as a heavily disturbed shell midden with numerous lithics scattered on the beach. Though the site is currently accessible by water only, it was used for a period of 30 years in the late 1900s, which lead to a significant amount of historic disturbance, not only in the construction of buildings but also in the subsequent cleanup attempt using large, earth-moving machines.

Though the site was first recorded in 2001, investigation of the area did not begin until 2010 when a team from the University of Toronto mapped the site as part of a larger archaeological survey of Salmon Inlet. Inspection of the site as part of this survey led to the discovery of ground stone and shell beads eroding out of a bank that had been cut to construct an access road. Beads are not uncommon in Northwest Coast archaeological assemblages, but they have a known relation to burial contexts and so their presence suggested the presence of human remains. The potential of a burial led to a discussion between the University team and the shíshálh Chief and Council with a decision to excavate the area and to remove and rebury any humans remains encountered. The ensuing excavation involved constant

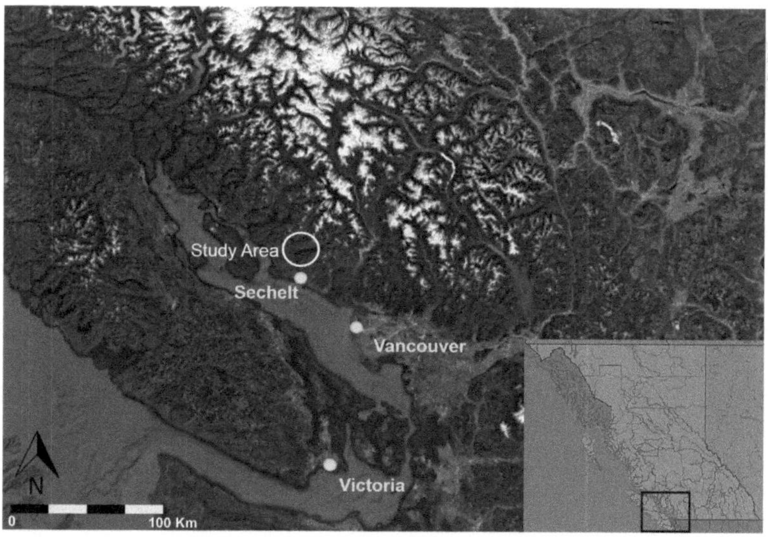

FIGURE 4.1 Study area map. Inset map of British Columbia by NordNordWest licensed under CC BY-SA 3.0, https://commons.wikimedia.org/w/index.php?curid = 7667685 (changed to black and white image).

communication between the archaeological team, Chief and Council, elders, and community members about the excavation, disposition, and handling of the remains discovered, as well as the involvement of Indigenous youth as members of the excavation team.

The initial excavation in 2010 revealed a single individual, buried with 360,000 hand ground stone and shell beads, representing the most bead-rich burial on the Northwest Coast. The richness of this burial, dated to approximately 4000 years ago, lends credence to the interpretation that this represented a shíshálh Chief. Discussions with Chief and Council resulted in a shared decision to continue excavation of the area to establish context for this individual. Altogether, excavation of the site occurred over three seasons and revealed five individuals in four discrete interments (Table 4.1). Buried with all but one individual were large numbers of hand ground stone and shell beads. This site represents not only the largest bead-rich burial found on the Northwest Coast, but also the largest grouping of bead-rich burials. While important academically, the richness of this site also made it spiritually and culturally important to the shíshálh people. Multiple individuals buried in bead-rich burials with no evidence of long-term occupation supported the idea that this was a cemetery for high-status individuals and used solely as a ceremonial site. Further description of the cultural context of the burials and summary of grave inclusions have been discussed in Coupland et al. (2016).

Understanding the People

Once excavated, the remains were placed in cedar boxes and sent to the CMH for analysis. Preparation for shipping was done following shíshálh rules for handling of the dead, which involved following particular proscriptions and placing cedar boughs with remains. The results of the analysis of the four adults and one infant are described in Table 4.1.

Extensive discussion with Chief, Council, and community members allowed the sARP team to proceed with traditional osteological analysis and minimal invasive testing, which took the form of isotopic analysis and carbon dating. The community was interested in knowing the age of these ancestors, where they had potentially come from, and any details of their lives that could be ascertained from their skeletal remains. In-depth descriptions of what could be gleaned from each type of investigation were presented to the Council, and team members were present at meetings to answer any questions that arose. The goal of this discussion was to ensure that Council and community were aware of and consented to what would happen at each step of the project and to ensure that team members understood where the boundaries were and the types of information that the community was interested in obtaining. The team wanted to avoid any miscommunication over what was permissible in the analysis. The understanding that these

TABLE 4.1 Osteological descriptions of the five individuals excavated from Kwenten Makw'ali.

Individual[a]	RC dating	Sex	Age	Stature	Description
Burial 1	3634–3910 cBP	M	50 +	171.50 ± 3.18 cm	Moderate preservation, degenerative joint disease, compression fracture of L3
The chief	3559–3811 cBP				
Burial 2	3420–3685 BP	F	19–23	150.22–160.70 cm	Moderate preservation
					Enamel hypoplasia, right rib fracture
Burial 3	3577–3832 BP	M	20–25	171.26 ± 3.25 cm	Good preservation
Possible twin					Metopic suture, impacted 3rd molar, linear enamel hypoplasia, heavy tooth attrition, enlargement of insertion of *oppenens digiti minimi*
Burial 4	3401–3637 BP	M	20–25	166.94 ± 4.14	Poor preservation
Possible twin					Metopic suture, impacted 3rd molar, linear enamel hypoplasia, heavy tooth attrition, enlargement of insertion of *oppenens digiti minimi*
Burial 5		Unknown	3–6 months	–	Good preservation

[a]*Detailed information on the remains recovered from Kwenten Makw'ali is presented in Coupland et al. (2016), Cybulski (2011), Holland (2014a, 2014b, 2014c), Williams (2011).*

were shíshálh ancestors rather than research specimens was made a fundamental focus of the partnership and helped ensure that remains were treated with respect at all times. As part of this understanding, no photos of the remains were to be displayed, and as a result there are no images of the human skeletal remains contained in this chapter. However, a unique exception to this agreement arose when the shíshálh were invited to participate in the creation of a new exhibit at the CMH.

Building the Display

With the transition to a new name and mandate in 2012 the CMH undertook an ambitious project to create the largest and most comprehensive permanent exhibition ever developed about the history of Canada. Key to the development of the Canadian History Hall was the implementation of six "guiding principles" (Amyot, Leblanc, & Morrison, 2017, p. 21), the result of extensive consultation with the public, experts, and communities. These included: National narrative, legacy, authenticity, human experience, multiple perspectives, and participation. These principles ensured/demanded that the museum told real (not meta) histories grounded in objects and documents, which spoke to the stories of real individuals with personal histories. The principles also dictated that the stories be told from multiple perspectives, not just the perspective of museum professionals or archaeologists, and that the stories needed to show a legacy from the past which persisted to the modern day.

These guiding principles posed significant challenges in the first gallery of the Canada History Hall, which focused primarily on archaeological evidence of the earliest Indigenous occupations of what is now Canada. The goal was to show how individuals lived, rather than focusing on populations. The bioarchaeological evidence gained during the sARP excavations provided a medium to highlight individual lives within the context of a population. The existing relationship between the sARP team and the CMH (one member of the team was an exhibition curator) allowed the CMH to engage in discussions with the shíshálh Chief and Council about the possibility of incorporating the excavated shíshálh Chief and ancestors into the CMH display.

Understandably the remains of the Chief represented a deeply sensitive topic, and initial consultations began tentatively; the history of positive collaboration between sARP and the shíshálh Chief and Council proved beneficial to these discussions. sARP had been active in the Sechelt region for the past 10 years, though the notion of collaboration had undergone an evolution from the early days of research in the area. However, it was this long history and evolving focus on collaboration that had led to the establishment of trust between the archaeologists and the community that laid the basis for a larger-scale collaboration with the CMH. The shíshálh Nation, in consultation with elders, carefully considered the proposal, and responded with a draft memorandum of understanding, which outlined the steps to be taken in the project, and which asserted the rights of the shíshálh Nation over the care and interpretation of their ancestor's remains.

Internationally, museums have displayed human remains in a variety of ways, including the direct placement of skeletal remains into exhibits that can be seen by the public, renderings of remains, and the display of grave goods. Many of these methods were decided with little or no consultation with the cultural groups who identified with these individuals, especially when many of these collections were amassed without permission from Indigenous persons (Fforde & Hubert, 2006; Walker, 2007). The decision of how to display skeletal remains is a difficult and sensitive topic as they are the physical embodiment of ancestors. In this case a decision was made to make use of the new technologies that have become available in digital forensic facial reconstruction. The use of technology as a tool in archaeological knowledge translation has stimulated discussion recently, especially as a mechanism for not only disseminating knowledge of Indigenous culture to the public, but also as a way of repatriating knowledge back to Indigenous communities (Dawson, Levy, & Lyons, 2011). The skulls of the four adults were reassembled, 3D scanned, and digitally reconstructed to represent the individuals.

Creation of the Reconstructions

Each individual was given a neutral designation for the project: Individual one (male Chief), Individual two (female), Individual three (male brother one), and Individual four (male brother two). The infant burial did not have any individualizing characteristics and was not reconstructed. The first step in the facial reconstruction involved osteologists reconstructing the damaged skulls using standard anthropological techniques. The reconstruction was done as respectfully as possible, in the presence of the cedar boxes and cedar boughs provided by the community, in a private room inaccessible to nonessential museum staff. The remains were covered in blankets when they were not being actively studied. The reconstructions for Individuals two and three proceeded very smoothly as the skulls were much better preserved than the others. Individual one, however, proved particularly challenging. While both the entire cranium and mandible were present, both elements were highly fragmentary. As the skull was reassembled, an asymmetry was introduced that could not be rectified as the reconstruction proceeded (it was hoped that this issue could be digitally addressed during the facial reconstruction).

Unfortunately, Individual four proved to be impossible to reconstruct due to the highly fragmented nature of the remains and the absence of certain critical portions of the skull. Due to the osteological evidence that Individuals three and four were probably brothers and likely twins (Coupland et al., 2016; Cybulski, 2011; Holland, 2014a, 2014b, 2014c; Williams, 2011), the team decided to use the Individual three skull as a substitute for his twin brother. Our hope was that we could modify the appearance of Individual four through the reconstruction of his soft tissue (e.g., body weight) and hairstyle to provide him the individuality he deserved.

Following the reconstruction of the crania and mandibles, these elements were digitized using a NextEngine HD laser scanner set at maximum resolution. Textures of the remains were recreated in addition to the capture of 3D data, leaving a permanent record of the skulls prior to reburial. The remains were also photographed with a high-resolution digital single-lens reflex (SLR) camera. In addition to the physical remains, the burial objects, including shell necklaces, bone ear spools, and stone beads, were 3D scanned. The community wished for the Chief to be wearing his beaded robe, therefore, a 10 cm × 10 cm section of the cape was reconstructed on a fabric backing using real burial beads. The section was then 3D scanned to serve as a reference for reconstructing the larger beaded cape. In addition, the community wished Individuals two, three, and four to be wearing cedar bark capes. A Salish cedar bark cape from the Museum's collection (specific provenience unknown) was selected as an avatar for the capes, and it was scanned using the same protocols used for the burial remains and objects.

The digital data were then transferred to Phillipe Froesch of VISUALFORENSIC. The forensic digital facial reconstruction began with significant community input where the community assembled a large package of historic photographs and drawings to be used as reference for facial expressions, skin color, hairstyles, and posture. A schedule was instituted so that feedback would be given at each stage of the facial reconstruction process. The artist submitted images digitally to the team, and these were then presented to community elders and experts for comments.

The skulls were delivered to VISUALFORENSIC as digital obj. files, which were then imported for work in ZBRUSH and Cinema 4D. The first steps of the reconstruction were guided by the physical anthropology reports created for each skeleton, as the age, sex, and major pathological lesions were critical to the reconstruction and individualization of each face. Individual one had a significant asymmetry in the left side of the cranium, resulting from the physical reconstruction of the remains. This was corrected digitally before any forensic reconstruction took place. The digital reconstruction process mimics the physical facial reconstruction process (Wilkinson, 2004) in its methodology, but with several important adaptations, as described later.

The first step of the methodology consisted of adding 3D soft tissue depth markers of appropriate thickness on the digital crania and mandibles. Data for these markers were derived from Peckman, Manheim, Listi, and Fournier (2013, Tables 2 and 3) for Individuals two, three, and four. For Individual one the "Male, Normal" thicknesses from Rhine (1983) were used. For each cranium, 10 depth markers were positioned onto the sagittal axis and nine

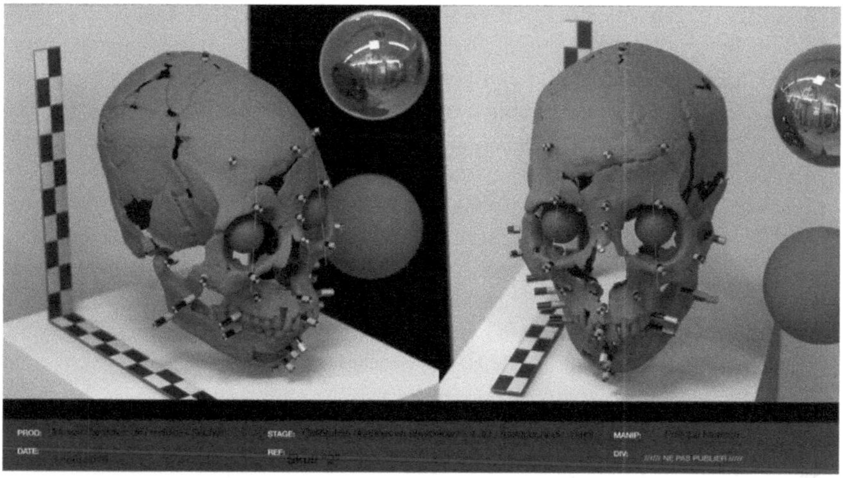

FIGURE 4.2 Tissue markers.

more on each side (Fig. 4.2). These virtual markers provided the visual approximation for the epidermis outline, just as wood or rubber tissue depth markers do for physical reconstructions using clay.

The reconstruction proceeded using a unique and progressive system which incorporated the following elements:

The anatomical facial muscles: Insertion marks were located on the digital remains and the following groups of muscles were created in 3D, following a methodology similar to that described in Wilkinson (2004): buccinator, masseter, risorius, zygomaticus major and minor, frontalis, temporalis, procerus, corrugator, orbicularis oculi, nasalis, levator labii, depressor labii, mentalis, levator anguli, and orbicularis oris.

Eyes and eyelids: Each eye was assigned an estimated diameter of 24.6 mm, and centered in the orbits (Wilkinson, 2004; Wilkinson & Mautner, 2003). In lateral view the iris plane was positioned tangential to an axis touching the superior and inferior orbit ridges (Wilkinson, 2004; Wilkinson & Mautner, 2003).

Insertion of the eyelids: The palpebral ligament of the external canthus was attached to the malar tubercle zone, 9 mm under the fronto-zygomatic suture and the internal ligament was connected to the lacrimal crest zone (Whitnall, 1921). The palpebral foil was positioned in an axis replicating the superior orbit ridge direction (Balueva & Veselovskaya, 2004). The eyelid aperture was set to represent 70% of the maximum width of the orbit.

Nasal volume: Nasal reconstruction was accomplished using the Gerasimov method and the "two tangents" method (Gerasimov, 1955, 1971) as modified by Rynn and Wilkinson (2006). A craniometric method based on trigonometry (Rynn, Wilkinson, & Peters, 2010) was used to calculate the correct nasal width by applying a 1.65 factor to the maximum nasal aperture. The equations specific to this method were not used as there is no appropriate reference measurement for this population available. The piriform aperture of the bony structure provided the inferior and superior limits of the nostrils (Gerasimov, 1955; Rynn et al., 2010).

Lips and mouth: Modiolus points were located on a radiant axis spreading out from the canine/premolar contact (Gerasimov, 1955; Wilkinson, 2004). Lip thickness was determined by the "upper" and "lower" lip depth markers, and vermillion was based on incisor enamel height. The philtrum width was estimated by the medium axis of the central incisors (Gatliff, 1984; Rynn et al., 2010).

3D skin texture: A standard 3D epidermis was placed on top of the markers, muscle, and the nose/mouth structure for each skull, and sculpted inside ZBRUSH. The sculpting process was conducted at a pore and wrinkle level, estimating a skin complexion for the corresponding ages and harsh environmental conditions, especially for the adult male subject. This process was conducted with significant community input.

Facial hair and hairstyles: Eyebrows, eyelids, and hairs were hand created and sculpted in 3D, according to the bone topology and documentation related to the shíshálh community. The hairstyle and especially facial hair were of specific concern for the community, and dozens of iterations were required for each individual before the reconstructions were finalized (Fig. 4.3).

Illumination and shooting: Forensic facial reconstructions result in portraits, which means that some subjective decisions were necessary, such as choosing the angle of camera, framing, lightning, facial expression,

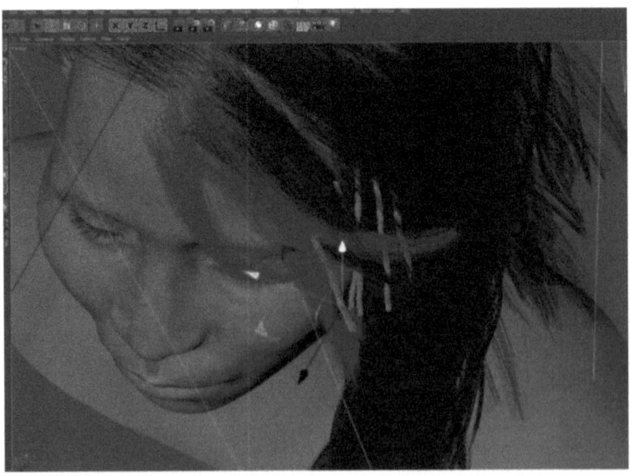

FIGURE 4.3 Hair sculpting.

and tilting of the head. Those decisions were made by the artist, who attempted to create "proud" and "powerful" attitudes in accordance with the wishes of the shíshálh Nation. Again, many iterations and community consultations were required to perfect the expressions and lighting.

Rendering of the final videos/images: Consistent with the Canadian History Hall principle of participation the team decided to attempt to animate the individual portraits in the hopes of making the images more engaging and lifelike. The goal was to have the heads turn slightly, the eyes to blink naturally, and the faces to "fix" the visitor in their gaze. Armatures were added to specific portions of the renderings to facilitate movement and animations produced in ZBRUSH. Because of the resolution inherent in a 4K rendering for such a large screen, processing requirements were significant. Each frame was composed of 2,073,600 pixels and required 50 min of rendering on an Apple Mac Pro with 32GB Ram and 12 cores at 2.66 GHz. At the target of 30 frames/s, to ensure natural movement, and at a 20 s video window (to be displayed on a loop), this required nearly 500 h of rendering for each individual. Each video was then finally edited into a single composite video by the CMH audiovisual studio.

The goal of this recreation was to display the individuals on a module, consisting of a 60-in. 4k television monitor to show the faces at slightly larger than life size. A smaller touch screen monitor was embedded in the plinth below the main monitor, which both activates and plays the video. The centerpiece of the module would include digital forensic facial reconstructions of the four individuals, presented as a family. This would be augmented by several text panels and a video that highlighted the community collaboration and the digital reconstruction process. The text used was created by the team, in consultation with shíshálh Chief and Council. A unique feature of this project, which particularly embodies collaboration, was the creation of two modules. One module would remain at the CMH in the Canadian History Hall and the other would be displayed in the Tems Swiya Museum in Sechelt, for the shíshálh Nation. During the recreation of the individuals, there was regular contact with the nation; shíshálh Nation Protector of Culture, Steven Feschuk, was the primary contact.

Documenting the Collaboration

While the facial reconstructions were ongoing, work began on the video of the collaboration and facial reconstruction. Following the guiding principles of multiple perspectives, authenticity, and legacy, the goal for this video project was to provide a platform for the community to discuss the project, their contemporary relationship to the individuals, and the history the individuals represent. Because this was a sensitive subject, it was considered important for the community to also discuss why they wanted to move forward with such a collaboration. Filming took place at the Tems Swiya Museum and at Kwenten Makw'ali over two days in late August 2016. The filming took the form of interviews with (then) Chief Calvin Craigan, elder Lori Dixon, elder Jamie Dixon, and Steven Feschuk, as well as the project director. The final video was compiled and edited by Northern Lights productions, under contract to the museum. As with the facial reconstructions, the editing process involved significant collaboration and feedback from the community as it was assembled.

Unveiling the Faces

The *te shíshálh hewhiwus ʔe shewelh x̱wux̱wulh*—The ancient chiefs of shíshálh module were first previewed to the community at an event at the CMH on May 17, 2017 (Fig. 4.4). shíshálh Chief and Council members attended the gathering, gifts were exchanged, and the module was blessed by elders.

Following the public event, media could view the faces for the first time in the presence of community members. The response by the community was overwhelming and immediate. As Chief Warren Paull has indicated: "When we returned on Friday, it was like we brought back the Stanley Cup... There were a lot of high-fives and a lot of happy people. It was a great and wonderful thing. It's unifying...and I hope it's unifying for everybody on the Coast" (Eckford, 2017). The connection to the community was highlighted by Tems Swiya curator Raquel Joe, a member of the exhibit team: "everybody got choked up when they first saw it, including myself. You come around the corner and you're looking into the faces of people...

FIGURE 4.4 Faces of the ancient chiefs.

FIGURE 4.5 Exhibition at Tems Swiya museum.

You can see portions of different [shíshálh] family members in the facial features of every one of those renderings" (Eckford, 2017).

The modules opened officially in both National museums on July 1, 2017 (Fig. 4.5). These animations representing some of the most influential and powerful Indigenous people ever to live in Canada are the first real historic individuals that visitors meet in the Canadian History Hall, an exhibition that is replete with paintings and photographs of other later influential historical figures. This is a story that could only be told through a deep collaboration using the most sensitive of archaeological deposits, and it is a story that only the shíshálh Nation could tell.

Conclusion

The sARP partnership arose during a time of increasing awareness and support for Indigenous rights over their lands and heritage. It was also a time when archaeologists were grappling with issues of a colonial past and attempting to decolonize the discipline in which they worked, while still engaging in archaeological research with First Nations communities. The sARP has tried to balance the needs and desires of the shíshálh community with academic archaeology. This project highlights the success of collaborative research when the value of this work is clearly evident to the community. In this case the shíshálh Nation was willing and proud to share the story of their ancient chiefs and viewed archaeology as a way of accessing a history that had been lost to them. Including the community in the decision to excavate, analyze, and finally how to disseminate and portray their ancestors represents a positive step away from the colonial control that academia has held over Indigenous people's representations of their own history. Far from being the marginalized objects of study, the shíshálh community were the agents of their own storytelling. The importance of these types of collaborations cannot be overstated, but the success of this project is rooted in known principles essential for collaboration. For Indigenous peoples to devote their time and knowledge to archaeological research, the questions must have relevance to them and there must be a benefit to the community. In this case the benefit is more tangible than most, but it can stand as an important representation that a project must give back to the community. This community is able to look into the eyes of their ancestors and see themselves, to see a visible representation of their history tied physically to the land. While not all projects will create a physical token of remembrance, they can contribute to strengthening community and historical knowledge, and supporting spiritual and physical connections to their lands provided they are doing research that shifts community members from objects of study to engaged partners in design, collection, and dissemination of research.

References

Amyot, C., Leblanc, L., & Morrison, D. (Eds.), (2017). *Stories of Canada: The Canadian history hall*. Ottawa: Library and Archives Canada.

Atalay, S. (2012). *Community based archaeology: Research with, by and for Indigenous and local communities*. Berkeley, CA: University of California Press.

Balueva, T. S., & Veselovskaya, E. V. (2004). New developments in facial reconstruction. *Archaeology, Ethnology and Anthropology of Eurasia, 1*, 143–152, [Russian and English].

Canadian Museum of Civilization. (2011). *Repatriation policy*. Canadian Museum of Civilization Corporation. Retrieved from https://www.historymuseum.ca/wp-content/uploads/2015/09/REPATRIATION-POLICY.pdf

Coupland, G., Bilton, D., Clark, T., Cybulski, J. S., Frederick, G., Holland, A., & Williams, G. (2016). A wealth of beads: Evidence for material wealth-based inequality in the Salish Sea region 4000–3500 cal BP. *American Antiquity, 81*(2), 295–315.

Cybulski, J. S. (2011). *The osteology of an early pacific human skeleton from the Bible Camp Site (DjRw-14), Sechelt, British Columbia*. Manuscript on file, Library Archives (Archaeology Ms. 5240). Gatineau: Canadian Museum of History.

Dawson, P., Levy, R., & Lyons, N. (2011). "Breaking the fourth wall": 3D virtual worlds as tools for knowledge repatriation in archaeology. *Journal of Social Archaeology, 11*(3), 387–402.

Eckford, S. (2017, May 18). Shíshálh ancestors come to life. *Coast reporter*. Retrieved from http://www.coastreporter.net/news/local-news/sh%C3%ADsh%C3%A1lh-ancestors-come-to-life-1.20034046

Fforde, C., & Hubert, J. (2006). Indigenous human remains and changing museum ideology. In P. J. Ucko, R. Layton, S. Shennan, & P. G. Stone (Eds.), *A future for archaeology: The past in the present* (pp. 83–96). London: University College London Press.

Gatliff, B. P. (1984). Facial sculpture on the skull for identification. *American Journal of Forensic Medicine and Pathology, 5*(4), 327–332.

Gerasimov, M. M. (1955). Reconstruction of the face from the basic structure of the skull. *(W. Tshernezky, Trans.)*. Russia: Publishers Unknown.

Gerasimov, M. M. (1971). *The face finder*. New York: Lippincott.

Holland, A. (2014a). *The osteology of Burial 3 at DjRw-14, Sechelt, British Columbia*. Manuscript on file. Gatineau: Canadian Museum of History.

Holland, A. (2014b). *The osteology of Burial 4 at DjRw-14, Sechelt, British Columbia.* Manuscript on file. Gatineau: Canadian Museum of History.

Holland, A. (2014c). *The osteology of Burial 5 at DjRw-14, Sechelt, British Columbia.* Manuscript on file. Gatineau: Canadian Museum of History.

Kakaliouras, A. M. (2012). An anthropology of repatriation: Contemporary physical anthropological and Native American ontologies of practice. *Current Anthropology, 53*(S5), S210–S221.

Kenrick, J., & Lewis, J. (2004). Indigenous people's rights and the politics of the term "indigenous". *Anthropology Today, 20*(2), 4–9.

Peckman, T. R., Manheim, M. H., Listi, G. A., & Fournier, M. (2013). In vivo facial tissue depth for Canadian Aboriginal children. *Journal of Forensic Science, 58*(6), 1429–1438.

Rhine, S. (1983). Tissue thickness of southwestern Asian-derived American Indians. Maxwell Museum of Anthropology: Lab of Physical Anthropology, unpublished report.

Rynn, C., & Wilkinson, C. M. (2006). Appraisal of traditional and recently proposed relationship between the hard and soft dimensions of the nose in profile. *American Journal of Physical Anthropology, 130*(3), 364–373.

Rynn, C., Wilkinson, C. M., & Peters, H. L. (2010). Prediction of nasal morphology from the skull. *Forensic Science, Medicine and Pathology, 6*(1), 20–34.

Supernant, K., & Warrick, G. (2014). Challenges to critical community-based archaeological practice in Canada. *Canadian Journal of Archaeology, 38*(2), 563–591.

Walker, P. L. (2007). Bioarchaeologicalethics: A historical perspective on the value of human remains. In M. A. Katzenberg, & S. R. Saunders (Eds.), *Biological anthropology of the human skeleton* (pp. 1–40). New Jersey: Wiley.

Whitnall, S. E. (1921). *Anatomy of the eye and orbit.* London: Oxford Medical Publications.

Wilkinson, C. M. (2004). *Forensic facial reconstruction.* Cambridge: Cambridge University Press.

Wilkinson, C. M., & Mautner, S. A. (2003). Measurement of eyeball protrusion. *Journal of Forensic Science, 48*(1), 1–5.

Williams, G. (2011). *The osteology of individual 2 from the Bible Camp Site, DjRw-14, Sechelt, British Columbia.* Gatineau: Canadian Museum of Civilization, Submitted to Archaeology and History Division. Available from Canadian Museum of Civilization, Gatineau.

Further Reading

Arcas Consulting Archaeologists. (1994). *Archaeological investigations at Tsawwassen, B.C. (Volume II).* Submitted to British Columbia Archaeology Branch, Victoria. Copies available from British Columbia Archaeology Branch, Victoria.

Arcas Consulting Archaeologists. (1999). *Archaeological investigations at Tsawwassen, B.C. (Volume IV).* Submitted to British Columbia Archaeology Branch, Victoria. Copies available from British Columbia Archaeology Branch, Victoria.

Katzie Development Corporation Archaeology. (2010). *Archaeological excavations at DhRp-52: Final report.* Submitted to British Columbia Archaeology Branch, Victoria. Copies available from British Columbia Archaeology Branch, Victoria.

Matson, R. G., & Coupland, G. (1995). *The prehistory of the Northwest Coast.* San Diego, CA: Academic Press.

Chapter 5

"Officially absent but actually present": bioarchaeological evidence for population diversity in London during the Black Death, AD 1348–50

Rebecca Redfern[1] and Joseph T. Hefner[2]

[1]*Centre for Human Bioarchaeology, Museum of London, London, United Kingdom,* [2]*Department of Anthropology, Michigan State University, East Lansing, MI, United States*

Chapter Outline

Introduction

Lewis' (2016, p. 109) statement, "officially absent but actually present," encapsulates the situation which instigated our research, whereby for the past 15 years, colleagues and visiting researchers to the Museum of London and Museum of London Archaeology have been anecdotally observing the

Bioarchaeology of Marginalized People. DOI: https://doi.org/10.1016/B978-0-12-815224-9.00005-1

presence of people with Black ancestry and dual heritage in the Medieval cemetery populations from London. Writing today, we can see that by not formally recording their presence, we have significantly contributed to their "official absence" and further served to marginalize them from mainstream knowledge and academic discourse. During those years, recording strategies and research interests held a different focus, and much of the scientific analyses used to reconstruct osteobiographies were in their infancy or had yet to be created (e.g., ancestry methods, light stable isotopes, ancient DNA analysis of genomes). These are not excuses, but gentle reminders that bioarchaeology, Medieval archaeology, and history had only just begun to more widely integrate gender, feminist, and life-course theories, as well as evidence for diversity into scholarship—the momentum for books and articles on these issues gathered pace in the 1990s to early 2000s thanks to earlier ground-breaking research (e.g., Hall, 1993; Miller, 1961; Phillips Jr, 1985). Since then, bioarchaeological scholarship in these areas has flourished but crucially physical anthropology has also sought to critically examine diversity and inclusion within the discipline itself (e.g., Antón, Malhi, & Fuentes, 2018; Turner et al., 2018). Events at the 2017 International Medieval Congress paint a different story (Chan, 2017), and with the increasing interest by the far right in Medieval history, it means that it is more important than ever to ensure that everyone is "present and correct" (S.N., 2017) (see also Hahn, 2001; Hsy & Orlemanski, 2018). The situation is summarized by Ramey (2014, p. 38): "[i]f the medieval period is allowed to in essence 'get away with' its part in the history of prejudice, whether classist or racist or sexist, because of its distance from today, then other times and places can also come to be seen as nonessential to the course of human history."

In researching this work, we also encountered further "official absences," as there is a paucity of Medieval scholarship about population diversity in the British Isles between AD 1000 and 1500, produced by biases in the primary sources and research of this period having focused on other areas, a situation eloquently described by Habib (2008, p. 9): "what is little looked for, and what is therefore non-existent, is also what is/should be unknown because it cannot be known... reinforc[ing] the conventional contemporary mistruth...the period is race innocent." Consequently, we have had to rely on later, 15th–17th century sources and secondary works, particularly about communities and urban centers in Iberia (Spain) and Italy to explore and understand the bioarchaeological evidence from London during AD 1348–50, a situation we recognize as being far from ideal. However, during the 14th century, the need for free and cheap labor after the first and second waves of the Black Death in Europe was instrumental in increasing the number of enslaved people present in Medieval Europe (Fynn-Paul, 2014). Therefore this work helps clarify the background against which these later shifts in economic activities took place.

Within British archaeology and bioarchaeology, an absence also exists with respect to published light stable isotope studies of migration and population movement, as these have focused on the Anglo-Saxon period (5th–11th centuries AD) (e.g., Groves et al., 2013). A few childhood residency results have been published for the later Medieval period, and have identified a handful of people from the Baltic region, with the majority of people found to be local to their region of burial or to the British Isles (Millard, Roberts, & Hughes, 2005; Roberts et al., 2013). However, a number of projects researching dietary and childhood residency stable isotopes in British Medieval cemetery populations are ongoing but to the best of our knowledge, these have not integrated skeletal evidence for ancestry into their research designs. Furthermore, we were unable to find any published skeletal ancestry studies of later Medieval British populations although a person believed to be from Tunisia has been communicated in the media (Williamson, 2014). The lack of bioarchaeological ancestry studies is discussed later.

Our chapter investigates diversity from the perspective of human variation as expressed phenotypically—the physical characteristics of an individual/population—using the macromorphoscopic ancestry method. It aims to substantiate the "actually present," with the discussion focusing on individuals of non-White European ancestry. It seeks to establish the ancestry of a subsample of 41 individuals buried in the Black Death cemetery of East Smithfield, unite these data with published light stable isotope work on childhood residency (Kendall, Montgomery, Evans, Stantis, & Mueller, 2013) and extant mitrochondrial DNA (mtDNA) data (Klunk & Poinar, personal communication, 2017), and to combine these data with the osteological evidence for disease and indicators of stress. In order to understand and interpret these data, we have used the concept of marginalization, a paradigm which proposes that for many people and societies, they are unable to improve their conditions because of social, political, economic, physical, and environmental barriers (Chand, Nel, & Pelc, 2017). Torres (2008) focuses this definition further, by identifying that it can be applied to a specific group or community of people who are singled out by the dominant group as having a certain negative social demographic characteristic, and notes that from the early Modern period, marginalization is associated with specific human phenotypes. To a certain extent, this concept suggests homogeneity and large-scale analysis, and therefore when constructing new osteobiographies for two individuals, we also employ intersectionality theory (Crenshaw, 1991). This theory recognizes that different forms of oppression, inequality, and injustice (amongst others, racism, sexism, disability, and socioeconomic statuses) interact and interrelate, and importantly raises the suggestion that there is no one experience of identity (Cho, Crenshaw, & McCall, 2013; Nash, 2008). That is to say, the experience of a person with Black ancestry in Medieval London would have varied according to their gender and age, if they had been born in the city or not, if they were free or a servant/enslaved, whether they were rich or poor, and if they had a physical impairment or not. There is no one way of being, as Lorde (2007, p. 138) wrote, "[t]here is no thing as a single-issue struggle because we do not live single-issue lives."

Background to Studying Diversity in the Medieval World

There is a wealth of scholarship concerned with diversity in the Medieval world, which investigates cultural, religious, linguistic, and ethnic variation (e.g., Borgolte, 2014; Cohen, 2008; Jäschke & Schrenk, 2013), with many studies focusing on migrants, often integrating evidence for ethnic and population differences (e.g., Weeda, 2016, 2017; see also https://blackcentraleurope.com/). Research from the 1960s onward has shown that Medieval Europe was not exclusively populated by people with White European ancestry although this myth continues to be perpetuated in the public's imagination (Habib, 2008; Kaufman, 2017), leading one scholar to propose that the "absence" of evidence is a consequence of the "still evolving effects of European colonisation" (Lowe, 2010a, p. 3). This period of history is critical to understanding the later trans-Atlantic slave trade as it sees the rise in the capture and transport of people from Africa to Europe, the beginnings of sugar cultivation, and the origin of plantations (Miller, 2002; Phillips Jr, 1985). Work by Ramey (2014) shows that our understanding of population diversity in this period directly contributes to contemporary views, which are increasingly being influenced by alt-right media opinions (see Introduction). It is worth noting that DNA analysis of contemporary southern Mediterranean populations reveals the contribution of people from north Africa over many generations (Capelli et al., 2009), again revealing the frequent disconnect seen today between a person's genomes, skin color, and ethnic/population identity (amongst others, Banda et al., 2015; Cardena et al., 2013; Shraga et al., 2017).

In Medieval primary sources, differences in cultural practices and physical appearances between communities and populations are mentioned, such as dress and language (Bartlett, 2001). The words used to describe people also reflect the blurring of these concepts, with "Ethiopian," "Black," and "Blackamoor" being used to describe anyone with Black ancestry, and "Saracen" and/or "Moor" for people from the Islamic world, many of whom had Black ancestry (Brann, 2009; Habib, 2008; Ramey, 2014; Ray, 2007). Primary sources also use the phrases "dark skin" or "black skin" to describe people who did not have a "white" or "pale skin" color, but care must be taken to understand the context in which these occur, as their meaning differs between poetry, religious texts, and other sources (see Braude, 1997; Ramey, 2014), all of which make researching this topic fraught with difficulty (Habib, 2008). Heng (2007, 2011a, 2011b) has been very direct in her assertion that racism was present in the Medieval world, and that this was employed by state and religious institutions to create social and economic inequalities, but also to provoke and carry out violent persecutions of minority communities. Such events reached crisis-point during the Black Death, and across Europe minorities such as Jews, Muslims, foreigners, pilgrims, and the poor were accused of creating and spreading the disease, often being physically beaten or killed as a result (Nirenberg, 2015). Although we must be mindful of the nuanced differences in language and between types of primary source documents, it is clear that having Black ancestry could result in a person experiencing racist abuse, prejudice, and discrimination (Lowe, 2010a). Similar to Nirenberg (2015), Lowe (2010b) observes that there was a pan-European reaction to people of African ancestry during the Renaissance (14th–17th centuries AD). Although the majority of the sources Lowe uses were created after AD 1500, she notes that having a "black skin" became synonymous with being a slave (despite the presence of many slaves with White ancestry), differences between people of African ancestry (e.g., language, presence of culturally prescribed piercings, and cicatrices) were ignored and the community was homogenized. Above all, many of the later trans-Atlantic slavery stereotypes seem to have originated in the Medieval world, with Black servants/enslaved being described as lazy, childlike, prone to criminality, drunkenness, and sexual promiscuity (Lowe, 2010b); as one Florentine tax return from AD 1480 states, "One black female slave aged 18 or 20 for domestic work who works badly and is of little worth; she is lazy as are all black females" (Archivio di stato; Lowe, 2010b, p. 28).

Enslavement and Mobility in the Medieval World

There were no slaves in northern Europe in the later Middle Ages, let alone Black ones.

Spufford (2002, p. 339)

Key to understanding enslavement in the Medieval world is to recognize the connections between west and north Africa, the Black Sea region, the Islamic World, and the Christian communities in Mediterranean port cities (Miller, 2002; Phillips Jr, 1985). These regions and communities became bound together by trade and politics, with slavery being part of Islamic succession, whereby conquests during the 10th–15th centuries AD generated huge numbers of enslaved people, usually women and children. Slaves were converted to Islam and considered to be property. Women were mainly used as domestic servants, artisans, and assistants, and if men were enslaved, they often joined the military (Miller, 2002; Phillips Jr, 1985). Phillips Jr (1985) makes the important observation that the Islamic world was a slave society rather than being a society that uses slaves.

In west Africa, warriors and elites used slaves and sold captives (usually female) to consolidate their political power and to buy horses. The captured were transported across the Sahara Desert into north Africa, where they were bought by Arab traders and then sold on in markets particularly in Iberia (Spain). The north African territory, now comprising the Republic of Sudan and South Sudan, also played a very influential role, trading gold and slaves, commodities which were regarded as both expensive and luxurious by Mediterranean merchants. By the 9th century AD, Sub-Saharan Africans were brought by Islamic caravan traders into the Mediterranean ports under their control, which meant that places like Islamic Spain had access to slaves (Phillips Jr , 1985); there is also a report that Black slaves from Morocco were sold in Ireland during the AD 860s (Ray, 2007). By the beginning of the 11th century AD, people from the Sub-Sahara were being transported and sold into Europe; during this century, North African Berbers were also enslaved in Islamic Spain, and a century later the numbers of enslaved Sub-Saharan Africans reaching Spain and Portugal declined (Phillips Jr, 1985). This long-distance movement of people is also attested archaeologically; three light stable isotope studies, from France and Spain of individuals from Muslim burial contexts dating to the 7th–10th centuries AD, identified migrants from the southern Mediterranean and north Africa (Dury et al., 2018; Gleize et al., 2016; Guede et al., 2017; see also Zakrewski, 2011); no anthropological analyses of ancestry were undertaken in these studies.

Work by Austen (1979) suggests that between AD 1100 and 1400 an average of 5500 people per year and a total of 1,650,000 individuals had been transported by the trans-Saharan slave trade. Slavery was not confined to Africa, with Islamic traders also buying slaves from the Black Sea region, from even before the 10th century AD, with Slavs being the most numerous enslaved people (Phillips Jr, 1985). Merchants from Italy, southern France, and Catalonia had strong relationships with north African ports, meaning that by the 12th century AD routes into Christian Europe had been created. However, it is also worth noting that English, Dutch, and French corsairs (pirates) operated in the Mediterranean Sea, attacking Islamic merchant shipping and enslaving any people they captured, thereby providing another route for Sub-Saharan Africans into northern Europe (Phillips Jr, 1985).

Analysis of Italian mercantile primary sources reveals that through their connections to the Islamic World, captured people from the Black Sea area (Tatars, Circassians, Russians, Bulgarians, Armenians, and Albanians) and the Mediterranean islands, as well as Sub-Saharan Africa were being sold—analysis of Genoese records between AD 1126 and 1186 shows that 17 males and 13 females described as "Muslims" were sold (3/17 and 1/13 are recorded as being of Black ancestry), and 3 male and 10 females from Sardinia (Phillips Jr, 1985). The involvement of Medieval Christians in the slave trade was a contradictory situation, and one to which the Medieval Church was ambivalent, whereby it did not object to the institution of slavery, and allowed Christian owners to have their slaves baptized and given new Christian names (Hernæs & Iversen, 2002; Phillips Jr, 1985). But on the other hand the Papacy also disapproved, with primary sources revealing criticism of Catalan Christians owning Islamic slaves, particularly those who had converted from the Muslim faith, with some enslaved people only obtaining their freedom upon the death of their owner (Fynn-Paul, 2014; Hernæs & Iversen, 2002). The Church's teaching was also central to the social and legal convention for married couples in elite households to maintain monogamous relationships (Fynn-Paul, 2014). Nevertheless, there is considerable evidence for extra-marital affairs and for (often dual heritage) illegitimate children being born to servant/enslaved and owners—often these children were formally recognized and included in wills (Mazo Karras, 2017; McKee, 2004).

Adding to the highly complex situation in the Christian world is the perspective offered by legal documents. These trace a continuity in slave owning from the Roman to Medieval worlds; they also show that in many southern Mediterranean port cities, legislation allowed slaves to be imported and kept (Fynn-Paul, 2014; Hernæs & Iversen, 2002). Another determining factor in the free and/or forced movement of people across the Islamic and Christian worlds was the Crusades (11th–13th centuries AD), and again Italian mercantile (particularly Venice and Pisa) activities greatly benefitted from these wars. They were involved in the transport of enslaved people from the Islamic world and eastern Europe to slave markets in the Holy Land, such as the Crusader principality of Acre (today in Israel), where they were predominantly used as domestic staff, but also in the cultivation of sugar cane on plantations (Phillips Jr, 1985). At present, only one light stable isotope study has been published on human remains from this region and date; the analysis of childhood residency in 20 individuals from Caesarea (12th–13th centuries AD) found that at least 13 people had spent their childhoods in Europe (Mitchell & Millard, 2009).

Studies of primary sources (e.g., wills and mercantile records) from southern Europe suggest that the majority of enslaved people lived in urban centers, especially those associated with long-distance trade. They worked in a domestic setting and regardless of origin were further outward examples of their owner's wealth and luxury (Phillips Jr, 1985). Miller (2002) suggests that because of their rarity, people from Sub-Saharan Africa were more highly valued by their owners because of their exoticism (i.e., often those with cicatrices on their face and torso [Phillips Jr, 2013]), becoming another visible signifier of their owner's status. The uptake of luxury elite European lifestyles began when the Crusades had ended and people were reliant upon the use of slaves to create, maintain, and signal status (Phillips Jr, 1985). However, this research and other studies of population diversity, particularly post-AD 1500s in England and Europe, challenge the extent to which these individuals were actually rare (Austen, 1979; Earle & Lowe, 2010; Kaufman, 2017).

Although many individuals with Black ancestry living in Europe were enslaved, a minority of people were not; evidence from wills shows that the enslaved could be manumitted following the death of their owner (Phillips Jr, 2013). Unfortunately, the majority of primary source evidence for free and manumitted people come from the 16th century AD and later. These tell us that free people traveled to Europe as ambassadors or pilgrims from Christian Ethiopia; many were also involved in martial activities, the playing of instruments, or were artisans concerned with ivory carving, jewelry making, and basket weaving (Lowe, 2010b).

Archaeological Context: The Black Death and Medieval London

Medieval London was the largest and most important urban center in Britain, and throughout the period the city underwent substantial changes, reflecting an increasing population and its role as the center for government, trade, and commerce (Porter, 1998). This success was achieved in part because of its docks. The city becoming self-governing in the 12th–13th centuries AD, which coincided with the Royal capital moving from Winchester to Westminster, a change which reinforced the political power and resources held and exercised by The Guilds, which were incorporated societies of merchants, professionals, or skilled craftsmen, who still exist today (Barron, 2005; Thomas, 2002; Williams, 2007). By the 14th century AD the inhabitants of London are proposed to have numbered approximately 80,000 individuals, and primary records and light stable isotope analysis show that people had migrated to the city from elsewhere in the British Isles, particularly from eastern counties such as Kent. Because of its importance as a trading center, merchants and people also came from Ireland and across Europe, including France, the Low Countries, Germany, the Baltic region, Italy, and Spain (Barron, Carlin, & Rosenthal, 2017; Kendall et al., 2013; Thrupp, 1989; Williams, 2007). Archaeologically excavated material culture (e.g., pottery) also supports trading connections with these areas (Thomas, 2002).

Analysis of primary source documents reveals that between AD 1336 and 1584, 17,376 individuals of foreign origins were present in London and included people from India, Greece, and Iceland, in addition to people from the regions/countries listed earlier. The majority were male ($N = 13{,}952$), with 487 foreign-born servants to 222 migrant families (Lutkin, 2016). Many of them were temporary residents, and as well as merchants, there were sailors, members of the Church and religious orders, soldiers, and ambassadors (Lutkin, 2016). With regard to the mercantile classes, the most prominent community were the Italians. These men were accompanied by their families and servants, and if merchants, they joined Guilds, with some achieving Royal patronage. Many of these people came from the important mercantile cities of Genoa, Venice, and Florence (Guidi-Bruscoli, 2016; Thrupp, 1989). These sources, as well as a chronicle written by Richard of Devizes (1192), a monk, reveal that London had a diverse population well before AD 1500, with the latter noting that London contained many "undesirable" people, including "moors." Another important source has been published in a little-known article, which reveals that in AD 1259, King Henry III testified a writ brought by a Sicilian knight, Roger de Lyntin, which stated that an "Ethiopian" who was his "Saracen slave" had run away and de Lyntin was trying to recapture him (Ray, 2007).

These trading connections and highly mobile populations helped facilitate the spread of the Black Death, a pandemic which affected numerous countries in Asia and Europe (Ziegler, 2016a, 2016b). Ancient DNA work has shown that the Black Death was caused by the bacteria *Yersinia pestis* whose reservoir is a number of rodent species (e.g., marmots), with fleas acting as the vector (Bos et al., 2011, 2012; Dean et al., 2018) (alternative perspectives are offered by, amongst others, Bolton, 2013; Ditrich, 2017; see also Welford & Bossak, 2010; Ziegler, 2016a, 2016b).

Primary source evidence shows that the Royal Household and Church were very aware of the devastation and turmoil created by the Black Death on the Continent from AD 1347. By late September–early October AD 1348 the disease had arrived in the British Isles, reaching London in the autumn. One source recorded All Saints Day as the beginning of the first visible signs of disease in the city, but other accounts record its first appearance in Stepney during December (Llwellyn Smith, 1939; Sloane, 2011). In response, during late AD 1348, King Edward III closed all ports (including London) and made arrangements for the governance of the kingdom during the emergency (Sloane, 2011; Williams, 2007). An estimated 290 people died every single day in London until the disease petered out in AD 1351, with a proposed 60% loss of population during the plague years (Byrne, 2012; Horrox, 1994; Sloane, 2011). Despite the economic and social instability caused by the loss of population, London continued to operate. In contrast to many cities on the Continent, no formal ordinances were issued by the authorities with respect to the handling and burying of the dead (Sloane, 2011).

Evidence from wills and other primary sources from London show that Black Death victims were buried in one of over 100 parish cemeteries in the city (e.g., St Botolph Aldgate), but the Royal Household, Church, and City's knowledge of how devastating the disease could be led them to organize two emergency burial grounds, East and West Smithfield (Sloane, 2011). West Smithfield's cemetery has been recently excavated ahead of the Crossrail infrastructure project, but the skeletal sample is not available for study at the present time (Dick et al., 2015; Pfizenmaier, 2016).

The second emergency burial ground at East Smithfield was created because the authorities were concerned that the West Smithfield burial ground could not cope with the high mortality rates (Grainger, Hawkins, Cowal, & Mikulski, 2008). The cartulary of Holy Trinity (Aldgate) described the location and size of the East Smithfield site and mentions a clerk called

John de Corey as one of the landholders. de Corey was actually a servant of Edward the Black Prince, Prince of Wales, and had "at the instigation of substantial men of the City... asked... the Bishop of London to consecrate a toft... as a burial ground" (Holy Trinity Priory, 1971, p. 186; Grainger et al., 2008). The consecration is likely to have occurred in early AD 1349 as Andrew Cros' (a fishmonger) will requests that he be buried there (Grainger et al., 2008). A decade later the site also included a chapel and gatehouse, and ownership had passed from King Edward III to the Cistercian abbey of St Mary Graces. The abbey also acted as memorial to the plague's victims and had its own burial ground, which partly overlaid the western burial area and may have been used to bury victims of later plague outbreaks between AD 1369 and 1479–80 (Grainger et al., 2008). Following the dissolution of the monasteries in AD 1550 during the reign of Henry VIII, the area was used as a manor house, then as a victualing yard for the Royal Navy, and later for yards and tenements. Development did not take place until the early 19th century AD, when the site was used for manufacturing by the Royal Mint, whose disposal of waste metals and chemicals into the soil resulted in the contamination of many individuals (Grainger et al., 2008).

The most recent phase of development occurred in the late 1980s, when the area was subject to property development. From 1984 to 1988, trial and full excavations were carried out by the Museum of London's Department of Greater London Archaeology, which uncovered approximately 20,000 m^2 of the cemetery, with an estimated 40%–50% of burial ground remaining in situ because of extant buildings, now known as Royal Mint Court (Grainger et al., 2008). The archaeological work found that mass and individual graves were concentrated in two areas (Table 5.1), and the internments had been carried out following normative funerary practices, with bodies carefully placed and organized in the mass graves. Several people had been buried on a layer of ash, adults and subadults had been interred in wooden coffins, and the finding of two coin purses and other dress accessories showed that many people had been clothed, but also that valuables had not been removed from the bodies before burial (Grainger et al., 2008). The communities and areas of London represented in the burial population are unknown, although wills, such as Andrew Cros', show that it does include local people.

Materials and Methods

Selection of a Subsample

The subsample of individuals chosen for ancestry analysis was initially selected based on the individuals chosen by Kendall et al. (2013) in their light stable isotope study of early childhood residency in the East Smithfield population. This gave a total of 30 individuals from the site whose dental enamel had been analyzed for strontium and oxygen, which provide information about

TABLE 5.1 Summary of the funerary context (Grainger et al., 2008).

Area of the cemetery	Description	Burial type	Description
Eastern cemetery (OA3)	Area badly truncated by 19th Royal Mint buildings; four north-south parallel rows of individuals and one mass burial trench (MBT 3)	Parallel row of single burials	97 grave cuts arranged in four rows but only 90 individuals were extant because of contamination. 50 individuals had been interred in coffins, one of whom had been buried with a layer of charcoal
	Majority of skeletons were contaminated by chemicals from the Royal Mint. South, west, and east limits of the burial were identified. No grave or boundary markers found	Mass burial trench (MTB3)	Greater than 125 m in length, average width of 2 m, maximum surviving depth of 0.75 m. Truncation by later building works meant that only 102 individuals were excavated, 13 had been interred in coffins
	Individuals interred extended, head at west and feet at east ends of the grave (s)		
Western cemetery (OA2)	50%–60% of the total area was fully excavated (c.75 × 30 m). The cemetery's edges are archaeologically defined by the absence of burials. No trace of boundary or grave markers or graveyard structures	Large mass burial trench (MBT 1)	67 m in length, orientated north-south, average width of 2 m and a maximum surviving depth of 1.25 m. The northern and southern limits were defined; burials at the southern end were heavily truncated
	Burials in this area consisted of two mass burial trenches, a mass burial pit, and graves laid out in 11 parallel north-south rows. One of the rows contained graves and one small mass burial trench (MTB2), and a mass burial pit (MTB1). The trenches were long rectangular cuts aligned north-south, all features were stratigraphically contemporary		Individuals were carefully placed in the trench but packed very close-together and laid up to 5 deep; subadults were used to fill the spaces between adults. The remains of 242 or 243 individuals were excavated, and one male had been buried in a flexed position [11618]. 36 individuals were buried in coffins and of these, three had ash/charcoal in their coffins
	Individuals interred extended, head at west and feet at east ends of the grave(s)		

(*Continued*)

TABLE 5.1 (Continued)

Area of the cemetery	Description	Burial type	Description
		Small mass burial trench (MTB2)	All of this feature was excavated. It was 9.50 m in length, orientated north-south, average width was 2.0 m and a maximum surviving depth of 1.66 m. 50 individuals were excavated, who had been densely laid in the trench and stacked up to 5 deep, two subadults were interred in coffins, and one adult [12510] was buried prone—likely to be accidental
		Western rows of single burials: 1–4, 6, 9	Excavation of the 11 rows revealed 262 graves with 268 individuals present. The majority of burials likely to have been interred in coffins; six double-graves were identified containing the remains of adults and/or adults and subadults. 10 burials contained ash/ charcoal, and 1 individual had been buried with a coin purse

underlying geology and drinking water values (Budd, Montgomery, Evans, & Chenery, 2001; Evans, Chenery, & Montgomery, 2012; Evans, Montgomery, Wildman, & Boulton, 2010; Lightfoot & O'Connell, 2015; Montgomery, 2010; Montgomery, Evans, & Cooper, 2007). At the time of recording, one of the individuals who had been sampled for light stable isotope analysis (skeleton 5326) could not be found. Three of these individuals (skeletons 5281, 5902, 6531) had also been sampled for full genome ancient DNA (aDNA) analysis, which meant that their mtDNA had been sequenced (Klunk & Poinar, personal communication, 2017). Despite the majority of the extant human remains from the site recorded as being of "good" preservation (Centre for Human Bioarchaeology, 2007), it was evident that at least half this group either had the requisite features necessary for estimating ancestry absent, or they were damaged postmortem making observations impossible. Therefore the Wellcome Osteological Research Database (WORD) was queried to retrieve individuals with skull measurements present. This list was further filtered to identify those who also had craniofacial measurements and 11 individuals from that list were randomly selected for recording. In total, 41 individuals had ancestry observations recorded, but only eight had complete crania present.

Osteology

The extant human remains ($N = 636$) from the East Smithfield cemetery (site code MIN86) were recorded onto the WORD database by the Centre for Human Bioarchaeology between 2003 and 2007 using the standards created by the Museum of London (Powers, 2012), which are based on the widely employed professional standards of Buikstra and Ubelaker (1994) and Brickley and McKinley (2004). The first author used the WORD database to retrieve records about the 41 individuals for: sex determination, estimation of age-at-death, specific infectious and metabolic diseases, and indicators of stress (cribra orbitalia, periosteal new bone formation, and enamel hypoplastic defects). Femoral length data were also retrieved in order to calculate stature according to ancestry group using the formulae described in Bass (1995). Evidence for body modification was also investigated during ancestry recording, such as head-shaping or decoration of the dentition, as the latter is attested in individuals of Black ancestry found in 8th century AD Spain (Prevedorou, Díaz-Zorita Bonilla, Romero, Buikstra, & Knudson, 2010) and 15th–17th centuries AD Portugal (Wasterlain, Neves, & Ferreira, 2016). No such changes were observed, but because the population is affected by heavy ante- and postmortem loss of the anterior dentition, such evidence may have been lost (Centre for Human Bioarchaeology, 2007).

Ancestry

The recording methods employed by the Centre for Human Bioarchaeology and Museum of London Archaeology, as well as other archaeological contractors working in London, do not include the determination of ancestry as part of standard data collection (Powers, 2012); a database code for ancestry was introduced nearly a decade ago for work undertaken by the first author's research on Roman-era human remains. This approach is not unique to London, it is one determined by the business orientation and time pressures of archaeological work undertaken by contractors, and also the recording standards adopted by professionals over the past 14 years (Brickley & McKinley, 2004). These standards have just been updated to include ancestry (Mitchell & Brickley, 2017), but it is not clear whether this will be adopted by contractors, as the increase in data collection will impact on their costings. Furthermore the methods chosen for recording ancestry are reliant on high levels of skeletal completeness, and are ones not frequently used by forensic anthropologists or bioarchaeologists.

Reference Data

Temporally and geographically appropriate craniometric and macromorphoscopic reference data for comparison to the cemetery population from MIN86 are not currently available. Therefore we implemented datasets approximating worldwide references for our comparisons. For the craniometric comparisons, data were obtained from the Forensic Anthropology Databank (FDB) for 2990 individuals from around the world, including a large majority of the Howells Dataset comprising craniometric measurements taken from 2524 human crania from 28 populations and compiled between 1965 and 1980 (Howells, 1973, 1989, 1995). The Howells data were obtained from Auerbach (2018). The FDB data were obtained from Dr. Richard Jantz (personal communication, 2018). For the macromorphoscopic data comparisons, 1537 individuals were selected from the Macromorphoscopic Databank (MaMD, see Hefner, 2018) representing populations from around the world. For our purposes the geographic origin [three-group ancestry, see Hefner (2018) for explanation] was selected from the MaMD. To ensure clarity in how we describe these populations, we elected to maintain the relative population descriptors from the FDB, MaMD, and the Howells dataset when describing the populations. Since we are working within pooled, geographic samples, all groups with ancestors originating from Africa (e.g., American Black, East African) are termed "Black African" to distinguish those groups from so-called "White Africans"; all groups with ancestors originating from Europe (e.g., American white, Zalavar) are termed "White European"; and all groups with ancestors originating from Asia (e.g., China, Japan) and Southeast Asia (e.g., Thailand, Philippines) are included under the umbrella term "Asian."

Missing Data Imputation

As with most archaeologically derived skeletal material, the MIN86 sample suffered postmortem damage leading to fragmentation and missing data. To perform the most robust analyses possible and to maximize sample sizes, we elected to impute missing data. Little and Rubin (2014) explained the goal of data imputation as the generation of plausible values over more accurate values. However, Kenyhercz and Passalacqua (2016) argued that, for ancestry estimates, the most accurate imputation method is also the most favorable. We followed their suggestion for craniometric and macromorphoscopic data and utilized the k nearest neighbor algorithm to estimate missing values for the MIN86 sample. Pairwise deletion of variables would have resulted in a very small sample size, nearing zero. Instead, we developed a conservative approach for imputation using an unpooled worldwide dataset to determine the k nearest neighbors to all MIN86 individuals based on their observable data. Once these neighbors are identified in multivariate space, the missing values for the MIN86 sample are replaced with values taken from the closest neighbors. Fig. 5.1 presents the distribution of missing values for the total sample, including the worldwide reference data used for the imputation, to illustrate overall missingness for the total sample. Table 5.2 provides the distribution of missingness, by individual burial. Once imputation was complete the MIN86 sample was separated from the reference data for all subsequent analyses.

Canonical Analysis of the Principal Coordinates

To assess potential members of different ancestries within the MIN86 sample and to better understand the craniofacial morphology of the entire population, we performed a canonical analysis of the principal coordinates (CAP) using reference data derived from the MaMD (Hefner, 2018). Legendre and Legendre (1998) proposed a canonical discriminant analysis performed on

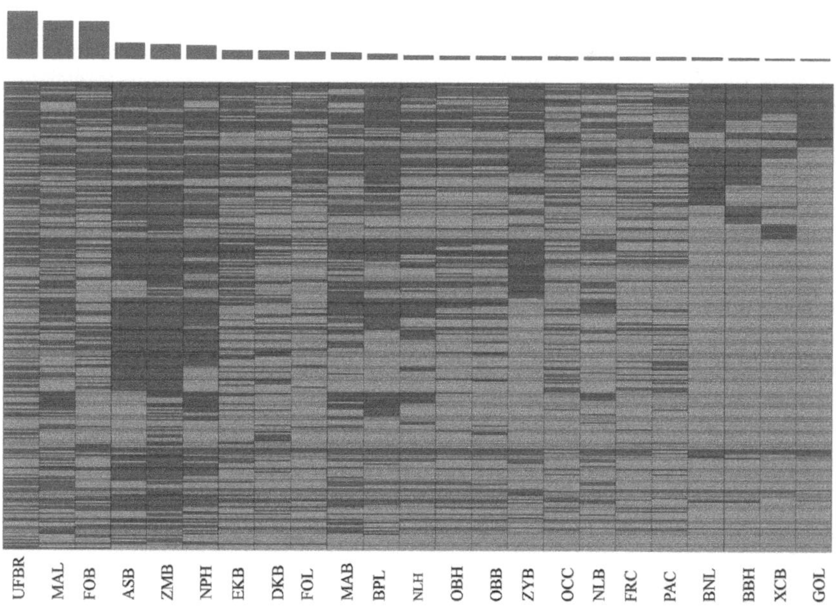

FIGURE 5.1 Combinations of missing data values for the entire sample (MIN86 and worldwide reference database).

TABLE 5.2 Percent of missing data in the East Smithfield (MIN86) sample.

MIN86 no.	%	MIN86 no.	%	MIN86 no.	%
5272	65.2	8277	4.3	11627	64.7
5281	88.2	8343	61	11857	69.5
5283	47.1	8427	78.3	11914	47.1
5291	88.2	9540	30.4	11944	23.5
5741	56.5	9807	69.6	12566	86.9
5902	58.8	11108	4.3	12567	86.9
5960	91.3	11108	0	12643	78.3
6428	73.9	11109	64.7	12700	0
6467	82.3	11115	47.1	12790	91.3
6532	43.6	11118	91.3	12813	86.9
7065	43.5	11193	52.2	12814	95.6
7094	35.3	11244	0	12815	58.8
7163	82.6	11430	0	20003	58.8
7831	58.8	11625	56.5		

the transformed values of the principal coordinates, using anyone of several distance measures (Anderson & Willis, 2003). A CAP essentially transforms categorical variables into continuous, normally distributed variables and is highly effective for dealing with macromorphoscopic data. CAP enables classification and visualization of the groups in a manner approximating craniometric analyses. To that end the chi-square distance metric (Anderson, 2006) was used to calculate interindividual similarities (and a distance matrix) within each imputed dataset. Permutations ($N = 4999$) were applied on the resulting similarity matrices. For the interpretation of significance, we considered permutation P-values as the permutation number (4999) is considered high (Anderson, 2006). An evaluation of the cross-validated (leave-one-out) classification accuracies and the distribution of posterior probabilities provide a robust measure of these classifications. Diagnostic plots (Figs. 5.2 and 5.3) and classification tables (Tables 5.3–5.6) are provided for each analysis.

Quadratic Discriminant Function

Quadratic discriminant analysis (QDA) is closely related to linear discriminant analysis, requiring many of the same assumptions. Unlike linear

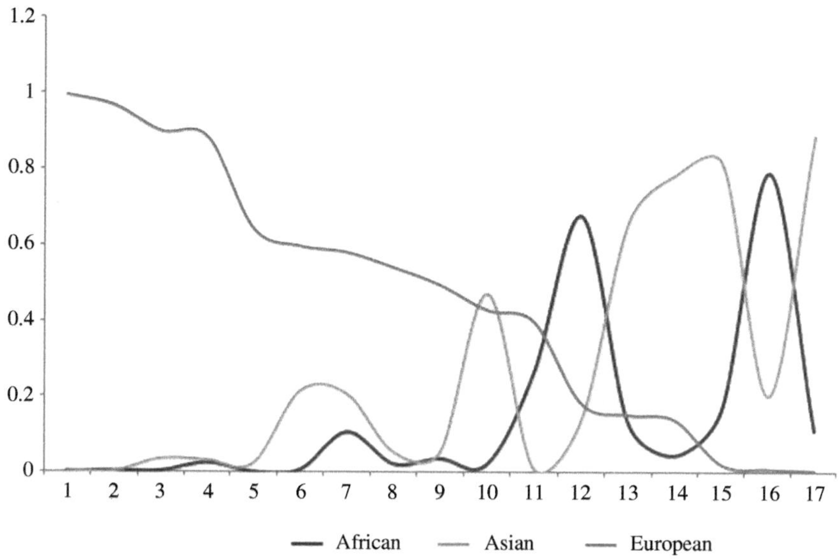

FIGURE 5.2 Distribution of posterior probabilities among MIN86 females, calculated from a canonical analysis of the principal coordinates (distance = χ^2 metric; $m = 4$).

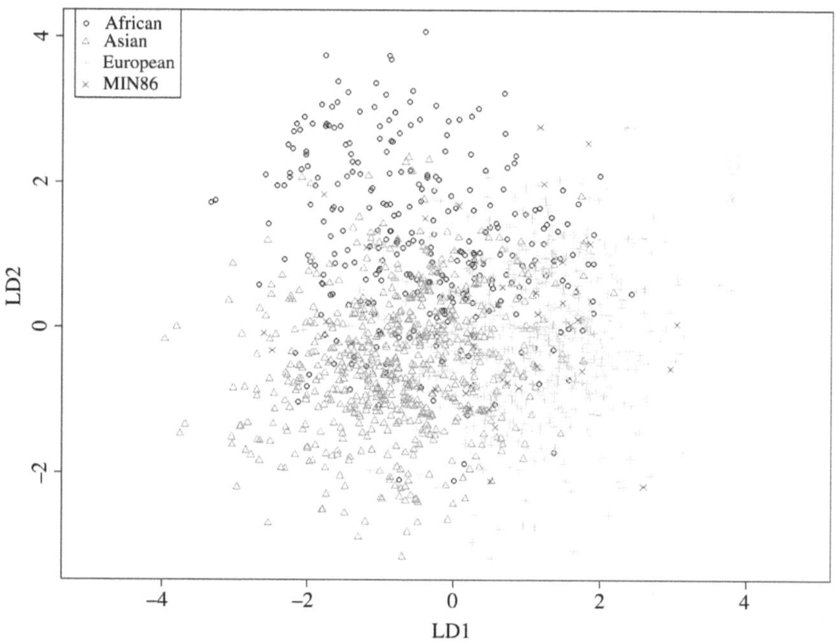

FIGURE 5.3 Constrained ordination plot of the MIN86 sample ("X"), compared to a worldwide sample of African, Asian, and European groups. *Reference data from the Macromorphoscopic Databank (Hefner, J.T. (2018). The macromorphoscopic databank. American Journal of Physical Anthropology. https://doi.org/10.1002/ajpa.23492).*

TABLE 5.3 Classification matrix from a canonical analysis of the principal coordinates using macromorphoscopic data (distance = χ^2 metric; $m = 4$; 4999 permutations, $P < .001$).

Group	African	Asian	European
African	153	83	69
Asian	45	544	90
European	22	85	446
MIN86	5	13	23
Total	225	725	628

TABLE 5.4 Classification of the East Smithfield (MIN86) pooled sample.

MIN86 no.	Ancestry	Classification		Strength
		Craniometric	Macromorphoscopic	
12566	White European	European	European	Strong
12700	White European	European	European	Strong
12643	White European	European	European	Strong
12814	White European	European	European	Strong
12813	White European	European	European	Strong
11118	White European	European	European	Strong
11857	White European	European	European	Strong
12567	White European	European	European	Strong
5272	White European	European	European	Strong
8427	White European	European	European	Strong
5960	White European	European	European	Strong
9807	White European	European	European	Strong
11430	White European	European	European	Strong
8277	White European	European	European	Strong
6428	White European	European	European	Strong
6532	White European	European	European	Strong
11108	White European	European	European	Strong

(*Continued*)

TABLE 5.4 (Continued)

MIN86 no.	Ancestry	Classification		Strength
		Craniometric	Macromorphoscopic	
7163	White European	European	European	Strong
8343	White European	European	European	Strong
11193	White European	European	European	Strong
7065	White European	Asian	European	Moderate
12790	African/European	African	European	Weak
5741	African	African	African	Strong
9540	African/Asian	African	Asian	Moderate
11244	African/Asian	African	African/Asian	Moderate
11625	Asian/European	Asian	European	Moderate
5902	African/Asian	–	Asian	Strong[a]
7094	European	–	European	Strong
12815	European	–	European	Strong
11944	European	–	European	Strong
20003	European	–	European	Strong
11914	European/Asian	–	European/Asian	Moderate
11115	European/Asian	–	European/Asian	Moderate
11627	European	–	European	Weak
5291	African	–	African	Weak
5281	African	–	African	Weak
6467	European	–	European	Strong
5283	European	–	European	Strong
11109	European	–	European	Strong
7831	Asian	–	Asian	Moderate
11108	Asian	–	Asian	Strong

[a]*Haplotype: U5b2a5.*

discriminant analysis, however, in QDA there is no assumption that the covariance of each of the classes is identical. All QDAs were calculated in R (R Core Team, 2018) using the base package and the aforementioned reference data from the FDB. Diagnostic plots (Figs. 5.4–5.6) and summary tables (Tables 5.7–5.10) are provided for each analysis.

TABLE 5.5 Classification of the MIN86 female sample.

African	Asian	European	MIN86 context no.
0.001954	0.003206	0.99484	9807
0.00351	0.001194	0.967126	12643
0.002564	0.033722	0.900143	7163
0.023882	0.030165	0.882289	6467
0.000251	0.022298	0.641016	12814
0.005926	0.212625	0.59555	8427
0.105172	0.204243	0.57906	12790
0.021469	0.051395	0.5393	11430
0.034967	0.05084	0.4932	5283
0.020359	**0.469143**	0.427062	5902[b]
0.262749	0.007742	0.395772	11109[b]
0.674903	0.136157	0.181555	5741[a]
0.129436	**0.657505**	0.151121	12700[b]
0.043362	**0.782319**	0.137219	7381[b]
0.166067	**0.813393**	0.020205	11244[b]
0.788604	0.199817	0.008381	6428[b]
0.110685	**0.88501**	0.004267	11108[b]
0.072951	**0.918498**	0.004266	6532[b]

"Misclassification" denoted by bold numbers.
[a]*Classified as African using both craniometric and macromorphoscopic data.*
[b]*Conflicting classifications from craniometric and macromorphoscopic data.*

Results

Funerary Context

Individuals with White European ancestry were buried in all but one of the funerary context types; none were identified from grave row one in the Western cemetery. Those with non-White European ancestry were buried in the majority of funerary contexts apart from grave rows four, six, and nine in the Western cemetery (Table 5.11).

Light Stable Isotopes and Mitochondrial DNA

The interpretation of stable isotope values from London is very difficult, because the Medieval city relied upon a large hinterland for resources, as

TABLE 5.6 Classification of the MIN86 male sample.

African	Asian	European	MIN86 context no.
0.030203	0.057512	0.910481	11857
0.003128	0.03793	0.904388	7094
0.011598	0.024693	0.850735	7065
0.113647	0.060085	0.787462	11193
0.00062	0.003023	0.685592	12815
0.011682	0.207744	0.677469	5960
0.135186	0.10101	0.607171	5272
0.049186	0.061595	0.572109	11944
0.033426	0.357061	0.545836	12567
0.143883	0.261981	0.526507	11625
0.006913	0.047971	0.52512	20003
0.015793	0.113416	0.453975	5285
0.004736	**0.570763**	0.42334	11914[a]
0.053154	**0.503076**	0.391383	11115[a]
0.106215	**0.436935**	0.384229	8343[a]
0.025112	**0.598713**	0.359849	11118[a]
0.318637	0.029542	0.33435	11627[a]
0.071094	**0.388537**	0.326037	12813[a]
0.641095	0.015287	0.216453	5291[a]
0.025416	**0.451939**	0.107657	8277[a]
0.588245	0.186558	0.086609	5281[a]
0.536858	0.412963	0.039763	9540[a]
0.107792	**0.850644**	0.033095	12566[a]

"Misclassification" denoted by bold number.
[a]*Conflicting classifications from craniometric and macromorphoscopic data.*

well as imports from Continental Europe (such as olive oil, wine, and dried fruits, e.g., Gutiérrez, 2007) for its resources. Therefore Kendall et al. (2013) have been appropriately cautious in the interpretation of their results and suggest that eight of the individuals in our study were nonlocal to the London region: skeletons 5281, 5285, 5291, 6467, 7163, 8427, 11627, and 11944. Balancing the results of the strontium and oxygen light stable isotopes, they suggest that a male with Black African ancestry

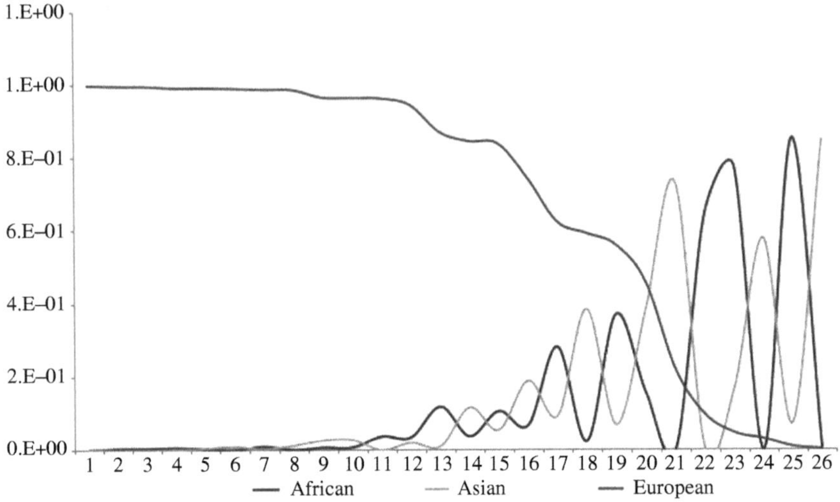

FIGURE 5.4 Distribution of posterior probabilities for the pooled MIN86 sample, calculated from a quadratic discriminant function.

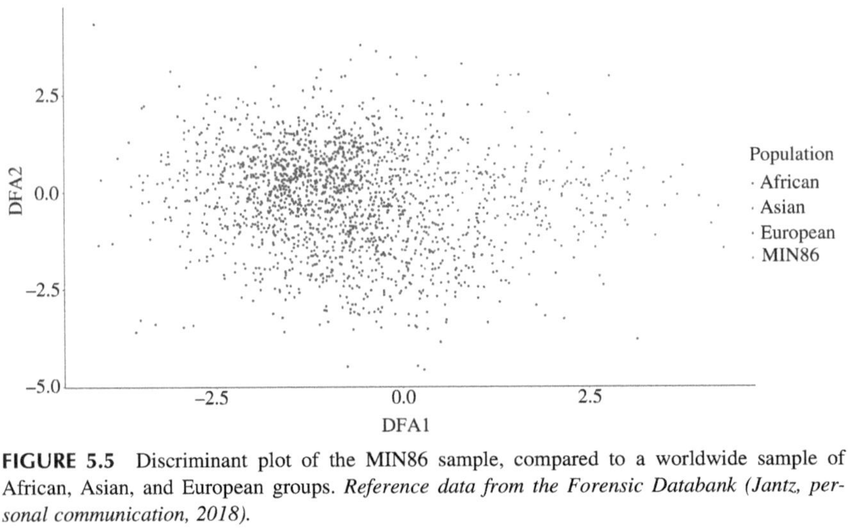

FIGURE 5.5 Discriminant plot of the MIN86 sample, compared to a worldwide sample of African, Asian, and European groups. *Reference data from the Forensic Databank (Jantz, personal communication, 2018).*

(skeleton 5281), and a female (skeleton 7163) and male (skeleton 11944) with White European ancestry were from western Britain. Two other people are proposed to have migrated from the west: a female (skeleton 7163) and a male (skeleton 11944) with White-European ancestry are proposed to have migrated from Devon, Cornwall, the Welsh coast, and the extreme western fringe of the Western Isles of Scotland. A male (skeleton 5285) and a female (skeleton 6467) with White European ancestry are suggested to have spent

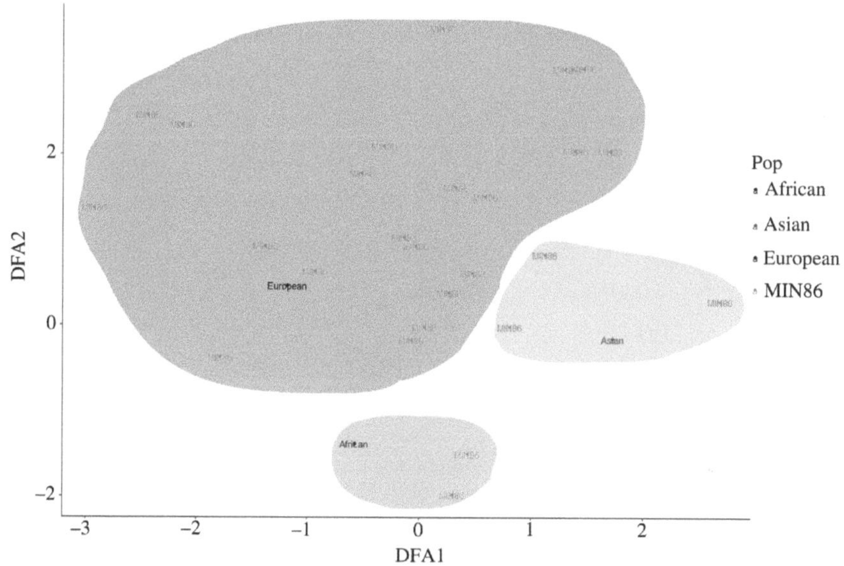

FIGURE 5.6 Discriminant plot of the MIN86 sample, compared to the centroids from a world-wide sample of African, Asian, and European groups. *Reference data from the Forensic Databank (Jantz, personal communication, 2018).*

their childhoods in an area which includes eastern Scotland, York and its immediate environs, and to the south of York.

The aDNA analysis had been undertaken on skeletons 5281 (male with Black African ancestry), 5902 (female with Black African/Asian ancestry), and 6532 (female with White European ancestry), but because of preservation Klunk and colleagues were only able to sequence the mtDNA from 5902. The haplotype of this female with Black African/Asian ancestry was U5b2a5, which is commonly found in England, Finland, and Tajikistan (Hay, 2017). Given their light stable isotope results, it is most likely that their maternal ancestry was from the British Isles. This result suggests that although these individuals are matching people with Black African/Asian ancestry in the macromorphoscopic database, in fact they may have had diverse heritage.

Ancestry

Ancestry analysis identified seven potential different population affiliations (Tables 5.5, 5.6, and 5.10). The majority of the population (70.7%) classified closest to the samples of White Europeans (17 males and 12 females). Two adult females (4.9%) had craniofacial morphologies most similar to the Asian sample (skeletons 7381 and 11108), one male (2.4%) classified between the Asian and White European samples (skeleton 11625), and two males (4.9%) (skeletons 11115 and 11914) classified as being dual heritage, White

TABLE 5.7 Group means of the discriminant functions and the original variables.

Variable	Group			
	African	Asian	European	MIN86
DF1	−0.5742	1.7299	−1.1779	0.0130
DF2	−1.3867	−0.1580	0.4643	1.0863
DF3	0.4192	−0.4283	−0.8178	0.7866
GOL	183.1	175.9	183.1	178.8
BNL	100.4	98.5	101.2	98.7
BBH	131.8	134.7	135.6	131.5
XCB	134.9	138.6	139.2	138.5
ZYB	127.4	129.6	127.5	127.3
ASB	107.5	108.2	111.2	111.3
BPL	100.7	96.7	94.4	96.8
NPH	67.8	68.3	67.0	62.4
NLH	50.2	50.6	51.5	51.2
NLB	26.0	25.1	23.8	24.4
MAB	64.5	63.8	60.4	63.0
MAL	55.5	51.0	52.1	49.7
OBH	34.5	34.6	33.8	34.8
OBB	39.2	38.9	39.7	38.0
DKB	23.5	25.7	21.3	24.8
ZMB	92.6	96.2	89.8	92.4
EKB	98.8	102.5	96.8	98.8
FRC	110.1	109.0	111.9	109.0
PAC	116.3	110.4	115.7	112.6
OCC	95.8	99.0	97.8	97.0
FOL	35.9	36.5	36.3	35.4
UFBR	104.8	105.1	103.2	102.7

GOL, Glabella-Occipital Length; BNL, Basion-Nasion Length; BBH, Basion-Bregma Height; XCB, Maximum Cranial Breadth; ZYB, Bizygomatic Breadth; ASB, Asterionic Breadth; BPL, Basion-Prosthion Length; NPH, Nasion-Prosthion Height; NLH, Nasal Height; NLB, Nasal Breadth; MAB, Maximum Alveolar Breadth; MAL, Maximum Alveolar Height; OBH, Orbit Height; OBB, Orbit Breadth; DKB, Dacryon Breadth; ZMB, Zygomaxilare Breadth; EKB, Ectoconchion Breadth; FRC, Frontal Chord; PAC, Parietal Chord ; OCC, Occipital Chord; FOB, Foramen Magnum Breadth; UFBR, Upper Facial Breadth.

TABLE 5.8 Standardized quadratic discriminant function coefficients.

Variable	Function		
	1	2	3
GOL	−0.06837	−0.00867	0.012757
BNL	−0.03056	0.040972	0.01001
BBH	0.051508	0.006285	−0.0525
XCB	−0.01217	0.055648	−0.02194
ZYB	−0.00744	−0.0112	−0.0105
ASB	−0.03105	0.072989	0.044105
BPL	0.038279	−0.00974	0.074776
NPH	0.084099	−0.11891	−0.09588
NLH	−0.06455	0.179019	0.01242
NLB	−0.01756	−0.17499	0.10178
MAB	−0.00716	−0.00532	0.059574
MAL	−0.09256	−0.12512	−0.00759
OBH	0.011731	−0.09782	0.146018
OBB	−0.08205	−0.00568	−0.09848
DKB	0.114641	0.013085	0.123832
ZMB	0.060005	0.011154	−0.01225
EKB	0.150104	0.012944	−0.0629
FRC	−0.02736	−0.00473	−0.00656
PAC	−0.02388	−0.0164	0.009047
OCC	0.048687	−0.00062	−0.01337
FOL	0.05058	−0.00028	−0.03801
UFBR	−0.05973	−0.04518	−0.01216

GOL, Glabella-Occipital Length; BNL, Basion-Nasion Length; BBH, Basion-Bregma Height; XCB, Maximum Cranial Breadth; ZYB, Bizygomatic Breadth; ASB, Asterionic Breadth; BPL, Basion-Prosthion Length; NPH, Nasion-Prosthion Height; NLH, Nasal Height; NLB, Nasal Breadth; MAB, Maximum Alveolar Breadth; MAL, Maximum Alveolar Height; OBH, Orbit Height; OBB, Orbit Breadth; DKB, Dacryon Breadth; ZMB, Zygomaxilare Breadth; EKB, Ectoconchion Breadth; FRC, Frontal Chord; PAC, Parietal Chord ; OCC, Occipital Chord; FOB, Foramen Magnum Breadth; UFBR, Upper Facial Breadth.

European and Asian. Four females and three males (17.1%) had craniofacial morphologies with conflicting results (dual heritage: African/White European/Asian) (skeletons 12790, 9540, 11244, 5902) or were morphologically similar to the samples with Black African ancestry (skeletons 5741, 5291, 5281).

TABLE 5.9 Classification matrix derived from a quadratic discriminant function using craniometric data.

Group	African	Asian	European
African	*481*	37	56
Asian	13	*183*	4
European	10	33	*1142*
MIN86	3	3	20
Total	507	256	1222

Note: *Italicized* numbers denote correct classifications within each group.

Health Variables

The most frequently observed disease variables were indicators of stress. The majority of the sample had enamel hypoplastic defects ($N = 36$) present, which were observed in all ancestry groups, with more males than females affected (Fig. 5.7 and Table 5.12). The second most frequently occurring condition was cribra orbitalia ($N = 16$); all of these individuals had at least one orbit present. More males than females were affected (Fig. 5.7), but it was not observed in males with Black African and Black African/Asian ancestries, or in one female with Black African/White European ancestry. Note that porotic hyperostosis was not recorded for any individuals in the sample. Periosteal new bone formation was observed in six individuals, the majority of whom had White European ancestry (Fig. 5.7). A single female from each of the Black African/Asian, Black African/White European ancestry groups had this condition present (5.6%), and only males with White European ancestry ($N = 3$, 13%) were affected. Only two individuals had evidence for a specific infectious disease. One Black African/Asian male (skeleton 9540) had potential evidence for brucellosis in his lumbar spine, where lytic lesions were observed, and a White European male (skeleton 11118) had evidence for a healed tubercular infection to his left wrist joint, which had ankylosed the carpals into a single mass, as well as fusing the bases of the second and third metacarpals to the trapezoid and capitate bones. A male with Asian/White European ancestry had lateral bowing to the proximal third of his left tibia, which could potentially reflect residual rickets.

Those with White European ancestry were the only group to have all three indicators of stress present, and they also had the highest frequencies of these changes. Unfortunately, due to the small sample size, it was not possible to apply statistical tests to these data.

TABLE 5.10 Classification of the MIN86 pooled sample.

African	Asian	European	MIN86 no.
0.0066140	0.001326	0.998607	12566
0.003166726	0.000506	0.996783	12700
0.003730441	0.000102	0.996167	12643
0.005989564	0.001958	0.992053	12814
0.00310901	0.005124	0.991767	12813
0.00009	0.009566	0.990338	11118
0.009064537	0.003269	0.987666	11857
0.0000845	0.013311	0.986605	12567
0.006504959	0.02732	0.966175	5272
0.007022249	0.028545	0.964433	8427
0.037078439	4.76E-05	0.962874	5960
0.034408482	0.020621	0.94497	9807
0.118420276	0.010767	0.870813	11430
0.037471285	0.116794	0.845734	8277
0.105851818	0.055383	0.838765	6428
0.067441457	0.189207	0.743351	6532
0.281762897	0.093605	0.624632	11108
0.023044186	0.384185	0.592771	7163
0.370452858	0.068896	0.560651	8343
0.155875763	0.385471	0.458653	11193
0.000338332	**0.729585**	0.218674	**7065**[b]
0.647226801	0.00089	0.095532	**12790**[b]
0.774730837	0.172495	0.045854	**5741**[a]
0.000874915	**0.578404**	0.028917	**9540**[b]
0.854888472	0.074261	0.007754	**11244**[b]
0.006117526	**0.84736**	0.000366	**11625**[b]

"Misclassification" denoted by bold numbers.
[a]*Classified as African using both craniometric and macromorphoscopic data.*
[b]*Conflicting classifications from craniometric and macromorphoscopic data.*

TABLE 5.11 Summary of the subsample by archaeological context, ancestry group and sex (% of total sample).

Archaeological context	Total, *N*	Asian females	Asian/ White European males	Black African males	Black African females	Black African/ Asian males	Black African/ Asian females	Black African/ White European females	White European males	White European females	White European/ Asian males
Eastern cemetery: grave rows	4 (9.7)				1		1		1	1	
Eastern cemetery: mass burial trench 3	5 (12.2)			2					2	1	
Western cemetery: mass burial trench 1	9 (21.9)						1	1	6	1	
Western cemetery: mass burial trench 2	9 (21.9)	1	1						3	3	1
Western cemetery: grave row 1	1 (2.4)										1
Western cemetery: grave row 2	2 (2.4)					1				1	

Western cemetery: grave row 3	3 (7.3)	1							1	1	
Western cemetery: grave row 4	2 (4.9)									2	
Western cemetery: grave row 6	5 (12.2)								3	2	
Western cemetery: grave row 9	1 (2.4)								1		
Total	41	2	1	2	1	1	2	1	17	12	2

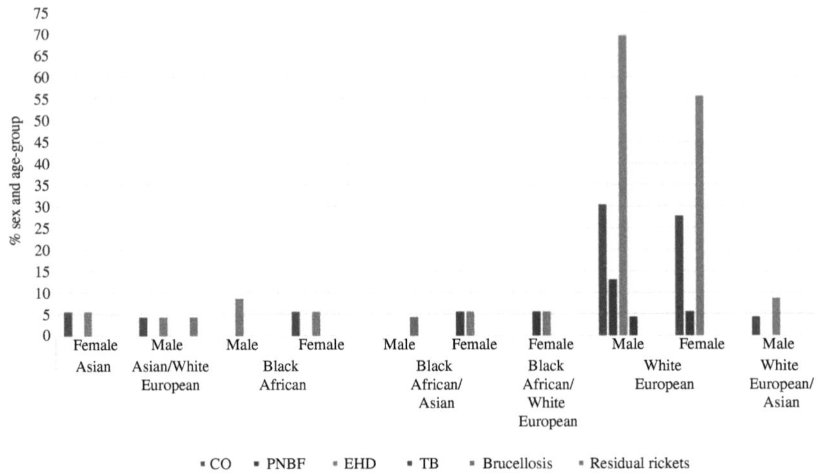

FIGURE 5.7 Health variables by ancestry and sex groups. *CO*, cribra orbitalia; *PNBF*, periosteal new bone formation; *EHD*, enamel hypoplastic defects; *TB*, tuberculosis.

TABLE 5.12 Indicators of stress by ancestry and sex grouping.

Ancestry group	Sex	CO	PNBF	EHD
Asian	Female	5.6	–	5.6
Asian/White European	Male	4.3	–	4.3
Black African	Male	0.0	–	8.7
	Female	5.6	–	5.6
Black African/Asian	Male	–	–	0.0
	Female	–	5.6	5.6
Black African/White European	Female	–	5.6	5.6
White European	Male	30.4	13.0	69.6
	Female	27.8	5.6	55.6
White European/Asian	Male	4.3	–	8.7

CO, Cribra orbitalia; PNBF, periosteal new bone formation; EHD, enamel hypoplastic defect.

Stature could be calculated for 20 individuals and where individuals had been assigned dual heritage, the first ancestry group was used to calculate stature (Table 5.13). The majority ($N = 16$) were of White European ancestry, with males having an average stature of 167.7 ± 3.94 cm, and females 153 ± 3.72 cm. The only male with Black African/Asian ancestry was calculated to be 160.6 ± 3.91 cm, and as shown in Table 5.13, this result falls

TABLE 5.13 Stature data by ancestry and sex groups (Bass, 1995).

Ancestry group	Sex	Context	Femoral length and side	Data (cm)	Equation (cm)	± cm
Asian/ White European	Male	11625	FeL1 R	47.2	–	–
Black African/ Asian	Male	9540	FeL1 R	42.1	160.6	3.91
Black African/ Asian	Female	11244	FeL1 R	42	155.5	3.41
Black African/ White European	Female	12790	FeL1 R	42.1	155.7	3.41
				Average	155.6	
White European	Female	6467	FeL1 R	43.5	161.5	3.72
	Female	6532	FeL1 L	38.4	148.9	3.72
	Female	7163	FeL1 R	40.6	154.4	3.72
	Female	11430	FeL1 R	37.7	147.2	3.72
	Female	12700	FeL1 R	38.9	150.2	3.72
	Female	12814	FeL1 R	41.2	155.9	3.72
				Average	153.0	
White European	Male	5960	FeL1 L	44.9	169.7	3.94
	Male	8277	FeL1 R	42.7	164.6	3.94
	Male	8343	FeL1 R	43.8	167.1	3.94
	Male	11118	FeL1 L	44.9	169.7	3.94
	Male	11627	FeL1 R	46.4	173.2	3.94
	Male	11944	FeL1 R	41.7	162.3	3.94
	Male	12566	FeL1 R	44	167.6	3.94
	Male	12567	FeL1 L	43.7	166.9	3.94
	Male	12813	FeL1 R	42.7	164.6	3.94
	Male	12815	FeL1 R	45.5	171.1	3.94
				Average	167.7	

below the White European male data. In contrast the two females with dual heritage had an average stature of 155.6 ± 3.41 cm, a result higher than the average for White European females (153 ± 3.72 cm), although the majority of that group were shorter than 155 cm (Table 5.13). Again, due to disparities in sample sizes, it was not possible to apply statistics to these data.

Discussion

Our study of a subgroup of individuals from MIN86 identified the potential for seven population groups and provides circumstantial evidence for the presence of males and females with Black African ancestry and dual heritage. These data are primary evidence for these people being "actually present" in Medieval London. However, the data provided a very unexpected result as it designated several individuals as having full or dual Asian ancestry. We propose that these results are a false positive, foremost because comparable temporally and geographically appropriate craniometric and macromorphoscopic reference data are not available. Cranial index data from Medieval London, covering the 12th to early 16th centuries AD, did not see any changes over time and found that both sexes were brachycephalic—broad/round headed (Connell, Gray Jones, Redfern, & Walker, 2012). Craniofacial metric data from Medieval and post-Medieval London also reveals that people's faces, particularly in the mid-line, nasal, and jaw areas, are wider/broader in the Medieval period and become narrower over time (WORD, 2018). It is worth noting that morphological changes have also been observed in forensic data collected from individuals who have died within the past 100 years (Forensic Anthropology Centre, 2018). Consequently, we suggest that some individuals are being falsely identified as having Asian ancestry because their faces are wider than individuals of other ancestry groups in the comparable datasets. Importantly, we observed a disconnect between a person's morphological affiliation (when observed macroscopically), and their statistical population affiliation. For example, skeleton 11108 is an adult female who, macroscopically, has Black African ancestry (Fig. 5.8) (e.g., nasal guttering) but is grouped as having Asian ancestry, and female skeleton 6428 who macroscopically also corresponds to Black African populations but statistically matches White European populations (Fig. 5.9). We believe this also to be the case for female skeleton 5902, who was determined as having Black African/Asian ancestry but her mtDNA suggests dual White European/Black African/Asian heritage—again, most likely because the wider/broader faces of people from Medieval London are more closely matching Asian populations in the database, creating a false-positive result. As with any classification statistic, solutions will always be provided by the algorithm, even when the comparison is between individuals derived from older populations to more recent, nearly modern reference data.

FIGURE 5.8 Anterior view of adult female 11108 whose cranium was classified as Asian. © *Museum of London.*

Secular change is well documented between samples and must be considered when interpreting these results.

The Medieval written sources, and much of the resulting scholarship from its study, suggest that the majority of people with Black African ancestry in Europe were enslaved, or even if they had been freed or were born free, continued to be marginalized, affected by a manifold of social and economic inequalities. Bioarchaeological analysis is adept at tracing the consequences of these inequalities in the remains of past people, particularly using indicators of stress, and our initial thoughts were that the frequencies of these indicators could be higher in non-White Europeans. Although the possibility that some people in that ancestry group could have been enslaved cannot be ruled out, it is beyond our reach at the present time. Bioarchaeological research on enslavement in the Roman period

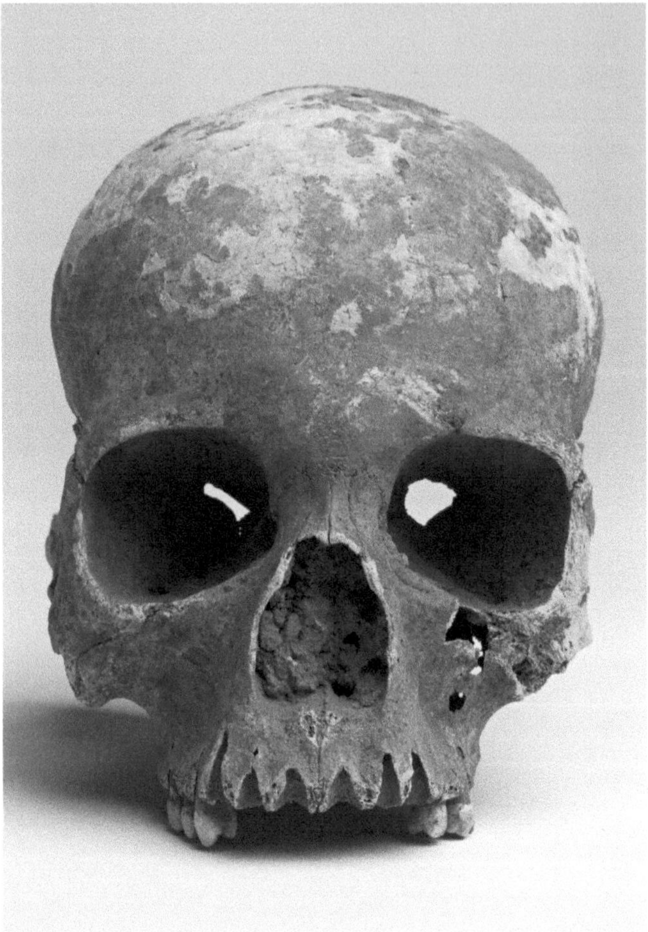

FIGURE 5.9 Anterior view of adult female 6428 whose cranium was classified as Asian. © *Museum of London.*

suggests that it may well be impossible to differentiate this status group from free but impoverished individuals (Redfern, 2018). Nevertheless, in both the Roman and Medieval periods, the occupations and responsibilities of the enslaved were incredibly varied and therefore much of the bioarchaeological research on captured and enslaved individuals with Black African ancestry (Table 5.14, see Redfern, 2018) is judged to have limited application to our present study, unlike other funerary contexts in Medieval Europe (e.g., Martiniano et al., 2014).

However, an osteobiographic approach, as advocated by Robb (2017), brings the life histories of two individuals to the fore when viewed through the lens of intersectionality. One is the 36–45-year-old Asian female,

TABLE 5.14 Bioarchaeological evidence associated with captivity and enslavement.

Age-group: social and biological ages	Bioarchaeological evidence
Subadults: those not living as an "adult" in the Medieval life course	Infanticide
	Mortality: high infant mortality; atypical demographic profile: juvenile and adolescent individuals
	Morbidity: increased risk
	Delayed puberty and skeletal maturation
	Delayed or compromised growth
	Death in childbirth at a young age
Adults: those living as an "adult" in the Medieval life course	Mortality: catastrophic profile; older adults
	Morbidity: increased risk
	Short stature
Both groups	Stable isotope analysis: evidence for dietary and physiological stress; evidence for breastfeeding and weaning strategies
	Stable isotope analysis: mobility
	aDNA analysis: oral microbiome evidence for disease and stress; disease and virus evidence
	Ancestry: haplotype and other genomic information; skeletal morphology and metrics
	Diet: skeletal and dental evidence for metabolic diseases cause by nutritional insufficiencies
	Skeletal and dental malformations associated with sexually transmitted diseases (e.g., syphilis)
	Death in childbirth at a young age
	Congenital and developmental defects associated with maternal health being compromised during pregnancy and reflecting genetic inheritance
	Nonspecific indicators of stress: cribra orbitalia, new bone formation, dental enamel hypoplastic defects, reduced vertebral dimensions

(*Continued*)

TABLE 5.14 (Continued)

Age-group: social and biological ages	Bioarchaeological evidence
	Injuries (ante and perimortem): stress fractures particularly to load-bearing joints; presence of multiple fractures; fractures to the head, teeth, face, and bones of the torso; injury patterning that conforms to child abuse, domestic violence, assault, or elder abuse
	Injury healing: evidence for insufficient treatment outcomes (e.g., poor apposition); evidence for poor care vs recommendations provided by the Index of Care
	Biomechanical and musculoskeletal changes associated with high levels of physical activity
	Respiratory conditions: sinusitis and rib lesions
	Localized areas of inflammation and injury to wrists, ankles, and neck suggesting use of restraints and collars
	Dental health and morphology: carious lesions; calculus; antemortem tooth loss; periodontal disease; dental asymmetry; malocclusion; reduction in tooth size between different phases of burial
	Infectious disease (specific and nonspecific): tuberculosis, osteomyelitis, malaria, ear infections, endocranial lesions
	Parasites

Source: *After Redfern, R. C. (2018). Blind to chains? The potential of bioarchaeology for identifying the enslaved of Roman Britain. Britannia. https://doi.org/10/1017/S0068113X18000119.*

skeleton 11108—as stated earlier, we reject the statistical population affiliation, and suggest she has Black African ancestry. Analysis of her skeleton reveals the presence of spinal osteoarthritis, a Schmorl's node in a thoracic vertebra, and rotator cuff disease of the left shoulder joint, changes that suggest not only age-related degeneration but also over-use because of activity-patterns (Clayton & Court-Brown, 2008) (we are mindful of the work of Henderson & Alves Cardoso, 2013)—note only one other individual, a possible male (skeleton 8393) had this condition reported in the MIN86 population. She also has heavy dental wear and bilateral temporomandibular joint disease, which are likely to be associated with her pronounced prognathism (see Fig. 5.8). The 36–45-year-old male, skeleton

9540, with Black African/Asian ancestry, in addition to possibly having brucellosis (see Section "Results"), also has osteoarthritis to his left ankle joint and spine, Schmorl's nodes in his lumbar vertebrae, and a healed Colles' fracture to his right radius with secondary osteoarthritic changes to the right wrist joint, and a healed fracture to one rib. Although fractures caused by accidental and violent mechanisms are frequently encountered in the MIN86 and other populations from Medieval London (Krakowka, 2017a, 2017b; Walker, 2012), taken as a whole, we glimpse two people with multiple conditions, which would have compromised their movement, mobility, and gait, and may have occurred because of their marginal status as a social outsider, a factor driven by socioeconomic inequalities based on their ancestry.

Our inability to interrogate the data using statistical techniques requires us to be very cautious in our assertions, particularly as research by DeWitte (2009, 2010a, 2010b, 2014a, 2014b, 2015, 2018), DeWitte and Hughes-Morey (2012), and DeWitte and Wood (2008) has demonstrated that older people, those with indicators of stress, and of shorter stature were more likely to die from the Black Death. This is further compounded by the presence of many migrants in the sample, whose disease frequencies will also influence the patterns seen in this population (see Redfern, DeWitte, Montgomery, & Gowland, 2018). Our results suggest, in line with other primary evidence, that the majority of London's population were of White European ancestry, and despite the small size of our sample, it appears that this population's health status is strongly influencing the results of earlier studies. Rather than comparing frequencies, it is perhaps the lack of evidence for multiple indicators of stress, principally the absence of cribra orbitalia and periosteal new bone formation in males of Black African or Black African/Asian ancestry that raises important questions: was their health compromised by their social status to such an extent that they were unable to create a bony response (DeWitte & Stojanowski, 2015)? Did their status as newcomers to London (e.g., skeleton 5281 from western Britain) further increase their mortality risk during the Black Death epidemic?

Our results also reveal the need to revisit the interpretation of certain diseases observed in this population, in particular the proposed case of brucellosis in a male of Black African/Asian ancestry (skeleton 9540) (Aufderheide & Rodriguez-Martin, 1998). Although we do not know whether or not they were a migrant to Britain, until that question is resolved we must widen our interpretation to include the possibility that he was infected in his country of origin rather than in Britain. The presence of diverse ancestry groups and long-distance migrants in the MIN86 sample also means that the pathways of transmission for the evidence of tuberculosis have to give more weight to the role of migrants in how this disease is understood to have been acquired and transmitted in Medieval London (see Redfern et al., 2018; see also Müller, Roberts, & Brown, 2014).

Conclusions

Our study of the Black Death population from East Smithfield aimed to examine the evidence for people with Black African ancestry in Medieval London using the theoretical approach of intersectionality. The analysis of ancestry groupings in the city identified several individuals with Black African ancestry or dual heritage, a result which supports the limited 14th century AD primary source evidence. Our research suggests that these and later sources may actually be under-representing population diversity in the city, given that in our sample of 41 individuals, 29% were people with non-White European ancestry. The osteobiographies of two such people may provide a glimpse into the health consequences of social and economic inequalities, whereby their degenerative osteoarthritic changes could have been caused or exacerbated by manual labor. The absence of evidence for some indicators of stress in males with Black African ancestry could, potentially, also support such a situation. However, there were no clear differences in health, either between the sexes in each ancestry group or between each ancestry group. These findings contrast with other bioarchaeological studies of status differences in Medieval London (DeWitte, Boulware, & Redfern, 2013; Walter & DeWitte, 2017). Therefore it may well be, that similarly to the Roman period, it could be impossible to differentiate between the enslaved and the poverty-stricken at the present time.

We propose that the lack of distinction in health-statuses between ancestry groups is in part due to our inability to apply statistical tests to the data, but foremost because of the far-reaching and significant impacts of multiple famines during the 14th century AD, which created a vulnerable population who was subsequently decimated by the Black Death. These environmental catastrophes and disease epidemics were not limited to Britain and affected all socioeconomic groups across Europe. Although those hardest hit by inequalities would have borne the brunt of these events, we suggest that the decline in health at the population level seen during this period is masking any underlying differences, and we suggest that more work combing ancestry and health data, with incremental dietary isotope results and evidence for migration should be undertaken in order to disentangle the evidence.

Acknowledgments

We are most grateful to the editors for inviting us to contribute to this publication, and for all their help and support throughout the process. Thanks are also given to the reviewers whose insightful comments were most welcome and helpful in the revision of this manuscript. RR is most grateful to the members of the WORD project for all their work on the MIN86 population, and to MoL Photographers for taking the images used in this work. RR would also like to thank Jennifer Klunk and Hendrik Poinar (McMaster University) for sharing unpublished mtDNA information, and Jeff Fynn-Paul (Leiden University) for sharing research. JTH is grateful to R.L. Jantz for providing access to the FDB dataset for reference material and B. Auerbach for access to the Howells data. JTH would also like to acknowledge the MaMD for providing reference data.

References

Anderson, M. J. (2006). Distance-based tests for homogeneity of multivariate dispersions. *Biometrics*, *62*(1), 245–253.

Anderson, M. J., & Willis, T. J. (2003). Canonical analysis of prinicipal coordinates: A useful method of constrained ordination for ecology. *Ecology*, *84*, 511–525.

Antón, S. C., Malhi, R. S., & Fuentes, A. (2018). Race and diversity in U.S. Biological Anthropology: A decade of AAPA initiatives. *American Journal of Physical Anthropology*, *S65*, 158–180.

Auerbach, B. M. (2018). The William W. Howells craniometric data set. Retrieved from https://web.utk.edu/~auerbach/HOWL.htm.

Aufderheide, A. C., & Rodriguez-Martin, C. (1998). *The Cambridge encyclopedia of human paleopathology*. Cambridge: Cambridge University Press.

Austen, R. A. (1979). The trans-Saharan slave trade: A tentative census. In H. A. Gemery, & J. S. Hogendorn (Eds.), *The uncommon market: Essays in the economic history of the Atlantic slave trade* (pp. 23–76). New York: Academic Press.

Banda, Y., Kvale, M. N., Hoffmann, T. J., Hesselson, S. E., Ranatunga, D., Tang, H., & Risch, N. (2015). Characterizing race/ethnicity and genetic ancestry for 100,000 subjects in the Genetic Epidemiology Research on Adult Health and Aging (GERA) cohort. *Genetics*, *200* (4), 1285–1295.

Barron, C. (2005). *London in the later Middle Ages: Government and people, 1200-1500*. Oxford: Oxford University Press.

Barron, C., Carlin, M., & Rosenthal, J. T. (2017). *Medieval London: Collected papers of Caroline M. Barron*. Western Michigan University: Medieval Institute Publications.

Bartlett, R. (2001). Medieval and modern concepts of race and ethnicity. *Journal of Medieval and Early Modern Studies*, *31*(1), 39–56.

Bass, W. M. (1995). *Human osteology, a laboratory and field manual* (4th ed.). Columbia: Missouri Archaeological Society, Special Publication No. 2.

Bolton, J. L. (2013). Looking for *Yersinia pestis*: Scientists, historians and the Black Death. In L. Clark, & C. Rawcliff (Eds.), *The fifteenth century XII-society in an age of plague* (pp. 15–38). Woodbridge: Boydell Press.

Borgolte, M. (Ed.), (2014). *Migration im Mittelalter: ein Handbuch*. Berlin: De Gruyter.

Bos, K. I., Schuenemann, V. J., Golding, G. B., Burbano, H. A., Waglechner, N., Coombes, B. K., … Krause, J. (2011). A draft genome of *Yersinia pestis* from victims of the Black Death. *Nature*, *478*(7370), 506–510.

Bos, K. I., Stevens, P., Nieselt, K., Poinar, H. N., Dewitte, S. N., & Krause, J. (2012). *Yersinia pestis*: New evidence for an old infection. *PLoS One*, *7*(11), e49803.

Brann, R. (2009). The Moors? *Medieval Encounters*, *15*(2–4), 307–318.

Braude, B. (1997). The sons of Noah and the construction of ethnic and geographical identities in the Medieval and Early Modern Periods. *The William and Mary Quarterly*, *54*(1), 103–142.

Brickley, M., & McKinley, J. (Eds.), (2004). *Guidance to the standards for recording human skeletal remains*. Reading: Institute of Field Archaeologists, British Association of Biological Anthropology and Osteoarchaeology. Retrived from http://www.babao.org.uk/assets/Uploads/HumanremainsFINAL3.pdf.

Budd, P., Montgomery, J., Evans, J., & Chenery, C. (2001). Combined Pb-, Sr-and O-isotope analysis of human dental tissue for the reconstruction of archaeological residential mobility. *Special Publications of the Royal Society of Chemistry*, *267*, 311–326.

Buikstra, J. E., & Ubelaker, D. H. (1994). Standards for data collection from human skeletal remains. In *Proceedings of a seminar at the field museum of natural history organized by Jonathan Haas*. Arkanas: Arkansas Archaeological Survey Research Series No. 44.

Byrne, J. P. (2012). *Encyclopedia of the Black Death*. Santa Barbara, CA: ABC-CLIO LLC.

Capelli, C., Onofri, V., Brisighelli, F., Boschi, I., Scarnicci, F., Masullo, M., ... Gusmao, L. (2009). Moors and Saracens in Europe: Estimating the medieval North African male legacy in southern Europe. *European Journal of Human Genetics*, *17*(6), 848–852.

Cardena, M. M., Ribeiro-Dos-Santos, A., Santos, S., Mansur, A. J., Pereira, A. C., & Fridman, C. (2013). Assessment of the relationship between self-declared ethnicity, mitochondrial haplogroups and genomic ancestry in Brazilian individuals. *PLoS One*, *8*(4), e62005.

Centre for Human Bioarchaeology. (2007). *East Smithfield Black Death cemetery summary*. Retrieved from https://www.museumoflondon.org.uk/collections/other-collection-databases-and-libraries/centre-human-bioarchaeology/osteological-database/medieval-cemeteries/east-smithfield-black-death-medieval.

Chan, J. C. (2017, July 16). Medievalists, recoiling from white supremacy, try to diversify the field. *The Chronicle of Higher Education*. Retrieved from https://www.chronicle.com/article/Medievalists-Recoiling-From/240666.

Chand, R., Nel, E., & Pelc, S. (2017). Introduction. In R. Chand, E. Nel, & S. Pelc (Eds.), *Societies, social inequalities and marginalization. Marginal regions in the 21st century* (pp. 1–9). Switzerland: SpringerLink.

Cho, S., Crenshaw, K. W., & McCall, L. (2013). Toward a field of intersectionality studies: Theory, applications, and praxis. *Signs: Journal of Women in Culture and Society*, *38*(4), 785–810.

Clayton, R. A. E., & Court-Brown, C. M. (2008). The epidemiology of musculoskeletal tendinous and ligamentous injuries. *Injury, International Journal of the Care of the Injured*, *39*, 1338–1344.

Cohen, J. (Ed.), (2008). *Cultural diversity in the British Middle Ages. Archipelago, Island, England*. New York: SpringerLink.

Connell, B., Gray Jones, A., Redfern, R. C., & Walker, D. (2012). *Spitalfields: A bioarchaeological study of health and disease from a medieval London cemetery. Archaeological excavations at Spitalfields Market 1991-2007. Museum of London Archaeology Monograph 60*. London: Museum of London Archaeology.

R Core Team. (2018). *R: A language and environment for statistical computing*. Vienna: R Foundation for Statistical Computing. Retreieved from https://www.R-project.org/.

Crenshaw, K. (1991). Mapping the margins: Intersectionality, identity politics, and violence against women of color. *Stanford Law Review*, *43*(6), 1241–1299.

Dean, K. R., Krauer, F., Walløe, L., Lingjærde, O. C., Bramanti, B., Stenseth, N. C., & Schmid, B. V. (2018). Human ectoparasites and the spread of plague in Europe during the Second Pandemic. *Proceedings of the National Academy of Sciences*, *115*(6), 1304–1309.

DeWitte, S. N. (2009). The effect of sex on risk of mortality during the Black Death in London, A.D. 1349–1350. *American Journal of Physical Anthropology*, *139*(2), 222–252.

Dewitte, S. N. (2010a). Age patterns of mortality during the Black Death in London, A.D. 1349–1350. *Journal of Archaeological Science*, *37*(12), 3394–3400.

DeWitte, S. N. (2010b). Sex differentials in frailty in Medieval England. *American Journal of Physical Anthropology*, *143*(2), 285–297.

DeWitte, S. N. (2014a). Differential survival among individuals with active and healed periosteal new bone formation. *International Journal of Paleopathology*, *7*, 38–44.

DeWitte, S. N. (2014b). Health in post-Black Death London (1350–1538): Age patterns of periosteal new bone formation in a post-epidemic population. *American Journal of Physical Anthropology*, *155*(2), 260–267.

DeWitte, S. N. (2015). Setting the stage for medieval plague: Pre-black death trends in survival and mortality. *American Journal of Physical Anthropology, 158*(3), 441–451.

DeWitte, S. N. (2018). Stress, sex, and plague: Patterns of developmental stress and survival in pre- and post-Black Death London. *American Journal of Human Biology, 30*(1). Available from https://doi.org/10.1002/ajhb.23073.

DeWitte, S. N., & Hughes-Morey, G. (2012). Stature and frailty during the Black Death: The effect of stature on risks of epidemic mortality in London, A.D. 1348–1350. *Journal of Archaeological Science, 39*(5), 1412–1419.

DeWitte, S. N., & Stojanowski, C. M. (2015). The osteological paradox 20 years later: Past perspectives, future directions. *Journal of Archaeological Research, 23*(4), 397–450.

DeWitte, S. N., & Wood, J. W. (2008). Selectivity of Black Death mortality with respect to preexisting health. *Proceedings of the National Academy of Sciences of the U.S.A, 105*(5), 1436–1441.

DeWitte, S. N., Boulware, J. C., & Redfern, R. C. (2013). Medieval monastic mortality: Hazard analysis of mortality differences between monastic and nonmonastic cemeteries in England. *American Journal of Physical Anthropology, 152*(3), 322–332.

Dick, H. C., Pringle, J. K., Sloane, B., Carver, J., Wisniewski, K. D., Haffenden, A., ... Cassidy, N. J. (2015). Detection and characterisation of Black Death burials by multi-proxy geophysical methods. *Journal of Archaeological Science, 59*(1), 132–141.

Ditrich, H. (2017). The transmission of the Black Death to western Europe: A critical review of the existing evidence. *Mediterranean Historical Review, 32*(1), 25–39.

Dury, G., Lythe, A., Marquez-Grant, N., Garcia-Rubio, A., Graziani, G., Mari, J., ... Schulting, R. (2018). The Islamic cemetery at 33 Bartomeu Vicent Ramon, Ibiza: Investigating diet and mobility through light stable isotopes in bone collagen and tooth enamel. *Archaeological and Anthropological Sciences*, 1–18.

Earle, T. F., & Lowe, K. J. P. (Eds.), (2010). *Black Africans in renaissance Europe*. Cambridge: Cambridge University Press.

Evans, J., Chenery, C., & Montgomery, J. (2012). A summary of strontium and oxygen isotope variation in archaeological human tooth enamel excavated from Britain. *Journal of Analytical Atomic Spectrometry, 27*(5), 754–764.

Evans, J., Montgomery, J., Wildman, G., & Boulton, N. (2010). Spatial variations in biosphere $^{87}Sr/^{86}Sr$ in Britain. *Journal of the Geological Society, 167*(1), 1–4.

Forensic Anthropology Centre. (2018). Forensic Anthropology Databank (FDB). Retrieved from https://fac.utk.edu/background/.

Fynn-Paul, J. (2014). Reasons for the limited scope and duration of 'Renaissance slavery' in southern Europe (ca. 1348-ca. 1750): A new structuralist analysis. In S. Cavciocchi (Ed.), *Schiavitù e servaggio nell'economia europea, secc. XI-XVII • Serfdom and slavery in the European Economy, 11th-18th Centuries. Atti delle "Quarantunesima Settimana di Studi", 14-18 aprile 2013. Ed. Simonetta Cavaciocchi (Atti delle "Settimane di Studi" e altri Convegni, 45; Fondazione IstitutoInternazionale di Storia Economica "F. Datini"). no. 45* (pp. 337–350). Florence: Florence University Press.

Gleize, Y., Mendisco, F., Pemonge, M.-H., Hubert, C., Groppi, A., Houix, B., ... Breuil, J.-Y. (2016). Early Medieval Muslim graves in France: First archaeological, anthropological and palaeogenomic evidence. *PLoS One, 11*(2), e0148583.

Grainger, I., Hawkins, D., Cowal, L., & Mikulski, R. (2008). The Black Death cemetery, East Smithfield, London. MoLAS Monograph Series 43. London: Museum of London Archaeology.

Groves, S. E., Roberts, C. A., Lucy, S., Pearson, G., Gröcke, D. R., Nowell, G., ... Young, G. (2013). Mobility histories of 7th–9th century AD people buried at early medieval

Bamburgh, Northumberland, England. *American Journal of Physical Anthropology, 151*(3), 462–476.

Guede, I., Ortega, L. A., Zuluaga, M. C., Alonso-Olazabal, A., Murelaga, X., Pina, M., ... Iacumin, P. (2017). Isotope analyses to explore diet and mobility in a medieval Muslim population at Tauste (NE Spain). *PLoS One, 12*(5), e0176572.

Guidi-Bruscoli, F. (2016). London and its merchants in the Italian archives, 1380-1530. In M. Allen, & M. Davies (Eds.), *Medieval merchants and money: Essays in honour of James L. Bolton* (pp. 113–136). London: Institute of Historical Research.

Gutiérrez, A. (2007). Portuguese coarsewares in early modern England: Reflections on an exceptional pottery assemblage from Southampton. *Post-Medieval Archaeology, 41*(1), 64–79.

Habib, I. H. (2008). *Black lives in the English archives, 1500-1677: Imprints of the invisible.* Farnham: Ashgate Publishing, Ltd.

Hahn, T. (2001). The difference the Middle Ages makes: Color and race before the Modern World. *Journal of Medieval and Early Modern Studies, 31*(1), 1–37.

Hall, K. (1993). Reading what isn't there: 'Black' studies in early Modern England. *Stanford Humantities Review, 3*(1), 23–33.

Hay, M. (2017). *Haplogroup U5 (mtDNA).* Retrieved from https://www.eupedia.com/europe/Haplogroup_U5_mtDNA.shtml#distribution.

Hefner, J. T. (2018). The macromorphoscopic databank. *American Journal of Physical Anthropology.* Available from https://doi.org/10.1002/ajpa.23492.

Henderson, C. Y., & Alves Cardoso, F. (2013). Special issue entheseal changes and occupation: Technical and theoretical advances and their applications. *International Journal of Osteoarchaeology, 23*(2), 127–134.

Heng, G. (2007). Jews, Saracens, 'Black Men', Tartars: England in a world of racial difference. In P. Brown (Ed.), *A companion to Medieval English literature and culture c.1350–c.1500* (pp. 247–269). Oxford: Wiley-Blackwell Publishing Ltd.

Heng, G. (2011a). The invention of race in the European Middle Ages I: Race studies, modernity, and the Middle Ages 1. *Literature Compass, 8*(5), 315–331.

Heng, G. (2011b). The invention of race in the European Middle Ages II: Locations of Medieval Race 1. *Literature Compass, 8*(5), 332–350.

Hernæs, P. O., & Iversen, T. (Eds.), (2002). Slavery across time and space: Studies in slavery in Medieval Europe and Africa. Trondheim: Norwegian University of Science and Technology, Department of History.

Holy Trinity Priory. (1971). The cartulary of Holy Trinity Priory, Aldgate. In G. A. J. Hodgett (Ed.), *London record society* (Vol. 7). British History Online. http://www.british-history.ac.uk/london-record-soc/vol7.

Horrox, R. (1994). *The Black Death.* Manchester: Manchester University Press.

Howells, W. W. (1973). *Cranial variation in man. A study by multivariate analysis of patterns of differences among recent human populations. Papers of the Peabody Museum of Archaeology and Ethnology* (Vol. 67). Cambridge, MA: Peabody Museum.

Howells, W. W. (1989). *Skull shapes and the map. Craniometric analyses in the dispersion of modern homo. Papers of the Peabody Museum of Archaeology and Ethnology* (Vol. 79). Cambridge, MA: Peabody Museum.

Howells, W. W. (1995). *Who's who in skulls. Ethnic identification of crania from measurements. Papers of the Peabody Museum of Archaeology and Ethnology* (Vol. 82). Cambridge, MA: Peabody Museum.

Hsy, J., & Orlemanski, J. (2018). *Race and Medieval studies: A partial bibliography*. Retrieved from https://docs.google.com/document/d/18JClsma1BMKYCxvgeWqwPej3ZSCrQXlAlXbL0CdqWmE/edit.

Jäschke, K.-U., & Schrenk, C. (Eds.). (2013). *Vieler völker städte. Polyethnizität und migration in Städten des Mittlealters- chancen und gefahren*. Stadtarchiv Heilbronn. Retrieved from <https://stadtarchiv.heilbronn.de/fileadmin/daten/stadtarchiv/online-publikationen/12-vieler-voelker-staedte.pdf>.

Kaufman, M. (2017). *Black Tudors. The untold story*. Great Britain: Oneworld.

Kendall, E. J., Montgomery, J., Evans, J. A., Stantis, C., & Mueller, V. (2013). Mobility, mortality, and the middle ages: Identification of migrant individuals in a 14th century black death cemetery population. *American Journal of Physical Anthropology*, *150*(2), 210–222.

Kenyhercz, M. W., & Passalacqua, N. V. (2016). Missing data imputation methods and their performance with biodistance analyses. In M. A. Pilloud, & J. Hefner (Eds.), *Biological distance analysis* (pp. 181–194). New York: Elsevier.

Krakowka, K. (2017a). Violence-related trauma from the Cistercian Abbey of St Mary Graces and a late Black Death Cemetery. *International Journal of Osteoarchaeology*, *27*(1), 56–66.

Krakowka, K. (2017b). Patterns and prevalence of violence-related skull trauma in Medieval London. *American Journal of Physical Anthropology*, *164*(3), 488–504.

Legendre, P., & Legendre, L. (1998). *Numerical ecology. Developments in environmental modelling 20* (2nd ed.). New York: Elsevier.

Lewis, T. E. (2016). 'Like Devils out of Hell': Reassessing the African presence in Early Modern England. *Black Theology*, *14*(2), 107–120.

Lightfoot, E., & O'Connell, T. C. (2015). On the use of biomineral oxgyen isotope data to identify human migrants in the archaeological record: Intra-sample variation, statistical methods and geographical considerations. *PLoS One*, *11*(4), e0153850.

Little, R. J., & Rubin, D. B. (2014). *Statistical analysis with missing data* (2nd ed.). New York: John Wiley & Sons.

Llwellyn Smith, H. (1939). *The history of east London from the earliest times to the end of the eighteenth century*. London: Macmillan.

Lorde, A. (2007). *Sistexr outsider: Essays and speeches by Audre Lorde*. Berkely: Crossing Press.

Lowe, K. J. P. (2010a). The Black African presence in Renaissance Europe. In T. F. Earle, & K. J. P. Lowe (Eds.), *Black Africans in Renaissance Europe* (pp. 1–14). Cambridge: Cambridge University Press.

Lowe, K. J. P. (2010b). The stereotyping of black Africans in Renaissance Europe. In T. F. Earle, & K. J. P. Lowe (Eds.), *Black Africans in Renaissance Europe* (pp. 17–47). Cambridge: Cambridge University Press.

Lutkin, J. (2016). Settled or fleeting? London's Medieval immigrant community revisited. In M. Allen, & M. Davies (Eds.), *Medieval merchants and money: Essays in honour of James L. Bolton* (pp. 137–150). London: Institute for Historical Research.

Martiniano, R., Coelho, C., Ferreira, M. T., Neves, M. J., Pinhasi, R., & Bradley, D. G. (2014). Genetic evidence of African slavery at the beginning of the trans-Atlantic slave trade. *Nature, Scientific Reports*, *4*, 5994.

Mazo Karras, R. (2017). *Sexuality in Medieval Europe. Doing unto others* (3rd ed.). London: Routledge.

McKee, S. (2004). Inherited status and slavery in late Medieval Italy and Venetian Crete. *Past & Present*, *182*, 31–53.

Millard, A., Roberts, C., & Hughes, S. (2005). Isotopic evidence for migration in Medieval England: The potential for tracking the introduction of disease. *Society, Biology and Human Affairs*, *70*(1), 9–13.

Miller, J. C. (2002). The historical contexts of slavery in Europe. In P. O. Hernæs, & T. Iversen (Eds.), *Slavery across time and space: Studies in slavery in Medieval Europe and Africa* (pp. 1–57). Trondheim: Norwegian University of Science and Technology, Department of History.

Miller, W. E. (1961). Negroes in Elizabethan England. *Notes & Queries*, *206*, 138.

Mitchell, P. D., & Brickley, M. (2017). *Updated guidelines to the standards for recording human remains*. Reading: Chartered Institute for Archaeologists, British Association for Biological Anthropology and Osteoarchaeology. Retrieved from https://www.archaeologists.net/sites/default/files/14_Updated%20Guidelines%20to%20the%20Standards%20for%20Recording%20Human%20Remains%20digital.pdf.

Mitchell, P. D., & Millard, A. R. (2009). Migration to the medieval Middle East with the crusades. *American Journal of Physical Anthropology*, *140*(3), 518–525.

Montgomery, J. (2010). Passports from the past: Investigating human dispersals using strontium isotope analysis of tooth enamel. *Annals of Human Biology*, *37*(3), 325–346.

Montgomery, J., Evans, J. A., & Cooper, R. E. (2007). Resolving archaeological populations with Sr-isotope mixing models. *Applied Geochemistry*, *22*(7), 1502–1514.

Müller, R., Roberts, C. A., & Brown, T. A. (2014). Genotyping of ancient *Mycobacterium tuberculosis* strains reveals historic genetic diversity. *Proceedings of the Royal Society B*, *281* (1781), 20133236.

Nash, J. C. (2008). Re-thinking intersectionality. *Feminist Review*, *89*(1), 1–15.

Nirenberg, D. (2015). *Communities of violence. Persecution of minorities in the Middle Ages*. Oxford: Princeton University Press.

Pfizenmaier, S. (Ed.), (2016). *Charterhouse square: Black Death cemetery and Carthusian monastery, meat market and suburb. Crossrail Series 7*. London: Crossrail and Museum of London Archaeology.

Phillips, W. D., Jr (2013). *Slavery in medieval and early modern Iberia*. Philadelphia, PA: University of Pennsylvania Press.

Phillips, W. D., Jr (1985). *Slavery from Roman times to the early transatlantic trade*. Manchester: Manchester University Press.

Porter, R. (1998). *London: A social history*. Harvard: Harvard University Press.

Powers, N. (Ed.), (2012). *Human osteology method statement*. London: Museum of London. Retrieved from https://www.museumoflondon.org.uk/application/files/4814/5633/5269/osteology-method-statement-revised-2012.pdf.

Prevedorou, E., Díaz-Zorita Bonilla, M., Romero, A., Buikstra, J. E., Paz de Miguel Ibáñez, M., & Knudson, K. J. (2010). Residential mobility and dental decoration in Early Medieval Spain: Results from the eighth century site of Plaza del Castillo, Pamplona. *Dental Anthropology*, *23*(2), 42–52.

Ramey, L. T. (2014). *Black legacies: Race and the European Middle Ages*. Gainesville, FL: University Press of Florida.

Ray, M. (2007). A Black slave on the run in thirteenth-century England. *Nottingham Medieval Studies*, *51*, 111–119.

Redfern, R., DeWitte, S., Montgomery, J., & Gowland, R. (2018). A novel investigation into migrant and local health-statuses in the past: A case study from Roman Britain. *Bioarchaeology International*, *2*(1), 20–37.

Redfern, R. C. (2018). Blind to chains? The potential of bioarchaeology for identifying the enslaved of Roman Britain. *Britannia*. Available from https://doi.org/10/1017/S0068113X18000119.

Richard of Devizes. (1192). *Chronicon de rebus gestis Ricardi Primi*. Retrieved from https://archive.org/details/chroniconricardi01rich.

Robb, J. (2017). Osteobiography: A conceptual framework. In Society for American Archaeology 82nd *annual meeting*, Vancover, BC. Retrieved from https://core.tdar.org/document/430621/osteobiography-a-conceptual-framework

Roberts, C. A., Millard, A., Nowell, G., Gröcke, D., Macpherson, C., Pearson, D., & Evans, D. (2013). Isotopic tracing of the impact of mobility on infectious disease: The origin of people with treponematosis buried in Hull, England, in the late Medieval period. *American Journal of Physical Anthropology*, *150*(2), 273–285.

S.N. (2017, January 2). The far right's new fascination with the Middle Ages. *The Economist*. Retrieved from https://www.economist.com/blogs/democracyinamerica/2017/01/medieval-memes.

Shraga, R., Yarnall, S., Elango, S., Manoharan, A., Rodriguez, S. A., Bristow, S. L., ... Puig, O. (2017). Evaluating genetic ancestry and self-reported ethnicity in the context of carrier screening. *BMC Genetics*, *18*(1), 99.

Sloane, B. (2011). *The Black Death in London*. Stroud: The History Press Ltd.

Spufford, P. (2002). *Power and profit: The merchant in Medieval Europe*. London: Thames & Hudson.

Thomas, C. (2002). *The archaeology of Medieval London*. Stroud: The History Press Ltd.

Thrupp, S. L. (1989). *The merchant class of Medieval London, 1300-1500*. Ann Arbor, MI: University of Michigan.

Torres, M. (2008). Marginalization. In R. T. Schaefer (Ed.), *Encyclopedia of race, ethnicity, and society* (pp. 871–872). London: SAGE Publications.

Turner, T. R., Bernstein, R. M., Taylor, A. B., Asangba, A., Bekelman, T., Cramer, J. D., ... Vogel, E. (2018). Participation, representation, and shared experiences of women scholars in biological anthropology. *American Journal of Physical Anthropology*, *S165*, 126–157.

Walker, D. (2012). Trauma. In B. Connell, A. Gray Jones, R. Redfern, & D. Walker (Eds.), *Spitalfields: A bioarchaeological study of health and disease from a medieval London cemetery. Archaeological excavations at Spitalfields Market 1991-2007* (Vol. 3, pp. 88–108). London: Museum of London Archaeology, Monograph 60.

Walter, B. S., & DeWitte, S. N. (2017). Urban and rural mortality and survival in Medieval England. *Annals of Human Biology*, *44*(4), 338–348.

Wasterlain, S. N., Neves, M. J., & Ferreira, M. T. (2016). Dental modifications in a skeletal sample of enslaved Africans found at Lagos (Portugal). *International Journal of Osteoarchaeology*, *26*(4), 621–632.

Weeda, C. (2016). The fixed and the fluent: Geographical determinism, ethnicity, and religiou c. 1100-1300 CE. In R. Futo Kennedy, & M. Jones-Lewis (Eds.), *The Routledge handbook of identity and the environment in the Classical and Medieval worlds* (pp. 93–113). London: Routledge.

Weeda, C. (2017). Characteristics of bodies and ethnicity c.900-1200. *Medieval Worlds*, *5*, 95–112.

Welford, M., & Bossak, B. (2010). Body lice, *Yersina pestis* orientalis, and Black Death. *Emerging Infectious Diseases*, *16*(10), 1649–1651.

Williams, G. A. (2007). *Medieval London*. Oxford: Routledge.

Williamson, V. (2014). *Evidence for Medieval Black History in England*. Retrieved from http://decodedpast.com/evidence-medieval-black-history-england/5433.

WORD. (2018). *Wellcome Osteological Research Database downloads*. Museum of London.

Zakrewski, S. R. (2011). Population migration, variation and identity: An Islamic population in Iberia. In S. C. Agarwal, & B. A. Glencross (Eds.), *Social bioarchaeology* (pp. 183–211). Chichester: Wiley-Blackwell.

Ziegler, M. (2016a). *Plague dialogues: Monica Green and Boris Schmid on plague phylogeny (II)*. Retrieved from https://contagions.wordpress.com/2016/06/29/plague-dialogues-monica-green-and-boris-schmid-on-plague-phylogeny-ii/.

Ziegler, P. (2016b). *The Black Death*. Rockville, MD: American Heritage Publishing.

Chapter 6

Marginalized by choice—Kayenta Pueblo communities in the Southwest (AD 800–1500)

Debra L. Martin
Department of Anthropology, University of Nevada, Las Vegas, NV, United States

Chapter Outline

Introduction

The Kayenta region during the 8th through 13th centuries was populated by Ancestral Pueblo people who shared aspects of material culture, architecture, and ideology with groups living in nearby regions such as Mesa Verde and Chaco Canyon. Both Mesa Verde and Chaco Canyon have been the foci of extensive archaeological investigations and retrieval of artifacts and burials since the 1950s (Cordell & McBrinn, 2012). The archaeological sites in these regions are replete with large, dense communities with visibly spectacular architecture and trade goods from groups outside of the Southwest. At the same time, there were aspects of life in the Kayenta area, which were distinctive, ranging from unique architectural features and settlement patterns to differences in subsistence activities, trade and networking. For example, Kayenta is one of the only regions where there were relatively few trade items or exotic nonlocal artifacts from groups outside of the region (Euler, 1988). Yet the Kayenta communities were not socially isolated or cut-off from other groups. The distinctive pottery produced in Kayenta (e.g., several

Bioarchaeology of Marginalized People. DOI: https://doi.org/10.1016/B978-0-12-815224-9.00006-3

styles of black on white and multiple versions of polychromes and orange wares) is found at Mesa Verde, Chaco Canyon, and other places (Dean, 2002).

Marginality in this paper is explored and addressed as a label that characterizes not only the geographically remote location and environmentally dry and sparse land, but also the lack of sociocultural complexity within the region that is seen in the dearth of trade items found at archaeological sites and the simplicity of the architecture within habitation areas. Scholars themselves have not made Kayenta a priority in terms of excavation, retrieval, and analysis making its remoteness even more so. Archaeologists have always described the region as marginal, and this label of marginality is first and foremost based on the dry desert environment but also on the lack of exotic trade items and monumental architecture that is seen at contemporaneous sites outside the region (Geib, 2011). The geographic location within a maze of washes, arroyos, and uneven landscapes has been linked to the lack of resources and cultural development.

For example, Kayenta was originally referred to as a "provincial backwater" (Gumerman, Westfall, & Reed, 1972, p. 198) when compared to the more impressive architecture and artifacts found at Mesa Verde and Chaco Canyon. Archaeologists have referred to the Kayenta groups as "insular, conservative folk" (Ambler, 1983, p. 125) who have "an overall simple-looking social fabric" (p. 124). There are no high status burials from any of the core areas of Kayenta (Dean, 2002). Kayenta lacks sociocultural complexity when compared to their counterparts in Mesa Verde and Chaco Canyon and this is a recurrent theme (Cordell & McBrinn, 2012). Archeologists who have spent decades doing studies in Kayenta suggest that it was neither part of a major population center, nor a "focal point for trade or... cultural innovation" (Gumerman, 1984, p. 6). It is explicit in many of these summaries of the Kayenta Region that environmental marginality placed constraints on cultural development. But cultural development and complexity at Kayenta are always measured against other regions and found wanting based on these kinds of comparisons.

The environmental and cultural features that archaeologists use to distinguish Kayenta as marginalized may have been the saving grace for the people living there because bioarchaeological data suggest a generally robust, high-fertility population that was well-adapted and that lived successfully without violence or warfare over several centuries. These Kayenta communities challenge the notion that environmental marginality limits cultural innovation and produces poorer health. Earlier assessments of Kayenta as poverty-stricken and less developed when compared to other Ancestral Pueblo people living at Mesa Verde and Chaco Canyon have proven to be a misleading way to characterize the particulars of social organization and cultural processes operating throughout the occupation (c. AD 800–1300) at Kayenta. The argument posited here is that the people living in the Kayenta Region should be recast as an innovative and sustainable culture composed of interconnected communities that drew upon themselves and their local resources in creative ways (Dean, 2002; Geib, 2011). A nuanced reading of the literature suggests that it was precisely the provincial and parochial nature of those living there, with their inward-focused (but not insular) political economy, strong local identity, and their local and extra-local social networks, that permitted Kayenta groups to respond quickly to problems unencumbered by rigid and hierarchical social structures (Dean, 1996). Dean and Clark (2013, pp. 22–23) stated that "although they never exhibited the degree of social complexity of their Mesa Verde and Chacoan contemporaries, their less elaborate organization and remarkable ability to organize, dissolve, and reconfigure communities in different ways endowed them with the flexibility necessary to adapt to a wide array of social and environmental opportunities and challenges."

Why the Kayenta region is so important in the distribution of Ancestral Pueblo groups across the Colorado Plateau area is that it offers an alternative narrative for thinking about marginalization and sustainability. No one disagrees that most of the Kayenta region is extremely environmentally marginal, and that being farmers in a desert fraught with both seasonal cycles of unpredictability and multiple-year droughts was challenging. As Gieb notes, people survived in spite of "less food, less water" over long periods of time (2011, p. 202). Yet, people stayed in the Kayenta region instead of migrating to places where resources were more plentiful, and where trade items were more diverse. Bioarchaeological data on demography and disease provides a way to investigate the various ways marginality may have affected individuals and communities. Unpredictable crop yields and sparse natural resources can affect fertility, health and community resilience, and this can be assessed through analysis of human remains. Linking these data on health with a reconstruction of biocultural factors such as trade networks, alliance formation, and other political-economic choices provides a more complete picture of what life was like within Kayenta.

Kayenta Region

The border of the Kayenta Region is both naturally and culturally defined, and the criteria used to define it vary across archaeological studies. Kayenta covers an area of approximately 10,000 square miles (Gumerman, 1984) bounded geographically by the Colorado River on the west, the Chinle Wash on the east, the San Juan River to the north, and the Little Colorado River in the south (Dean, 1996; Geib, 2011) (Fig. 6.1). The Kayenta region takes its name from the nearby modern town of Kayenta, Arizona. The northern part is considered to be the core area where population was most pronounced, and the more southern part consists of the First, Second, and Third Mesas as well as Antelope Mesa and this is where Pueblo communities that self-identify as Hopi continue to live today.

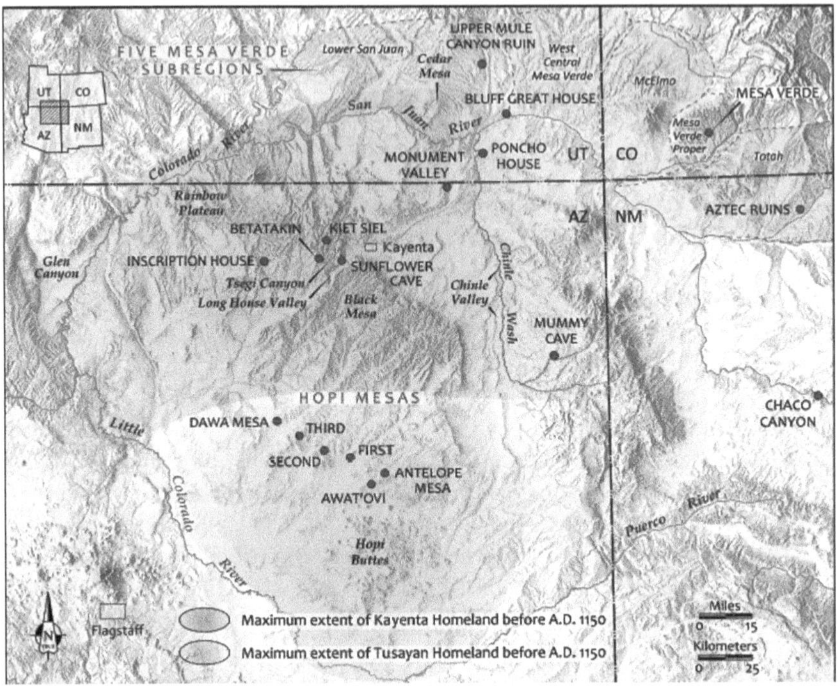

FIGURE 6.1 Map illustrating the maximum extent of Kayenta Homeland before 1150 AD. Drawn by Catherine Gilman for the Archaeology Southwest Magazine (2013, Volume 27, Number 3, Page 17).

This area has provided researchers with excellent tree-ring samples, so that both cutting dates and annual rainfall are available for many of the archaeological sites within this region (Dean, 2002). Added to this are pottery analyses that demonstrate stylistic changes that also denote specific time periods. Dates for most of the archaeological sites can be provided, which are to within 50 years for most of the occupation, and to within 25 years for the last century of occupation (Haas & Creamer, 1993). Environmental conditions have been reconstructed based on analyses of tree rings, pollen and hydrology data along with extensive chronostratigraphic studies of floodplain deposits, arroyo cutting, and alluvial ground water levels (Dean, 2002).

The pattern in general for architecture in Kayenta was that of nuclear and extended family households. These were linked by kinship and residence in villages that ranged in size from 2 to 12 households (Dean, 2002). Small hamlets were interconnected in ways that formed dispersed communities. This type of arrangement meant that communities could grow larger or they could fission off and move toward less dense and smaller hamlets (Cordell & McBrinn, 2012). This flexibility is not seen in neighboring regions such as Mesa Verde and Chaco Canyon. The basic social unit was comprised of living areas, an open courtyard, and storage areas. Some larger communities were situated around a larger household unit with a kiva which is a large subterranean pit-structure that was often the focal point for ceremonial and political activities. The presence of kivas suggests that communities came together at times, and then spread out into smaller community hamlets at other times. Kayenta masonry in general was somewhat nondescript, and it did not borrow stylistic elements from Mesa Verde or Chaco Canyon (Neitzel, 2000).

Biodistance studies aiming to clarify the genetic relatedness of Kayenta people with other groups such as Mesa Verde, Chaco Canyon, Cibola, Rio Grande, and Mogollon have been conducted with varying degrees of success. All of the studies demonstrate that Kayenta people shared genetics with all the other Ancestral Pueblo peoples (Corruccini, 1972) but were distinguishable from groups farther away (such as Rio Grande groups). The inherent genetic consistency found across all Ancestral Pueblo groups suggests that none of the regional areas were exclusively endogamous for any length of time.

What seemed to connect people across villages within the Kayenta system was trading, networking, and shared ceremonial spaces. The connections outside of Kayenta were more likely based on networking, trading Kayenta pottery for information or food, and perhaps mate exchanges (Dean, 2002). The sites within the core were also connected in social- and political-economic ways with Kayenta sites on the periphery, such as those in the Glen Canyon area on the northwest, Monument Valley to the north, and the sites within Canyon de Chelly and Canyon del Muerto to the east (Powell, 2002). During the transition period (AD 1150–1250), there is a shift from smaller dispersed hamlet-like settlements across the core region to larger more aggregated and interdependent communities within the core. People emigrated out of the peripheral areas as the populations began concentrating in the core. The upland mesas were also depopulated (such as northern Black Mesa) by AD 1150. This was likely because the valleys and canyon localities in lower elevations were more favorable in terms of arable land and water than the mesa tops.

In summary, up to the major emigrations out of the region in the AD 1300s, Kayenta communities were strategically versatile, responsive to environmental changes and flexible in how habitation areas were formed and abandoned. These patterns are distinctive from those at Mesa Verde and Chaco Canyon where there appears to be much more conformity and lack of diversity in habitation patterns and food procurement. Geib (2011) and Powell (2002) have shown that there is evidence based on midden contents, storage features, ethnobotanical and faunal analyses, alliance formations, and artifact distributions across the region that there was an established system of egalitarianism that was underscored by interconnected communities. Thus multiple lines of evidence suggest that they consciously crafted a largely egalitarian and cooperative way of living. This permitted communities to be able to respond quickly and efficiently to the vicissitudes of seasonal and annual climate changes. There is evidence that while they were primarily farmers, they also were strategic in how they exploited natural plant and animal species maintaining a highly diverse diet that included an abundance of rabbit, rodents, amaranth and chenopodium, and other foraged and hunted food sources (Euler, 1988). While experienced farmers, their reliance on wild plants and seeds, and small mammals and other animals maximized subsistence productivity and this permitted relatively healthy communities to increase their fertility especially during the AD 1100s (Dean, 2002).

Another sign of the egalitarian nature of Kayenta groups is that they were creative with their in-house ceramics and stylistics and they crafted unique items such as seed bowls, colanders, and ladles with distinctive handles with distinctive styles such as Tusayán White Ware and Tsegi Orange Ware, creating a strong Kayenta identity (Lyons, 2013). Spielmann (2004, p. 227) suggests that specialized production of decorated serving bowls (such as the large Tsegi Orange Ware polychrome bowls used in community feasts) make for a "compelling case for the power of place...potters have created novel bowl forms as an expression of, and vessel for ceremonial feasting." All of these things created a particular and unique Kayenta identity that was temporally and spatially maintained within Kayenta right up to the end of their grand experiment in living off the grid, so to speak, from their counterparts in Chaco Canyon and Mesa Verde.

People from Kayenta did eventually emigrate out of the area in the AD 1200s, but not due to any one factor such as warfare, disease, or droughts (Dean, 2002). In terms of factors that might have pushed people out of Kayenta, Dean (2002) and Geib (2011) have suggested that it might have been that they were pulled toward something better than what they could hope to have at Kayenta. Kayenta enclaves have been well documented in Hohokam groups to the south and to Mogollon groups to the west (Geib, 2011).

Population Growth and Paleodemography

Based on several different archeological estimates of population size across the occupation of Kayenta, population size is seen to have increased markedly between AD 1100 and AD 1150 (Dean, 2002). Dean (1996) provides summary data suggesting that for the Kayenta region in AD 1100, there was minimally 2000 people living in dispersed hamlets and this increased to almost 4000 people in the early AD 1200s, and then dropped off precipitously in the AD 1280s. In the aggregated rock shelter sites of Betatakin and Kiet Siel, population increased from AD 1220 to AD 1300 going from zero to almost 500 people in three generations (Euler, 1988).

Information on the nature of the household is an important line of evidence for examining the ways that households acted as effective buffers.

Using agent-based modeling for the Long House Valley communities in the core Swedlund, Sattenspiel, Warren, Meindl, and Gumerman (2016) utilized households as one focus of study because their research suggested to them that decisions about where to farm and when to move are made at that level.

A detailed paleodemographic study was carried out for 178 Kayenta burials retrieved from communities living on Black Mesa (AD 800–1150) (Martin, Goodman, Armelagos, & Magennis, 1991). Using life table analyses and other demographic measures, population growth is well documented based on the area of floor space per site and the number of sites over time, with estimates ranging from a population of approximately 200 in AD 800, rising steadily to a peak of 3200 by AD 1050, and then a slow decline in population until AD 1150 when there was a slow movement of people from Black Mesa into the surrounding valleys and canyons (Powell, Andrews, Nichols, & Smiley, 1983; Swedlund & Sessions, 1976). It was estimated based on the number of household units in the study area that the households went from having an average of 4.5 people in AD 800 to 7.5 in AD 1000–1075, with the number decreasing to 3.6 and then 1.5 by the end of the occupation (Swedlund & Sessions, 1976). The ability to support more people at the household level may have positively affected the survival of infants and children who then became helpers with food production. The authors suggest that it was an increase in fertility that drove the growth of population on Black Mesa, not an influx of migrants. This is supported by the fact that burial practices never changed over time and neither did pottery types.

Despite the challenges of an unpredictable and marginal environment where droughts were common, there is no indication of increased mortality or morbidity during the worst of the dry seasons. Black Mesa households and villages may have coped by being able to accommodate environmental hardships (Martin et al., 1991). Life table analyses suggested that the mortality experience for Black Mesa does not change over time (c. AD 900–1150). The pattern of deaths is relatively similar in both the earlier and later groups. The mean age at death for the earlier versus the later groups is similar: 25.4 and 24.9 (Martin et al., 1991).

Diet, Health, and Trauma

What is known about Kayenta subsistence, and diet is reconstructed through a diverse set of paleoenvironmental, ethnobotanical, faunal, midden, and coprolite analyses (Dean, 2002). Although in a marginal environment not particularly well suited to agriculture, Kayenta communities were well adapted to their local ecologies in terms of their settlement patterns and subsistence strategies. Being a farmer in this region was always fraught with risk, but the hamlet-style settlements meant that wild plants and animals could be continuously exploited since the density of people at any given location was not large (Dean, 2002; Powell et al., 1983). Another suggestion regarding the challenge of producing or foraging for enough food is that Powell (2002) suggested that pottery exchange seemed to go in only one direction, from the Kayenta region to Mesa Verde, Sinagua, and Mogollon. Powell (2002) suggests that this leaves open the possibility that ceramics from Kayenta were traded with neighboring regions for perishable items such as food and cotton.

Geib (2011) summarizes the work of Powell et al. (1983) and suggests that in the core Kayenta areas, the dispersed hamlets were never permanent sites of full-time habitation. Groups hunted for small game, gathered wild plants and nuts, tended to farm plots, and moved around the landscape to maximize exploitation of all of these food sources. Utilizing both farming and foraging, or farmaging, would have minimized the risks of depending too much on any one source for food (Diehl, 2005). According to Diehl (2005), farmaging is an intentional subsistence strategy that is the primary motivating factor regarding the layout and organization of community units within a region. This combination of farming and foraging is not in evidence in other regions within the Southwest and seems to be unique to Kayenta. The flexibility in the settlement patterns noted for Kayenta also permitted mobility to move during winter seasons to exploit wild resources, and to be more sedentary during summers (Powell et al., 1983). This is not to downplay the importance of maize in the Kayenta diet because it did form an underlying base of the diet (Geib, 2011), but the ethnobotanical diversity seen in coprolites and middens suggests a mixed diet of farming and foraging (Martin et al., 1991; Reinhard, Geib, Callahan, & Hevly, 1992).

This farmager subsistence pattern worked synergistically with the flexible semisedentary settlement patterning and seasonal mobility in the northern core region of Kayenta. The less rigid Kayenta social organization combined with ceremonial cycles allowed for them to adjust accordingly, and this meant changing the size, layout, and location of their hamlet-style communities, as well as strengthening ties with other Kayenta communities as needed.

Nutritional Anemia

The measures of poor health that can be linked inferentially through clinical and experimental data are nutritional anemias (manifested in the skeleton as porosities in the orbit or vault area of the cranium) and childhood growth disruption (measured by counting the number of linear enamel hypoplasias (LEH) in an individual's dental enamel). Because several of the major studies have presented these data together or sequentially and examined their cooccurrence, they will be discussed together here. Both are very difficult to compare across studies because of the different ways that they are scored, tallied, and presented in various charts and tables.

During AD 900–1150, adults would have been preoccupied with a wide range of potential stressors relating to diet (e.g., food production, food shortages, potential wild sources) not so much because of difficult environmental conditions but due more to higher fertility, increased numbers of infants and children, and overall population growth. Two of the more well-studied indicators for general nutritional inadequacy are porotic hyperostosis and cribra orbitalia (Walker, Bathurst, Richman, Gjerdrum, & Andrushko, 2009). Any bone that is involved in the production of red blood cells has the potential to be affected by a nutritional deficit that leads to anemia. Walker (1985) and Walker et al. (2009) have argued that porotic hyperostosis, and the related pathology cribra orbitalia, are the result of a complex interaction between factors such as food intake, metabolism, and infectious disease. Thus these lesions most likely signal problems with the consumption or utilization of key nutrients, but there is no way of knowing what these exact nutrients are. McIlvaine (2013) makes a good case for not needing to differentiate between things such as B12 or iron deficiencies: both can result from a diet lacking in meat and they often cooccur. Anemia is a common health problem in both industrialized and nonindustrialized countries, with its bony expression being more pronounced in children, adolescents, and women during childbearing years (Oxenham & Cavill, 2010).

One of the best datasets for assessment of this pathology for AD 900–1150 comes from the Black Mesa burials with a sample size of 172. The data show that for the 172 burials retrieved from many small hamlet sites, a majority of the men, women, and children experienced mild to moderate nutritional problems. Porotic hyperostosis is present in 84.7% of the total collection. In terms of severity, only 10.3% of the cases are severe in expression; 64.3% are more moderate in expression and 25.2% are mild (Martin et al., 1991). These data suggest chronic nutritional inadequacies that may have been episodic or seasonal and that were widespread throughout the groups living on Black Mesa. There were no statistically significant differences when comparing rates during AD 900–1030 with those dated to AD 1070–1150. Comparing overall population rates across Kayenta sites and with frequencies from other regions shows that they are mostly similar although there are sites with lower frequencies (Table 6.1). In addition to this, 85% of adults from Black Mesa showed childhood physiological growth disruptions on their teeth, called LEH that peaked between the ages of 2 and 5 (Martin et al., 1991). The picture that emerges is one of endemic, mild to moderate nutritional stress that had an impact on all segments of the population, even adult males.

Ryan's (1977) dissertation was focused on health over time. He utilized Wade's (1970) Puerco Pueblo Cibola sample (close proximity to but not within Kayenta) in addition to burials from 34 other Kayenta and Sinagua (again, neighboring but not within Kayenta) sites and one historic Hopi site (Old Walpi, AD 1300–1700). Some of these burials were from the general Glen Canyon dam area and the Lake Powell region of southern Utah at the northern periphery of the Kayenta region. Additional burials were from the

TABLE 6.1 Reconstructed frequencies of porotic hyperostosis.

Site	Date	Porotic hyperostosis
Black Mesa, Kayenta	AD 900–1150	84.7% (50/59)
Canyon de Chelly, Kayenta (Basketmaker)	AD 400–700	72.0% (36/50)
Canyon de Chelly, Kayenta	AD 700–1300	88.2% (15/17)
Kayenta sites	AD 1150–1250	46.7% (7/15)
Inscription House, Kayenta	AD 1250–1300	63.6% (7/11)
Old Walpi (Hopi), Tusayán	AD 1350s	60.0% (3/5)
Chaco Canyon, Chaco	AD 900–1156	83.3% (10/12)

Sample size (*n*) is based on the presence of a well-preserved cranium.
Source: From Walker (1985, pp. 143–144); Martin, D. L., Goodman, A. H., Armelagos, G. J., & Magennis, A. L. (1991). *Black Mesa Anasazi health: Reconstructing life from patterns of death and disease* (p. 154). Carbondale: Southern Illinois University Press.

Klethla Valley and Inscription House. His total sample consisted of 353 burials representing AD 800–1500s. Unfortunately the way that Ryan collected data by using a scale of 0–5 and reporting frequencies per frontal, orbit, parietal, and occipital bone makes it very difficult to compare his findings with other collections. Ryan found no statistically significant differences among the various skeletal series (Ryan, 1977). However, he found a significant *decrease* in the frequency of infants with porotic hyperostosis over time in two Kayenta skeletal series which seems to go from about 20% to 0% (1977). In general, he found about a 60% rate of porotic hyperostosis for adults at Kayenta (Ryan, 1977), and this is comparable to the findings in Table 6.1.

El-Najjar, Lozoff, and Ryan (1975) and El-Najjar, Ryan, Turner, and Lozoff (1976) published a cross-regional study of porotic hyperostosis for burials from two Kayenta areas (Canyon de Chelly and Inscription House) and Chaco Canyon. Their data are also difficult to pull for comparative purposes because of the way they are presented. They divided sites/skeletal collections based on two ecological types, canyon bottoms (considered to have been relying on maize agriculture) and sage plains sites (considered to be farmagers reliant upon mixed maize and foraging). Out of a combined sample size of 539 intact crania, 34% (185/539) demonstrated the presence of porotic hyperostosis. In canyon bottom sites, where there was more of an emphasis on maize, 54% (146/270) of the individuals died with cases of porotic hyperostosis. In the sage plains where maize does not grow as well and the diet was more of a mixed domesticated/wild farmager strategy, only 14.5% (39/269) of the population showed signs of the lesion. These differences were statistically significant (El-Najjar et al., 1976).

The mild to moderate nature of the nutritional anemia suggests that communities faced daily health-related challenges that included widespread but low-level nutritional inadequacies. Individuals with porotic hyperostosis likely presented as "subclinical" in terms of their symptoms, meaning while they may have felt more tired, by itself anemia is serious but it is not life threatening unless there are other issues (Walker et al., 2009). It becomes problematic when other diseases are present that can take advantage of a somewhat compromised immune response that comes with any chronic illness (Oxenham & Cavill, 2010). Based on these data, there was no rampant malnutrition or starvation, no apocalyptic spike in deaths.

Nonspecific Inflammation

Periosteal reactions show up on long bones due to inflammation of the external membrane when there is some systemic body-wide health problem. Usually the actual causative agent cannot be pinpointed (Weston, 2012), but these reactions are often due to common bacterial infections such as *Staphylococcus* or *Streptococcus*. Active periosteal reactions at the time of death appear as smooth, irregular, lattice-like layers of new bone formed over the existing bone (Weston, 2012). The amount of raised bone gives an indication of the severity and longevity of the infection. A healing bone will still display irregular and pitted lesions but will eventually return to normal texture through the remodeling process.

At Black Mesa periosteal reactions were found on 49.7% of the total population with the majority of these cases in the infants and children ($n = 58$); 70.7% of the infants and children showed some form of periosteal reactions indicating nonspecific generalized infections (Martin et al., 1991). The status of these lesions was noted to be slight or moderate (Table 6.2). There were no severe cases of periosteal reactions within the infants and children

TABLE 6.2 Black Mesa nonspecific inflammation/infection in the subadults.

Age (years)	None, *n*	Slight, *n*	Moderate, *n*	Severe, *n*
Nb–1.9	23.8% (5)	57.1% (12)	19.5% (4)	0.00%
2.0–6.9	31.2% (5)	37.5% (6)	31.2% (5)	0.00%
7.0–12.9	40.0% (6)	46.7% (7)	13.3% (2)	0.00%
13.0–16.9	16.7% (1)	66.7% (4)	16.7% (1)	0.00%
Total	29.3% (17)	50.0% (29)	20.7% (12)	0.00%

Source: Adapted from Martin, D. L., Goodman, A. H., Armelagos, G. J., & Magennis, A. L. (1991). Black Mesa Anasazi health: Reconstructing life from patterns of death and disease (p. 132). Carbondale: Southern Illinois University Press.

suggesting that while this was a mild but chronic problem contributing to morbidity, the expression of it was subclinical and likely not life threatening.

For Kayenta individuals from the Rainbow Bridge collection (RB568), Berry (1983) found only one case of bone inflammation. Ryan's (1977) data on nonspecific infections for Kayenta groups is quite different and more in line with the findings at Rainbow Bridge. He reports that for the sample from Glen Canyon, there are no cases of lesions suggestive of infections and he also found no cases at Old Walpi. Ryan (1977, p. 191) concludes that "the long bone inflammations were probably not of much consequence and have the appearance of being healed."

For the Kayenta Region in general, long bone inflammation rates are very low except for Black Mesa for which the cases scored presented as mostly slight and moderate in expression. This pathology is hard to score when bone surfaces have been etched or eroded through taphonomic processes. It is also often not recognized when it is mild in expression. Most of the Black Mesa cases were in children and they were mild to moderate in expression. If only the moderate cases were considered, it would bring the frequency down to 20% for the infants and children and 7.1% for the entire population (Martin et al., 1991).

In a large comparative study looking at the relationship between subsistence strategy and infections, Wade (1985) reviewed the literature on infectious diseases from European skeletal collections and calculated the frequency as 13% for foragers, 36% for small-scale agriculturalists, and 50% for state-level farmers. He emphasizes the relationship between transmissible bacterial diseases and increased population density, trade networks, and social stratification. In light of this, the few cases found in the Kayenta Region are revelatory of the generally lower population density (even as population increased).

Dental Disease

Analysis of dental disease would include the frequency of dental caries, dental attrition, and antemortem tooth loss. Because dental attrition and antemortem tooth loss are age-dependent phenomena, a relatively large sample size is necessary so that frequencies can be compared across relatively small age categories. Very few collections in the Kayenta region have presented detailed analyses of the full range of dental pathologies. Most only note the number of carious lesions or missing teeth. For the studies that do report dental pathology with some specificity, the highest frequencies of reported dental disease in terms of carious lesions are reported by Bernor, Ponnech, and Miller (1972) for burials from the Rainbow Bridge sites (AD 1200–1300), where 85% of available dentition had one or more carious lesions at the time of death. For Black Mesa about 26% of available dentition had carious lesions (Martin et al., 1991). For comparison, Wade (1970) reported a 12% caries rate for the Puerco Pueblo Cibola burials. Berry (1983) compared Rainbow Bridge Kayenta frequencies with those from Mogollon sites for several dental pathologies and found them to be similar. El-Najjar et al. (1976) noted that 14% of individuals from Canyon de Chelly have one or more carious lesions.

Several studies attempting to look temporally at the frequencies of caries show that there are increases over time (Martin et al., 1991). This relates to the increased consumption of cariogenic food, such as maize. Thus this one indicator of dental health may relate to a shift in a diet that becomes increasingly based on maize. Crittenden et al. (2017) point out that caries are increasing in Hadza foragers, who are currently undergoing shifts in diet induced by globalization with an increase in carbohydrates and a decrease in foraged food. They state, "our results showed that women living in villages consuming a mostly agricultural diet exhibited more caries and periodontal disease than those living in the bush consuming a mostly wild-food diet" (Crittenden et al., 2017, p. 1). Caries rates are thus a good indicator of what people are eating, or at least the amount of sticky cariogenic properties the food has. Caries do not often cause people to die, but they can cause suffering and infections until the bad tooth is extracted or until the nerve dies and the tooth falls out on its own. In this case the increase in frequency in the later Kayenta phase tells us less about overall health than about what people were eating.

Perimortem Trauma

Haas and Creamer (1993) discuss one isolated cranium that was recovered from Kin Klethla with perimortem trauma to the frontal bone and cut marks on the back from a site dating to the late AD 1200s that was burned down and abandoned. Another site within Long House Valley called the Brown Star Site produced a male buried face down and flexed who was found in a midden near another burial of a female with grave goods. This male burial is in a flexed position without a cranium. There are no signs of perimortem trauma, cut marks, or beheading. In an another Kayenta burial, a young adult male from Betatakin (Site 73) was located in a kiva and had cut marks on the cranium in locations that suggest it could have been scalped (Turner & Turner, 1999).

There are a number of explanations for why an adult female or male might be killed and scalped. Witchcraft accusations often resulted in death for the accused and these practices have been written about widely for the Ancestral Pueblo (Darling, 1998; Walker, 2009; Whiteley, 2008). Ritualized violence associated with malfeasance is found liberally in Hopi oral tradition (Whiteley, 2008) and scalpings also have been noted for a number of non-Kayentan sites (Kohler, Varien, Wright, & Kuckelman, 2008) with a number of motivations and interpretations. The relatively small number of these cases suggest that whatever the causes, the practice was not widespread.

Antemortem Trauma

At Black Mesa the frequency of well-healed traumatic fractures was about 20% of the population (Martin et al., 1991). These are found largely on the top and back of the cranium, and there are more on adult females than males. It is possible that these represent women who may have fled from the more violent regions surrounding Kayenta, and these refugees may have contributed to the rapid population growth discussed earlier.

There is very little evidence for warfare and/or violence directed at certain villages or individuals within the Kayenta system, and while there are two possible cases of killing and scalping from a later phase of the occupation, these were isolated burials for which there is very little contextual information. The generally low frequencies of healed cranial depression fractures and other postcranial fractures suggest that interpersonal violence was not a problem at Kayenta.

Conclusions

In summary the health profile that emerges for Kayenta is one of a robust, demographically stable series of small interconnected villages spanning AD 800–1350. Kayenta people and their communities differ in that they never lived in large aggregated groups as they did at Mesa Verde and Chaco Canyon, and there is no evidence for the trading of extra-local or exotic trade items that are liberally found in sites outside of Kayenta. While raiding and low-level warfare have been documented for the other regions, there is no evidence for this at Kayenta.

While interactions with people outside of their area seem limited, there is evidence that the communities within the Kayenta region were extremely well connected and that settlements shared ritual and stylistic knowledge that increased over time. Integration between Kayenta communities has been analyzed by looking at the ratio between population size and the number of kivas which provides a rough estimate of local integration (Hegmon, 1986). The similarity in the unique Kayenta design elements on bowls and pitchers throughout the Kayenta region indicates strong communication and connectivity among the villages. When there are changes in the design element, it is adopted simultaneously by groups within and across the Kayenta region (Haas, 2001).

There is no bioarchaeological evidence of increasing stratification or elites based on mortuary patterns or health differentials between subgroups by age or sex. The lack of interest in exotic trade items and in what was going on at Chaco Great Houses and later at Mesa Verde suggests a more inward-focused philosophy. At some sites like Kiet Siel, there was an increase in households attempting to store food, whereas in other areas there was an increase in sharing food across communities. This could be interpreted as always having backup plans for when resources got scarce. It also suggests strong social networks that can be called upon to help redistribute food to kin groups that need it.

The biometric, paleodemographic, and paleopathology data demonstrate that being farmagers in an unpredictable marginal desert environment like Kayenta was not easy, but it was actually better than life in regions to the north and east that were experiencing more health problems and low-level warfare, even though food was likely plentiful. Kayenta groups had to work hard, endure suffering, and have strategic plans to get them through hard times as the droughts came and went for varying periods of time. Bioarchaeology has offered an alternative view to thinking about marginality. Sometimes living a harder life in more marginal environments may be better than living within hierarchical and larger communities where flexibility is not possible. The conscious choice made to stay in a marginalized environment and adapt to its vicissitudes was likely what Kayenta groups did.

References

Ambler, J. R. (1983). Kayenta Anasazi archaeology on Central Black Mesa, Northeastern Arizona: The Pinon Project. *Kiva*, *49*(1–2), 124–126.

Bernor, R., Ponnech, S., & Miller, P. (1972). *Human skeletal report: Pathologies and anomalies for RB-MV 568, a Tesgi phase site near Kayenta, AZ*. Los Angeles: Laboratory of Skeletal and Faunal Analysis, University of California, MS on File.

Berry, D. (1983). Skeletal remains from RB 568. In H. Crotty (Ed.), Honoring the dead: Anasazi ceramics from the Rainbow Bridge Monument Valley expedition *(Monograph Series 22)* (pp. 64–69). Los Angeles: Museum of Cultural History.

Cordell, L. S., & McBrinn, M. E. (2012). *Archaeology of the Southwest* (3rd ed.). Walnut Creek: Left Coast Press, Inc.

Corruccini, R. S. (1972). The biological relationships of some prehistoric and historic Pueblo populations. *American Journal of Physical Anthropology*, *37*(3), 373–388.

Crittenden, A., Sorrentino, J., Moonie, S., Peterson, M., Mabulla, A., & Ungar, P. (2017). Oral health in transition: The Hadza Foragers of Tanzania. *PLoS One*, *12*(3), e0172197.

Darling, A. J. (1998). Mass inhumation and the execution of witches in the American Southwest. *American Anthropologist, New Series*, *100*(3), 732–752.

Dean, J. S. (1996). Kayenta Anasazi settlement transformations in Northeastern Arizona, AD 1150 to 1350. In M. Adler (Ed.), The prehistoric Pueblo world, AD (pp. 29–47). Tucson: University of Arizona Press.

Dean, J. S. (2002). Late Pueblo II-Pueblo III in Kayenta—branch prehistory. In S. Powell, & F. E. Smiley (Eds.), *Prehistoric culture change on the Colorado Plateau: Ten thousand years on Black Mesa* (pp. 121–159). Tucson: University of Arizona Press.

Dean, J. S., & Clark, J. J. (2013). Understanding the Kayenta, from beginning to end. In J. S. Dean, & J. J. Clark (Eds.), *Before the Great Departure, the Kayenta in their homeland* (Vol. 27, pp. 21–23). Tucson: Archaeology Southwest Magazine. (no. 3).

Diehl, M. W. (2005). Epilogue: "Farmaging" during the Early Agricultural Period. In M. W. Diehl (Ed.), *Subsistence and resource use strategies of early agricultural communities in*

Southern Arizona (pp. 181–184). Tucson: Center for Desert Archaeology, Anthropological Papers No. 34.

El-Najjar, M. Y., Lozoff, B., & Ryan, D. J. (1975). The paleoepidemiology of porotic hyperostosis in the American Southwest: Radiological and ecological considerations. *American Journal of Roentgenology, 125*(4), 918–924.

El-Najjar, M. Y., Ryan, D. J., Turner, C. G., II, & Lozoff, B. (1976). The etiology of porotic hyperostosis among the Prehistoric and Historic Anasazi Indians of Southwestern United States. *American Journal of Physical Anthropology, 44*, 477–488.

Euler, R. C. (1988). Demography and cultural dynamics on the Colorado Plateau. In G. J. Gumerman (Ed.), *The Anasazi in a changing environment* (pp. 192–229). Cambridge: Cambridge University Press.

Geib, P. (2011). *Foragers and farmers of the Northern Kayenta region*. Salt Lake City: University of Utah Press.

Gumerman, G. J. (1984). *A view from Black Mesa: The changing face of archaeology*. Tucson: University of Arizona Press.

Gumerman, G. J., Westfall, D., & Reed, C. S. (1972). *Archaeological investigations on Black Mesa, the 1969-1970 seasons*. Prescott: Prescott College Press.

Haas, J. (2001). Early Anasazi. In P. N. Peregrine, & M. Ember (Eds.), *Encyclopedia of prehistory* (Vol. 6, pp. 34–42). New York: Springer.

Haas, J., & Creamer, W. (1993). *Stress and warfare among the Kayenta Anasazi of the thirteenth century A.D.* Fieldiana Anthropology, New Series, No. 21, Publication 1450.

Hegmon, M. (1986). Information exchange and integration on Black Mesa, Arizona, AD 931–1150. In S. Plog (Ed.), *Spatial organization and exchange: Archaeological survey on northern Black Mesa* (pp. 256–281). Carbondale: Southern Illinois University Press.

Kohler, T. A., Varien, M. D., Wright, A. M., & Kuckelman, K. A. (2008). Mesa Verde migrations: New archaeological research and computer simulation suggests why ancestral Puebloans deserted the northern Southwest United States. *American Scientist, 96*, 146–153.

Lyons, P. D. (2013). Jeddito yellow ware, migration, and the Kayenta Diaspora. *Kiva, 79*(2), 147–174.

Martin, D. L., Goodman, A. H., Armelagos, G. J., & Magennis, A. L. (1991). *Black Mesa Anasazi health: Reconstructing life from patterns of death and disease*. Carbondale: Southern Illinois University Press.

McIlvaine, B. (2013). Implications of reappraising the iron-deficiency anemia hypothesis. *International Journal of Osteoarchaeology, 25*(6), 997–1000.

Neitzel, J. (2000). What is a regional system? Issues of scale and interaction in the Prehistoric Southwest. In M. Hegmon (Ed.), *The archaeology of regional interaction* (pp. 25–40). Boulder: University Press of Colorado.

Oxenham, M. F., & Cavill, I. (2010). Porotic hyperostosis and cribra orbitalia: The erythropoietic response to iron-deficiency anaemia. *Anthropological Science, 118*(3), 199–200.

Powell, S. (2002). The Puebloan florescence and dispersion: Dinnebito and beyond, AD 800–1150. In S. Powell, & F. E. Smiley (Eds.), *Prehistoric culture change on the Colorado Plateau: Ten thousand years on Black Mesa* (pp. 79–117). Tucson: University of Arizona Press.

Powell, S., Andrews, P. P., Nichols, D. L., & Smiley, F. (1983). Fifteen years on the Rock: Archaeological research, administration, and compliance on Black Mesa, Arizona. *American Antiquity, 48*(2), 228–252.

Reinhard, K. J., Geib, P. R., Callahan, M. M., & Hevly, R. H. (1992). Discovery of colon contents in a skeletonized burial: Soil sampling for dietary remains. *Journal of Archaeological Science*, *19*(6), 697–705.

Ryan, D. J. (1977). *The paleopathology and paleoepidemiology of the Kayenta Anasazi Indians in northeastern Arizona*. Unpublished PhD thesis. Arizona State University, Tempe.

Spielmann, K. A. (2004). Communal feasting, ceramics and exchange. In B. J. Mills (Ed.), *Identity, feasting and the archaeology of the Greater Southwest* (pp. 210–232). Boulder: University Press of Colorado.

Swedlund, A. C., & Sessions, S. E. (1976). A developmental model of prehistoric population growth on Black Mesa, Northeastern Arizona. In G. J. Gumerman, & R. Euler (Eds.), *Papers on the archaeology of Black Mesa, Arizona* (pp. 136–148). Carbondale: Southern Illinois University Press.

Swedlund, A. C., Sattenspiel, L., Warren, A., Meindl, R. S., & Gumerman, G. J., III (2016). Explorations in paleodemography: An overview of the Artificial Long House Valley agent-based modeling project. In M. K. Zuckerman, & D. L. Martin (Eds.), *New directions in biocultural anthropology* (pp. 403–428). Hoboken: John Wiley & Sons.

Turner, C. G., II, & Turner, J. A. (1999). *Man corn: Cannibalism and violence in the prehistoric American Southwest*. Salt Lake City: University of Utah Press.

Wade, W. D. (1970). Skeletal remains of a prehistoric population from the Puerco Valley, eastern Arizona. Unpublished PhD dissertation, University of Colorado, Boulder.

Wade, W. D. (1985). Disease and predation: The comparative ecology of predators and parasites. In C. Merbs, & R. Miller (Eds.), *Health and disease in the Prehistoric Southwest*. Tempe: Arizona State University, Anthropological Research Papers No. 34.

Walker, P. L. (1985). Anemia among Prehistoric Indians of the American Southwest. In C. F. Merbs, & R. J. Miller (Eds.), *Health and Disease in the Prehistoric Southwest* (pp. 139–164). Arizona State University, Tempe, Anthropological Research Papers No. 34.

Walker, P. L., Bathurst, R. R., Richman, R., Gjerdrum, T., & Andrushko, V. A. (2009). The causes of porotic hyperstosis and cribra orbitalia: A reappraisal of the iron-deficiency-anemia hypothesis. *American Journal of Physical Anthropology*, *139*, 109–125.

Walker, W. H. (2009). Warfare and the practice of supernatural agents. In A. E. Nielsen, & W. H. Walker (Eds.), *Warfare in cultural context: Practice, agency, and the archaeology of violence* (pp. 109–138). Tucson: University of Arizona Press.

Weston, D. A. (2012). Nonspecific infection in paleopathology: Interpreting periosteal reactions. In A. Grauer (Ed.), *A companion to paleopathology* (pp. 492–512). Chichester: John Wiley & Sons.

Whiteley, P. M. (2008). The discourse of cannibalism at awat'ovi. In D. L. Nichols, & P. L. Crown (Eds.), *Social violence in the Prehispanic American Southwest* (pp. 184–215). Tucson: University of Arizona.

Further Reading

De Harport, D. L. (1951). An archaeological survey of Canon de Chelly: Preliminary report of the field sessions of 1948, 1949, and 1950. *El Palacio*, *58*(1), 35–48.

Finan, T. J., West, C. T., Austin, D., & McGuire, T. (2002). Processes of adaptation to climate variability: A case study from the US Southwest. *Climate Research*, *21*(3), 299–310.

Judd, N. M. (1930). *The excavation and repair of Betatakin*. Washington, DC: Smithsonian Institution.

Kennedy, K. A. R. (1998). Markers of occupational stress: Conspectus and prognosis of research. *International Journal of Osteoarchaeology*, *8*, 305–310.

Reinhard, K. J., Hevly, R. H., & Anderson, G. A. (1987). Helminth remains from prehistoric Indian coprolites on the Colorado Plateau. *The Journal of Parasitology*, *3*(3), 630–639.

Yoffee, N. (1994). Memorandum to Murray Gell-Mann Concerning: The complications of complexity in the prehistoric Southwest. In G. J. Gumerman, & M. Gell-Mann (Eds.), *Understanding complexity in the Prehistoric Southwest* (pp. 341–358). Reading: Addison-Wesley.

Chapter 7

Marginalized bodies and the construction of the Robert J. Terry anatomical skeletal collection: a promised land lost

Carlina de la Cova
Department of Anthropology, University of South Carolina, Columbia, SC, United States

Chapter Outline

Introduction

In recent years, bioarchaeologists have become increasingly interested in studying the biological impact marginalization has on skeletal biology and health. Marginalization can be defined in a plethora of ways. In bioarchaeology it is based on skeletal analyses and examination of perceived class, sociocultural, and biological differences observed in the archaeological, iconographic, ethnographic, and/or historical record. Particular groups, or individuals, may experience extreme ostracism by a society's dominant culture, who view these persons as deviant due to their different ancestral backgrounds, religious beliefs, cultural practices, or perceived (dis)abilities. This marginalization works on social and political levels, resulting in limited access to resources needed for survival such as food, shelter, medical care,

Bioarchaeology of Marginalized People. DOI: https://doi.org/10.1016/B978-0-12-815224-9.00007-5

and social mobility, ultimately impacting the individual's or group's skeletal health. It is the task of the bioarchaeologist to examine contemporaneous documentary, cultural, or archaeological evidence to tease out these complex relationships between marginalization, disease, and skeletal biology in the respective groups that they are studying. When paired with a biocultural and theoretical framework that engages contextual research from different lines of evidence, the bioarchaeologist can paint a rich picture of how marginalization literally cuts to the bone (Mant & Holland, 2016). Thus bioarchaeologists are in a unique position to not only highlight consistent diachronic themes associated with marginalization, but they can be strong advocates of social justice.

As a marginalized person in a discipline that still suffers from diversity issues, I have spent most of my career studying what I term the *marginalized others*. For me the marginalized others are individuals peripheralized to the margins of a society by those in power due to their ancestry, low social status, class differences, or attributes tied to what the dominant society viewed (or continues to view) as deviant. Deviance can be tied to social perceptions about "race," mental status, and social class. Most of my career has been focused on how these power dynamics play out amongst the marginalized and invisible others in the Hamann-Todd, Robert J. Terry, and William Montague Cobb anatomical collections (de la Cova, 2011, 2012, 2014). Whilst these collections are some of the most utilized in our discipline and form the very core of our forensic and bioarchaeological identification methods, we know very little about the individuals that comprise them. Sadly, their experiences and circumstances—including the social and political power dynamics that resulted in their dissection and subsequent curation—have been silenced. Even their identities have been erased and replaced with "cadaver" numbers. As anthropologists, especially bioarchaeologists, have increasingly focused on understanding the lifeways of nonelites and marginalized groups, we have failed to turn our lens inward to our own discipline and examine those whose bodies literally built the major anatomical collections that aided in the birth of American physical/biological anthropology. This chapter will ascertain who the individuals that comprise the Robert J. Terry Anatomical Skeletal Collection were and examine the relationship between marginalization, anatomization, and discrimination in the series. I argue that the Terry Collection contains the most socially and culturally marginalized persons in St. Louis, MO, and conveys vital narratives about the relationships between structural violence, poverty, Blackness, and anatomization.

The Robert J. Terry Anatomical Skeletal Collection: Robert J. Terry and the Origins of His Collection

The Robert J. Terry Anatomical Skeletal Collection, colloquially known amongst scholars as the Terry Collection, is one of the most utilized series, next to the Hamann-Todd Collection, in biological anthropology. Standardized methods tied to stature and ageing were (and continue to be) developed from the series (Kindschuh, Dupras, & Cowgill, 2010; Trotter & Gleser, 1952). It was amassed by Robert J. Terry, Professor and Chair of the Anatomy Department at Washington University School of Medicine (WUSM), between 1910 until his retirement in 1941. By this time Terry had collected 80% of the series (Hunt & Albanese, 2004). Dr. Mildred Trotter, a WUSM colleague of Terry's and instructor of human anatomy, as well as one of the earliest female skeletal biologists, continued Terry's work. She expanded the collection to the large series it is today and balanced its demographic profile by the inclusion of more females, which had previously been unavailable due to social and economic factors tied to beliefs about dissection and financial circumstances (Hunt & Albanese, 2004). As Trotter was expanding the series, Missouri passed its Willed Body Law in 1955, which legalized body donation to medical schools (Trotter, 1981). This resulted in a demographic shift in the collection from unclaimed persons to those that elected to donate their bodies to medicine (Trotter, 1981). Trotter continued to build the series until her 1967 retirement when she was able to transfer it to the Smithsonian Institution for curation.

The series is comprised of 1728 individuals born between 1822 and 1943, which were dissected at WUSM. It is one of a handful of documented anatomical collections in existence. Ages, biological sex, cause of death, place of death, and pathologies are recorded for most individuals (Hunt & Albanese, 2004; Trotter, 1981). Place of birth, occupation, medical histories, clinical diagnoses, and photographs also exist for some persons. In addition to this demographic data, somatological information (body shape and physique) including photographs, anatomical measurements at death, bone and teeth inventories, and data about postmortem fracturing and bone loss is also present (Hunt & Albanese, 2004).

The Terry Collection has its origins in the early 20th century, a period when anatomists and physical anthropologists eagerly collected skeletal remains and pathological examples of people sans permission or ethical implications. In the late 19th century, whilst Ales Hrdlička, the father of American Physical Anthropology and curator of physical anthropology at the Smithsonian Institution, and Franz Boas, father of American anthropology and curator of anthropology at the American Museum of Natural History, were engaged in a race to acquire (or pillage) by any means necessary the most diverse skeletons to fill their bone rooms, Robert J. Terry started to amass human remains (Redman, 2016). His first foray into collecting the dead began in 1898, but this sample was destroyed by fire (Hunt & Albanese, 2004; Trotter, 1981). He started a second series, but whilst he was on a teaching fellowship at Harvard from 1906 to 1907, elements were lost or commingled (Hunt & Albanese, 2004; Trotter, 1981). Terry did not initiate the collection that currently bears his name until 1910.

Numerous influences spurred Terry to collect the dead. He completed the first year of his medical studies (1892) at the College of Physicians and Surgeons, Columbia University in New York (Hunt & Albanese, 2004). Here, he was mentored by Dr. George S. Huntington, who believed that skeletons amassed from documented medical school cadavers could contribute new data to anatomical research (Hunt & Albanese, 2004; Pearlstein, 2015). Huntington would eventually assemble his own collection from his anatomy classes. Today this series, known as the George Huntington Anatomical Collection, comprises over 3600 individuals for whom nationality, age, sex, and cause of death are known. Most were poor, unclaimed European immigrants and New York City inhabitants that died between 1892 and 1920 (Pearlstein, 2015).

The Financial Panic of 1893 forced Terry to abandon his medical education at Columbia and return to his native St. Louis to complete his education at Missouri Medical College (Hunt & Albanese, 2004). He graduated *cum laude* in the spring of 1895 (Trotter, 1981). In 1898 he started post-graduate studies in anatomy at the University of Edinburgh, Scotland, under the supervision of Sir William Turner, who gave a "stimulating and interesting course in physical anthropology which included lectures and laboratory training in methods" (Terry qtd. in Trotter, 1981, p. 505). Terry was so captivated by this introduction that he ultimately pursued a research agenda in the discipline and was inspired to "establish the osteological collection and a course in physical anthropology" at Washington University (Terry qtd. in Trotter, 1981, p. 505).

Although Sir Turner served as the impetus for Terry's interest in physical anthropology, Trotter (1981, p. 506) believes that it was Dr. Ales Hrdlička's "mesmerism" that "persuaded" Terry to make physical anthropology his primary research focus. Hrdlička and Terry corresponded frequently about skeletal research, human variation, and skeletal collections. A 1926 exchange between the men reveals how supportive Hrdlička was of Terry, who expressed an interest in studying somatotypes and gene flow amongst American Blacks. Hrdlička (1926) responded reassuringly, stating that: "[a] good somatological study of the American Negro and his mixtures is very desirable and I shall back you all I can. . .you doubtless have your own plans which I will be glad to help you with when ready."

The two also exchanged human remains, a common practice for physical anthropologists during the late 19th and early 20th centuries. Hrdlička (1927) offered Terry skulls, presumably for teaching and research, indicating that the Smithsonian could spare "1 skull of an Eskimo; 1 underformed skull of an Indian [from California]; 3 skulls of prehistoric Indians showing three types of artificial deformation; 1 skull of an Egyptian; and 1 skull of a Polynesian (Hawaii)." Terry (1927) responded to Hrdlička the following month indicating that "it is not our plan to attempt a general collection of anthropological material. We are content to pursue the collection of negro material and are making progress." However, Terry (1927) felt the "specimens" Hrdlička offered in his "letter of Nov. 25 would be most acceptable" as his program needed "a few types to be used for our course of instruction in physical anthropology."

Ultimately, Terry's reasons for initiating a collection were similar to those of Boas, Hrdlička, and other physical anthropologists of his time period: he was interested in human biological, morphological, and pathological variation as the aforementioned statement as well as his research and publication record illustrates (Terry, 1932, 1942, 1959). However, Terry was not focused on the archaeological past. He was more concerned with the contemporary biological present. Like his Columbia mentor, Dr. George Huntington, he saw the value of "documented human osteological/anatomical specimens from which skeletal biology, anatomy, and pathology could be investigated" (Hunt & Albanese, 2004, p. 407). Terry knew the importance of individual context and its impact on skeletal variation and believed proper studies of human variation had to address this. As he stated in 1940, "fundamental to any morphological research is proper documentation of the material to be studied. If a dissecting room cadaver is to be used for observations to be applied to physical anthropology, a description of the individual is in order before dissection is begun" (Terry, 1940, p. 433).

To properly document his collection, Terry conscientiously recorded names, ages, places of birth (when possible), occupations, and the origins of the persons that comprised his series. Terry often contacted the institutions in which his subjects died and requested any demographic information he felt was missing from the data provided with each body that entered his laboratory. Ultimately, Terry knew the exact names and social circumstances of the persons that comprised his collection. This issue is addressed later as it is important in regard to reframing how biological anthropologists should engage with these collections.

Amassing the Terry Collection: A Biological Archive of the Marginalized and Socioculturally Disappeared

By the 20th century, most states had passed anatomical legislation that (nonconsensually) legalized the anatomization of the unclaimed poor. Missouri was no different. The state's current Revised Statutes, Chapter 194, in regard to Death and Disposition of Dead Bodies, Section 194.150, entitled Disposal of paupers' bodies, which has not been modified since 1929, states:

> *Superintendents or wardens of* ***penitentiaries, houses of correction and bridewells, hospitals, insane asylums and poorhouses, and coroners, sheriffs, jailers, city and county undertakers, and all other state, county, town or city officers having the custody of the body of any deceased person required to be buried at public expense****, shall be and hereby are required immediately to*

> *notify the secretary of the [state anatomical] board, or the person duly designated by the board or by its secretary to receive such notice, whenever any such body or bodies come into his or their custody, charge or control, and shall, without fee or reward, deliver, within* ***a period not to exceed thirty-six hours after death****, except in cases within the jurisdiction of a coroner where retention for a longer time may be necessary, such body or bodies into the custody of the board and permit the board or its agent or agents to take and remove all such bodies, or otherwise dispose of them; provided, that each educational institution receiving a body from the* ***board shall hold such body for at least thirty days, during which time any relative or friend of any such deceased person or persons shall have the right to take and receive the dead body from the possession of any person in whose charge or custody it may be found, for the purpose of interment, upon paying the expense of such interment****.*
>
> MO Rev Stat § 194.150 (2013), (emphasis added).

In other words, friends and family of persons who died in taxpayer-funded (or state-funded) institutions, such as city hospitals, poor farms, infirmaries, state mental hospitals, and other charitable institutions meant to help the poor and disabled (and who were to be buried at public expense in a pauper's grave) had (and still have) 36 hours to claim their loved ones. Bodies meeting this criterium (with cost to the taxpayer being key), not claimed within this designated interval, were sent to the state anatomical board and distributed to medical institutions for dissection. Ultimately, this legislation allowed for the amassment of the Terry Collection. In Robert J. Terry's own words, at the pinnacle of his collecting, between 1910 and 1940, "material" for research was "secured through the State Anatomical Board of Missouri. Between 100 and 123 cadavers, of which approximately half are negroes, are brought annually to the laboratory" (Terry, n.d.). He acknowledged that males outnumbered females and far more Black women were anatomized than white females. Most "white cadavers are above 45 years of age; cadavers under 21 years are very seldom received. . .at the present time the average age of negro cadavers is much lower than that of white, and bodies in the second decade, women as well as men, are not uncommon; a circumstance explained by the recent immigration of strangers into the community and by hard times" (Terry, n.d.). The immigration which Terry was probably referencing was the Southern Diaspora and the Great Migration, movements that expanded the African American and poor white population of St. Louis.

Individuals associated with the aforementioned taxpayer funded institutions were often poor, recent migrants without family or friends in the city, or mentally ill. Thus anatomical collections comprised of these individuals were created in a structurally violent nature, supported by the law, through the nonconsensual harvesting of the destitute: those deemed socially deviant and marginalized by society due to class, race, perceived criminality, and mental health. Structural violence is a form of violence in which social structures "suppress agency and prevent individuals, groups, and societies from reaching their social, economic, and biological potential" (Klaus, 2012, p. 31). These factors are considered structural "because they are embedded in the political and economic organization of our social world; they are violent because they cause injury to people" (Farmer, Nizeye, Stulac, & Keshavjee, 2006, p. 1686). Nonconsensual dissection can be viewed as a structurally violent act as the state exerts control over someone's body and denies burial to the poor and marginalized, effectively erasing their identity.

Identifying and Unsilencing the Marginalized: Demography, Dissection, and the Terry Collection

To ascertain how Missouri anatomical legislation targeted St. Louis' most marginalized groups and to comprehend the composition of the Terry Collection as a broader reflection of discrimination and structural violence at the political and legal level, 621 individuals born between 1822 and 1877 were demographically and historically researched (Table 7.1). This birth interval was chosen as it focused on the earlier part of the Terry Collection and encompassed unclaimed nonwilled persons who did not elect to donate their bodies to medicine. Only unclaimed individuals were studied. Morgue data accompanying each individual, death records from the state of Missouri, and United States census records were examined for all persons in the sample to ascertain their origins, including occupation, place of birth, and last known address or institution of death. Although these individuals were born in the 19th century, all died between 1910 and 1959, with the majority being amassed between 1925 and 1940.

An examination of the sample reveals that it is biased toward whites, especially white males (Table 7.1). However, it should be noted that available demographic data on *the entire* Terry Collection show a bias toward Black males and White females. During 1930, African Americans comprised 8.78% of the St. Louis population; in 1940 this number was 7.5% (Gibson & Kay, 2005). This contrasts sharply to the percentage of Blacks in the entire Terry Collection as well as the sample researched in this study. In both cases, there are more than four times the number of African-descended individuals in the Terry collection when compared to St. Louis' population. This overrepresentation of people of color was further confirmed by Terry above when he indicated that of the 100–123 "cadavers" brought to his laboratory annually, half were Black (Terry, n.d.). If African-descended individuals comprised less than 10% of the St. Louis population, it is problematic that they make up over 50% of the entire Terry Collection.

Research from combined death and census records for the sample revealed that most individuals had low income or unskilled jobs (Fig. 7.1).

TABLE 7.1 Individuals in the Terry Collection.

	Distribution of Terry Collection sample used in this study			Distribution of the entire Terry Collection[a]		
Race	Males (%)	Females (%)	Total (%)	Males (%)	Females (%)	Total (%)
Black	116 (18.7)	110 (17.7)	226 (36.4)	546 (31.6)	392 (22.7)	938 (54.3)
White	253 (40.7)	142 (22.9)	395 (63.6)	461 (26.7)	323 (18.7)	784 (45.4)
Total	369 (59.4)	252 (40.6)	621 (100.0)	1007	715	1722

[a] *There are also five Asiatic males (0.289%) and one unknown origin (0.06%).*

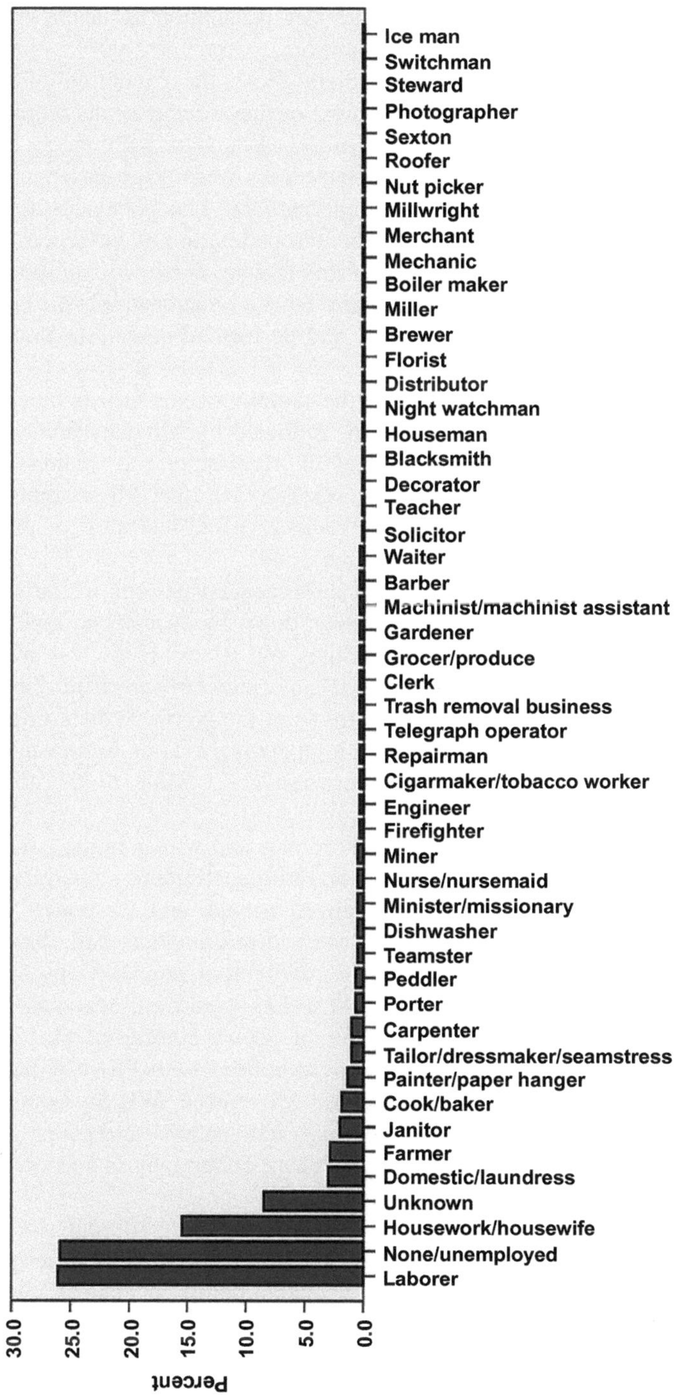

FIGURE 7.1 Occupation of individuals in Terry Collection sample studied.

The majority were laborers, had no known occupation at death, or were unemployed. Others were farmers, janitors, carpenters, cooks, painters, tailors/seamstresses, porters, and peddlers. With the exception of cooks, carpenters, and clothing-related jobs, most of these occupations required no training or skill, and were predominantly associated with those of low socioeconomic status (SES). Many of these jobs were wage based and may have been transitory, seasonal, or nonpermanent. The presence of housewives and domestics/laundresses reflects the perception of gendered female roles during this period. It is unclear if this is what these women did for all of their lives as during this period many worked clandestinely from home as seamstresses, cleaners, child-sitters, and performed other jobs that could provide income.

The place of birth of individuals in the sample reveals further bias tied to dissection. Most were born in Missouri, followed by Illinois, Pennsylvania, Ohio, Kentucky, and the southern states of Mississippi and Tennessee, the latter of which would have been accessible via the Mississippi River (Fig. 7.2). A regional analysis (Fig. 7.3) also revealed that most of the sample was from the Midwest followed by the South.

Given the high frequencies of African-descended persons in the sample, place of birth analyses were further broken down by ancestry to ascertain if regional differences existed amongst whites and Blacks (Figs. 7.4 and 7.5). Results revealed that most of the Terry Blacks studied were from the South and not Midwestern-born. Very few were from the North. Whites originated from the Midwest, but there were also high frequencies of European immigrants; the proportion of white southerners versus white northerners was similar.

These differential origins for people of color and whites in the collection, especially in regard to Southern Blacks and European immigrants, raised further questions about targeting marginalized groups and warranted further investigation into the relationship between discrimination and dissection. Additional demographic analyses of states and countries of birth by ancestry were performed; they indicated that most whites were from Missouri, neighboring Illinois, and Germany (Fig. 7.6). St. Louis comprised the German Triangle, a migratory settlement pattern associated with German nationals that included all towns and cities between Milwaukee, WI; St. Louis, MO; and Cincinnati, OH, including Chicago and Indianapolis (Bergquist, 2008). This may explain why there are higher rates of Germans in the collection when compared to other immigrant groups.

The Black narrative in the Terry Collection told a different story. The majority were from Missouri, Tennessee, Mississippi, Kentucky, and Alabama, all of which were slaveholding states before and during the Civil War (Fig. 7.7). To ascertain if there were differences in Black birth/migration patterns before and after the Civil War, the sample was divided into Enslaved (1800–65) and Liberated (1866–77) Black birth cohorts.

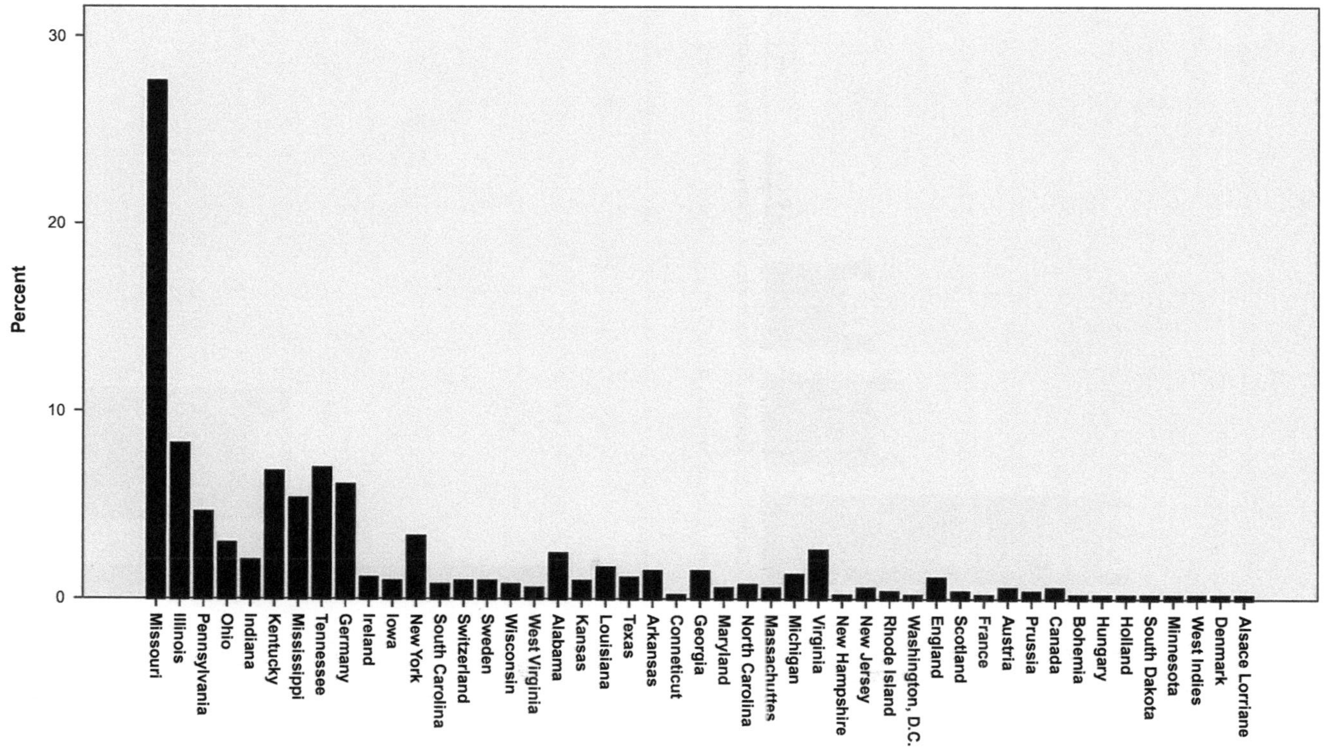

FIGURE 7.2 Places of birth of the individuals in the Terry Collection sample studied.

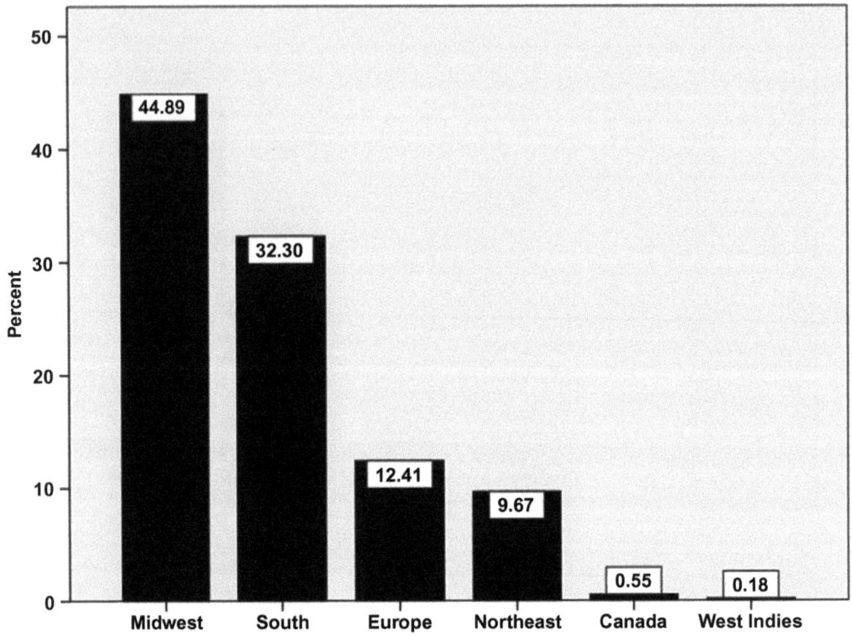

FIGURE 7.3 Regions of birth of the individuals in the Terry Collection sample studied.

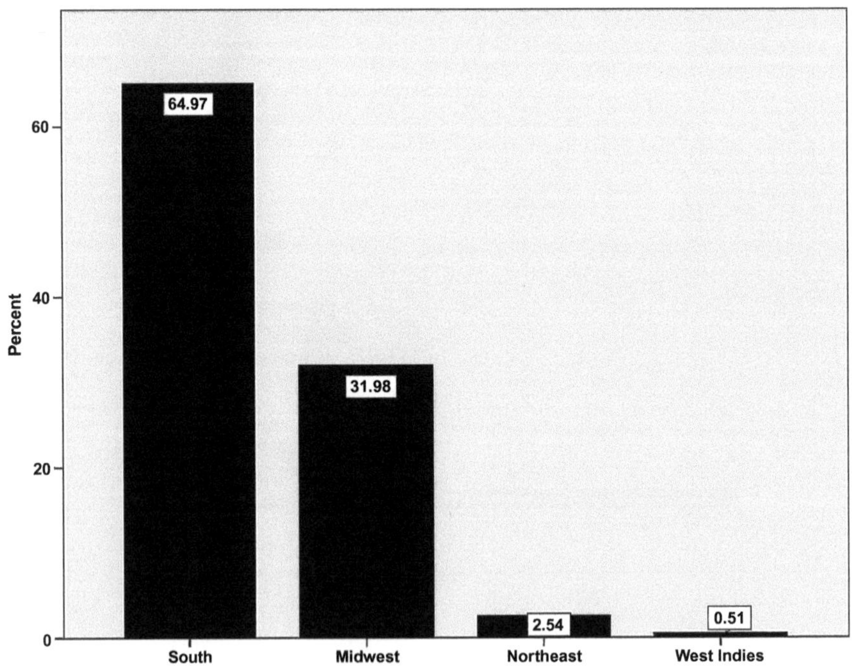

FIGURE 7.4 Birth regions of Blacks examined in the Terry Collection sample studied.

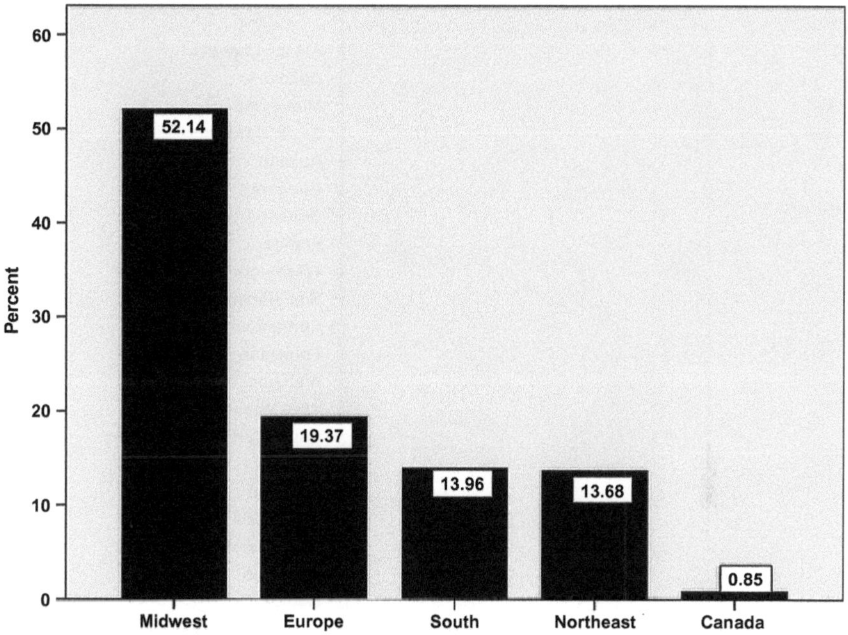

FIGURE 7.5 Birth regions of whites examined in the Terry Collection sample studied.

The Enslaved Black cohort (Fig. 7.8) has a strong emphasis on locality with most African-descended individuals born in Missouri, followed by Kentucky, Mississippi, Tennessee, and Alabama, all of which were slaveholding states. The Liberated Black cohort, however, reveals increased migration from the South. Most individuals were born in Tennessee, Mississippi, and Alabama (Fig. 7.9).

A Promised Land Lost: The Great Migration, Structural Violence, Anatomization, and the Terry Collection

The aforementioned demographic analyses of individuals from the Terry Collection, born between 1800 and 1877, illustrate how they are the most marginalized persons within their communities. All were of low SES, most had menial, wage-earning jobs, and many were either in-migrants from other regions of the United States, or European immigrants. Particularly disturbing is the high frequencies of African-descended individuals in the series, especially when compared to the general St. Louis population. Furthermore, the majority of these persons were Southern-born, indicating that they were in-migrants to the community. During the period in which the collection was amassed the Great Migration (1916–70) was impacting St. Louis (de la Cova, 2011, 2014). I have no doubt that the Southern-born African

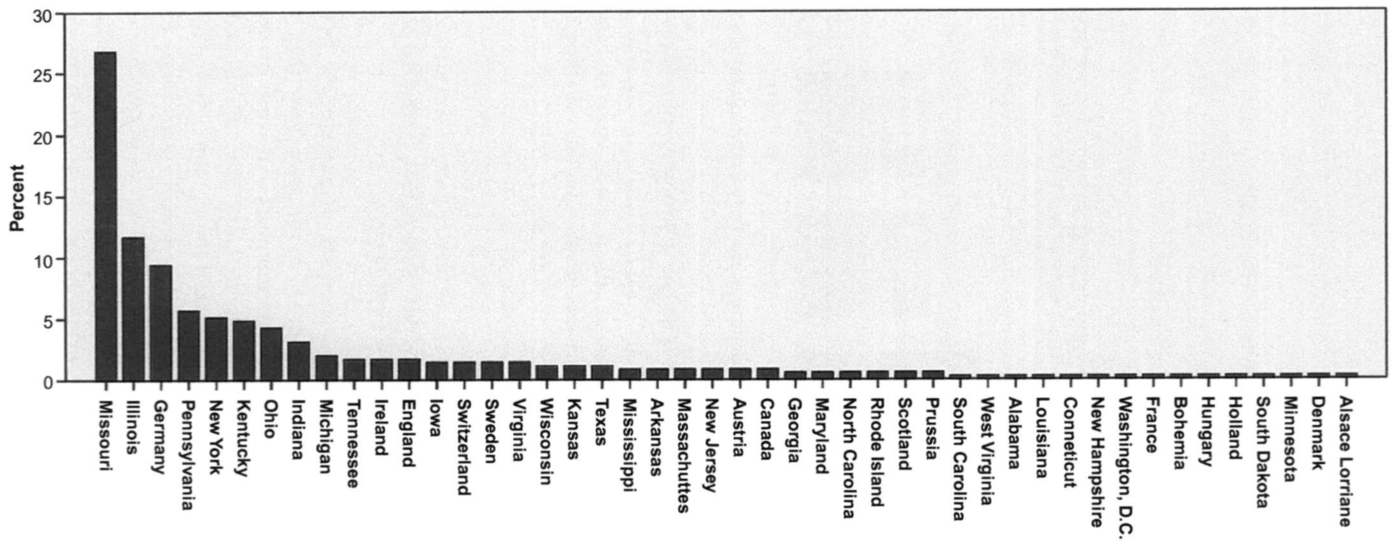

FIGURE 7.6 Places of birth of whites examined in the Terry Collection sample studied.

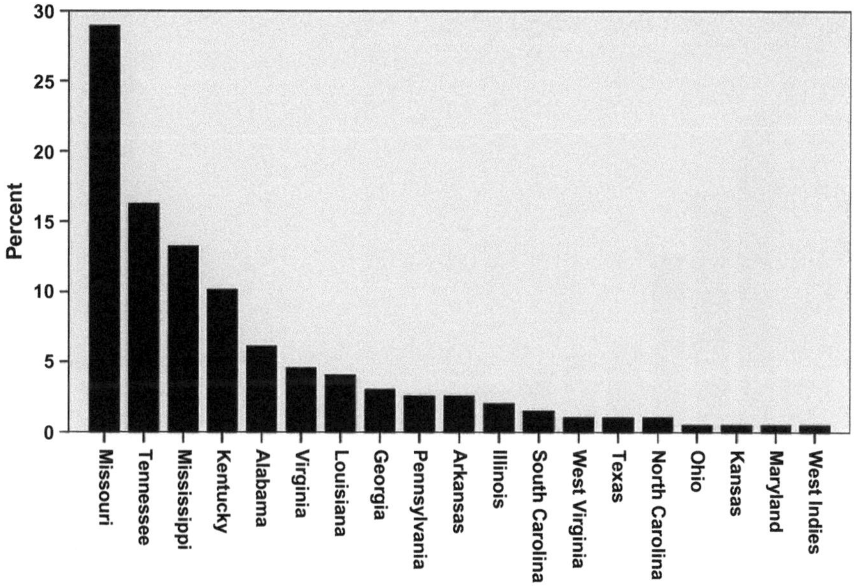

FIGURE 7.7 Places of birth of Blacks examined in the Terry Collection sample studied.

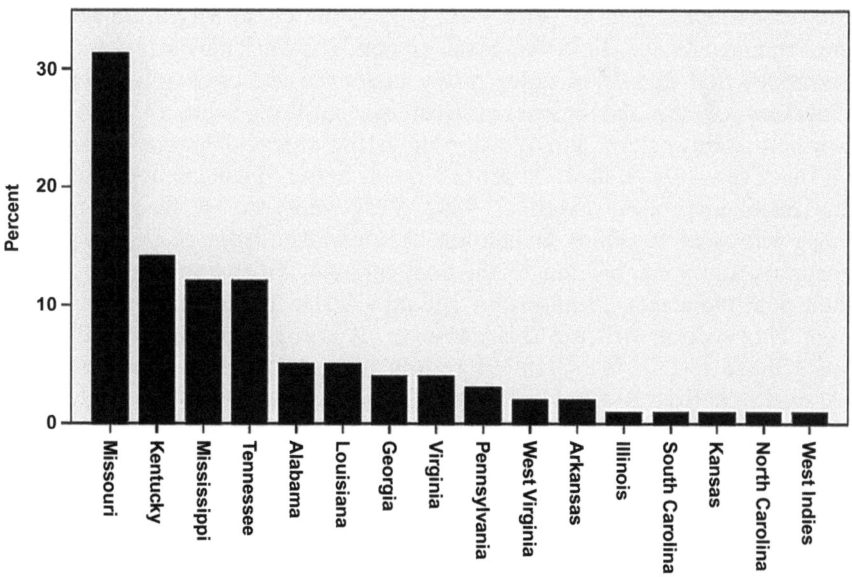

FIGURE 7.8 Places of birth of Enslaved Blacks born from 1800 to 1865 examined in the Terry Collection.

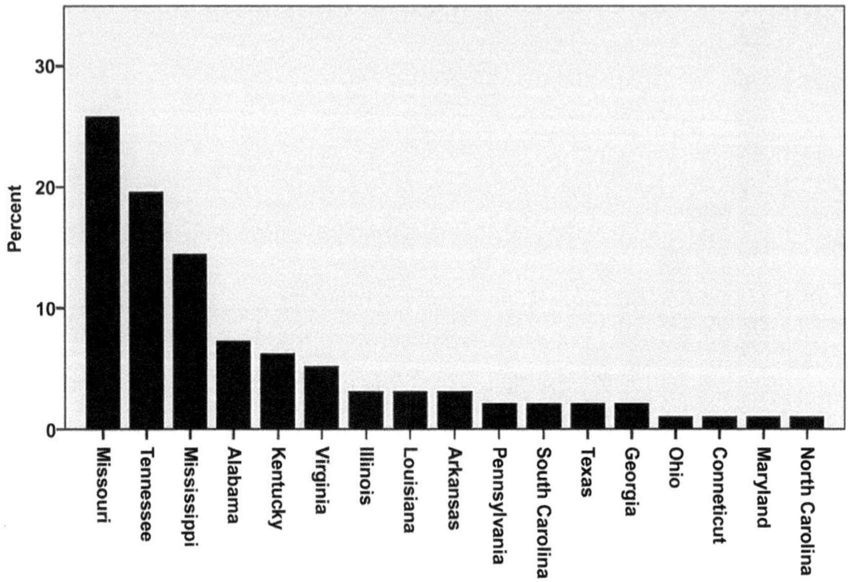

FIGURE 7.9 Places of birth of Liberated Blacks born from 1866 to 1877 examined in the Terry Collection.

Americans represented in Terry were part of the Great Migration north to the Promised Land. However, these anatomized individuals represent the narratives that people of color rarely hear. We are often told about the successes of the movement of over six million Southern Blacks to Northern, Midwestern, and Western industrial cities wishing to break free of Jim Crow in search of improved lives, better financial opportunities, and racial integration (Marks, 1989). Very rarely do we hear stories of those who were so impoverished that they perished from disease in public hospitals and were offered to medical schools for anatomization to pay their debt to society because they sought assistance from a public institution. This section will tell this narrative. It is my hope that it will unsilence those lost in the Great Migration to anatomization. Cobb (1935), the nation's first Black biological anthropologist, also addressed these issues with the Hamann-Todd Collection. However, when one considers the number of active medical schools in the many cities African Americans migrated to during the great exodus to the Promised Land, the grim reality is that we may never know how many in-migrant brethren were the victims of nonconsensual, state-mandated dissection. The Terry Collection is merely a small sample from one medical school, nevertheless it provides us with a historical window into the devastating impact the Great Migration had on Black mortality, as demonstrated by the demography of the series.

Going to the Promised Land: Hopes for Migration and Grim Realities Encountered

Racial violence, the harsh sharecropping system, Jim Crow laws, and weevil epidemics that impacted crop productivity served as major push factors for the exodus of African Americans to Northern and Midwestern cities like St. Louis (Phillips, 1999; Tolnay & Beck, 1990). War-time losses of white unskilled workers in steel mills, foundries, railroads, and other industries opened up jobs in northern industry which were previously unavailable to African Americans (Giffin, 2005; Phillips, 1999; Tolnay & Beck, 1990; Wilkerson, 2010). These new opportunities, as well as the desire to escape the Jim Crow South, served as major pull factors for Black Southerners to relocate to the North and Midwest (Mandle, 1978). According to Missouri's *Moberly Evening Democrat* (Little, 1923), about 30,000 Black in-migrants had settled in St. Louis during the first eight months of 1923. They were described as carrying all of their possessions in "a paper bundle. A few carry cheap pasteboard suitcases" (Little, 1923, p. 1). Most were from Arkansas, Tennessee, Mississippi, Alabama, and Texas and were described as "penniless," and a "large proportion" were "between 17 and 19 years of age" (Little, 1923, p. 1). Males had been lured by "the high wages offered by industrial plants through labor agencies" (Little, 1923, p. 1).

The Great Migration ultimately changed the demographics of St. Louis. Blacks comprised 6.4% of the city's population in 1910, numbering 43,960 (Gibson & Kay, 2005). By 1920, this figure increased to 69,854, or 9%. During 1930, African Americans comprised 11.4% or 93,580 of the total St. Louis population (Gibson & Kay, 2005). Southern in-migrants continued to pour into the city, and by 1960 St. Louis was home to 214,377 Blacks, who comprised 28.6% of the city's population (Gibson & Kay, 2005).

Whites in general, especially those of low SES, did not eagerly welcome these new in-migrants as both competed for jobs (Bonacich, 1972, 1975). As the labor movement and striking began in the early 20th century, industrial corporations utilized Southern Black in-migrants as strikebreakers to fill labor losses, often traveling to southern states to recruit males (Phillips, 1999). This exacerbated growing racial tensions as Euro-Americans felt African American Southerners, who often worked longer hours for lower wages, were stealing their jobs. These sentiments erupted in violence during the summer of 1917 and the Red Summer of 1919 as race riots gripped the United States (Bonacich, 1972, 1975; Wilson, 1978). The 1917 East St. Louis Riots, the bloodiest of all the unrests, ended in the recorded deaths of 39 African Americans and nine whites (Congressional Edition, 1918).

In addition to job competition and racially driven violence, many African American Southern in-migrants faced the major obstacle of finding housing (Giffin, 2005; Phillips, 1999). The large influx of Black in-migrants, combined with European immigrants and World War I soldiers returning home, resulted in housing shortages, tenement overcrowding, and homelessness (Giffin, 2005; Kusmer, 1978; Phillips, 1999). St. Louis became overwhelmed in 1923 by the migration of 30,000 African American Southerners, which "brought the city face to face with two big problems—that of housing the newcomers and. . .halting the invasion of disease" as 17 cases of smallpox had occurred that year (Little, 1923, p. 1). A population surge, combined with housing shortages prompted landlords to increase rent, often targeting African Americans in-migrants for higher rates (Giffin, 2005). During 1928, rent in a St. Louis Black tenement district increased "from 20 to 40 per cent" (Little, 1923, p. 1). These in-migrants were also discriminated against and marginalized to specific districts and tenements with poor sanitation and infrastructure. Missouri's *St Joseph's Observer* ("Losing out in North", 1921, p. 5) noted that many of "the new negro residents" were "living in crowded and extremely uncomfortable quarters, and even if there were not a housing shortage the prejudice against their entering many neighborhoods would prevent relief from this condition."

Whilst the Great Migration has traditionally been viewed as a means by which impoverished Southern-born African Americans fled oppressiveness and racial persecution and resettled in the Northern "Promised Land," sadly the challenges, discrimination, and grim reality African Americans experienced during this exodus is directly reflected in the Terry sample. That the series has more African Americans that are mostly Southern-born than Euro-Americans is a direct indicator of the stresses of the Great Migration and the broader structural violence and institutionalized racism directed at Southern in-migrants in St. Louis from the 1910s to 1960s. Their higher death frequencies and representation in the Terry Collection can be attributed to a number of issues tied to structural and institutional violence that plagued both the Great Migration, as discussed earlier, and African Americans in general. Impoverished, lacking the means for good health care, and discriminated against in a Missouri hospital system that was segregated by race, poor and transient African Americans had few choices for health care and probably experienced little sympathy as they were viewed as unwanted invaders in the broader St. Louis community. As many Black Southerners, especially males, migrated to the city in a solitary, transient nature with no local kin, they would have been more vulnerable to being unclaimed at death. With little resources, lacking close relations, and the inability to find family members within the brief time allotted by anatomical legislation, African Americans Southerners would have been at high risk for anatomization. Sadly, with so few resources, they could have done little to circumvent this fate as it was (and still is) the law. Ultimately the postmortem journey their bodies took resulted in the biological embodiment of their social and cultural circumstances.

Remembering Those Lost in the Quest for the Promised Land

This chapter has illustrated how the persons that comprise the Robert J. Terry Anatomical Skeletal Collection were from the invisible and marginalized classes of society. This was especially true for Great Migration-era African Americans, many of whom hoped to find the Promised Land. The sad reality is that death and the anatomist's scalpel shattered this dream. These individuals, although legally dissected, did not consent to the anatomization of their bodies. Their experiences and the use of their bodies in medical dissection speaks to broader issues in American society tied to class, race, and structural violence. Historically, African Americans were more vulnerable, and targeted more often than whites in regard to anatomization and medical experimentation (Savitt, 1978, 1982; Skloot, 2010; Washington, 2007). Southern medical schools, many of which still function today, such as the Medical College of South Carolina (Medical University of South Carolina), the Medical College of Georgia, and the Medical College of Virginia (Virginia Commonwealth University School of Medicine) boasted in adverts to potential students about the ready availability of bodies for study, referred to as *materia medica*, comprised of the Black enslaved or factory-working populations (Savitt, 1978). In Antebellum Kentucky, about 80% of all dissection subjects were African American (Savitt, 1982). Records from Johns Hopkins University indicate that between 1898 and 1904, of the 1200 cadavers the university received, two-thirds were Black (Humphrey, 1973). In addition to legal appropriation of cadavers (as people of color had no legal control over their bodies after death), body snatchers also illegally shipped the bodies of dead Southern Black men North to desperate anatomy professors into the 20th century (Humphrey, 1973).

This medical abuse of Black bodies generated fear in Black communities about physicians performing nonconsensual medical experiments or intentionally causing death for the purpose of autopsy or dissection (Savitt, 1978). These fears were so real that they permeated African American folklore. Children were instructed not to play near physician offices, residences, or hospitals so "Night Doctors" would not kidnap them for medical experimentation or anatomization (Savitt, 1978; Skloot, 2010). Even today, the Black community has not forgotten J. Marion Sims' experiments on enslaved women sans anesthesia, Tuskegee, or Henrietta Lacks.

Ultimately, anatomical collections demonstrate the continued exploitation of Black bodies in early 20th century American medicine. This may not have been the intention of Robert J. Terry, but anatomy legislation and embedded institutional racism worked against African American Southern migrants hoping to find better lives in St. Louis. Marginalized by society and viewed as the subhuman, socially, and intellectually inferior other, dissection became an invisible and normalized form of structural violence inflicted upon African Americans, who had little financial, social, or political power to resist, reject, or circumvent anatomical legislation that preyed on the marginalized. Structural violence not only occurred at the level of legislation, but also with the physical act of dissection. Bioarchaeologist Kenneth Nystrom (2014, p. 765) has argued, "[c]onceptualizing dissection as a manifestation of structural violence extends the concept to encapsulate postmortem manifestations of social inequality." Even if the dead no longer live, this does not mean their social identity should be erased; the deceased still play important roles within broader social networks (Hallam, Hockey, & Howarth, 1999; Nystrom, 2014). In many cultures, including those within America, death does not destroy identity (Scheper-Hughes, 2011). For the unfortunate Great Migration migrants in the Terry Collection, dissection was used as a means to not only force these persons to "pay" a debt to society, but it simultaneously resulted in the permanent erasure of their identities from public memory. This erasure continues into the present day as anatomists and forensic anthropologists utilize select elements of these persons in their research but never acknowledge the individual, or who they were. Ironically, in a subtle manner of subconscious structural violence, these persons are only known by the cadaver numbers their collectors inked on their remains, not their actual names or the circumstances that resulted in their inclusion into the collection.

How can we remember those lost in the Great Migration and those whose remains comprise not only the Terry Collection but other anatomical series? As bioarchaeologists that frequently engage with these collections, we must be conscientious about restoring identity to the individuals we study. Remember who they were. They were more than humeri, pelvii, skulls, and metacarpals. These were individuals that traveled to St. Louis with hopes of finding better lives and deserve to be known for who they were, not just numbers in a collection. To be ethically engaged with anatomical collections means that anthropologists must avoid the repeated silencing of the experiences of these persons since this continues the cycle of structural violence initiated over 100 years ago. As bioarchaeologists, we have the ability to be strong advocates for social justice for both past and present marginalized groups. Anatomical collections should not be precluded from our reflexive gaze as their very existence is dependent on discriminatory anatomical legislation that preyed, and continues to prey, upon the poor and those that live on the margins of society. The stories of these individuals continue to inform the political present, as the social marginalization and structural violence they experienced still exists today in American society. We should reconstruct their identities, share their stories, and in so doing reveal how their past reflects our present.

References

Bergquist, J. (2008). *Daily life in immigrant America, 1820–1870*. Westport: Greenwood Press.

Bonacich, E. (1972). A theory of ethnic antagonism: The split labor market. *American Sociological Review*, *37*(5), 547–559.

Bonacich, E. (1975). Abolition, the extension of slavery, and the position of free Blacks: A study of split labor markets in the United States, 1830–1863. *American Journal of Sociology*, *81* (3), 601–628.

Cobb, W. M. (1935). Municipal history from anatomical records. *Scientific Monthly*, *40*, 157–162.

Congressional Edition. (1918). *House of representatives 65th congress 2nd session document #1231* (Vol. 7444). Washington, D.C.: United States Government Printing Office.

de la Cova, C. (2011). Race, health, and disease in 19th-century-born males. *American Journal of Physical Anthropology*, *144*(4), 526–537.

de la Cova, C. (2012). Patterns of trauma and violence in 19th-century-born African American and Euro-American females. *International Journal of Paleopathology*, *2*(2), 61–68.

de la Cova, C. (2014). The biological effects of urbanization and in-migration on 19th-century-born African Americans and Euro-Americans of low socioeconomic status: An anthropological and historical approach. In M. K. Zuckerman (Ed.), *Are modern environments bad for human health? Revisiting the second epidemiological transition* (pp. 243–266). Hoboken: Wiley-Blackwell.

Farmer, P. E., Nizeye, B., Stulac, S., & Keshavjee, S. (2006). Structural violence and clinical medicine. *PLoS Medicine*, *3*(10), e449:1686-1691.

Gibson, C., & Kay, J. (2005). *Historical census statistics on population totals by race, 1790 to 1990, and by Hispanic origin, 1970 to 1990, for large cities and other urban places in the United States*. U.S. Census Bureau of the Census, Population Division, Working Paper No. 76.

Giffin, W. W. (2005). *African Americans and the color line in Ohio, 1915–1930*. Columbus: Ohio State University Press.

Hallam, E., Hockey, J., & Howarth, G. (1999). *Beyond the body: Death and social identity*. London: Routledge.

Hrdlička, A. (1926, March). [Letter to Robert J. Terry]. Robert James Terry Papers, Series 9: Office correspondence by subject, 1899-1957, American Association of Physical Anthropologists 1926-1955 (Box 9, Folder 5), Missouri History Museum Archives, St. Louis, MI.

Hrdlička, A. (1927, November). [Letter to Robert J. Terry]. Robert James Terry Papers, Series 7: Personal correspondence, 1903-1952 (Box 7, Folder 11:H), Missouri History Museum Archives, St. Louis, MI.

Humphrey, D. C. (1973). Dissection and discrimination: The social origins of cadavers in America, 1760-1915. *Bulletin of the New York Academy of Medicine*, *49*(9), 819–827.

Hunt, D. R., & Albanese, J. (2004). History and demographic composition of the Robert J. Terry anatomical collection. *American Journal of Physical Anthropology*, *127*(4), 406–417.

Kindschuh, S. C., Dupras, T. L., & Cowgill, L. W. (2010). Determination of sex from the hyoid bone. *American Journal of Physical Anthropology*, *143*(2), 279–284.

Klaus, H. D. (2012). The bioarchaeology of structural violence: Theoretical model and case study. In D. L. Martin, R. P. Harrod, & V. R. Perez (Eds.), The bioarchaeology of violence: Small-scale conflict, warfare, and ritualized violence in the pas*t* (pp. 29–62). Gainesville: University Press of Florida.

Kusmer, K. L. (1978). *A ghetto takes shape: Black Cleveland, 1870–1930*. Urbana: University of Illinois Press.

Little, H. (August 29, 1923). North seeking a solution of its new Negro problem. *Moberly Evening Democrat*, p. 1.

Losing out in North. (January 15, 1921). *St. Joseph Observer*, p. 5.

Mandle, J. R. (1978). *The roots of Black poverty: The southern plantation economy after the Civil War*. Durham: Duke University Press.

Mant, M., & Holland, A. (Eds.), (2016). *Beyond the bones: Engaging with disparate data sets*. Boston: Academic Press.

Marks, C. (1989). *Farewell—we're good and gone: The Great Black Migration*. Bloomington: Indiana University Press.

Nystrom, K. (2014). The bioarchaeology of structural violence and dissection in the 19th-century United States. *American Anthropologist, 116*(4), 765–779.

Pearlstein, K. E. (2015). *Health and the huddled masses: an analysis of Immigrant and Euro-American skeletal health in 19th century New York City*. Unpublished doctoral dissertation. American University, Washington, D.C.

Phillips, K. L. (1999). *Alabama North: African-American migrants, community, and working-class activism in Cleveland, 1915–1945*. Urbana: University of Illinois Press.

Redman, S. J. (2016). *Bone rooms: From scientific racism to human prehistory in museums*. Cambridge: Harvard University Press.

Savitt, T. L. (1978). Medicine and slavery: The diseases and health care of Blacks in antebellum Virginia. Chicago: University of Illinois Press.

Savitt, T. L. (1982). The use of Blacks for medical experimentation and demonstration in the old south. *Journal of Southern History, 48*, 331–348.

Scheper-Hughes, N. (2011). Dissection: The body in tatters—Dismemberment, dissection, and the return of the repressed. In F. E. Mascia-Lees (Ed.), *A companion to the anthropology of the body and embodiment* (pp. 172–206). Malden: Wiley-Blackwell, Blackwell Companions in Anthropology Series.

Skloot, R. (2010). *The immortal life of Henrietta Lacks*. New York: The Crown Publishing Group.

Terry, R. J. (December 8, 1927). [Letter to Ales Hrdlička]. Robert James Terry Papers, Series 7: Personal correspondence, 1903-1952 (Box 7, Folder 11:H), Missouri History Museum Archives, St. Louis, MI.

Terry, R. J. (1932). The clavicle of the American negro. *American Journal of Physical Anthropology, 16*(3), 351–379.

Terry, R. J. (1940). On measuring and photographing the cadaver. *American Journal of Physical Anthropology, 26*(1), 433–447.

Terry, R. J. (1942). Absence of superior gemellus muscle in American Whites and Negroes. *American Journal of Physical Anthropology, 29*(1), 47–56.

Terry, R. J. (1959). Sprengel's deformity and club-foot: An anthropological interpretation. *American Journal of Physical Anthropology, 17*(4), 251–271.

Terry, R. J. (n.d.) Biological investigation of the American Negro. Unpublished manuscript. Robert James Terry Papers, Missouri History Museum Archives, St. Louis.

Tolnay, S. E., & Beck, E. M. (1990). Black flight: Lethal violence and the Great Migration, 1900 to 1930. *Social Science History, 14*, 347–370.

Trotter, M. (1981). Robert J. Terry (1871–1966). *American Journal of Physical Anthropology, 56*(4), 503–508.

Trotter, M., & Gleser, G. C. (1952). Estimation of stature from long bones of American whites and negroes. *American Journal of Physical Anthropology*, *10*(4), 463–514.

Washington, H. A. (2007). *Medical apartheid: The dark history of medical experimentation on Black Americans from Colonial Times to the present*. New York: Anchor Books.

Wilkerson, I. (2010). *The warmth of other suns: The epic story of'America's Great Migration*. New York: Random House.

Wilson, W. J. (1978). *The declining significance of race*. Chicago: University of Chicago Press.

Chapter 8

Health inequity and spatial divides: infant mortality during Hamilton, Ontario's industrial transition, 1880–1912

Natalie C. Ludlow and Paul Hackett
Department of Geography and Planning, University of Saskatchewan, Saskatoon, SK, Canada

Chapter Outline

Introduction

Over the span of the late 19th to early 20th centuries the economy of the province of Ontario, Canada shifted substantially as industrialization began to take hold in the country. At the same time, population growth, driven by rapid urbanization and immigration, led to the physical expansion of Canadian cities, itself partly driven by changes in the nature of urban transport technology. These changes were not without impact on the health of the local populations, but the question remains of how the health effects were manifested among those who were most vulnerable.

Historical health research can expose the multifaceted causes of health inequity both in the past and present, advancing our knowledge of health amongst marginalized populations. By marginalized we are referring to groups in a society that experience health inequities resulting from socioeconomic structures. Historical epidemiology is one approach to bettering knowledge of health inequity in the past (Hautaniemi, Swedlund, & Anderton, 1999; Herring, Abonyi, & Hoppa, 2003; Herring & Korol, 2012; Pelletier, Légaré, & Bourbeau, 1997; Sawchuk & Burke, 2003; Sawchuk, Herring, & Waks, 1985; Swedlund & Donta, 2003). Causes of health disparities are

Bioarchaeology of Marginalized People. DOI: https://doi.org/10.1016/B978-0-12-815224-9.00008-7

multifaceted and thus require an ecological lens that analyzes the complex interactions between population, behavior, and habitat. In this paper, we employ a mixed-method study design to better understand historical health inequities amongst infants living within an industrializing urban area.

In this case study, we explore the connections between shifting economic activity, urban development, mortality, and the social gradient of health. Using the city of Hamilton, Ontario, covering the years 1880–1912, a period of rapid industrialization centered on an emerging steel industry, we investigate the changing socioeconomic constructs of a society and urban development in a historical Canadian context, and how these factors contribute to spatiotemporal variations in working-class infant mortality patterns, specifically diarrheal and respiratory infectious diseases. We focus on the health of this marginalized population with an eye toward understanding how their health status changed due to industrialization. Further to this we explore how these health changes were manifested spatially in the expanding city as it underwent a period of rapid growth.

The choice of our study population provides an opportunity to gain insights into changes in the community as a whole. Infants are highly susceptible to the influences of the external environment in terms of their health—quality of sanitation, water, and housing, for example, may be manifested in infant health, for good or bad. Where the quality of the environment is poor as can be the case in marginalized communities or neighborhoods, infants are highly vulnerable to becoming sick or dying from diarrheal and infectious respiratory diseases. Moreover, infant mortality provides insights into the health of a society, the distribution of its resources, its socioeconomic structure, its urban development, and, in turn, its social gradient of health. According to Haines (2011), there is currently a 50%–150% penalty in terms of infant mortality for being in the lowest socioeconomic status group relative to the highest in the United States. Limited economic opportunities for specific populations increase potential health risks (Blane, 2006; Durkin, 1998), and thereby marginalizes those populations, presenting an inequity in population health. These undermining health patterns, as Labonte, Polanyi, Muhajarine, McIntosh, and Williams (2005) suggest, are reinforced by the history of social structure, economic relations, and ideological assumptions. Given these connections between health inequity and the social gradient, the change in socioeconomic and urban structure of Hamilton during industrialization likely affected the overall population health, and specific segments of the society more so than others. In our study, then, infants living in working-class neighborhoods of Hamilton during the turn of the 20th century emerge as a bellwether for the impacts of industrialization on the health of society's most vulnerable populations.

An ecological lens implemented through historical epidemiological studies can provide important insights into variability in health status within urban populations. For example, Sawchuk et al. (1985) found that differences in infant mortality rates between Jewish and non-Jewish populations in

Gibraltar during the period from 1870 to 1959 were related to weaning practices. Later weaning for Jewish infants protected them from bacteria in the water supply and unpasteurized milk that was harming non-Jewish infants (Sawchuk et al., 1985). Ludlow and Burke (2012) found that, in the early 20th century, single-industry urban locales in Nova Scotia created a capitalist/labor dynamic in company towns that created poor working and living conditions, which, in turn, significantly affected the rates of tuberculosis and accidental mortality for the working class. These health inequities can be expressed spatially within urban areas. Although some class integration was found in Detroit neighborhoods between 1880 and 1920, Zunz (1982) found urban development had a marked spatial inequality, connected to immigration status, ethnicity, class, and the distribution of public services. While municipal water supply was accessible throughout Detroit, providing service improvements in working-class areas was a low priority for the municipal government, leading to spatial differences in the quality of the water supply. Thus the east side constantly lagged in public improvements compared to the west side (Zunz, 1982). These examples show that historical epidemiology can identify the plausible interplay of the ecological interactions that may contribute to health inequity, placing some subpopulations at increased risk. In this case, we apply this ecological lens to better understand how ecological interactions in Hamilton contributed to health inequities among infants at the onset of industrialization.

Historical Background

Hamilton's industrialized development represents a major transition not only in the city's geography of economic activity, but also for Canada as a nation. The patterns of settlement in Hamilton in part reflect its urban growth toward industrial activity and increased class segregation over time. Rapid urban development due to the onset of industrial activity and the spatial divide amongst the classes may have manifested into unequal urban development in, for example, adequate public health infrastructure and possibly health disparities. Urban development and potential health risks for the city of Hamilton, therefore, must be examined together.

The dates selected for this research (1880–82 and 1910–12) span a transition in Hamilton's economic system whereby the city moved from predominately commercial and light industry toward heavy industry and manufacturing (primarily steel manufacturing), emerging by the end date as the most industrialized city in Canada (Harris & Sendbuehler, 1992; Nader, 1976). Although known for its steel industry, Hamilton attracted a wide variety of manufactories (Harris & Sendbuehler, 1992), which generated substantial growth, consequently introducing new stressors to the city. During the study period's 33 years, the city's urban landscape was radically transformed to reflect a highly industrialized economy, allowing for an examination of

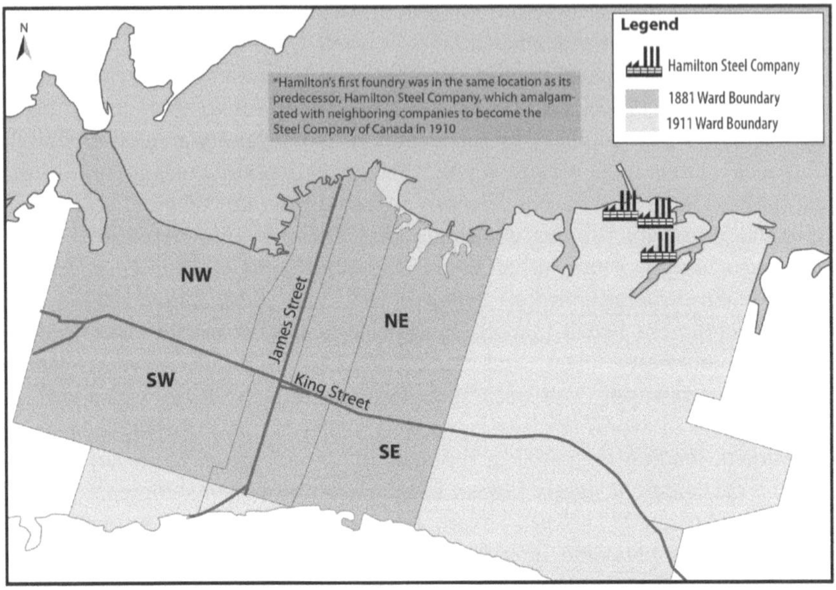

FIGURE 8.1 Map of Hamilton showing the physical growth from 1881 and 1911, and two major streets that divided the city.

life and death before and during heavy industrial activity. Nevertheless, physical growth of the city was uneven as the underlying physical geography and industrial needs (accessible water and transportation ease) constrained the patterns of urban growth eastwards. By the 1910s, two major streets divided the city—James Street signifying the east-west boundary and King Street as the north–south boundary (Fig. 8.1). Over time, Hamilton's physical layout and design reflected its growing industrial economy, but continued to illustrate spatial differences in the urban social landscape, leading to the marginalized working-class poor communities in the northern parts of the city. This economic transition, spatial urban development patterns, and increase in working-class communities make Hamilton an excellent case to examine infant mortality and the connections of these interrelated factors.

Materials and Methods

Infant mortality is often used as an indicator to measure health, well-being, and level of development in a society (Centers for Disease Control & Prevention, 2014; Vaid, Mammen, Primrose, & Kang, 2007). Thus examining the historical mortality patterns of infants over different time periods can inform the potential impact the changing economy had on urban development and spatiotemporal disparities of health in places like Hamilton, Ontario. To do so a mixed method design integrating multisourced information is used to quantitatively, qualitatively, and spatially examine life and death of infants in Hamilton at two periods in time, 1880–82 and 1910–12.

Our approach is structured as an explanatory sequential mixed method model, an iterative process that begins with a quantitative analysis and subsequently moves to a qualitative analysis. Toward this end, we analyze mortality patterns based on the civil death registry for each of the two subperiods (Government of Canada, 1869–1938). This study uses a multinomial logistic regression known as a mortality odds ratio to evaluate a specific cause of death and its relative distribution across variables when compared to all other causes of death in the sample. Results from the mortality odds ratio are then integrated into a historical geographic information science (HGIS) map to analyze spatial patterns of mortality for significant sample characteristics during the later period. Unfortunately, spatial mortality data were not available for the earlier time period. HGIS technique used in this study includes a number of historical maps to alter current GIS (Hamilton Ontario, 1911). The end result is a GIS map that replicates the city streets and street numbers during the study period. Lastly, historical images and historical written documents are synthesized to inform the quantitative and HGIS evidence and contextualize life and death in Hamilton.

Infant causes of death were coded by individual disease classification using the International List of Causes of Death (ILCD2) in consultation with the International Classification of Diseases (ICD 10) (Department of Commerce, & Labor, Bureau of the Census, & Durand, 1911; World Health Organization, n.d.). Where multiple primary causes were listed, the Index of Joint Causes of Death (Department of Commerce, Bureau of the Census, & Harris, 1914) and the Grammars of Death database (Hautaniemi Leonard, Anderton, Swedlund, Beemer, & Robinson, n.d.) were consulted. This coding process coincided with frequency analyses of causes to identify the cause of death groups for infant mortality and used to run chi-square tests for independence to determine independent variables for the mortality odds ratio. Independent variables coded from the mortality dataset to provide information on their potential as explanatory variables include date at death (seasonality), age at death, sex of the deceased, and birthplace. The infant sample was divided into two age categories: neonatal (up to 28 days after birth) and postneonatal (after 28 days to <1 year). These age categories follow the same age definitions as presented by mortality statistics from the Centers for Disease Control and Prevention (CDC) (Centers for Disease Control & Prevention, 2009). Date of death was coded into the following seasons: spring (March, April, and May), summer (June, July, and August), autumn (September, October, and November), and winter (December, January, and February) in order to assess potential seasonal patterns of mortality. These were used for a more in-depth examination into the characteristics of the infant mortality sample toward identifying plausible attributable cause for these infants dying of such causes.

Results

The logistic regression models presented in this study consider various characteristics in association with the likelihood of infants dying from diarrhea and respiratory infections compared to all other causes of death among the sample. Based on the chi-square test for independence, these two leading causes of death presented multiple independent variables (or predictors of mortality cause) and were therefore chosen for both the 1880–82 and 1910–12 infant samples. Infant mortality maps were then constructed as per the logistic regression model results. For the infant sample, 18.36% of the cases had no spatial attribute, leading to a smaller sample size for mapping cases (Table 8.1).

The logistic regression model for 1880–82 diarrheal cause mortality (Table 8.2) suggests that infant age and seasonality both significantly predict diarrheal-related mortality. Postneonatal infants were over five times more likely to die from a diarrhea cause ($OR = 5.9991$, $P < .001$) than neonatal infants (infants within their first month of life). Infants overall were 13 times more likely to die in summer of diarrhea ($OR = 13.140$, $P < .001$) than in winter. They were also six times more likely to die of diarrhea in autumn ($OR = 6.656$, $P < .001$) than in winter. This model suggests that there was a strong link between diarrheal cause mortality and postneonatal infant age as well as dying of diarrhea during the summer and autumn months. Summer seasonal deaths had the strongest link for infants dying from diarrhea than other independent variables.

Similarly, for the 1910–12 period, the logistic regression model for diarrheal cause mortality (Table 8.3) suggests that infant age and seasonality significantly predict diarrheal-related mortality. Postneonatal infants had over 15 times the odds of dying from a diarrheal cause ($OR = 15.592$, $P < .001$) when compared to neonatal infants. In the mortality sample the odds of an infant dying of a diarrheal cause in the summer was over four times ($OR = 4.367$, $P < .001$) the odds of dying from diarrhea in the winter. As well, the odds that death from diarrhea would occur in the autumn months

TABLE 8.1 Cause of death cases unmatched during geocoding for the infant sample (<1 year), Hamilton 1910–12.

Major cause of death	Number of cases	Cases missing spatial property (unmatched)	Percent of unmatched cases
Diarrheal cause	155	32	20.65
Infectious respiratory disease	101	15	14.85
Total	256	47	18.36

TABLE 8.2 Logistic regression predicting for diarrheal cause mortality, infant deaths (<1 year), Hamilton 1880–82.

Independent variables	Coeff.	Sig. (*P*)	Exp(*B*)	S.E.
Infant age				
Postneonatal (>28 days to >1 year)	1.790	0.000	5.991	0.395
Neonatal (≤28 days)[a]				
Seasonality				
Spring	−0.320	0.643		0.690
Summer	2.576	0.000	13.140	0.488
Autumn	1.882	0.000	6.656	0.512
Winter[a]				
Sample size	513			
−2 log likelihood	412.823			

Notes: Coeff., logistic regression coefficient; Sig.(*P*), significance levels; Exp(*B*), odds ratio; S.E., standard error.
[a]*Reference category.*

TABLE 8.3 Logistic regression predicting for diarrheal cause mortality, infant deaths (<1 year), Hamilton 1910–12.

Independent variables	Coeff.	Sig.(*P*)	Exp(*B*)	S.E.
Infant age				
Postneonatal (>28 days to >1 year)	2.741	0.000	15.592	0.428
Neonatal (≤28 days)[a]				
Seasonality				
Spring	−1.247	0.039	0.287	0.603
Summer	1.488	0.000	4.367	0.353
Autumn	1.432	0.000	4.136	0.360
Winter[a]				
Sample size	783			
−2 log likelihood	608.850			

Notes: Coeff., logistic regression coefficient; Sig.(*P*), significance levels; Exp(*B*), odds ratio; S.E., standard error.
[a]*Reference category.*

were over four times higher (OR = 4.136, $P < .001$) than in the winter season. The model suggests a strong link between postneonatal infant age and dying of diarrhea, especially during the summer and autumn months. Postneonatal age had the strongest link for infants dying from diarrhea compared to the other variables presented in the model. In the earlier period the model suggests that the strongest link was found between diarrhea and summer; however, in the later period the strongest link was found between diarrhea and postneonatal age.

The logistic regression model for diarrheal cause mortality predicted a relationship for both seasonality and age. Spatial distribution for summer and autumn is presented in Fig. 8.2 and Table 8.4. Summer and autumn make up 89.43% of geocoded diarrhea cases (51.22% and 38.21%, respectively). Most cases of diarrhea occurring in summer or autumn were located in the northeast. There were 40 (63.49%) summer cases and 21 (44.68%) autumn cases in the northeast. Similar findings can be found overall, with 56.10% ($n = 69$) of cases occurring in the northeast. With the northeast having the majority of cases, the range of cases for autumn was quite small ($n = 8-11$ cases). Summer did show a higher range of cases, with the smallest being 1.59% ($n = 1$) in the southeast and the second highest cases in the northwest (20.63%; $n = 13$). There was some weak sporadic clustering throughout the northeast, but the most pronounced cluster occurred across both northeast and northwest quadrants around the northern section of James Street.

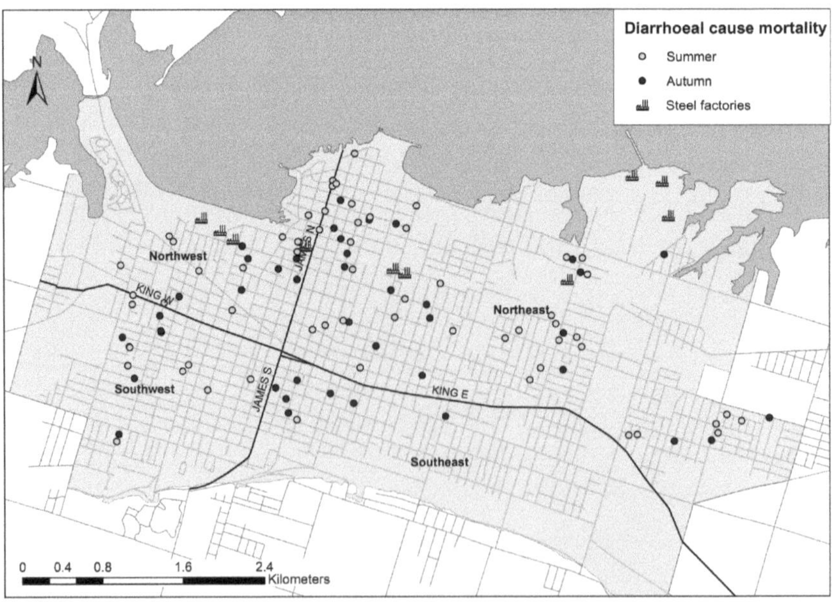

FIGURE 8.2 Infant diarrheal cause mortality by season, Hamilton 1910–12.

TABLE 8.4 Infant mortality by season, Hamilton 1910–12.

City quadrant	Cause of death			
	Diarrheal cause		Summer/autumn	
	%	*n*	%	*n*
NW	17.07	21	20.63	13
SW	19.51	24	14.29	9
NE	56.10	69	63.49	40
SE	7.32	9	1.59	1
Total[a]	100.00	123	100.00	63

[a]*Total of cases matched during geocoding.*

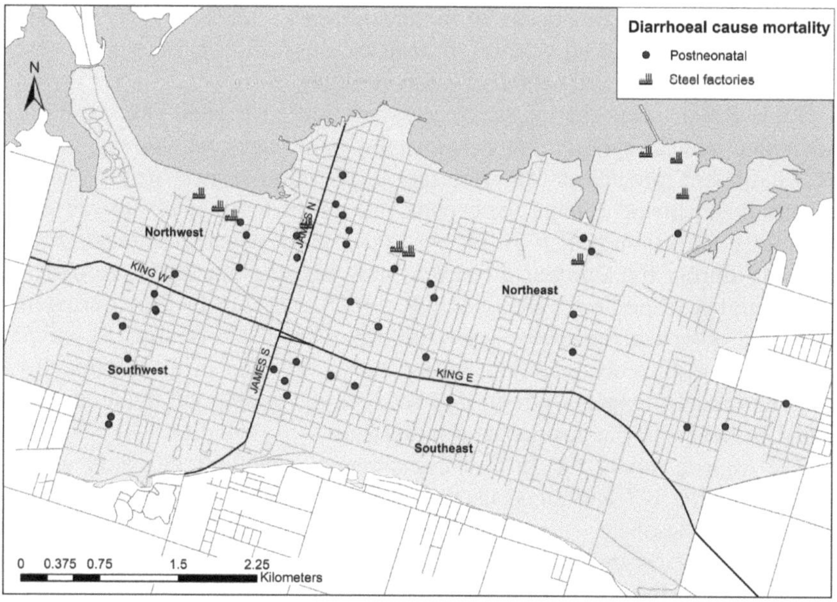

FIGURE 8.3 Infant diarrheal cause mortality by age, Hamilton 1910–12.

The spatial distributions of postneonatal age and diarrhea cases are examined in Fig. 8.3 and Table 8.5. Postneonatal age made up 36.59% ($n = 45$) of all geocoded cases of diarrhea. The majority of neonatal cases were found in the northeast (44.44%; $n = 20$), and a weak clustering can be found on the western side of this quadrant. Other cases in the northeast are sporadic. Across the other quadrants, cases range from eight to 11. Overall, however,

TABLE 8.5 Infant diarrheal cause mortality by age, Hamilton 1910–12.

City quadrant	Cause of death			
	Diarrheal cause		Postneonatal age (>28 days to >1 year)	
	%	*n*	%	*n*
NW	17.07	21	13.33	6
SW	19.51	24	24.44	11
NE	56.10	69	44.44	20
SE	7.32	9	17.78	8
Total[a]	100.00	123	100.00	45

[a] *Total of cases matched during geocoding.*

the least number of cases occurred in the southeast (7.32%; $n = 9$). Although the southeast only had eight cases geocoded, most of the postneonatal cases in this quadrant clustered near James Street South.

Table 8.6 presents the logistic regression model for 1880–82 respiratory infections, which suggests that postneonatal infant age and summer months are significant predictors for respiratory infection-related deaths among infants. Postneonatal infants were over five times more likely to die from respiratory infection (OR = 5.439, $P < .001$) than neonatal infants. Infant mortality during the summer, however, showed significantly lower odds of dying from a respiratory infection (OR = 0.181, $P < .001$) than during the winter. In other words, infants were five times more likely (1/0.181 = 5.53) to die from respiratory infection during the winter than in the summer season. The model suggests a strong link between the winter and dying of respiratory infections in the postneonatal infant age.

The logistic model for 1910–12 respiratory infections mortality is presented in Table 8.7 and suggests that postneonatal infant age and summer and autumn seasonality are significant predictors for infectious respiratory cause mortality. Postneonatal-aged infants had over nine times the odds of dying from respiratory infections (OR = 9.650, $P < .001$) than neonatal-aged infants. Infant mortality during the summer and autumn showed significantly lower odds for respiratory infections (OR = 0.150, $P < .001$ and OR = 0.060, $P < .001$, respectively) than in the winter. In other words, respiratory infections occurred over six times more often during the winter (1/0.150 = 6.67) than the summer. As with the earlier period, the model for 1910–12 suggests there is a strong link between dying of respiratory infections during the winter season and postneonatal infant age.

TABLE 8.6 Logistic regression predicting for infectious respiratory cause mortality, infant deaths (<1 year), Hamilton 1881–82.

Independent variables	Coeff.	Sig.(*P*)	Exp(*B*)	S.E.
Infant age				
Postneonatal (>28 days to >1 year)	1.694	0.000	5.439	0.397
Neonatal (≤28 days)[a]				
Seasonality				
Spring	0.336	0.309		
Summer	−1.707	0.000	0.181	0.400
Autumn	−0.919	0.018		
Winter[a]				
Sample size	513			
−2 log likelihood	380.901			

Notes: Coeff., logistic regression coefficient, Sig.(*P*), significance levels; Exp(*B*), odds ratio; S.E., standard error.
[a]*Reference category.*

TABLE 8.7 Logistic regression predicting for infectious respiratory cause mortality, infant deaths (<1 year), Hamilton 1910–12.

Independent variables	Coeff.	Sig.(*P*)	Exp(*B*)	S.E.
Infant age				
Postneonatal (>28 days to >1 year)	2.267	0.000	9.650	0.385
Neonatal (≤28 days)[a]				
Seasonality				
Spring	−0.304	0.311		
Summer	−1.899	0.000	0.150	0.339
Autumn	−1.350	0.000	0.060	0.318
Winter[a]				
Sample size	783			
−2 log likelihood	514.038			

Notes: Coeff., logistic regression coefficient; Sig.(*P*), significance levels; Exp(*B*), odds ratio; S.E., standard error.
[a]*Reference category.*

Seasonality and age also predicted infectious respiratory disease mortality. Cases of respiratory infections occurring in the winter are spatially presented in Fig. 8.4 and Table 8.8. Winter made up 34.88% ($n = 30$) of the geocoded cases ($n = 86$). Summer and autumn had lower odds (when compared to winter) of predicting for infectious respiratory cause mortality. While overall the northeast presented the highest number of cases (52.33%; $n = 45$), most cases that occurred in the winter were located in the northwest

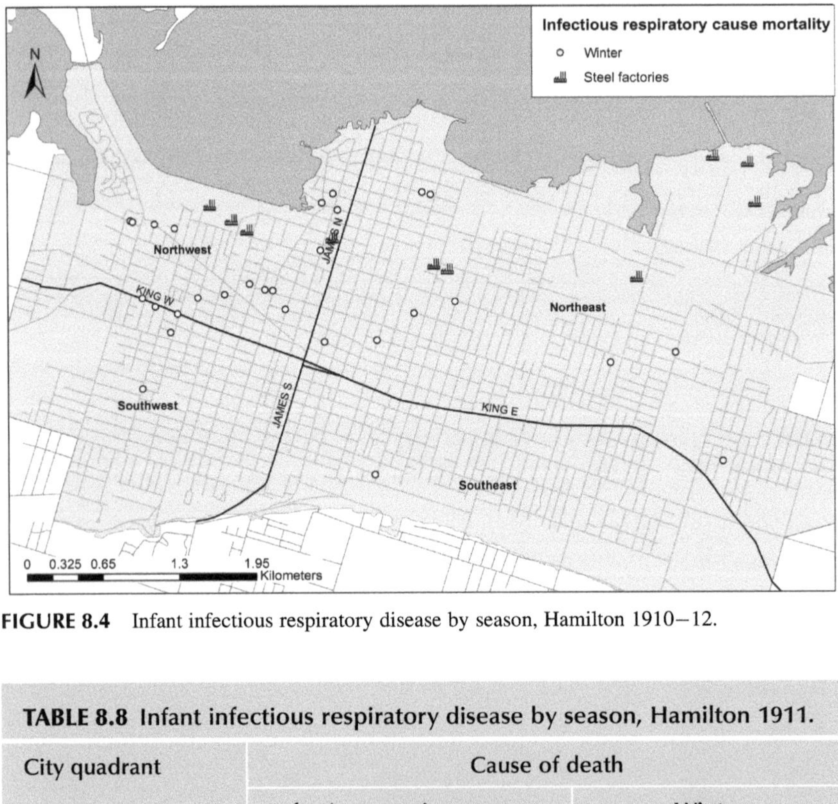

FIGURE 8.4 Infant infectious respiratory disease by season, Hamilton 1910–12.

TABLE 8.8 Infant infectious respiratory disease by season, Hamilton 1911.

City quadrant	Cause of death			
	Infectious respiratory cause		Winter	
	%	*n*	%	*n*
NW	32.0	8	50.0	4
SW	8.0	2	12.5	1
NE	52.0	13	25	2
SE	8.0	2	12.5	1
Total	100	25	100	8

(50.00%; $n = 15$). Three clusters can be found in this quadrant: north by James Street, near the center to the south, and in the northwest.

Spatial distributions were mapped for respiratory infections and age (Fig. 8.5 and Table 8.9). Of all the geocoded cases, postneonatal age made up 91.86% ($n = 79$) of the sample. The majority of these cases occurred in the northeast and the northwest (53.16% and 34.18%, respectively).

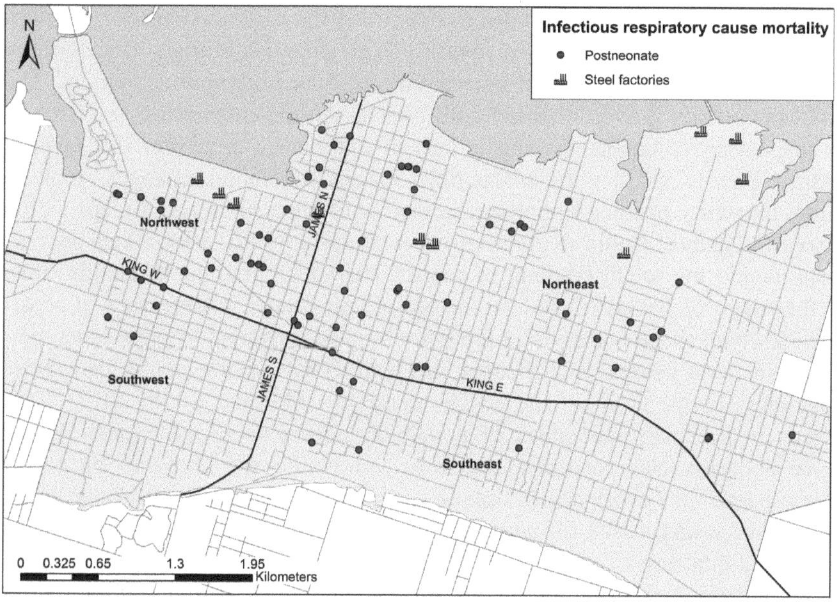

FIGURE 8.5 Infant infectious respiratory disease mortality by age, Hamilton 1910–12.

TABLE 8.9 Infant infectious respiratory disease mortality by age, Hamilton 1911.

City quadrant	Cause of death			
	Infectious respiratory		Postneonatal age (>28 days to >1 year)	
	%	*n*	%	*n*
NW	32.0	8	33.3	8
SW	8.0	2	4.7	1
NE	52.0	13	54.7	13
SE	8.0	2	8.3	2
Total	100	25	100	24

Clustering is less prevalent than the examination of winter cases. Most cases occurred above King Street, reinforcing the north/south divide, whereby both southern quadrants revealed only five cases each.

Discussion

Mortality as a health outcome in epidemiology can be used to describe and explain the potential distribution of disease between populations, especially when using a mortality odds ratio to determine the characteristics of the population that died of a specific cause. Over time Hamilton's demography changed with rapid population growth and increased urban development. The rapid population growth coupled with poor urban development manifested as an uneven environment, leaving infants in some areas at greater risk of poor health. Infants are highly susceptible to environmental changes, making infant mortality profiles important indicators of changes in social deprivation (Davies, Tocque, Bellis, Rimmington, & Davies, 1999), which can provide insights into the social gradient of health. The social gradient of health refers to the range of health related to socioeconomic status, manifesting in a pattern in which those occupying higher social positions tend to experience better health; as a general rule, people will tend to have worse health than those positioned above them in the social hierarchy (Marmot, 2006, 2012). This results in the marginalization of people in poorer social positions. Within those poorer social positions, the most vulnerable are likely to be at the greatest risk for poorer health outcomes, especially coupled with poor urban development and a lack of basic public health needs like quality water, sanitation, and housing. The result is an increased susceptibility to diseases attributed to a lack of public health infrastructure such as diarrhea and respiratory diseases. For infants, these diseases become a matter of life and death.

Infant diarrhea can be attributed to several distinct causes; however, it is often associated with an infectious pathogen that affects the intestinal tract. Diarrheal causes are predominately water-related and contracted when contaminated water is ingested (through the washing of food, direct consumption, watering down milk, or unhygienic/unsanitary practices) (Meade & Emch, 2010). The type of disease found in this category has a causal relationship with conditions found in the built environment and are often affiliated with overcrowded poverty-stricken locales where public health infrastructure is lacking, making the population highly susceptible to changes in the physical environment, such as seasonal droughts and flooding (Meade & Emch, 2010; World Health Organization, 2013).

Diarrhea is a known major cause of death occurring beyond the neonate period of infancy (Mulholland, 2007). Neonatal mortality is often due to endogenous causes (those occurring within the body due to genetic makeup), or circumstances before or during birth rather than environmental causes (Reid, 2001). In the United States, around the 1880s, women began to supplement breastmilk with cow's milk shortly after birth and began to wean babies before three months of age (Wolf, 2003). This practice in the early months of life may have caused an increase in deaths in the postneonatal ages. Thus time of weaning is an important factor to consider because breastfeeding can protect infants from external risks that may cause infectious diseases (Canadian Paediatric Society, 2004). While a shift in different countries has happened over time for infectious disease risk, diarrheal cause of infant death remains one of the leading causes of death for children under five years of age in middle- and lower-income countries (World Health Organization, 2013). Diarrheal causes of infant mortality were a constant risk to Hamilton's infant population in both periods and a manifestation of the human and physical environment.

The connection between seasonality and diarrheal infant mortality can be attributed, in part, to poor quality water supply (Sawchuk, Burke, & Padiak, 2002). Infantile cholera, a historical term for diarrhea, was also known as summer complaint due to its association with hot, humid weather (Swedlund, 2010). Contaminated milk caused by poor or nonexistent refrigeration, or cross-contamination of food and beverages with viruses and bacteria (Keusch et al., 2006; Leavitt, 1992; Meade & Emch, 2010) also contributed to infant diarrhea. Pasteurizing, introduced in North America in the early 20th century, was an attempt to address public health concerns in Canada and the United States (Block, 2009; Czaplicki, 2007; Speake, 2011). Pasteurization of milk, however, was not compulsory in Ontario until 1938 (Speake, 2011).

In both periods, postneonatal infant age showed a strong link to diarrheal cause mortality when compared to neonatal infant age. Ferrie and Troesken (2008) note that, while literature supports the connection between the reduction of infant mortality and the introduction of public water and sewer lines, the efficacy of these interventions varies. In Hamilton, while age and seasonality were linked to infant diarrheal causes, there was a temporal flip in the association with the independent factor, revealing an increased association with age by the later time period. This flip suggests that, during the earlier period, environmental causes such as seasonality and water quality were more influential than maternal practices, while, in the later period, maternal practices, such as the time of weaning and breastfeeding, had some influence in addition to the environmental factors and sanitary practices. This conclusion is supported by the northeastern spatial pattern for infant deaths caused by diarrhea.

The influence of environmental factors on diarrheal-related infant mortality in the early period reflects the challenges Hamilton had with its sewers. Reports from the city council between 1880 and 1882 indicate that sewer pipes were regularly clogged during heavy rains, water was overflowing onto people's properties, and sewers were discharging onto properties (City of Hamilton Council, 1878–1882). Concerns were raised about the abundance of privies and cesspools and the need to regularly collect night soil—or human fecal matter (City of Hamilton Council, 1878–1882; Harris, n.d.). During the 1880s the Province of Ontario also noted that the wells supplying water in the city could easily become contaminated by cesspools through porous soils and expressed the need for better sanitary reforms in the disposal of sewage (Province of Ontario, 1883). Thus Hamilton and the whole province of Ontario were greatly concerned with building an adequate system for water and sewage.

Like diarrheal causes, infectious respiratory diseases among infants have also shown a high correlation to environmental factors (Reid, 2002). Infectious respiratory diseases are caused by airborne viral and bacterial pathogens. Today, pneumonia is the leading cause of infectious mortality for children under the age of five years (World Health Organization, 2015). Whooping cough (pertussis), a highly contagious viral disease of the respiratory system, mostly affects infants and young children, but is especially fatal to infants under one year of age (Centers for Disease Control & Prevention, 2015) when vaccination is not practiced. Overcrowded conditions, weakened immune systems, nonbreastfeeding practices, and poor nutrition are key risk factors of infectious respiratory infant mortality (Cohen, Wilson, & Aiello, 2007; Mercer, 1986; Shulman, 2004; Weiss & McMichael, 2004). The highest risk of complications for seasonal flu patterns occurs in children under the age of two years (World Health Organization, 2014), and pneumonia in particular is known to have a postneonatal age association (Mulholland, 2007). Respiratory infections, such as pneumonia and bronchitis, are associated with infants who have been artificially fed at two months of age (Reid, 2002). Such behavioral and environmental risk factors were prevalent in the infant infectious respiratory mortality found in Hamilton at both periods in time.

Although infectious respiratory mortality declined in the later period in Hamilton, it nonetheless persisted as a major cause of infant death. In both periods, age and seasonality were significant predictors for infectious respiratory mortality. Age had the highest significant association predicting for death from infectious respiratory diseases at both time periods and showed a northeast spatial pattern for postneonates in the later period. Maternal feeding practices may have caused infant respiratory tract infections. Reports on weaning age and artificial feeding in Hamilton are scarce; however, the medical officer expressed concern about maternal education and infant feeding practices for new immigrant families in the industrial districts of the city (Roberts & City of Hamilton, 1910).

Seasonality also contributed to infant mortality. Winter showed slightly more occurrences in the northwest, followed closely with cases in the northeast. The pattern of seasonal flu epidemics occurring during the colder months is consistent with typical wintertime seasonal trends (Fisman, 2012; Lofgren, Fefferman, Naumov, Gorski, & Naumova, 2007), where overcrowded and poorly ventilated homes coupled with poor diet and a weakened immune system allowed for the spread of such diseases. Poorly ventilated overcrowded homes would increase susceptibility for seasonal flus and health reports in the city suggest that the houses in these industrial working-class areas were not suitable in the winter. Houses in these neighborhoods were in some cases condemned because of their unhealthy and overcrowded conditions (Fig. 8.6). Conditions in Hamilton basements were described as being poorly ventilated, lacking sunlight, and being cold and clammy (Bowman & City of Hamilton, 1912). In inspections, it was noted that 28 families were only able to afford to live in a single room used for living, cooking, and sleeping (Bowman & City of Hamilton, 1912). Such housing conditions in the industrial working-class neighborhoods in Hamilton presented a space where infectious respiratory conditions easily spread to the most susceptible population: infants. This would have especially been the

FIGURE 8.6 Hamilton 1910 Board of Health—"condemned home. *Note*: icicles from roof and ice on floor, plumbing bad." (Roberts & City of Hamilton, 1910). A family of 12 occupied this basement and two small rooms. *Image courtesy of the Hamilton Public Library, Local Archives & Archives.*

case if infants were weaned at an early age, removing the protective buffer provided through maternal breastfeeding.

Both diarrheal and infectious respiratory causes of death can be attributed to breastfeeding practices and the use of artificial milk. By the later period, 1910–12, the Hamilton Board of Health became increasingly concerned with maternal education and milk supply. Lack of sewerage and "primitive" methods for disposing of waste were still concerns raised, especially within the industrial districts (Roberts & City of Hamilton, 1910, p. 21). The annual report for the year 1909–10 even suggested an increase in inspectors during the summer and early fall to enforce sanitary rules on the construction, cleaning, and disinfection of privy vaults and dry earth closets (Roberts & City of Hamilton, 1910). According to health reports, the high death rate of infants was, however, also attributed to the lack of maternal education for women and the availability of low-quality cow's milk (i.e., unpurified/unpasteurized) (Roberts & City of Hamilton, 1910). To help, the Medical Health Officer suggested that Women's Health visitors who would instruct women in the care and feeding of children would benefit Hamilton, due to the large and increasing "foreign element" (Roberts & City of Hamilton, 1910, p. 4). The uncontrolled supply of milk was actually a larger contributor to infant morbidity (and plausibly infant mortality) and resulted from economic disparity rather than a lack of education in parenting.

Unsanitary cow barns, contaminated milk, and poor milk storage were significant risks to infants in the later period. Photographs document the state of unsanitary cow barns in Hamilton during the later period (Fig. 8.7). According to the health reports for the city of Hamilton, unsanitary cow barns heightened the risk of the consumption of low-quality raw milk (Bowman & City of Hamilton, 1912; Roberts & City of Hamilton, 1910). Awareness of the variations in milk quality led to the implementation of a certification process for dairies producing milk for human consumption (Roberts & City of Hamilton, 1910). The term *certified milk* meant that dairies fell within the standards and regulations of local authorities (Block, 2009; Czaplicki, 2007; Speake, 2011). Certified milk, however, was quite expensive for the consumer (Czaplicki, 2007; Speake, 2011). To alleviate some of the cost, families may have turned to watered-down milk. Sawchuk et al. (2002) suggest that poorer families in Gibraltar would have purchased watered-down milk because it was cheaper than the pure milk that was available. Including water in the milk increased the potential for contamination; both the water and milk supply contributed to infant diarrheal mortality. As infants were weaned or artificial feeding practices were used, infants' susceptibility to tainted milk, water, or food led to weanling diarrhea (Sawchuk et al., 2002). Thus the association of infant diarrheal mortality with age and season support two causal factors: an urban public health problem at the city level, and a behavioral problem of early weaning time and poor artificial feeding practices of Hamilton's residents.

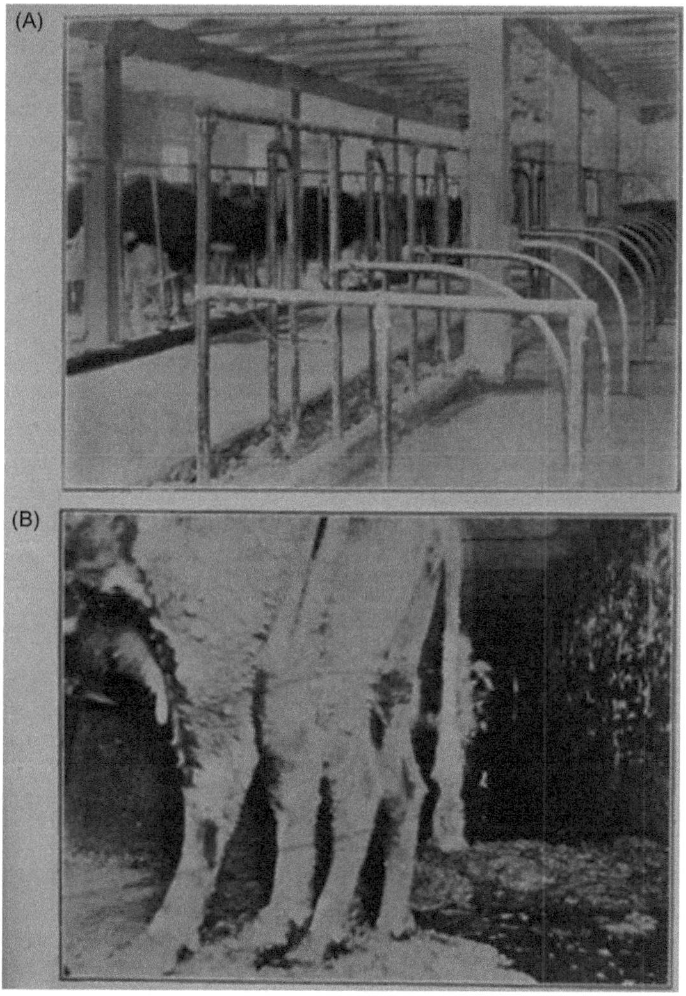

FIGURE 8.7 "Sanitary concerns about cow stables. (A) A sanitary cow barn. This enterprising young farmer has all the equipment for certified milk. (B) Unsanitary cow stable. Cows plastered with manure and floors filthy." (Roberts & City of Hamilton, 1910). *Image courtesy of the Hamilton Public Library, Local Archives & Archives.*

Environmental causes greatly contributed to the high death rates in Hamilton. The high rates of infectious respiratory causes and diarrheal causes in Hamilton were attributed to the unsanitary state of the industrial districts as described in the health reports (Bowman & City of Hamilton, 1912; Roberts & City of Hamilton, 1910). The 1910 city health report suggested both the lack of sewerage and the practices of the population were causal factors (Roberts & City of Hamilton, 1910). The HGIS results of this study revealed a north spatial pattern in 1911 for infant infectious respiratory diseases.

Herring and Korol (2012), in their study of the 1918 influenza pandemic, also found a prominent north–south divide in the city of Hamilton, with influenza occurring mostly in the northern wards. Infectious respiratory diseases tend to be most frequent in low-income areas (Corner, Dewan, & Hashizume, 2013; Kelly-Hope et al., 2007). The spatial patterning of mortality in the later period reinforces that health disparities existed in Hamilton and had a pronounced socioeconomic gradient; this gradient suggests that of the northern sections, the northwest revealed more infant mortality cases for both diarrhea and infectious respiratory diseases. These spatial observations revealed aspects of the mortality analysis that was not easily attainable without this tool.

Conclusions

Multiple logistic regression models predicting for infant mortality indicate a link between postneonatal age for both infant diarrheal causes and infectious respiratory causes of death that increased over time, while the relationship to seasonality for both causes decreased. These findings can be attributed to underlying mechanisms. At the height of the industrial activity, age was the strongest predictor for both infant diarrheal and infectious respiratory causes, suggesting that maternal practices, housing, and the state of public health infrastructure may have been causative factors. Infant diarrhea is highly associated with poor sanitation, poor water quality, the lack of breastfeeding/early weaning, and the quality of milk supply (Ferrie & Troesken, 2008; Sawchuk et al., 2002; Vaid et al., 2007). In the United States, infant mortality due to infectious respiratory diseases showed a higher peak in the winter months where unhealthy conditions and poverty persisted (Sakamoto-Momiyama, 1978). Maternal health plays an imperative role in infant health, especially during the preweaning stages, as breastfeeding usually acts as a protective buffer against environmental insults. When the health of the mother is compromised by external environmental factors, infants are also at risk (Black et al., 2008; Goodman & Armelagos, 1989). Furthermore, artificial feeding or weaning at earlier ages would increase infant health insult due to direct exposure to external environmental factors—poor housing, sanitation, and water supply, poor quality of milk—and the related infectious pathogens associated with these factors. Thus the compromise to health is rooted in the environmental, economic, and contextual factors that cause undernutrition, poverty, and increase the risk of infectious diseases (Black et al., 2008).

Understanding the spatial mortality patterns in the context of environmental and behavioral factors leads to better examination of the social gradient of health. Social hierarchies of advantaged/disadvantaged groups persist worldwide and contribute to divisions based on socioeconomic status, ethnic or religious groups, gender, age, geography, and health (Braveman & Gruskin, 2003). The increased significance of age in the later period for both diarrheal and infectious respiratory causes of infant death reflects the changing socioeconomic gradient of health in Hamilton. The expansion of the industrial working class meant more individuals were living in overcrowded housing with access to inadequate water supply and sanitation. This expansion would coincide with women in working-class families having to work outside the home and, therefore, needing to wean early and/or feed artificially. The higher cost for certified milk and options available for lower quality milk presents health inequities tied to the social gradient of the population in Hamilton. The social gradient in Hamilton presented a socioeconomic disadvantage to marginalized working-class families living in the industrial communities. This disadvantage was found amongst infants in these families, showing an increased vulnerability to diarrheal and infectious respiratory diseases. Thus this study extends the notion of the importance of examining the environment alongside human behaviors as the choices people make are not always due to a lack of education, but also what is and is not available in their environment.

References

Black, R. E., Victora, C. G., Walker, S. P., Bhutta, Z. A., Christian, P., de Onis, M., ... Uauy, R. (2008). Maternal and child undernutrition and overweight in low-income and middle-income countries. *The Lancet, 382*(9890), 427–451.

Blane, D. (2006). The life course, the social gradient, and health. In M. G. Marmot, & R. G. Wilkinson (Eds.), *Social determinants of health* (2nd ed., pp. 54–77). Oxford: Oxford University Press.

Block, D. R. (2009). Public health, cooperatives, local regulation, and the development of modern milk policy: The Chicago milkshed, 1900–1940. *Journal of Historical Geography, 35*(1), 128–153.

Bowman, F. B., & City of Hamilton. (1912). In L. Spectator Printing Co. (Ed.), *Annual report: 1911-1912 Board of Health*. Hamilton: Spectator Printing Co., Ltd.

Braveman, P., & Gruskin, S. (2003). Defining equity in health. *Journal of Epidemiology & Community Health, 57*, 254–258.

Canadian Paediatric Society. (2004). *Weaning from the breast* (Position Statement CP04-01). Retrieved from Ottawa: <https://www.cps.ca/en/documents/position/weaning-from-the-breast>

Centers for Disease Control and Prevention. (2009). Quickstats: Infant, neonatal, and postneonatal mortality rates*—United States, 1940–2006. Retrieved from <http://www.cdc.gov/mmwr/preview/mmwrhtml/mm5823a4.htm>

Centers for Disease Control and Prevention. (2014). Infant mortality. Retrieved from <http://www.cdc.gov/reproductivehealth/maternalinfanthealth/infantmortality.htm>

Centers for Disease Control and Prevention. (2015). Pertussis (Whooping cough). Retrieved from <http://www.cdc.gov/pertussis/>

City of Hamilton Council. (1878–1882). *City council minutes* (Vol. 13). Hamilton: City of Hamilton Council, December 9, 1978–January 9, 1882.

Cohen, J. M., Wilson, M. L., & Aiello, A. E. (2007). Analysis of social epidemiology research on infectious diseases: Historical patterns and future opportunities. *Journal of Epidemiology and Community Health, 61*(12), 1021–1027.

Corner, R. J., Dewan, A. M., & Hashizume, M. (2013). Modelling typhoid risk in Dhaka metropolitan area of Bangladesh: The role of socio-economic and environmental factors. *International Journal of Health Geographics*, *12*, 13.

Czaplicki, A. (2007). "Pure milk is better than purified milk": Pasteurization and milk purity in Chicago, 1908-1916. *Social Science History*, *31*(3), 411–433.

Davies, R. P. O., Tocque, K., Bellis, M. A., Rimmington, T., & Davies, P. D. O. (1999). Historical declines in tuberculosis in England and Wales: Improving social conditions or natural selection? *The International Journal of Tuberculosis and Lung Disease*, *3*(12), 1051–1054.

Department of Commerce., Bureau of the Census., & Harris, W. J. (1914). *Index of joint causes of death: Showing assignment to the preferred title of the International List of Causes of Death when two causes are simultanelously reported*. Washington: Government Printing Office.

Department of Commerce and Labor., Bureau of the Census., & Durand, D. E. (1911). *Manual of the international list of causes of death* (2nd ed.). Washington: Governement Printing Office.

Durkin, J. T. (1998). Immigration, assimilation and growth. *Journal of Population Economics*, *11*(2), 273–291.

Ferrie, J. P., & Troesken, W. (2008). Water and Chicago's mortality transition, 1850–1925. *Explorations in Economic History*, *45*(1), 1–16.

Fisman, D. (2012). Seasonality of viral infections: Mechanisms and unknowns. *Clinical Microbiology and Infection*, *18*(10), 946–954.

Goodman, A. H., & Armelagos, G. J. (1989). Infant and childhood morbidity and mortality risks in archaeological populations. *World Archaeology*, *21*(2), 225–243.

Government of Canada. (1869–1938). Ontario, Canada, deaths, 1869–1938 and deaths overseas, 1939–1947. Retrieved from <http://search.ancestry.ca/search/db.aspx?dbid = 8946>. <http://search.ancestry.ca/search/db.aspx?dbid = 8946>

Haines, M. R. (2011). Inequality and infant and childhood mortality in the United States in the twentieth century. *Explorations in Economic History*, *48*(3), 418–428.

Hamilton Ontario (Cartographer). (1911). Insurance plan of Hamilton, Ontario (Vols. 1–3). Retrieved from <http://library.mcmaster.ca/maps/collection/fire>

Harris, C. (n.d.). The health of Hamilton, 1880–1905. *Pamphlet File – Weaver*. Local History and Archives, Hamilton.

Harris, R., & Sendbuehler, M. P. (1992). Hamilton's east end: The early working class suburb. *The Canadian Geographer*, *36*(4), 381–386.

Hautaniemi Leonard, S., Anderton, D. L., Swedlund, A. C., Beemer, J. K., & Robinson, C. T. (n.d.). Grammars of death. Retrieved from <https://sites.google.com/a/umich.edu/grammars-of-death/home>

Hautaniemi, S. I., Swedlund, A. C., & Anderton, D. L. (1999). Mill town mortality: Consequences of industrial growth in two nineteenth-century New England towns. *Social Science History*, *23*(1), 1–39.

Herring, A. D., & Korol, E. (2012). The north-south divide: Social inequality and mortality from the 1918 influenza pandemic in Hamilton, Ontario. In M. Fahrni, & E. W. Jones (Eds.), *Epidemic encounters: Influenza, society, and culture in Canada, 1918-20* (pp. 97–112). Vancouver: University of British Columbia Press.

Herring, A. D., Abonyi, S., & Hoppa, R. D. (2003). Malnutrition among Northern Peoples of Canada in the 1940s: An ecological and economic disaster. In A. D. Herring, & A. C. Swedlund (Eds.), *Human biologists in the archives* (pp. 289–310). Cambridge: Cambridge University Press.

Kelly-Hope, L. A., Alonso, W. J., Thiem, V. D., Anh, D. D., Canh do, G., Lee, H., ... Miller, M. A. (2007). Geographical distribution and risk factors associated with enteric diseases in Vietnam. *American Journal of Tropical Medicine and Hygiene*, *76*(4), 706–712.

Keusch, G. T., Fontaine, O., Bhargava, A., Boschi-Pinto, C., Bhutta, Z. A., Gotuzzo, E., ... Laxminarayan, R. (2006). Diarrheal diseases. In D. T. Jamison, J. G. Breman, A. R. Measham, G. Alleyne, M. Claeson, D. B. Evans, P. Jha, A. Mills, & P. Musgrove (Eds.), *Disease control priorities in developing countries* (2nd ed., pp. 371–387). Washington, DC: World Bank.

Labonte, R., Polanyi, M., Muhajarine, N., McIntosh, T., & Williams, A. (2005). Beyond the divides: Towards critical population health research. *Critical Public Health*, *15*(1), 5–17.

Leavitt, J. W. (1992). "Typhoid Mary" strikes back: Bacteriological theory and practice in early twentieth-century public health. *ISIS*, *83*, 608–629.

Lofgren, E., Fefferman, N. H., Naumov, Y. N., Gorski, J., & Naumova, E. N. (2007). Influenza seasonality: Underlying causes and modeling theories. *Journal of Virology*, *81*(11), 5429–5436.

Ludlow, N. C., & Burke, S. D. A. (2012). Deadly occupations: Assessing tuberculosis and accidental mortality among male workers in Sydney and Glace Bay, Nova Scotia, 1909-1917. *Canadian Studies in Population*, *39*(3-4), 35–48.

Marmot, M. (2006). Introduction. In M. G. Marmot, & R. G. Wilkinson (Eds.), *Social determinants of health* (2nd ed., pp. 1–5). Oxford: Oxford University Press.

Marmot, M. (2012). Why should the rich care about the health of the poor? *Canadian Medical Association Journal*, *184*(11), 1231–1232.

Meade, M. S., & Emch, M. (2010). *Medical geography* (3rd ed.). New York: The Guildford Press.

Mercer, A. J. (1986). Relative trends in mortality from related respiratory and airborne infectious diseases. *Population Studies*, *40*(1), 129–145.

Mulholland, K. (2007). Perspectives on the burden of pneumonia in children. *Vaccine*, *25*(13), 2394–2397.

Nader, G. A. (1976). *Cities of Canada volume two: Profiles of fifteen metropolitan centres*. Toronto: MacMillan Company of Canada.

Pelletier, F., Légaré, J., & Bourbeau, R. (1997). Mortality in Quebec during the nineteenth century: From State to the cities. *Population Studies*, *51*(1), 93–103.

Province of Ontario. (1883). *First annual report of the Provincial Board of Health of Ontario 1882*. Toronto: C. Blackett Robinson.

Reid, A. (2001). Neonatal mortality and stillbirths in early twentieth century Derbyshire, England. *Population Studies*, *55*(3), 213–232.

Reid, A. (2002). Infant feeding and post-neonatal mortality in Derbyshire, England, in the early twentieth century. *Population Studies*, *56*(2), 151–166.

Roberts, J., & City of Hamilton. (1910). *Annual report: 1909-1910 Board of Health*. Hamilton: City of Hamilton, Canada.

Sakamoto-Momiyama, M. (1978). Changes in the seasonality of human mortality: A medico-geographical study. *Social Science & Medicine. Part D: Medical Geography*, *12*(1), 29–42.

Sawchuk, L. A., & Burke, S. D. A. (2003). The ecology of a health crisis: Gibraltar and the 1865 cholera epidemic. In A. D. Herring, & A. C. Swedlund (Eds.), *Human biologists in the archives* (pp. 178–215). Cambridge: Cambridge University Press.

Sawchuk, L. A., Burke, S. D. A., & Padiak, J. (2002). A matter of privilege: Infant mortality in the garrison town of Gibraltar, 1870-1899. *Journal of Family History*, *27*(4), 399–429.

Sawchuk, L. A., Herring, D. A., & Waks, L. R. (1985). Evidence of a Jewish advantage: A study of infant mortality in Gibraltar, 1870-1959. *American Anthropologist, 87*(3), 616–625.

Shulman, S. (2004). The history of pediatric infectious diseases. *Pediatric Research, 55*(1), 163–176.

Speake, S. W. (2011). Infectious milk: Issues of pathogenic certainty within ideational regimes and their biopolitical implications. *Studies in History and Philosophy of Science Part C: Studies in History and Philosophy of Biological and Biomedical Sciences, 42*(4), 530–541.

Swedlund, A. C. (2010). *Shadows in the valley: A cultural history of illness, death, and loss in New England, 1840-1916*. Amherst & Boston: University of Massachusetts Press.

Swedlund, A. C., & Donta, A. K. (2003). Scarlet fever epidemics of the nineteenth century: A case of evolved pathogenic virulence? In A. D. Herring, & A. C. Swedlund (Eds.), *Human biologists in the archives* (pp. 159–177). Cambridge: Cambridge University Press.

Vaid, A., Mammen, A., Primrose, B., & Kang, G. (2007). Infant mortality in an urban slum. *The Indian Journal of Pediatrics, 74*(5), 449–453.

Weiss, R. A., & McMichael, A. J. (2004). Social and environmental risk factors in the emergence of infectious diseases. *Nature Medicine, 10*(12 Suppl), S70–S76.

Wolf, J. H. (2003). Low breastfeeding rates and public health in the United States. *American Journal of Public Health, 93*(12), 2000–2010.

World Health Organization. (2013). Diarrhoeal disease. Retrieved from <http://www.who.int/mediacentre/factsheets/fs330/en/>

World Health Organization. (2014). Influenza (seasonal). Retrieved from <http://www.who.int/mediacentre/factsheets/fs211/en/>

World Health Organization. (2015). Pneumonia. Retrieved from <http://www.who.int/mediacentre/factsheets/fs331/en/>

World Health Organization. (n.d.). International Classification of Diseases – ICD 10. Retrieved from <http://www.who.int/classifications/icd/en/>

Zunz, O. (1982). The changing face of inequality: Urbanization, industrial development and immigration in Detroit, *1880-1920*. Chicago: University of Chicago Press.

Chapter 9

In the shadow of war: the forgotten 1916 polio epidemic in New Zealand

Heather T. Battles
Anthropology, School of Social Sciences, University of Auckland, Auckland, New Zealand

---

The shadow of war was enough – now we have a terror which is closer at hand

"Social gossip" (1916, p. 14).

Chapter Outline

Introduction

Poliomyelitis emerged as an epidemic disease in New Zealand and many other Western countries (e.g., Australia, Canada, the United States, and Sweden) in the late 19th and early 20th centuries, presumably from a prior state of endemicity in substantial populations with low levels of sanitation and hygiene (Smallman-Raynor, Cliff, Trevelyan, Nettleton, & Sneddon, 2006). Though New Zealand experienced small polio outbreaks in the 1880s–90s, the first large one occurred on the South Island in 1914, prior to the start of the First World War. A total of 268 polio cases were recorded

Bioarchaeology of Marginalized People. DOI: https://doi.org/10.1016/B978-0-12-815224-9.00009-9

that year, with incidence calculated at 2.46 per 10,000 population (New Zealand Department of Public Health, Hospitals, and Charitable Aid, 1916). When infantile paralysis, as it was commonly known then, emerged on the North Island two years later, it was not entirely unexpected. Alice Darragh (née McGuire) from Pukekawa (south of Auckland), who caught polio in 1916, recalls that her physician Dr. Dalziel had predicted an epidemic would come to New Zealand (Darragh, 1994). Alice recalls that "there had been warnings of a dreaded children's disease taking its toll overseas, especially in the war zones. I suppose most people would think 'It won't come here'; but it did" (1994, p. 29).

Apart from contemporary medical articles (e.g., in the *New Zealand Medical Journal*) about polio in New Zealand, particularly from the later epidemics (1930–50s), the historical literature is extremely limited. The existing historical works focus largely on the later epidemics and include a chapter in MacLean (1964), two Masters theses, an edited book by Karen Butterworth (1994) that records the stories of polio survivors (Butterworth is a polio survivor herself), and a book on the Duncan Hospital, which provided polio rehabilitation services from the 1940s to 1960s (The Duncan Family, 2011). One thesis presents the history of polio in New Zealand as a whole, including a short chapter on the 1916 epidemic (Ross, 1993, pp. 15–25) and the other examines only the Auckland region, specifically focused on the period 1925–62 with brief discussion of the events of 1916 (Simpson, 1993, pp. 11–12, 18–20). Even more than the once "forgotten" 1918 flu (as per Crosby, 2003 [1976]; see also Winter, 2006), there is a conspicuous historical silence about this 1916 epidemic, and an absence of remembrance in literature or in public memorials. It has been marginalized and overshadowed by its temporal proximity to the much larger death tolls of the New York polio epidemic the same year, the 1918 flu pandemic, and the First World War. In this chapter, I therefore define marginalized as contemporaneously deprioritized and only selectively engaged with (as filtered through the lens of the war), and subsequently forgotten in terms of commemoration and scholarly attention. Secondarily, an additional example of marginalization addressed here is the intersection of anti-German propaganda and paranoia ("Germanophobia") and fear of polio in the form of rumors of the deliberate spreading of polio germs. While it is beyond the scope of this chapter to fully consider this aspect, this is connected to the wider marginalization of Germans as a minority group in New Zealand during the war that lead to and included destruction of property during riots, dismissal from employment, and internment (see Francis, 2012, 2014).

Clues to addressing this historical marginalization of the 1916 polio epidemic in New Zealand can be found in the wave of new research on the 1918 flu that has examined how deeply the pandemic was connected to the First World War (see Phillips's 2014 review of this literature). This research has revealed how the war was a direct contributor to the pandemic; the new virulent strain of influenza spread through crowded trenches and hospitals and across oceans in troop transports, infecting bodies already under stress (see Oxford, Sefton, Innes, Daniels, & Johnson, 2002). Many have also examined how the pandemic's connection to the war contributed to the 1918 flu being largely forgotten, until recent decades, in terms of a lack of both public awareness and academic study (see, e.g., Honigsbaum, 2014; Youde, 2017). The same theme can be explored concerning the wartime polio epidemics.

In this chapter, I have two related questions: first, how was the 1916 infantile paralysis epidemic in New Zealand connected to the First World War, and second, what does this tell us about how this epidemic was marginalized and "forgotten" and how does it inform our understanding of marginalization and collective forgetting more broadly? There are two aspects to the first question. The first of these asks about the biological features of the epidemic among the Pāhekā (non-Māori or white) population: given that the epidemic was first reported among civilians in and near Auckland, did troops bring the virus into the country and assist its spread? Were soldiers, especially those coming from rural areas with less exposure to childhood diseases, affected by this epidemic as they crowded into the training camps? The second aspect follows on from this, considering the social and psychological responses to the epidemic among Pāhekā: in what ways did the war shape the experiences of grieving families, survivors, and the public? And why was this epidemic largely "forgotten" in public memory and academic history?

To begin to answer these questions, first, I will establish that proportional to New Zealand's population the epidemic was comparable in severity to the one that hit the eastern United States later that year, and thus the historical forgetting of this event is not explained by a relatively small death toll. Second, I will examine the demographic distribution of mortality in the epidemic to determine who was most impacted and whether this indicates a role of the war in shaping these patterns. Third, I will examine the social perception and reaction to the epidemic, particularly how it was framed in relation to the war during which it appeared—a war that dominated New Zealand life and media at the time. As historical records such as newspapers and survivor memories indicate, this epidemic became closely intertwined with the war—and yet marginalized by it. I conclude by discussing what these findings suggest about why this epidemic was "forgotten" and what further questions they raise.

Sources and Methods

Individual and household-level data were collected from the non-Māori death registrations from the Registry of Births, Deaths and Marriages held by the Department of Internal Affairs in Wellington. Access permission was granted by the Registrar-General, and the research approved by the University of Auckland Human Participants Ethics Committee (UAHPEC). Access to Māori death registrations was not requested at this time due to different requirements, including Māori consultation to ensure that research is "developed and conducted in a culturally appropriate way and in a way that is responsive to Māori" (UAHPEC, 2017, p. 74). Therefore Māori death registrations were not included at this stage. However, the presence of probable Māori names among the deaths registrations I examined suggests that some Māori who were not identified as such (e.g., those from mixed families) were likely included in this analysis.

The 1916 Census of New Zealand provided population numbers by age, sex, geographic divisions, and ethnicity (European, Māori, and so-called "race aliens"). The *New Zealand Official Yearbook, 1917* provided numbers of polio cases and deaths in 1916, while MacLean (1964) had calculated attack rates and death rates. The US Mortality Statistics 1916 (US Department of Commerce, 1918) provided comparative information (polio deaths by age, sex, and state, as well as population numbers by age and state) allowing for calculation of polio death rates. Statistical tests of this quantitative data included chi-square and Pearson's chi-square.

Historical newspapers, magazines, journals, and parliamentary papers were accessed between September 2017 and February 2018 through the searchable online database Papers Past. Search terms included "infantile paralysis," "poliomyelitis," and in some instances the names of specific individuals or places identified from the initial searches (such as Nurse Bevilaqua, who became a central figure in the epidemic). The articles were surveyed and examined in relation to existing research questions (e.g., any mentions of polio among troops) and for emergent themes. Additional sources include government documents (e.g., Parliamentary records and public health reports), and published and unpublished survivors' and families' recollections in secondary sources (e.g., Ross's 1993 thesis) and, in one case, a personal communication.

1916 by the Numbers

Population

New Zealand's 1916 European Census recorded a population of just over one million, with 35% living in the four major metropolitan areas of Auckland, Wellington (the capital city), Christchurch, and Dunedin (see Fig. 9.1). One-third of the European population was under 15 years of age. The 1916 Census captured a snapshot of a wartime population, with many people not at the usual places of residence; for example, many were recorded either near or in the military training camps on the North Island, while thousands of troops and additional personnel were already deployed overseas.

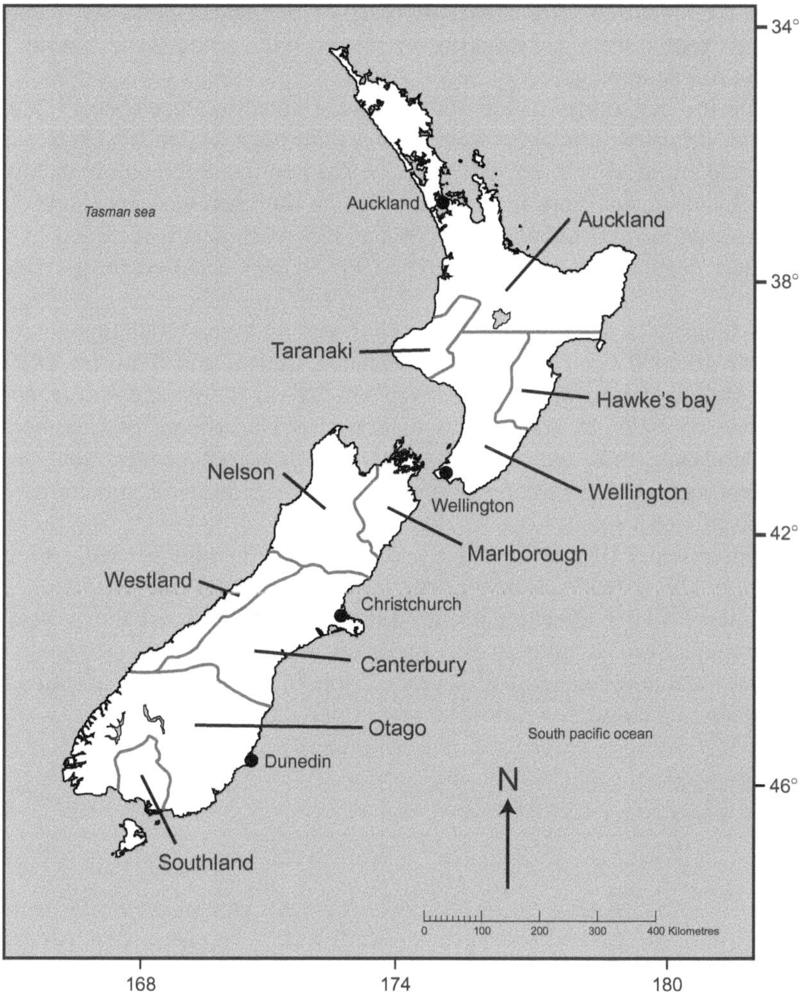

FIGURE 9.1 Map of New Zealand depicting the provincial district divisions and locations of the four major cities (created by Briar Sefton).

The Census noted that 42,666 troops were abroad on Census night (New Zealand Census and Statistics Office, 1920).

Polio Mortality

Polio is an enterovirus spread through contaminated water or food, person-to-person via droplets, or via the fecal-oral route. Polio is typically asymptomatic or causes mild flu-like symptoms, but in a small minority of those infected the virus invades the nervous system and attacks the anterior horn cells of the spinal cord, causing temporary or permanent paralysis. Fatality typically results from encephalitis or issues with respiration, leading to asphyxia or pneumonia.

While the beginnings of the outbreak were noted in December 1915, the epidemic occurred primarily from January through April of 1916, with deaths peaking in March (see Fig. 9.2). Deaths continued through November, including many survivors infected during the summer who succumbed to complications several months later. Of the 125 polio deaths recorded in the non-Māori death registrations in 1916, 106 (84.8%) occurred on the North Island.

New Zealand's polio death rate for 1916 was 11.4 per 100,000 population (13.3 per 100,000 aged 0–49) (New Zealand Census and Statistics Office, 1920). This is comparable to the 1916 US Death Registration Area polio death rate of 10.0 per 100,000 population (US Department of Commerce, 1918). However, since the 1916 US epidemic was largely concentrated along the Atlantic coast, calculation of regional death rates provides a more useful comparison (see Table 9.1).

Children under five years of age had the highest number of deaths of any age group (49 deaths). However, the majority of polio deaths (60.8%) in New Zealand's 1916 epidemic occurred in those aged five and above. Age at death ranged from as little as six weeks up to 49 years, with a median of nine years and an average of 11.4 years. Table 9.2 shows the distribution by age and sex, including sex ratios.

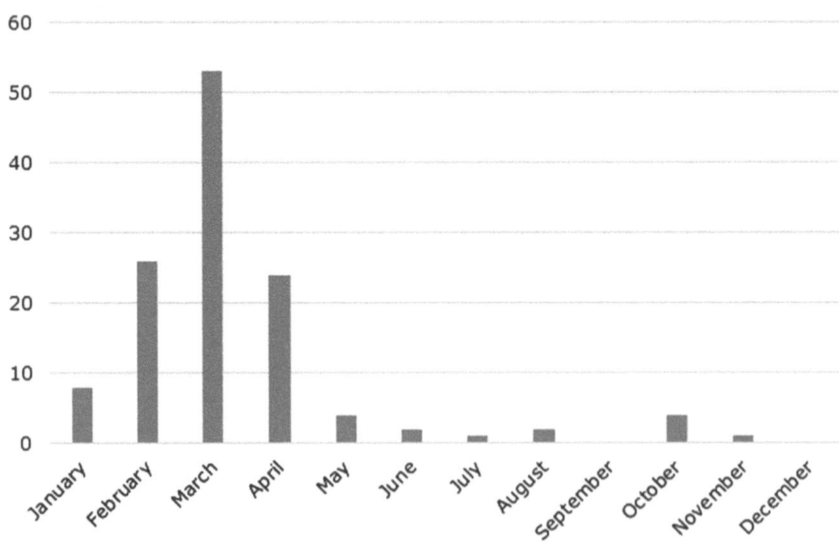

FIGURE 9.2 1916 polio deaths by month. *New Zealand Death Registrations (1916).*

TABLE 9.1 Polio death rates by region for the United States and New Zealand in 1916.

Country	Region (NZ = provincial districts; US = census divisions)	Polio deaths (count)	Population (NZ = census; US = estimated)	Polio death rate per 100,000 pop.
United States[a]	New England (six states)	811	7,156,734	11.3
	Middle Atlantic (three states)	5246	21,743,409	24.1
	South Atlantic (four states out of eight, with D.C. excluded)	258	7,583,039	3.4
	Combined	*6315*	*36,483,182*	*17.3*
NZ[b]	Auckland	62	308,766	20.1
	Taranaki	12	55,925	21.5
	Hawke's Bay	10	54,267	18.4
	Wellington	23	232,114	9.9
	Marlborough	4	16,608	24.1
	Nelson	2	43,251	4.6
	Westland	0	15,502	0.0
	Canterbury	5	181,869	2.7
	Otago–Otago portion	0	131,518	0.0
	Otago–Southland portion	7	59,629	11.7
	Combined (national)	*125*	*1,099,449*	*11.4*
	Combined—districts with zero polio deaths excluded	*125*	*952,429*	*13.1*
	North Island	*107*	*651,072*	*16.4*
	South Island	*18*	*448,377*	*4.0*

[a]*US Dept. of Commerce, Bureau of the Census.* Mortality Statistics 1916. *17th Annual Report. Washington (1918).*
[b]*New Zealand Death Registrations (1916); New Zealand Census (1916).*

TABLE 9.2 Non-Māori polio deaths in New Zealand, 1916.[a]

Age group	Number of deaths	Sex ratio (M:F)
0–4	49	1.9 (32:17)
5–9	17	1.1 (9:8)
10–14	10	1.0 (5:5)
15–19	23	3.6 (18:5)
20–44	25	1.3 (14:11)
45–49	1	–(1:0)
Total	125	1.7 (79:46)

[a]*New Zealand Death Registrations 1916.*

The difference in total male versus female deaths was statistically significant: χ^2 (1125) = 8.712, $P = .003$, $\varphi = .26$. Median age at death was eight years for males and 7.5 years for females. The high sex ratio in the 0–4 age group points to a biological sex-based susceptibility for males, which is seen in many other childhood infectious diseases. A male-biased sex ratio has been consistently (but not universally) reported for polio mortality (see Battles, 2013; Mortimer & Cherry, 2004). Since case fatality increases with age, the slightly older age at death in the males might indicate one source of the higher male mortality, which represents gendered exposure. The highest sex ratio is found in the 15–19 age group, but it is possible this is a chance occurrence due to the relatively small numbers.

MacLean (1964, p. 329, Table 7) provides some breakdown of the polio cases and deaths, including attack rates and death rates (Māori excluded). However, his information is uneven. Percentage distributions of cases and deaths by age combine those aged 20 and above into a single category (20 +). In presenting attack and death rates, though MacLean begins with five-year age groups (0–4, 5–9, and so on), he combines the 15–24-year-olds into one age group, followed by ages 25–34, and ages 35 + . As the military enlistment age in New Zealand during the First World War was 20–44 years, it was necessary to calculate my own age-specific death rates using data from the 1916 Census. For comparison, Table 9.3 displays my calculations alongside MacLean's, for both his age groups and mine.

MacLean's numbers showed a relatively high death rate in his 15–24 age group. However, Table 9.3 shows that after the 0–4 age group, the next highest death rate is found at ages 15–19, with a much lower rate in the 20–44 age group. Therefore the higher death rates were occurring prior to enlistment age.

TABLE 9.3 Polio cases, deaths, and rates per 10,000 population in 1916.

Age group	Cases (%)[a]	Deaths (%)[b]	Attack rate[a]	Death rate (Maori excl.)[a]	Death rate (Maori excl.)[b]
0–4	61.3	**39.2**	43.1	3.94	**3.71**
5–9	17.5	**13.6**	15.8	1.22	**1.38**
10–14	8.2	**8.0**	7.6	0.91	**0.92**
15–19	6.3	**18.4**	4.8		**2.52**
20 +	6.7	**20.8**	1.2		
15–24				1.72	**1.78**
25–34				0.76	**0.88**
35 +				0.07	**0.08**
20–44					**0.59**
45–49					**0.16**
All	100%	**100%**	9.4		**1.33**

Numbers from MacLean (1964) in plain text; numbers from this study in bold text.
[a]*MacLean (1964, p. 329, Table 7):* N_{cases} *= 1018,* N_{deaths} *= 123.*
[b]*New Zealand Death Registrations (1916) (*N_{deaths} *= 125); New Zealand Census (1916).*

Comparing the death rates by sex, the apparently high death rate in the 15–19 age group is mainly the result of male deaths in that age group (Fig. 9.3). It is unclear if this is simply due to chance, however, given the small numbers (18 males, five females in that age group) statistical testing with Pearson chi-square found no evidence of a difference between males and females ($\chi^2 = 4.393$, df = 4, $P = .355$).

This analysis shows that there were few deaths in the enlistment age group. Furthermore, none of the 125 polio death registrations had "soldier" listed as an occupation. This supports historical reports that infantile paralysis did not affect the troops in the training camps (Lawson, 1916).

Polio and the Great War

Impact of the War on the Public Health Response

The war was feared to have had a negative impact on New Zealand's ability to respond to the epidemic. Medical resources, both in terms of funds and personnel, were diverted to the war effort, leaving serious gaps in civilian public health. Just as the polio epidemic was beginning, the *Poverty Bay Herald* carried news from England of worries of a doctor shortage, with warning of the potential danger: "If these young men are all sent away, we

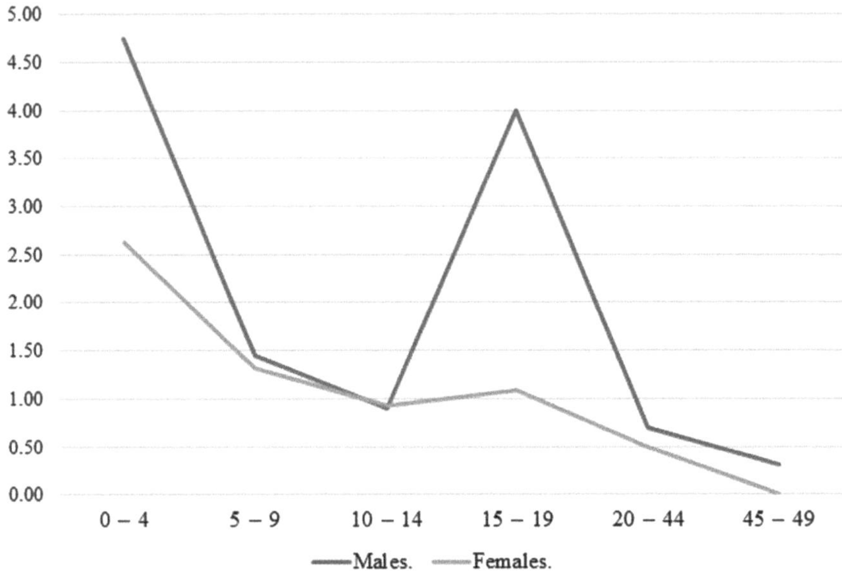

FIGURE 9.3 1916 polio death rate per 10,000 population by age group. *New Zealand Death Registrations (1916); New Zealand Census (1916).*

shall have nobody training but a few women, who will be badly handicapped to cope with any of those epidemics which often occur after a war" ("Shortage of doctors," 1916, p. 10). New Zealand soon felt the effects of similar pressures. As the epidemic took hold, the *New Zealand Tablet* reported that Auckland Hospital had been unsuccessful in its efforts to hire a bacteriologist and that the Inspector-General of Hospitals had advised the Board "to wait until after the war, as most of the best qualified men were now at the front" ("Interprovincial," 1916, p. 36).

The war was also blamed for holding back progress in public health that otherwise would have been implemented as demonstrated in these comments directed toward the Palmerston North Borough Councilors:

> *In view of the epidemic of infantile paralysis now in existence in New Zealand... [t]he suggestion is that the municipality should appoint a medical officer of health to act in conjunction with the lay health officer.... Something on these lines was indicated as necessary by the Hon. R. H. Rhodes when Minister for Public Health, and no doubt, if the war had not intervened, a scheme would have been propounded with a view to this end*
>
> "Wanted – a medical officer" (1916, p. 4).

Sydney Smith, in his report on the epidemic in his health district, lamented that misdiagnosis was a problem and that "unfortunately, we have no opportunity of serologically examining these cases, owing to the absence of monkeys and other facilities" (Smith, 1916, p. 44). New Zealand would not obtain monkeys for medical research on polio until the time of the next major infantile paralysis epidemic in 1925 (Ross, 1993). While I am not able to demonstrate empirically that these diverted resources had a direct effect on epidemic control and patient survival, the lack of available resources was clearly a concern for contemporary public health officials whose work came second to military needs.

Grief Upon Grief: Mourning Polio Victims in Wartime

> *Death, the reaper, has not been content with his harvest on the battlefields of Europe*
>
> "The country" (1916, p. 27).

Newspapers and other periodicals reveal glimpses of how the polio epidemic became enmeshed with people's experiences of the war. The epidemic began just as the Gallipoli campaign ended, with its resultant loss of 2721 New Zealanders. While sending their sons (and often daughters) overseas with high risk of death, they were finding home was not safe either. In the *Waiapu Church Gazette*, Reverend J. Hobbs observed this upon the death of one of his parishioners:

> *During the year ending last June only two funerals were recorded; since then we have already had nine of our friends laid in the grave. The last, and one specially touching, was that of a boy of fifteen, Philip Bishoprick, the son of our lay reader who was at his work in the Post Office on Tuesday, carried away with infantile paralysis on Friday, and laid in the grave on Sunday afternoon. The sudden shock warned parents forcibly that the epidemic might at any moment take their own healthy boys. The fact that the bereaved had only the last week bidden "farewell" to two other sons leaving for Trentham [the military training camp near Wellington], swelled the public sympathy*
>
> Hobbs (1916, p. 12).

In another example, Timothy John McCarthy's obituary in the *New Zealand Tablet* (an Irish Catholic periodical) mentions his brother being "in camp"—presumably in a military training camp ("Kaponga–Eltham," 1916, p. 27). The gendered emphasis on boys as potential polio victims, rather than both boys and girls, seems to reflect the high risk to the men in the war. It might also reflect the high sex ratio of polio deaths in this epidemic.

Not only did those who died of polio in 1916 leave behind grieving families and friends, but those who survived the disease often faced a long convalescence and adjustment to lasting paralysis. With 1018 notified cases and 125 deaths, the epidemic left behind nearly 900 polio survivors (at least). New Zealand's nursing journal *Kai Tiaki* was keenly aware of this, observing that "it is after the acute time of the epidemic that the results are most apparent, and that the convalescent victims begin to show the deformities left by this dread disease" ("Infantile paralysis," 1916b, p. 40).

"Hunnish Plots and Intrigues": Fear, Blame, and Anti-German Paranoia

Unlike during the 1918 flu pandemic, there is no evidence that news of either the polio epidemic in New Zealand, or the one that followed in the United States, was censored. The newspaper coverage of the 1916 epidemic was broadly similar in terms of placement and prominence to that of the 1914 outbreak, but somewhat more extensive—as might be expected from an epidemic concentrated in the more populous North Island. The public awareness of the epidemic was cited as one reason the disease was feared out of proportion to its impact: "From New York to Auckland the telegraphs and cables have kept us advised as to the daily toll of victims, in a way which was quite unknown formerly" ("Our babies," 1916, p. 10).

Fears of polio (an invisible enemy at home) became entangled with fears of the military enemy abroad. The Women's Anti-German League was among the first to attribute the epidemic to the actions of enemy forces—reported with some skepticism and amusement in the *Otago Witness*:

> *[T]hey have a notion in their hearts that the epidemic of infantile paralysis now in Auckland, or said to be, is caused by the machinations of German scientific persons sent here for the purpose by the Kaiser to prevent the strength of the New Zealand armies of the future from growing formidable. They have a prodigious respect for the intellectual and malevolent powers of the German Huns"*
>
> "Table talk" (1916, p. 66).

The prospect of bioterrorism seems to have been a recurring theme in the newspapers. *The Colonist* reported the comments of John Payne, then a Member of Parliament for Grey Lynn (Auckland), that "outbreaks of cerebro-spinal meningitis in camp and infantile paralysis all over the country lent color to the suspicion that Germans intended to liberate disease cultures" ("News of the day," 1916, p. 4). Further examples were reported in the *Observer* in May, the correspondent taking a skeptical stance on a report that a foreign doctor was spreading polio germs via his car's exhaust pipe and the suggestion that the epidemic was caused by poison gas drifting all the way from the battlefields of Europe ("The fretful porcupine," 1916). In its "It is Town Talk" column, comprised of brief bits of mixed news and gossip, the *Free Lance* included the snippet: "that on the other side they are blaming the Huns for the prevalence of cerebro-spinal meningitis. Can our own mysterious infantile paralysis be a further propagation of Hun kultur?" ("It is Town Talk," 1916, p. 22). It is not clear what is meant by "the other side"—perhaps Britain or continental Europe. Francis (2014) identifies the *Observer* and *Free Lance* as particularly vehement in their anti-German rhetoric during the war, leading calls for the internment of German-born residents. Whether the rumors and conspiracies in New Zealand during this epidemic were inspired from similar stories elsewhere is uncertain; in any event, such ideas were not unique.

In late 1916, a full year after New Zealand's polio epidemic began, the story of an incident in a suburb of Christchurch was carried with varying levels of detail in multiple newspapers throughout the country. The *Sun*'s report was perhaps the most embellished and editorialized—not unexpected, as the *Sun* was known for its "energetic" reporting ("The Sun," 2018)—but does not factually differ from the other papers' reports:

> *In these days of strife and strain the police are exercising even more than their usual vigilance in order that this outpost of Empire might be rendered immune from Hunnish plots and intrigues. It was reported to them the other day that two German spies had been seen liberating in St. Albans Park, flies infected with the germs of infantile paralysis*
>
> "Local and general" (1916, p. 15).

This story seemed to bear out the earlier fears of John Payne. However, it turned out that the "spies" were members of the local Microscopical Society collecting fly specimens for classification purposes. That polio germs should be singled out in this mistaken incident of bioterrorism, suggests that the fear of that disease generated by the previous summer's epidemic was still strong.

Infantile Paralysis as Threat to the State

Elsewhere in the British Empire, the First World War (like the Boer War before it) heightened "imperialist anxiety" and focused attention on infant and child health—particularly infant mortality—as the massive loss of life and high rates of rejection of potential troops as physically unfit was often linked to their childhood health (Walsh, 2017, p. 17; see also Dwork, 1987; Sutherland, 2000). Overall, in New Zealand, there was seemingly little politicization of the infantile paralysis epidemic—unlike the overt politicization of infant mortality in Ireland in the First World War described by Walsh (2017). There were passing mentions in the newspapers of instances in which polio could be cited as affecting troop recruitment; one article in the *Dominion* reported that a 36-year-old Auckland man had been rejected from the New Zealand forces due to the lasting effects of polio infection some 30 years earlier ("Camps and the men," 1916, p. 6).

Yet a degree of imperialistic or nationalistic baby-saving rhetoric can be found in the coverage of the epidemic—such as in the writing related to the four-month training tour of Miss Florence Bevilaqua, and controversy surrounding the implementation (or lack thereof) of her methods (see "Infantile paralysis," 1916a; "Rival systems," 1916). Physical therapy was identified early on as a key element in polio rehabilitation and prevention of deformity, and Bevilaqua, a Russian/Australian nurse-masseuse, was brought to New Zealand by the government for several months to provide training in the so-called "Mackenzie method." This method, named after Dr. William Mackenzie of Melbourne, combined splinting, hot packs, and passive exercises ("Almost a miracle," 1916; for more see Simpson, 1993). Bevilaqua was a "forceful personality" who attracted a fair amount of press interest (Maclean, 1932, p. 121). She described her child polio patients as "the little children we so need, and must be got well" ("Almost a miracle," 1916, p. 7). An account of a training session at Wellington Hospital contains a somewhat more direct statement that polio survivors, if cured, would make "fine available citizens" and so "in view of the present necessity for building up the nation in every possible way, to make up for the wastage caused by the war, facilities should certainly be given for skilled help and education" (Holmes, 1916, p. 9).

Rehabilitating Wounded Soldiers and Polio Survivors—and Rehabilitating Public Opinion?

> *The war has left many legacies, mostly bad, but there are some good ones*
>
> "The crippled child" (1921, p. 10).

The explicit linkages made between the epidemic and the war were not only about the children themselves as future soldiers valuable to the State, but also in how expertise and infrastructure related to the rehabilitation of polio survivors might be put to use in caring for the war wounded, and vice versa. For example, an article in *Kai Tiaki* talks about how the polio epidemic had led to an increase in interest in massage (though Bevilaqua repeatedly clarified that her treatment was not massage, but rather a method of isolating and exercising specific muscles) and notes that this knowledge and experience might be useful in the treatment of wounded returned soldiers ("Massage," 1916). Furthermore, as military hospitals were transitioned to civilian use after the war, military orthopedic expertise was turned to the needs of polio survivors and other "cripples." In discussing the treatment at Trentham military hospital of survivors of the 1916 epidemic, one *Press* article declares:

> *This is, however, but the beginning of a great work for the welfare of children, which deserves every support from the public and the State. To make out of poor human fragments, as it were, useful citizens in the community is a noble service to humanity, to which Colonel Carbery and his staff may well be proud to devote their lives.*
>
> "The crippled child" (1921, p. 10).

Demonstrating how much it was doing for both wounded troops and child infantile paralysis survivors was an opportunity for the government to rehabilitate its own tarnished image in the wake of public criticism of its handling of the epidemic and its aftermath.

In later 1916, as news of the New York polio epidemic kept the disease in the public's minds, an article in the *Free Lance* noted the worry about the potential for another polio epidemic the next summer and the need for continuing care of current polio survivors, calling for more training in polio rehabilitation ("Social gossip," 1916). Controversy erupted following a letter Bevilaqua wrote to the Wellington Hospital Board suggesting that they were failing in their duties regarding polio survivor rehabilitation ("Rival systems," 1916). However, this issue extended far beyond one hospital. One man wrote to the *Hawera and Normanby Star* to express his frustration:

> *A nephew of mine contracted the above fell disease and was taken to the hospital.... He was eventually, after about two months, sent home with a hand contorted, feet, toes, and legs likewise, and both legs completely paralysed.... All this could have been avoided the expert says, if his limbs had been put absolutely at rest in the first place, and exercises at the proper time given, and the result would have been that he would be walking about now.... There may be other such cases as this boy for all I know, and perhaps others to come, so it behoves the Board, if they have not already done so, to get a move on and keep pace with what they are on the Board for*
>
> Hughes (1916, p. 8).

Ross (1993) describes a number of cases in which hospital treatment was either denied in favor of home treatment, including that of a baby turned away from Auckland Hospital, or delayed for years. Many polio survivors and their families were disappointed by the treatment available (and availability of funding for it) and by the results. Alice from Pukekawa, quoted earlier, received physiotherapy at a clinic in Auckland and later, more than four years after the epidemic, spent six months in Rotorua at the King George V Hospital alongside dozens of other polio survivors—unfortunately in her case without much apparent effect (Darragh, 1994).

In 1920 and 1921 a series of newspaper stories drew attention to polio survivors from the 1916 epidemic receiving treatment at Rotorua and Trentham military hospitals. The treatment was not for profit, but there were fees. An article in the *Auckland Star* featured an extensive discussion with Wesley Spragg, a member of the Prices Investigation Tribunal who was at Rotorua in the course of an inquiry into the cost of orthopedic boots; Spragg appeared to be chastising parents for not taking up the opportunity to have their children receive rehabilitative treatment ("Crippled for life," 1920, p. 5). The article carried the subheadline: "Rotorua opens the door to hope – and no one knocks." The reporter declared, "it is evident that someone is to blame for the want of proper publicity." The following day, the same paper published a response from a father featuring the phrase, "knocking hard at the door of hope, but no one opens," in which he described his frustrated attempts to access such treatment for his child ("Crippled children," 1920, p. 5). The *Star* reporter defended Spragg and other officials, noting that Auckland General Hospital was also an option for treatment and that Rotorua's facilities were intended primarily for those from more rural areas.

A further article in January 1921 in the *Ashburton Guardian* covered an Auckland Hospital Board meeting at which greater action on the part of the national government was urged, in order to get more children sent to treatment at Rotorua ("Infantile paralysis," 1921). While the government appeared keen to downplay concerns and to stress that treatment was available, is not clear to what extent military needs took precedence and delayed treatment for polio survivors that otherwise might have happened sooner. It seemed that once the word was out about availability of spaces at Rotorua, those beds quickly filled; by May 1921, the *Auckland Star* noted that the wards were full, with a waiting list ("To help the children," 1921). The article explained that the waiting list could not be helped because "there are so many military patients being treated at present, that accommodation cannot be found for additional children" ("To help the children," 1921, p. 17).

The rehabilitation of polio survivors and wounded soldiers at the same sites shaped survivors' experiences in positive ways. For example, Julie Park, whose father Roy Mason contracted polio in Pihama, southern Taranaki in March 1916 at about age 10, recalls her father recounting his experience of undergoing rehabilitation treatment alongside wounded returned soldiers. He was told by the doctors that he would never walk again, but the returned men told him "bugger that!" and built him a set of parallel bars for walking practice; they encouraged and cheered him on as he made the effort to swing his legs forward (Park, personal communication, 2018). Heart-warming stories of soldier and child patient interactions appeared in the press, such as that of an elaborate dollhouse made by a soldier as a Christmas gift for the child polio patients at Trentham ("Local and general," 1921). The arrangement was depicted as one of mutual benefit. One *Press* article writer concluded:

> *so far as Trentham is concerned, it must be said that the presence of the children has had a most beneficial influence on the soldier-patients in taking them out of themselves in the contemplation of others' troubles. To the nurses it has added a new interest to their professional life*
>
> "The crippled child" (1921, p. 10).

The *Auckland Star* described "the sad plight of these little sufferers... whose present and future existence is very black" but who were fortunate because "the Government, on realizing this, decided to do all that was possible to bring back health and strength to the little ones" ("Little victims of infantile paralysis," 1921, p. 17). This appeared beside a prominent spread of seven photographs depicted smiling children receiving treatment at Rotorua ("Little victims of infantile paralysis," 1921). These photos also appeared in the *New Zealand Farmer* that July and in *Kai Tiaki* that October ("King George V Hospital, Rotorua," 1921). Frank Hockly, Member of Parliament for Rotorua, stood in Parliament on October 21, 1921 to pay "a tribute to the Government on the work being done at Rotorua for sick and crippled children suffering from infantile paralysis" (New Zealand Legislative Council and House of Representatives, 1921, p. 716). The positive press coverage would have been much welcomed by the government in the face of mounting public pressure over postwar economic troubles and spending cuts (see Clarke, 2007).

Discussion and Future Directions

This chapter has addressed the marginalization and historical forgetting of New Zealand's 1916 polio epidemic by examining the biological and social connections between the epidemic and the First World War. Biologically, historical sources state (both explicitly and by omission) that there were no outbreaks of infantile paralysis in the training camps—though cerebro-spinal meningitis did make an appearance. My investigation of the individual death registrations not only supports this but also shows a high sex ratio in these deaths. I suggest that this demographic pattern of mortality affected how the war was interpretively and experientially linked with the disease. The prevalence of older children and adolescents, particularly boys, among the epidemic's victims intersected with existing anxieties, many of which were heightened and exacerbated by the war, to shape the ways in which people responded to the epidemic and its resulting deaths. I identified and examined several of these here and will discuss them further, suggesting directions for future research.

In terms of biological links between the 1916 epidemic and the First World War, Gear (1952) states that polio was more prevalent during both World Wars and blames the South African epidemics of 1918 and 1944–45 on troops returning from the Middle East. Though this research has found no evidence of polio among New Zealand's troops in 1916, it has not investigated the possibility that the war contributed to the introduction of the virus into the country, perhaps a particularly virulent strain, and that the mass movements of people around New Zealand during the war (i.e., as families accompanied enlisted men to the training camp sites) contributed to its spread. Future work might be able to shed light on this possibility.

The negative civilian health impacts of the diversion of resources to the war effort have been examined in relation to the 1918 flu by several authors (e.g., Zylberman, 2003). However, here we have seen that there were positive effects as well, insofar as the response to the polio epidemic and its aftermath coincided with military-related goals such as the rehabilitation of injured troops and the safeguarding of a supply of future soldiers.

The patterns of blame for the spread of the disease in the first place and inadequate response to survivors' needs afterward contrast with those observed elsewhere. Rogers (1992) describes how the poor, particularly poor Italian immigrants, were scapegoated during the 1916 New York polio epidemic. Blaming of the poor, immigrants, and other marginalized groups within a society is such a common theme in epidemics throughout history that it has come to be expected. Similar to Jones's (2008) findings for the 1918 flu epidemic in Winnipeg, Canada, even though soldiers were suspected of spreading the disease, they did not become scapegoats—in the First World War, soldiers were revered. In New Zealand, rather than blame being directed primarily *inwards*, it was cast *outwards* at the wartime enemy, the Germans (but including the potential so-called "enemy within"), and, similar to what Washer (2010, p. 90) demonstrated regarding Britain's "Mad Cow" epidemic, *upwards* at governmental authorities. However, my research has not indicated how ethnic Germans living in New Zealand at this time were affected by this, in addition to how they were impacted by the war in general and the activities of groups such as the Women's Anti-German League (see Francis, 2012), and this topic merits investigation.

The connection between polio survivors (as "crippled" children) and the troops described here is also a theme in Koven's (1994) work on disabled children and wounded soldiers in Great Britain during the First World War. As in New Zealand, these two groups were brought together at specific facilities, and the orthopedic technology developed for one group was applied to the other (Koven, 1994). Koven also demonstrates the rhetorical and representational convergences between the "crippled warriors" and the "warrior cripples" (1994, p. 1193). Similarly the memoirs of survivors of the polio epidemics during the Second World War clearly describe how their experiences were directly linked with that war (see, e.g., Kriegal, 1991). War metaphors are salient in descriptions of survivors' experiences both during the Second World War and the subsequent Cold War period (see, e.g., Serotte, 2003; Sheed, 1999; Shell, 2005; Westbrook, 1996). Further work might explore these connections in other settings where wartime epidemics similarly occurred.

These findings regarding New Zealand's 1916 polio epidemic align in many aspects with those for the 1918 flu pandemic. For example, Spinney (2017, p. 293) observes that the war and the flu were "conflated or confounded" in multiple ways—such as in people's beliefs and fears that the flu was caused by biowarfare. The aforementioned investigation also yields some clues as to the reasons for the lack of memorialization of the epidemic or the lack of attention to it by historians and others since, which combined with the expanding literature on the 1918 flu pandemic provides some possible explanations. Among these is the idea that since the epidemic did not directly impact the military (i.e., no outbreak among enlisted troops), it received much less attention from authorities at the time and from historians since. Its impact was also subsumed by the casualties of the war and the mass morbidity and mortality from the 1918 flu—which itself was overshadowed by those military losses, its own marginalization and "forgetting" exacerbated by so many public memorial ceremonies and monuments to fallen soldiers (Honigsbaum, 2014). Furthermore, as suggested regarding the similar "forgetting" of the 1918 flu, it did not serve a purpose for the government to commemorate it (see Byerly, 2005; Youde, 2017). Indeed, there was considerable public criticism of the government and health boards for not doing enough by way of polio survivors' access to treatment. This criticism would likely have been especially unwelcome at a time when the losses of the war weighed heavily on those in positions of power.

In conclusion, this paper contributes to our understanding of what gets centered versus marginalized, and remembered versus forgotten. It supports the arguments advanced based on examinations of the 1918 flu pandemic that a lack of collective remembrance can be linked to: the demographic characteristics of the losses, the conflation of the event with the wider wartime experience, and the political purposes that remembrance would serve. The epidemic and its victims were marginalized except when and where they had relevance to the State. This marginalization took the form of under-resourcing of public health facilities during the war and restricted access to rehabilitative treatment, as child polio patients entered orthopedic wards only after soldiers had been taken care of. It also took the form of public expressions of grief and fear being shaped by the wartime context to such an extent that the epidemic and its victims themselves were no longer the focus—what mattered was their relevance to the war (and therefore the State). This helps us to explain why the epidemic was subsequently also "forgotten" in a public sense. Drawing from scholarship on the "forgetting" of the 1918 flu, I suggest first that the government would have been reluctant to memorialize the epidemic except in ways that reflected well upon itself, and that the epidemic was tied to a fair amount of criticism and bitterness toward the government. Second, I suggest that memories of the 1916 infantile paralysis epidemic would have been closely bound to memories of the war—and the memorialization of the war was overwhelming, leaving little room for memorialization of anything else (see Rice, 2005 regarding the lack of memorialization of the 1918 flu in New Zealand).

This research thus far focused on the Pākehā (NZ European) records. While New Zealand's first major polio epidemic has been forgotten and marginalized in historical memory, far more marginalized were, and are, the Māori affected by polio, about whom very little has been written. How was polio experienced by Māori individuals, families, and communities? I hope that future work, in collaboration and consultation with Māori, might address this.

References

Almost a miracle. (1916, August 5). *North Otago Times*. Retrieved from <http://paperspast.natlib.govt.nz/newspapers/NOT19160805.2.54>.

Battles, H. T. (2013). Examining mortality patterns in the epidemic emergence of poliomyelitis in southern Ontario, Canada (1900–1937). Unpublished doctoral dissertation. McMaster University, Hamilton, ON, Canada.

Buttersworth, K. P. (Ed.), (1994). *Mind over muscle: Surviving polio in New Zealand*. Palmerston North: The Dunmore Press.

Byerly, C. R. (2005). *Fever of war: The influenza epidemic in the U.S. Army during World War I*. New York: New York University Press.

Camps and the men. (1916, March 30). *The Dominion*. Retrieved from <http://paperspast.natlib.govt.nz/newspapers/DOM19160330.2.39>.

Clarke, S. (2007). Return, repatriation, remembrance and the Returned Soldiers' Association. In J. Crawford, & I. McGibbon (Eds.), *New Zealand's great war: New Zealand, the allies and the First World War* (pp. 157–180). Auckland: Exisle Publishing.

Hughes, D. J. (1916, September 13). Correspondence. Hawera hospital and infantile paralysis. *Hawera & Normanby Star*. Retrieved from <http://paperspast.natlib.govt.nz/newspapers/HNS19160913.2.39>.

Crippled children. (1920, October 14). *Auckland Star*. Retrieved from <https://paperspast.natlib.govt.nz/newspapers/AS19201014.2.58>.

Crippled for life. (1920, October 13). *Auckland Star*. Retrieved from <http://paperspast.natlib.govt.nz/newspapers/AS19201013.2.51>.

Crosby, A. W. (2003). *America's forgotten pandemic: The influenza of 1918*. Cambridge: Cambridge University Press.

Darragh, A. (1994). Alice's story: A full life. In K. P. Butterworth (Ed.), *Mind over muscle: Surviving polio in New Zealand* (pp. 29–35). Palmerston North: The Dunmore Press.

Dwork, D. (1987). *War is good for babies and other young children: A history of the infant and child welfare movement in England 1898–1918*. London: Tavistock.

Francis, A. (2012). 'To be truly British we must be anti-German': New Zealand, enemy aliens and the Great War experience, 1914–1919. Oxford: Peter Lang.

Francis, A. (2014). From 'proven worthy settlers' to 'lawless Hunnish brutes': Germans in New Zealand during the Great War. In P. Payani (Ed.), *Germans as minorities during the First World War: A global comparative perspective* (pp. 289–309). Abington: Routledge.

Gear, J. (1952). Immunity to poliomyelitis. *Annals of Internal Medicine*, *37*(1), 1–22.

Hobbs, J. (1916, March 1). Te Puke. *Waiapu Church Gazette*. Retrieved from <https://paperspast.natlib.govt.nz/periodicals/WCHG19160301.2.15.3>.

Holmes, C. (1916, August 16). Women in print. *Evening Post*. Retrieved from <http://paperspast.natlib.govt.nz/newspapers/EP19160816.2.143>.

Honigsbaum, M. (2014). *A history of the great influenza pandemics*. London: I. B. Tauris.

Infantile Paralysis. (1916a, August 18). *New Zealand Times*. Retrieved from <http://paperspast.natlib.govt.nz/newspapers/NZTIM19160818.2.65>.

Infantile Paralysis. (1916b, July 1). *Kai Tiaki*. Retrieved from <http://paperspast.natlib.govt.nz/periodicals/KT19160701.2.33>.

Infantile paralysis: an Auckland discussion. (1921, January 21). *Ashburton Guardian*. Retrieved from <http://paperspast.natlib.govt.nz/newspapers/AG19210120.2.16.1>.

Interprovincial. (1916, February 24). *New Zealand Tablet*. Retrieved from <http://paperspast.natlib.govt.nz/periodicals/NZT19160224.2.47>.

It is Town Talk. (1916, March 10). *Free Lance*. Retrieved from <http://paperspast.natlib.govt.nz/newspapers/NZFL19160310.2.52>.

Jones, E. W. (2008). *Influenza 1918: Disease, death, and struggle in Winnipeg*. Toronto: University of Toronto Press.

Kaponga—Eltham. (1916, March 30). *New Zealand Tablet*. Retrieved from <http://paperspast.natlib.govt.nz/periodicals/NZT19160330.2.33>.

King George V Hospital, Rotorua. (1921, October 1). *Kai Tiaki*. Retrieved from <http://paperspast.natlib.govt.nz/periodicals/KT19211001.2.21>.

Koven, S. (1994). Remembering and dismemberment: Crippled children, wounded soldiers, and the Great War in Great Britain. *American Historical Review*, *99*(4), 1167–1202.

Kriegal, L. (1991). *Falling into life*. San Francisco: North Point.

Lawson, W. (1916, June 8). Spinal meningitis. *Auckland Star*. Retrieved from <http://paperspast.natlib.govt.nz/newspapers/AS19160608.2.76>.

Little victims of infantile paralysis under treatment at Rotorua. (1921, May 14). *Auckland Star*. Retrieved from <http://paperspast.natlib.govt.nz/newspapers/AS19210514.2.127.1>.

Local and general. (1916, December 21). *The Sun*. Retrieved from <http://paperspast.natlib.govt.nz/newspapers/SUNCH19161221.2.108>.

Local and general. (1921, January 8). *Evening Post*. Retrieved from <http://paperspast.natlib.govt.nz/newspapers/EP19210108.2.25>.

MacLean, F. S. (1964). *Challenge for health: A history of public health in New Zealand*. Wellington: Government Printer.

Maclean, H. (1932). *Nursing in New Zealand: History and reminiscences*. Wellington: Tolan Printing Co.

Massage. (1916, July 1). *Kai Tiaki*. Retrieved from <http://paperspast.natlib.govt.nz/periodicals/KT19160701.2.34>.

Mortimer, E. A., & Cherry, J. (2004). Epidemiology of infectious diseases. In R. D. Feigin, J. Cherry, G. J. Demmler-Harrison, & S. L. Kaplan (Eds.), *Textbook of pediatric infectious diseases* (Vol. 1, pp. 114–139). Philadelphia: Elsevier.

New Zealand Census and Statistics Office. (1920). *New Zealand Census, 1916*. Retrieved from <https://www3.stats.govt.nz/historic_publications/1916-census/Report%20on%20Results%20of%20Census%201916/1916-report-results-census%20.html>.

New Zealand Dept. of Public Health, Hospitals, and Charitable Aid. (1916). Report on public health, hospitals and charitable aid. In *Appendices to the journals of the House of Representatives*. Retrieved from <http://paperspast.natlib.govt.nz/parliamentary/AJHR1916-I.2.2.5.44>

New Zealand Legislative Council and House of Representatives. (1921). *Parliamentary debates. Third session, twentieth parliament. Vol. 191. 22 September–2 November 1921*. Wellington: Government Printer.

News of the day. (1916, April 11). *The Colonist*. Retrieved from <http://paperspast.natlib.govt.nz/newspapers/TC19160411.2.22>.

Our babies. (1916, December 16). *Manawatu Standard*. Retrieved from <http://paperspast.natlib.govt.nz/newspapers/MS19161216.2.61>.

Oxford, J. S., Sefton, A., Innes, W., Daniels, R. S., & Johnson, N. P. (2002). World War I may have allowed the emergence of Spanish influenza. *Lancet Infectious Diseases*, *2*, 111–114.

Phillips, H. (2014). The recent wave of 'Spanish' flu historiography. *Social History of Medicine*, *27*(4), 789–808.

Rice, G. (2005). *Black November: The 1918 influenza pandemic in New Zealand* (2nd ed.). Canterbury, NZ: Canterbury University Press.

Rival Systems. (1916, August 18). *The Sun*. Retrieved from <http://paperspast.natlib.govt.nz/newspapers/SUNCH19160818.2.16>.

Rogers, N. (1992). *Dirt and disease: Polio before FDR*. New Brunswick, NJ: Rutgers University Press.

Ross, J. C. (1993). A history of poliomyelitis in New Zealand. Unpublished masters dissertation. University of Canterbury, New Zealand.

Serotte, B. (2003). Contagious. *Fourth Genre: Explorations in Nonfiction*, *5*(1), 118–135.

Sheed, W. (1999). *In love with daylight: A memoir of recovery*. New York: Akadine Press.

Shell, M. (2005). *Polio and its aftermath: The paralysis of culture*. Cambridge: Harvard University Press.

Shortage of doctors. (1916, January 8). *Poverty Bay Herald*. Retrieved from <http://paperspast.natlib.govt.nz/newspapers/PBH19160108.2.73.5>.

Simpson, D. J. (1993). "A persistent cloud on the human horizon": Polio in the Auckland Region 1925–1962. Unpublished masters dissertation. University of Auckland, New Zealand.

Smallman-Raynor, M. R., Cliff, A. D., Trevelyan, B., Nettleton, C., & Sneddon, S. (2006). *Poliomyelitis: A world geography. Emergence to eradication*. Oxford: Oxford University Press.

Smith, S. (1916). *Infantile paralysis in the Wellington Health District, New Zealand*. Wellington: Government Printer.

Social gossip. (1916, August 25). *Free Lance*. Retrieved from <http://paperspast.natlib.govt.nz/newspapers/NZFL19160825.2.38>.

Social gossip. (1916, February 18). *Free Lance*. Retrieved from <http://paperspast.natlib.govt.nz/newspapers/NZFL19160218.2.24>.

Spinney, L. (2017). *Pale rider: The Spanish Flu of 1918 and how it changed the world*. London: Jonathan Cape.

Sutherland, N. (2000). *Children in English-Canadian society: Framing the 20th-century consensus*. Waterloo: Wilfrid Laurier University Press.

Table talk. (1916, February 16). *Otago Witness*. Retrieved from <http://paperspast.natlib.govt.nz/newspapers/OW19160216.2.115.92.1>.

The country. (1916, June 14). *Otago Witness*. Retrieved from <http://paperspast.natlib.govt.nz/newspapers/OW19160614.2.79>.

The crippled child. (1921, March 29). *The Press*. Retrieved from <http://paperspast.natlib.govt.nz/newspapers/CHP19210329.2.70>.

The Duncan Family with Hunt, V., & McCrystal, J. (2011). *Otiwhiti station: The story of a hill country station and pioneering polio hospital*. Auckland: Random House.

The fretful porcupine. (1916, May 13). *Observer*. Retrieved from <http://paperspast.natlib.govt.nz/newspapers/TO19160513.2.25>.

The Sun. (2018). *Papers Past*. Retrieved from <http://paperspast.natlib.govt.nz/newspapers/sun>.

To help the children. (1921, May 14). *Auckland Star*. Retrieved from <http://paperspast.natlib.govt.nz/newspapers/AS19210514.2.126>.

UAHPEC. (2017). *Applicants' reference manual*. Retrieved from <https://cdn.auckland.ac.nz/assets/HumanEthics/Applicants%20Reference%20Manual.pdf>.

US Department of Commerce, Bureau of the Census. (1918). *Mortality statistics, 1916*. Washington: Government Printing Office, Seventeenth Annual Report.

Walsh, F. (2017). 'Every human life is a national importance': The impact of the First World War on attitudes to material and infant health. In D. Durnin, & I. Miller (Eds.), *Medicine, health and Irish experiences of conflict, 1914–45* (pp. 15–30). Manchester: Manchester University Press.

Wanted – a medical officer. (1916, March 9). *Manawatu Standard*. Retrieved from <http://paperspast.natlib.govt.nz/newspapers/MS19160309.2.13>.

Washer, P. (2010). *Emerging infectious diseases and society*. Basingstoke: Palgrave Macmillan.

Westbrook, M. T. (1996). Early memories of having polio: survivors' memories versus the official myths. In *Paper presented at the first Australian international post-polio conference, "Living with the Late Affects of Polio,"* Sydney, November 1996. Retrieved from <http://www.poliosurvivorsnetwork.org.uk/archive/lincolnshire/library/westbrook/mw1601.html>.

Winter, J. M. (2006). *Remembering war: The Great War between memory and history in the twentieth century*. Ann Arbor: Yale University Press.

Youde, J. (2017). Covering the cough? Memory, remembrance, and influenza amnesia. *Australian Journal of Politics and History, 63*(3), 357–368.

Zylberman, P. (2003). A holocaust in a holocaust: The Great War and the 1918 'Spanish' influenza epidemic in France. In H. Phillips, & D. Killgray (Eds.), *The Spanish influenza pandemic of 1918–19: New perspectives* (pp. 191–201). London: Routledge.

Chapter 10

Exploring the effects of structural inequality in an individual from 19th-century Chicago

Shelby L. Doubek[1,2] and Anne Grauer[1]

[1]*Department of Anthropology, Loyola University, Chicago, IL, United States,* [2]*Department of Anthropology, Field Museum of Natural History, Chicago, IL, United States*

Chapter Outline

Introduction

Human skeletons offer extraordinary insight into the past. The presence of disease and injury, the effects of environment, the ways humans used their bodies throughout life, and aspects of diet and nutrition may be evaluated through careful assessment of skeletal remains. Importantly, aspects of social interaction can also be inferred. Compendia by Baadsgaard, Boutin, and Buikstra (2011) and Agarwal and Glencross (2011), for instance, highlight research seeking to explore complex social interactions and aspects of human agency and identity in the past through the analysis of human remains. These studies find great success in focusing on the life of a single individual, an approach referred to as osteobiographical. Here, individual-level assessments are prioritized in order to develop an intimate narrative about life in the past, rather than aggregating data on a larger population. Furthermore, osteobiographies seek to move beyond simple description by exploring social identity linked to cultural belief and behaviors, and socio-economic and political structures that create differential access to resources, oppression,

Bioarchaeology of Marginalized People. DOI: https://doi.org/10.1016/B978-0-12-815224-9.00010-5

and inequality (Agarwal & Glencross, 2011; Gowland & Knüsel, 2006; Knudson & Stojanowski, 2008, 2009; Sofaer, 2006; Stodder & Palkovich, 2012). These social factors leave indelible traces on the body as pathological conditions, traumatic injuries, and as ante and postmortem body modification (Martin & Harrod, 2016; Martin, Harrod, & Pérez, 2013). Examining the social context of an individual's life and death through skeletal analysis can help identify the presence and ramifications of marginalization, a "complex and disputatious process by means of which certain people and ideas are privileged over others at any given time" (Tucker, 1990, p. 7). Marginalization can manifest as restriction or exclusion from social, economic, cultural, or political resources, and can lead to structural violence, whereby entrenched social structures harm individuals or groups (Farmer, Nizeye, Stulac, & Keshavjee, 2006; Nystrom, 2014).

In the 19th-century United States, the poor, mentally ill, the incarcerated, immigrants, African Americans, and Native Americans were just a few of the underprivileged groups to suffer the negative effects of marginalization. Individuals of Asian origin also experienced harmful differential treatment, isolating them from resources and restricting their legal rights. The immigration of Asian populations to the United States was well-established by the mid-19th century, with the majority settling in California and the Kingdom of Hawaii (Voss & Allen, 2008). Most immigrants were adult males, often farmers from Guangdong, a Southeastern province of China, specifically from areas surrounding the Pearl River delta (Mei, 1979; Voss & Allen, 2008). These areas sat near established seaports and suffered from slow industrial development. They offered few viable alternatives for work and contributed to increasingly impoverished populations (Mei, 1979). Seeking to escape economic and political turmoil, a steady flow of laborers left Southeast Asia for the United States.

In the United States, the start of the California Gold Rush in 1849 catalyzed large-scale Southeast Asian and Chinese immigration. Gold mining and the inception of the transcontinental railroad were associated with a sharp rise in immigration and were the primary sources of employment until the railroad's completion in 1869. While census records were inaccurate, as there was often under-enumeration of Chinese Americans (Chung, Frampton, & Murphy, 2005), it is estimated that by 1876 over 200,000 people had immigrated from China to the United States (Mei, 1979), and that the total Chinese population in the United States was just over 100,000 in 1880 (Chung et al., 2005; Voss & Allen, 2008). After the completion of the Transcontinental Railroad, thousands of workers of Asian descent were once again seeking employment and migrating eastwards to other industrial hubs (Voss & Allen, 2008).

This migration was met with intense anti-Asian sentiment, especially amongst European immigrants who were resentful of labor market competition (Chan, 1991; Voss & Allen, 2008). Nationwide, racism became codified by the Naturalization Act of 1870, which allowed for naturalization of people of European and African descent but excluded Native Americans and Asians from obtaining citizenship. Finally, in 1882, the Chinese Exclusion Act was passed, which specifically denied Chinese laborers entrance into the United States and placed added citizenship requirements onto those who had already entered the country (Voss & Allen, 2008). The effects of political sanctions, promulgated by overt racism, both intensified and maintained the social, political, and economic marginalization of Asian immigrants.

In 1898, 25 skeletons were brought into the Field Museum of Natural History by George A. Dorsey, Curator of Anthropology. They were assigned accession numbers and became a part of the permanent collection under the label "Rush Medical College." Curiously, information regarding the identity of the individuals and details pertaining to their acquisition are notably absent today, in spite of the fact that records pertaining to thousands of material objects and skeletons in the museum's collection exist. One individual, labeled with accession number "43855" (full accession 1898.0132.43855) is also marked with the racial moniker "Chinaman" on his bones. How this man lived and, perhaps, died, and why his bones became a part of the museum's collection are a reflection and embodiment of 19th- and 21st-century social inequities. Our goal is to analyze his remains as a means of contextualizing his life and death, and to provide a nuanced and humanized understanding of the presence and effects of marginalization.

Placing a Life in Historical Context

Incorporated as a city in 1837, Chicago profited from its geographical location on the Great Lakes and by serving as the hub of rail lines sprawling east and west. It soon became a national agro-industrial center, luring mobile wage-earning laborers to its streets. By 1850, a mere 13 years after incorporation, the city had grown in size from an estimated 4000 to 30,000 residents, and by 1870, the population was just under 300,000 (Hoyt, 2000). While there were benefits to rapid industrialization and urbanization nationwide, epidemics and extensive poverty followed (Nystrom, 2014). Perhaps not surprisingly, 19th-century urban centers concomitantly spawned the development and growth of medical colleges. Chicago was no exception. Rush Medical College, the first medical college in the city, was chartered in 1837, just days before the city became incorporated. By the 1860s, measures to establish a dental department within the school were initiated, resulting in the opening of the Chicago Dental Infirmary in 1883, later to be renamed the Chicago College of Dental Surgery. Here, doctors, after earning a medical degree, could continue their training in dental and oral surgery.

While no records exist indicating how Rush Medical College acquired cadavers for teaching, or how the Chicago Dental Infirmary acquired subjects to practice upon, at other medical institutions in the United States, the bodies of overtly disenfranchised people were used, both legally and illegally (see, e.g., Blakely & Harrington, 1997; Blakely, 1997; Grauer, Lathrop, & Timoteo, 2017; Hodge, 2013; Owsley, 1995; Pollack & Worne, 2014). In spite of a legislative act passed in 1825 by the State of Illinois designed to prevent the clandestine disinterment of the dead for medical investigation of any sort, a postscript to the Act offered sanctions under which bodies could be appropriated for dissection (Grauer et al., 2017); bodies could be used with permission from relatives. Grauer et al. state that "the overall subtext of the Act...is clear: the deceased with stable family ties were readily protected under the law, whereas recent immigrants, the disenfranchised poor, the homeless and mentally disabled, were not" (2017, p. 309). The passing of anti-grave robbing laws did little to curb the practice and proved to be insignificant protection to the populations most at risk: those marginalized due to their limited economic resources and/or race. These populations had neither the political nor the economic ability to protect their dead. Sixty years later, in 1885, the State of Illinois legalized the use of unclaimed bodies (usually of the poor with no economic resources or social ties) for medical study and practice.

Appreciating a Human Body

The individual labeled "43855" is represented by a virtually complete skeleton in excellent condition. The only missing elements include the 12th right rib, two hand phalanges, and four foot phalanges. It is possible that these elements were lost prior to arrival at the Field Museum, or were lost while on loan to other institutions after arriving at the museum. There were 24 teeth recovered with this individual, with seven lost antemortem (maxillary right lateral incisor, maxillary right central incisor, maxillary left central incisor, mandibular right second molar, mandibular right first molar, mandibular left central incisor, and mandibular left second molar), and one lost postmortem (left mandibular canine).

Based on a morphological analysis of the *os coxae* and the cranium, this individual appears to be male. His sciatic notch and subpubic angle are narrow, the ventral arc is absent, and the cranium displays a rugose nuchal crest, mastoid process, supraorbital margin, glabella, and mental eminence (Acsádi & Nemeskéri, 1970; Buikstra & Ubelaker, 1994; Walker, 2005). His age at death is estimated between 35 and 50 years old based on symphyseal and auricular surface morphology (Brooks & Suchey, 1990; Hartnett, 2010; Lovejoy, Meindl, Pryzbeck, & Mensforth, 1985; Osborne, Simmons, & Nawrocki, 2004). Ancestral data, based on osteometric analysis through FORDISC 3.1, suggest that this individual is morphologically similar to modern Vietnamese populations (posterior probability 0.989 and 0.082 Type F typicality) (Jantz & Ousley, 2005). However, FORDISC has limited applications since the database is designed primarily for use in modern forensic cases. The reference populations consist of individuals born after 1930, with limited Asian countries represented (FORDISC, n.d.). Given the complex social and political history of Vietnam and Southeast Asia, it is possible that the individual labeled "42855" might have been morphologically similar to modern Vietnamese groups, but was identified as Chinese upon arrival in the United States.

The cranial and postcranial elements of this individual display clear signs of antemortem stress from childhood through adulthood. Cranially, there is moderate well-remodeled porotic hyperostosis on the left and right parietal and frontal bones, appearing as remodeled coalescing foramina. Enamel hypoplasia is present on 11 of the 24 recovered teeth (45.8%). This individual also suffered from poor dental health (Fig. 10.1), displaying severe periodontitis and alveolar resorption on the maxilla and mandible. In total, there are six carious lesions (6/24, 25%) present, along with two abscesses (2/24, 8.3%). Interestingly, there are also a total of four crude dental restorations present on the left maxillary first molar, the left mandibular first molar, the right mandibular second premolar, and right mandibular third molar.

Postcranially, mild osteophytosis is present on the cervical vertebrae. The costal facet on the left side of T1 displays severe lipping, as well as considerable porosity on the right transverse facet. There is also severe lipping of the transverse facets of T2, T3, T4, and T5. Exostosis of the ligamentum flavum is present on T1, becoming moderate by T4, and continuing throughout the vertebral column to L2. Mild to moderate osteophytosis is present throughout the thoracic and lumbar vertebrae. Starting at L1, there is a slight

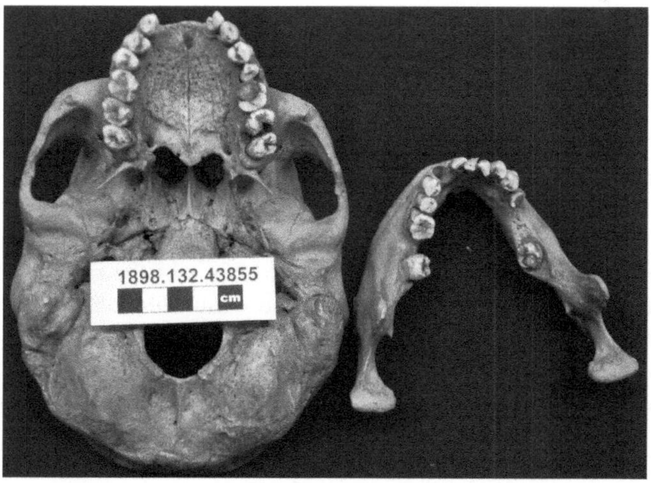

FIGURE 10.1 Maxillary and mandibular dental arcades displaying antemortem and postmortem tooth loss, six carious lesions, and four dental restorations. *Courtesy: The Field Museum, Cat. No. 43855, photographer Shelby Doubek.*

FIGURE 10.2 Endocranial view of the calotte; the craniotomy is the only postmortem cut mark on this individual. Arrow points to well-healed sharp force trauma on the ectocranial surface on the occipital bone near lambda. *Courtesy: The Field Museum, Cat. No. 43855, photographer Shelby Doubek.*

kyphotic curvature of the spine. The left tarsals and distal end of the left radius display moderate lipping. The diaphyses of the femora, tibiae, and fibulae display mild well-healed periosteal lamellar bone.

Evidence of antemortem trauma appears throughout the body of this individual. The cranium exhibits a well-healed facial fracture of the left zygomatic process, anterior to the temporal-zygomatic suture. Three shallow remodeled depression fractures appear on the right parietal bone (8.2 × 8.6 mm; 10.2 × 6.8 mm; 7.1 × 3.9 mm), and one on the left parietal bone (4.6 mm diameter). Additionally, on the occipital bone near lambda, there is a well-healed lesion (8.5 × 1.1 mm) likely caused by sharp force trauma (Fig. 10.2).

Postcranially, the right scapula displays a well-healed fracture on the medial aspect of the posterior spine. Numerous fractures of the ribs are apparent, with 12 out of the 23 extant ribs displaying evidence of fracture. The body of the 10th right rib displays a well-healed fracture with dense callus formation. The left 2nd, 3rd, 4th, 11th, 12th, and the right 2nd and 6th ribs all display healed fractures with some callus formation. More recent trauma occurred to the right 4th, 5th, 10th, 11th ribs, where there is periosteal reaction in and around the fracture site, but no callus formation.

Although cause of death or health issues leading to mortality cannot be inferred from the skeletal remains, it is apparent that a number of postmortem modifications were made to his skeleton. Quite prominently, the accession number "43855" is inscribed in ink on the anterior aspect of his left scapula, along with the racist moniker "Chinaman" (Fig. 10.3). The cranium exhibits a single postmortem transverse cut below lambda, extending through

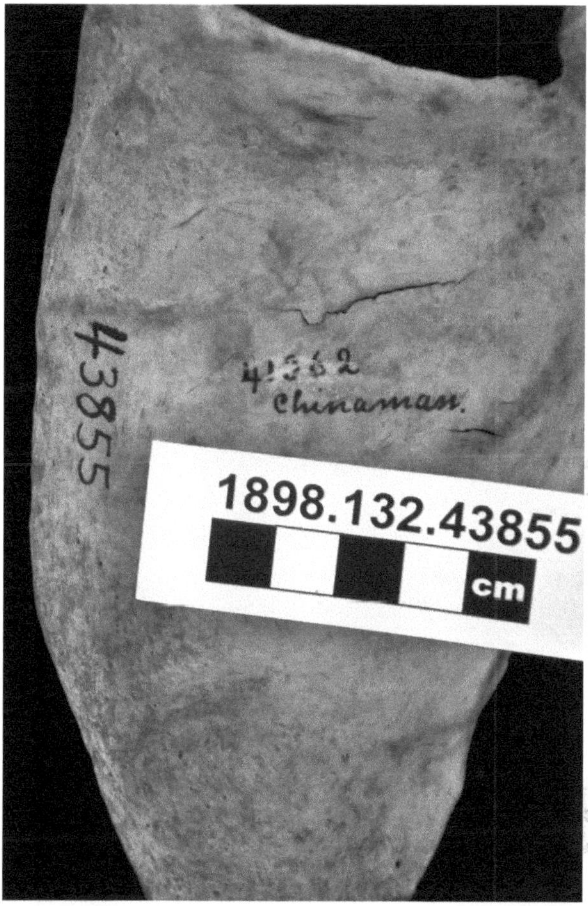

FIGURE 10.3 Ink markings on the anterior aspect of the left scapula provide the only accession information available. *Courtesy: The Field Museum, Cat. No. 43855, photographer Shelby Doubek.*

the parietals and frontal bones (Fig. 10.2). There are no postcranial cut marks present, but small drill holes into the proximal and distal ends of the humeri, ulnae, radii, femora, tibiae, and fibulae, as well as into the sternal end of the clavicles, are present (Fig. 10.4).

The Importance of Social Context

Examining the skeletal traces of life events of the individual labeled "43855" begins by evaluating evidence of childhood conditions. It appears that his childhood was difficult. The presence of dental enamel hypoplasia records periods of substantial childhood physiological stress, perhaps brought on by

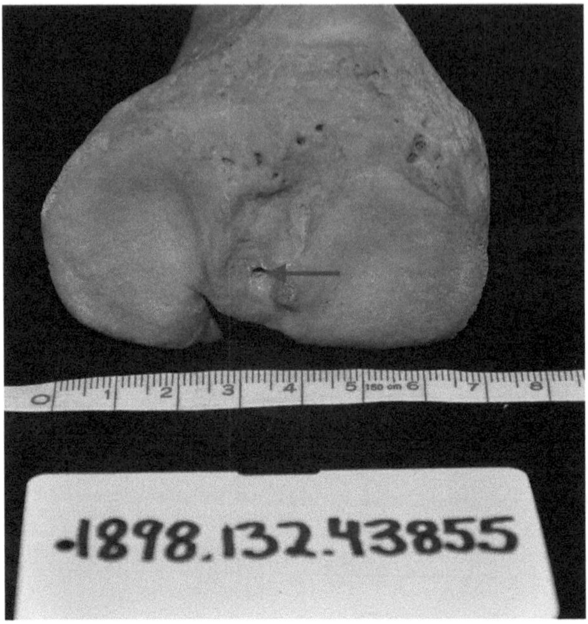

FIGURE 10.4 Arrow points to a drilled hole in the proximal aspect of the left tibia, the hole is likely evidence of rearticulation and display. *Courtesy: The Field Museum, Cat. No. 43855, photographer Shelby Doubek.*

inadequate nutrition and/or severe disease episodes. The presence of moderate porotic hyperostosis might also suggest the presence of nutritional stress or high pathogenic loads during childhood, contributing to anemia (Harrod & Crandall, 2015; Stuart-Macadam, 1985; Walker, Bathurst, Richman, Gjerdrum, & Andrushko, 2009). Lastly, a well-healed periosteal reaction, an indicator of infection and inflammation, was noted on the diaphyses of both his right and left femora, tibiae, and fibulae. Given the famine and rural poverty known to be present in mid-19th-century Indo-China, it is not surprising to find this suite of pathological lesions on the bones and teeth of this individual.

Stress followed this man into adulthood. Dental disease was pervasive, with antemortem tooth loss affecting his maxillary anterior teeth and three mandibular molars. Carious lesions affected 25% of his recovered teeth and were exacerbated by painful abscesses and periodontitis. Reconstructing the diet of this man is not possible from the nondestructive, macroscopic dataset, but with carious lesions known to be associated with bacterial fermentation of dietary carbohydrates, it is possible that his diet lacked essential nutritive contributors such as proteins and fats (Hillson, 1996; Temple, 2015).

Of particular interest is the fact that the individual labeled "43855" received treatment for caries. Four teeth retain dental fillings with three displaying restorations of large carious lesions. These fillings appear similar to amalgam restorations, which, despite the known harmful effects of mercury, remained popular from the early to the mid-19th century due to the malleability of the material compared to gold (Hyson, 2006; Lane, 1949). Regardless of the lesser price of amalgam restoration, access to dental care was usually limited to those with substantial economic resources (Chung et al., 2005; Harrod, Thompson, & Martin, 2012; Heffner, 2015). Hence, finding dental restorations in this individual seems unexpected. However, the individual labeled "43855," like many whose body legally or illegally became a medical specimen for practice or education, might have knowingly during life or unknowingly after death served as a dental subject for doctors (Richardson, 2000; White et al., 1883).

It is clear from his skeletal remains that this man endured multiple traumatic events, marked by healed cranial wounds and numerous fractured ribs, some broken shortly before death. Antemortem cranial wounds include well-healed depression fractures to the parietal bones, a remodeled sharp force traumatic lesion to the occipital bone, and a well-healed facial fracture of the left zygomatic process. Cranial trauma can have neurological impacts such as cognitive, motor, and speech problems, migraines, dizziness, difficulty concentrating, emotional instability, increased aggressiveness, and antisocial behavior (Center for Disease Control, 2017; Leon-Carrion & Ramos, 2003). These behavioral changes increase the risk of additional instances of violence and trauma. While the cause of the cranial fractures may be occupation related, in the case of individual "43855" perhaps mining or railway work, it is also possible that they are the result of interpersonal conflict. Harrod et al. (2012) and Walker (1989) assert that the head is a frequent target of interpersonal violence.

The individual labeled "43855" also displays evidence of numerous traumatic events to his body. Postcranially, the right scapula has a well-healed fracture on the medial aspect of the spine. His ribs have many fractures with varying degrees of callus formation, indicating that there were at least three separate instances of trauma (Fig. 10.5). A remnant of the first traumatic incident appears on the right 10th rib, midway along the body. Here, a well-healed fracture with considerable callus formation is present, suggesting that this traumatic event occurred months or years before death. The left 2nd, 3rd, and 4th ribs, along with the right 2nd and 6th ribs, display fractures at or near the sternal ends, immediately adjacent to the sternocostal junction. The shafts of the 11th and 12th left ribs display fractures midway along the body. These seven fracture sites display callus formation with retention of the fracture lines, suggesting that these fractures occurred more recently than the injury to the right 10th rib. The most recent instances of trauma, perhaps suffered days before this individual died, occur on the right 4th, 5th, 10th, and 11th ribs. These all display fractures with mild periosteal reaction in and around the clearly visible fracture site.

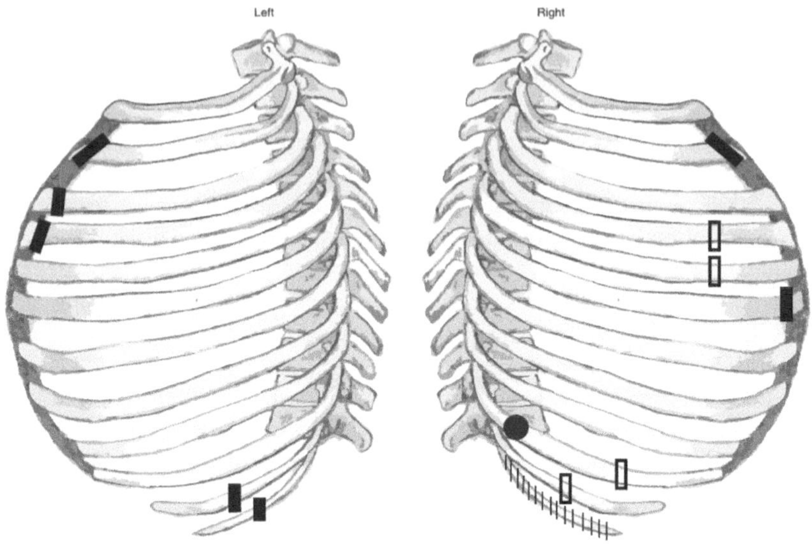

FIGURE 10.5 The locations of rib fractures and callus formation. Hash marks indicate missing bone, solid black circle indicates area displaying well-healed fracture accompanied by extensive callus formation, black rectangles indicate areas with visible fracture lines and development of some callus formation, open rectangles represent areas where fracture lines are clearly evident and only minimal periosteal reaction is present at the fracture site. *Image drawn by Shelby Doubek.*

The effects of these injuries on the individual labeled "43855" may have been profound. Alongside pain, rib fractures can lead to shortness of breath, damage to internal organs, pneumothorax (collapsed lung), and have been associated with increased morbidity for individuals over 45 years old (Holcomb, McMullin, Kozar, Lygas, & Moore, 2003). Although injuries to the postcranial skeleton are more often the result of accident or occupational injury, rather than violence (Harrod et al., 2012), the presence of multiple injury locations along the ribs of this man renders interpretation difficult. Rib fractures are commonly associated with blunt force trauma, especially with localized force across the transverse plane. Rib fractures in this individual appear to cluster toward the anterior aspects of the rib cage, suggesting that most force was direct and to the front of his body, leading to costochondral separation, and transverse, oblique, and greenstick fractures to multiple ribs on multiple occasions. Radiographic images were taken of all bones displaying traumatic lesions to assess if they occurred ante or postmortem, and to evaluate the pattern and progression of his injuries.

In spite of the difficulties in determining the exact causes of the fractures, the analyses of traumatic injury type and frequency can cautiously be used to gain insight into the life of the individual labeled "43855." For instance, social circumstances influence the types of injury and violence to which individuals are exposed (Harrod et al., 2012; Judd, 2002; Owsley, Orser, Mann, Moore-Jansen, & Montgomery, 1987; Watkins, 2012). Being of Southeast Asian descent during a time in United States history fraught with anti-Asian sentiment, the individual labeled "43855" might have become victim to racially motivated interpersonal violence, or might have been employed, as many Asians immigrants were, as a railway worker and suffered traumatic injuries related to his occupation. Railway work during the mid-19th century was dangerous (Harrod & Crandall, 2015), with injury incidence among rail workers higher than in any other industry (Friedman & Ladinsky, 1967). No matter the cause, it is clear that this man suffered from recidivistic trauma. Crandall and Harrod (2016) and Harrod et al. (2012) in their analysis of skeletal remains of 13 Chinese migrants employed as railway workers in Carlin, Nevada, during the 19th century, note that 10 out of 13 individuals suffered from multiple traumatic injuries. In their study, they found the pattern of injuries and stress similar to other historical cases of racialized labor exploitation. These injuries are similar in nature to that of the individual "43855" from Rush, with nine of the 13 individuals experiencing at least one cranial depression fracture, and five of 13 experiencing rib fractures (Crandall & Harrod, 2016; Harrod et al., 2012). In their study, injury recidivism was linked to harsh labor practices and hazards of railway work, poverty, and structural violence fueled by racism.

At some point during adulthood, skeletal changes consistent with arduous labor developed. This man developed arthritic changes in his spine, with mild to moderate osteophytes present throughout the entire vertebral column, and exostosis of the ligamentum flava, suggesting the presence of arduous stress placed upon his vertebrae. While these lesions have multiple etiologies, they are also consistent with stress indicators and trauma associated with racialized labor exploitation recorded in the bioarchaeological and historical record (Harrod et al., 2012; Harrod & Crandall, 2015).

Recognizing the Embodiment of Marginalization

This man, likely socioeconomically and politically disadvantaged in life, became further marginalized in death through the use of his body as a medical specimen. Bodies and anatomical elements chosen for use as medical specimens were predominantly from individuals with underprivileged backgrounds, lacking economic, social, and political power to determine the disposition of their bodies in death. This process inherently stripped these individuals of their autonomy, as well as their identity and personhood.

Three postmortem skeletal scars bear witness to 19th-century social attitudes toward Asian immigrants. The first is the surgical craniotomy across the frontal, parietal, and occipital bones to remove the calotte.

Nystrom (2014) and Crossland (2009) assert that the social status of an individual is reflected in the type of 19th-century postmortem examination, autopsy, or dissection, performed on a body after death. Autopsies were surgical procedures used to determine cause of death. They reflected and maintained an individual's personhood, or social identity since the goal was to seek an understanding of the death of the individual. Dissection, on the other hand, was used for anatomical study. The body was no longer associated with an individual, but rather, was simply an object from which to learn. Not surprisingly, marginalized individuals and groups with limited social, economic, or political power, such as African Americans, other racialized groups, and the poor, became the primary source of cadavers for medical study. Although the distinction between dissection and autopsy can be difficult to determine when analyzing skeletal remains due to methodological overlap between these two procedures, assessing the mortuary context of the remains can offer further insight (Nystrom, 2017).

The body of the individual labeled "43855" was subjected to a craniotomy, but no other cut marks are present indicating surgical practice or experimentation. However, other marks are present on his body which suggest that postmortem actions stripped him of his personhood and relegated him to "other" at a time in western history when desecration of the body was believed by many to deny the soul peace (Halperin, 2007). At some point after death, his body was macerated to remove all tissue, allowing others to view and use his bones. Lastly, small drill-holes were placed on the proximal and distal ends of his long bones; likely evidence of his body being deliberately rearticulated for display.

The marginalization of this individual continued when his body was brought to the Field Museum as a specimen. It is likely that here the word "Chinaman" was written indelibly on his scapula. The lack of documentation regarding the acquisition of this body and the other 24 bodies associated with Rush Medical College is also revealing. While both time and institutional changes might have led to the loss or destruction of accession records, it is telling that accession records and information regarding material objects in the Field Museum's collection are far more abundant. The negative space in the narrative of this individual's life and death reflects the social classification of immigrants as "other," and exacerbates the social, economic, and political effects of marginalization. Over the next century, the bones of the individual labeled "43855" were placed in a box and loaned out to other institutions as teaching material. Today, it is critical to note our own role in this system of structural inequality (Nystrom, 2014; Sappol, 2017) as it presents a paradox: human remains collections are filled with individuals who in life and after death were denied the socioeconomic and political power to refuse consent to be examined and collected, and thus we inadvertently continue to contribute to the postmortem process of marginalization.

Moving Forward

Taking an osteobiographical approach toward interpreting human skeletal remains offers a particularly poignant means of humanizing the past, as it places the lives of individuals into the social contexts in which they lived. For those who were socioeconomically and politically marginalized during life, the approach can bring inclusiveness and dignity. We do not know if the path taken to Chicago by the individual labeled "43855" was of his own volition or if this individual lived and died abroad and his remains were posthumously collected. There are no records of acquisition from the Rush Medical College, nor records retained by the Field Museum that would suggest that this individual's body was brought to Chicago directly from Asia. However, based on the great numbers of Asian immigrants into the United States in the mid- to late-19th century, it is not a stretch to assert that this individual was likely one of thousands of people who crossed the Pacific Ocean in hopes of starting a better life.

The individual labeled "43855" was a man who died sometime between the ages of 35–50 years old and was likely of Asian descent. Life for this individual appears to have been difficult. The presence of dental enamel hypoplasia suggests periods of profound stress during childhood, possibly triggered by famine and rural poverty occurring in the mid-19th-century Indo-China region (Mei, 1979). Later in life, arduous labor took a toll on his back. Dental disease became pervasive, and in spite of receiving crude restorative treatment for carious lesions, he suffered from extensive antemortem tooth loss, painful abscesses, and periodontal disease. He withstood at least three separate traumatic events in his life, marked by healed cranial wounds and numerous fractured ribs, some broken shortly before his death. While the context of this individual's death is unknown, it is possible that his body bears witness to rampant 19th-century animosity toward Indo-Chinese immigrants (Voss & Allen, 2008).

Following this individual's death, his skeleton continued to embody the effects of structural inequalities and the destruction of personal identity. His body was dissected at the Rush Medical College and, later, his bones were modified for display. Even at the Field Museum, where materials and artifacts are meticulously recorded upon accession, this individual was afforded nothing more than a number and a racist epitaph.

Now is the time for change. Chinese individuals, and other Asian American groups, are frequently overlooked in conversations about race and ethnicity in America (Shimpi & Zirkel, 2012). Despite being integral to building America's infrastructure, the voices of Asian immigrants remain eerily silent. Little is known from their perspectives or of their life experiences (Harrod & Crandall, 2015). There are no known written documents (letters or diaries) from Chinese transcontinental railway workers, leaving us to rely upon the perspectives of non-Chinese individuals (Harrod & Crandall, 2015;

Voss, 2015). The Historical Chinese Railroad Workers in North America Project (Chinese Railroad Workers in North America Project, 2012), as well as archaeological work to reconstruct the historical experience of Chinese laborers, seek to change this narrative (Harrod & Crandall, 2015; Ross, 2013; Voss & Allen, 2008). So, too, might our study of the life and death of a man labeled "43855."

Collections of human remains often have challenging histories, both in their acquisition and role within an institution. Recently, strides have been made to change the discourse involving human remains from referring to them as archaeological specimens, or objects, to appreciating their personhood and their unique lived experiences as individuals within larger social contexts. For those who were marginalized during life, the likelihood of becoming an object for study or display was intensified. Our goal has been to bring dignity to the individual objectified through the label "43855," and to contextually "map" and appreciate the life of this marginalized man.

Acknowledgments

The authors greatly thank Dr. Helen Robbins, Dr. Stacey Drake, and Emily Hayflick of the Field Museum of Natural History, and Kelsy Dorn and the Loyola University Chicago Bioanthropology Laboratory for assistance throughout this project.

References

Acsádi, G., & Nemeskéri, J. (1970). *History of human life span and mortality*. Budapest: Akadémiai Kiadó.

Agarwal, S. C., & Glencross, B. A. (Eds.), (2011). *Social bioarchaeology*. New York: Wiley-Blackwell.

Baadsgaard, A., Boutin, A. T., & Buikstra, J. E. (Eds.), (2011). *Breathing new life into the evidence of death: Contemporary approaches to bioarchaeology*. Santa Fe: School for Advanced Research Press.

Blakely, R. L. (1997). A clandestine past: Discovery at the Medical College of Georgia and theoretical foundations. In R. L. Blakely, & J. M. Harrington (Eds.), *Bones in the basement: Postmortem racism in nineteenth-century medical training* (pp. 3–27). Washington, DC: Smithsonian Institution Press.

Blakely, R. L., & Harrington, J. M. (Eds.), (1997). *Bones in the basement: Postmortem racism in nineteenth-century medical training*. Washington, DC: Smithsonian Institution Press.

Brooks, S., & Suchey, J. M. (1990). Skeletal age determination based on the os pubis: A comparison of the Acsadi-Nemeskeri and Suchey-Brooks methods. *Human Evolution, 5*(3), 227–238.

Buikstra, J. E., & Ubelaker, D. H. (1994). *Standards for data collection from human skeletal remains*. Fayetteville: Arkansas Archeological Survey, Research Series No. 44.

Center for Disease Control. (2017). Traumatic brain injury & concussion. National Center for Injury Prevention and Control. Retrieved from <www.cdc.gov/ncipc/tbi/TBI.htm> Accessed 07.01.18.

Chan, S. (1991). *Asian Americans: An interpretive history*. New York: Twayne Publishers.

Chinese Railroad Workers in North America Project. (2012). About our project. Chinese Railroad Workers in North America Project, Stanford University. Retrieved from <http://web.stanford.edu/group/chineserailroad/cgi-bin/wordpress/about-our-project/>.

Chung, S. F., Frampton, F. P., & Murphy, T. W. (2005). Venerate these bones: Chinese American funerary and burial practices as seen in Carlin, Elko County, Nevada. In S. F. Chung, & P. Wegars (Eds.), *Chinese American death rituals: Respecting the ancestors* (pp. 107–146). Lanham: Altamira Press.

Crandall, J. J., & Harrod, R. P. (2016). Witnessing exploited bodies: The bioarchaeology of violence recidivism and labor abuse in 19th-century Chinese America. In *Poster presented at the 2016 annual America association of physical anthropologists conference*, Atlanta, GA.

Crossland, Z. (2009). Acts of estrangement. The post-mortem making of self and other. *Archaeological Dialogues*, *16*(1), 102–125.

Farmer, P. E., Nizeye, B., Stulac, S., & Keshavjee, S. (2006). Structural violence and clinical medicine. *PLoS Medicine*, *3*(10), e449.

FORDISC: Help File Version 1.35. (n.d.). Retrieved 2018 from <http://math.mercyhurst.edu/~sousley/Fordisc/Help/Fordisc3_Help.pdf>.

Friedman, L. M., & Ladinsky, J. (1967). Social change and the law of industrial accidents. *Columbia Law Review*, *67*(1), 50–82.

Gowland, R., & Knüsel, C. (Eds.), (2006). *Social archaeology of funerary remains*. Oxford: Oxbow Books.

Grauer, A. L., Lathrop, V., & Timoteo, T. (2017). Exploring evidence of 19th century dissection in the Dunning Poorhouse cemetery. In K. Nystrom (Ed.), *The bioarchaeology of dissection and autopsy in the United States* (pp. 301–314). Cham, Switzerland: Springer.

Halperin, E. C. (2007). The poor, the black, and the marginalized as the source of cadavers in United States anatomical education. *Clinical Anatomy*, *20*(5), 489–495.

Harrod, R. P., & Crandall, J. J. (2015). Rails built of the ancestors' bones: The bioarchaeology of the overseas Chinese experience. *Historical Archaeology*, *49*(1), 148–161.

Harrod, R. P., Thompson, J. L., & Martin, D. L. (2012). Hard labor and hostile encounters: What human remains reveal about institutional violence and Chinese immigrants living in Carlin, Nevada (1885 – 1923). *Historical Archaeology*, *46*(4), 85–111.

Hartnett, K. M. (2010). Analysis of age-at-death estimation using data from a new, modern autopsy sample-Part I: Pubic bone. *Journal of Forensic Sciences*, *55*(5), 1145–1151.

Heffner, S. C. (2015). Exploring health-care practices of Chinese railroad workers in North America. *Historical Archaeology*, *49*(1), 134–147.

Hillson, S. (1996). *Dental anthropology*. Cambridge: Cambridge University Press.

Hodge, C. J. (2013). Non-bodies of knowledge: Anatomized remains from the Holden Chapel collection, Harvard University. *Journal of Social Archaeology*, *13*(1), 122–149.

Holcomb, J. B., McMullin, N. R., Kozar, R. A., Lygas, M. H., & Moore, F. A. (2003). Morbidity from rib fractures increases after age 45. *Journal of the American College of Surgeons*, *196*(4), 549–555.

Hoyt, H. (2000). *One hundred years of land values in Chicago: The relationship of the growth of Chicago to the rise of its land values, 1830-1933*. Washington, DC: Beard Books.

Hyson, J. (2006). Amalgam: Its history and perils. *Journal of the California Dental Association*, *34*(3), 215–229.

Jantz, R. L., & Ousley, S. D. (2005). Friedman 3.1: Computerized forensic discriminant functions. *Version 3.0*. Knoxville: The University of Tennessee.

Judd, M. (2002). Ancient injury recidivism: An example from the Kerma period of ancient Nubia. *International Journal of Osteoarchaeology*, *12*, 89–106.

Knudson, K. J., & Stojanowski, C. M. (2008). New directions in bioarchaeology: Recent contributions to the study of human social identities. *Journal of Archaeological Research, 16*(4), 397–432.

Knudson, K. J., & Stojanowski, C. M. (2009). *Bioarchaeology and identity in the Americas*. Gainesville: University Press of Florida.

Lane, J. R. (1949). A survey of dental alloys. *The Journal of the American Dental Association, 39*(4), 414.

Leon-Carrion, J., & Ramos, F. J. (2003). Blows to the head during development can predispose to violent criminal behavior: Rehabilitation of consequences of head injury is a measure for crime prevention. *Brain Injury, 17*(3), 207–216.

Lovejoy, C. O., Meindl, R. S., Pryzbeck, T. R., & Mensforth, R. P. (1985). Chronological metamorphosis of the auricular surface of the ilium: A new method for the determination of adult skeletal age at death. *American Journal of Physical Anthropology, 68*(1), 15–28.

Martin, D., & Harrod, R. (2016). The bioarchaeology of pain and suffering: Human adaptation and survival during troubled times. *Archeological Papers of the American Anthropological Association, 27*, 161–174.

Martin, D. L., Harrod, R. P., & Pérez, V. R. (2013). *Bioarchaeology: An integrated approach to working with human remains*. New York: Springer.

Mei, J. (1979). Socioeconomic origins of emigration: Guangdong to California, 1850-1882. *Modern China, 5*(4), 463–501.

Nystrom, K. C. (2014). The bioarchaeology of structural violence and dissection in the 19th-century United States. *American Anthropologist, 116*(4), 765–779.

Nystrom, K. C. (Ed.), (2017). *The bioarchaeology of dissection and autopsy in the United States*. Cham, Switzerland: Springer International Publishing.

Osborne, D. L., Simmons, T. L., & Nawrocki, S. P. (2004). Reconsidering the auricular surface as an indicator of age at death. *Journal of Forensic Sciences, 49*(5), 1–7.

Owsley, D. (1995). Contributions of bioarchaeological research to knowledge of nineteenth-century surgery. In S. R. Saunders, & A. Herring (Eds.), *Grave reflections: Portraying the past through cemetery studies* (pp. 119–151). Toronto: Canadian Scholars' Press.

Owsley, D. W., Orser, C. E., Mann, R. W., Moore-Jansen, P. H., & Montgomery, R. L. (1987). Demography and pathology of an urban slave population from New Orleans. *American Journal of Physical Anthropology, 74*, 185–197.

Pollack, D., & Worne, H. (Eds.), (2014). *Archaeological investigation of the Eastern State Hospital Cemetery (1839–1861)*. Fayette County, Kentucky: Kentucky Archaeological Survey, Research Report No. 11.

Richardson, R. (2000). *Death, dissection and the destitute*. Chicago: University of Chicago Press.

Ross, D. E. (2013). Overseas Chinese archaeology. In C. Smith (Ed.), *Encyclopedia of global archaeology* (pp. 5675–5686). New York: Springer.

Sappol, M. (2017). Forward II: The afterlife of death. In K. Nystrom (Ed.), *The bioarchaeology of dissection and autopsy in the United States* (pp. vii–xi). Cham, Switzerland: Springer.

Shimpi, P. M., & Zirkel, S. (2012). One hundred and fifty years of the Chinese question: An intergroup relations perspective on immigration and globalization. *Journal of Social Issues, 68*(3), 534–558.

Sofaer, J. R. (2006). The body as material culture: A theoretical osteoarchaeology. Cambridge: Cambridge University Press.

Stodder, A. L., & Palkovich, A. M. (2012). *The bioarchaeology of individuals*. Gainesville: University Press of Florida.

Stuart-Macadam, P. (1985). Porotic hyperostosis: Representative of a childhood condition. *American Journal of Physical Anthropology*, *66*(4), 391–398.

Temple, D. H. (2015). Caries: The ancient scourge. In J. D. Irish, & G. R. Scott (Eds.), *A companion to dental anthropology* (pp. 433–449). New Jersey: Wiley-Blackwell.

Tucker, M. (1990). Director's forward. In R. Ferguson (Ed.), *Out there: Marginalization and contemporary cultures* (pp. 7–8). Cambridge, MA: MIT Press.

Voss, B. L. (2015). The historical experience of labor: Archaeological contributions to interdisciplinary research on Chinese railroad workers. *Historical Archaeology*, *49*(1), 4–24.

Voss, B. L., & Allen, R. (2008). Overseas Chinese archaeology: Historical foundations, current reflections, and new directions. *Historical Archaeology*, *42*(3), 5–28.

Walker, P. L. (1989). Cranial injuries as evidence of violence in prehistoric southern California. *American Journal of Physical Anthropology*, *80*, 313–323.

Walker, P. L. (2005). Greater sciatic notch morphology: Sex, age, and population differences. *American Journal of Physical Anthropology*, *127*(4), 385–391.

Walker, P. L., Bathurst, R. R., Richman, R., Gjerdrum, T., & Andrushko, V. A. (2009). The causes of porotic hyperostosis and cribra orbitalia: A reappraisal of the iron-deficiency-anemia hypothesis. *American Journal of Physical Anthropology*, *139*, 109–125.

Watkins, R. (2012). Variation in health and socioeconomic status within the W. Montague Cobb skeletal collection: Degenerative joint disease, trauma and cause of death. *International Journal of Osteoarchaeology*, *22*(1), 22–44.

White, J. D., McQuillen, J. H., Ziegler, G. J., White, J. W., Kirk, E. C., & Anthony, L. P. (Eds.), (1883). *The dental cosmos* (Vol. 25). Philadelphia: SS White Dental Manufacturing Company.

Chapter 11

Down and out in postmedieval London: changes in welfare ideology and the impact on the health of workhouse inmates

Brittney K. Shields Wilford[1,2] and Rebecca Gowland[2]
[1]*NAGPRA Division, Southeast Archeological Center, National Park Service, Tallahassee, FL, United States,* [2]*Department of Archaeology, Durham University, Durham, United Kingdom*

Chapter Outline

Introduction

In AD 1834 the UK Government introduced the New Poor Laws, which centralized the existing parochial care of the poor into standardized Government Unions and abolished outdoor relief, in favor of a Union Workhouse. The impetus for these revisions was the shifting social and political climate in which poverty came to be perceived as an individual failing, rather than a matter of misfortune, and hence subject to public censure. Under the doctrine of the New Poor Laws, instead of providing a safety net, the workhouse became a place to "deter the idle, punish the immoral, reform the redeemable, and treat the physically unable" (Newman, 2013, p. 124). To achieve this a standardized regime was introduced into the workhouses that included mandatory hard labor and restricted diets. The aim was to instill the virtues of industriousness, while at the same time deterring those from seeking relief unless they were utterly destitute.

Bioarchaeology of Marginalized People. DOI: https://doi.org/10.1016/B978-0-12-815224-9.00011-7

Lower class and poorer inhabitants of Victorian London were increasingly vilified by the middle and upper classes of society and were marginalized as the gap between the rich and the poor widened, leading to stark inequalities in morbidity and mortality. While the social gradient of health affects all rungs of the social ladder, the exclusion and marginalization of the very poorest in society is known to have particularly profound and devastating consequences (Stuckler & Basu, 2013). In this work, marginalization is defined as the differential access to resources available to individuals who have been stigmatized by, and pushed to the periphery of, society (Burton & Kagan, 2003). This chapter aims to show the effects of welfare reforms on the health and well-being of London's poorest inhabitants through the analysis of diet, demography, and skeletal evidence for pathology. We hypothesize that a decline in health should be observable within the poorest social strata of Londoners during the mid-19th century as a consequence of the AD 1834 Poor Law Amendment. In particular, we examine changes in the workhouse diet, specifically the caloric content of the menus, and activities expected of inmates prior to and after the amendment. Using the osteological and historical evidence, we seek to investigate whether the new hardline approach toward London's very poorest inhabitants was visible in their skeletal remains. Given the decline in the nutritional quality and quantity of the union workhouse menu, along with the increase in physical activity, there should be a corresponding increase in the prevalence of pathological lesions. We examine changes in the prevalence of pathological conditions observable on the skeletons excavated from cemeteries known to be associated with workhouses and/or the poor following the New Poor Law of AD 1834.

Historical Background

As the population in England increased (Fig. 11.1), a series of laws were enacted in an attempt to stop the increasing numbers of itinerant poor who moved from parish to parish receiving alms (Pound, 1971). These early laws created the foundation of the Poor Laws, which culminated in AD 1601 with

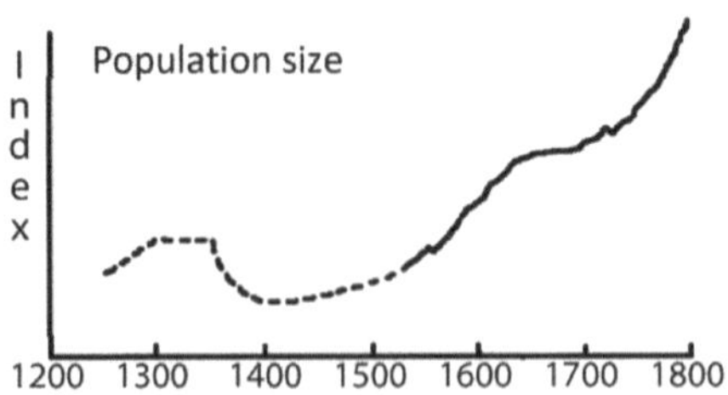

FIGURE 11.1 Increase of population in Preindustrial England as taken from Lee (1980). The dotted line indicates the rough estimate of the population from AD 1250 to 1540. The continuous line represents parish records from AD 1540 to 1800.

the *43 Elizabeth c.2* (Marshall, 1985). The Poor Laws stipulated that parishes should seek to administer outdoor relief for paupers and that the parish workhouse was to act as a "safety net" to provide indoor relief for the destitute. This legislation remained largely unchanged until the 19th century when attitudes toward the poor in Britain underwent a fundamental shift (Blaug, 1963; Englander, 1998). Across England the rising population, urban migration, and low employment led to an increase in those receiving aid. Instead of being seen as the "deserving poor" (Halper, 2012, p. 71), Victorians began to perceive the poor as a lazy and immoral underclass. The institution of the New Poor Laws in AD 1834 was a result of politically motivated demonization of the destitute that sought to change the function of the workhouse from being a "house of relief" to a deterrent, where only the very desperate would enter (Boyer & Schmidle, 2009, p. 250).

Changing Opinions of the Poor

The moniker of "pauper" was introduced into the English vernacular as the legal term, *in forma pauperis*, which first appeared in a statue dating to AD 1495 (Hollen Lees, 1998, p. 40). From the end of the 15th century, the term "paupers" was used to indicate individuals whose extreme need was deserving of charity (Miller, 2012, p. 448). By the 19th century, however, there was a marked shift in public perceptions of paupers; they were reconceptualized as a vector of urban pollution, disease, and immorality (Geber & Murphy, 2012). This perception peaked in the first two decades of the 19th century and "projected deep social fears of corruption and decay onto the bodies of the destitute" (Hollen Lees, 1998, p. 41).

Paupers were widely denigrated by a government who believed that the ready availability of outdoor relief offered under the Poor Laws system had "corrupted and demoralised the country's laborers" (Humphreys, 1995, p. 154) and "led the poor to think they had the right to relief" (Hilton, 2006, p. 341). This ultimately created a perception of the idle pauper who not only tolerated his/her chronic poverty, but embraced a life of State-subsidized dissolution (Hollen Lees, 1998). By AD 1834, pauperism carried a weighty moral charge, and punitive structural measures were thought necessary in order to ameliorate the "contagion" of poverty.

During the early AD 1830s, Parliament established a committee to examine the management of the Poor Laws. Assistant Commissioners were sent across England and Wales to compile reports and recommendations for reform. Ireland (Poor Laws established in AD 1838) and Scotland (Poor Laws established in AD 1845) were not included in the original investigation (Hilton, 2006). The inquiry was biased by preconceived notions regarding how the poor rate was being handled. The commissioners had set agendas to establish that outdoor relief served only to encourage fecklessness amongst the laboring classes (Rose, 1971), and that existing workhouses were ineffective in promoting the virtues of work (Longmate, 1974). The reports included statements testifying to the maladministration of parish welfare and emphasized the role of "outdoor relief" (Humphreys, 1995, p. 17) in the breakdown of the industrious spirit of the lower classes. A commissioner wrote within the *Report from His Majesty's Commissioners for Inquiring into the Administration and Practical Operation of the Poor Laws* that pauperism was "nearly as infectious as smallpox," and "without constant vigilance it would soon overspread the whole parish" (Hilton, 2006, p. 177). The final report resulted in the *Poor Law Amendment Act* of AD 1834, also referred to as the New Poor Laws, which had a substantial impact on the lives of the poor. Following AD 1834, 15,000 preexisting parishes across England and Wales were combined into approximately 600 unions (Hilton, 2006). Outdoor relief was removed, thereby forcing all those who needed aid into the workhouse (Carter, 2014).

The diet provided to workhouse inmates was also reformed to conform to the "less eligibility principle," which saw a reduction to the amount and nutritional quality of the food provided (Clarkson & Crawford, 2001, p. 185). In order to receive aid within the workhouse, paupers were also required to work, typically for lower wages and under more grueling conditions than independent laborers (Wakefield, Chandler, Lansbury, & Webb, 1909). The typical jobs within the workhouse were those of extreme physical labor and monotony, such as crushing bones, digging holes, breaking stone, and picking oakum (Hollen Lees, 1998).

As the structure of the welfare state changed, the workhouse became a barrier between poverty and death. It was deliberately designed to provide conditions that were worse than those experienced by the poorest laborer (Brown, 2016). Admission was a test of pure desperation and "want of the paupers" (Dunkley, 1981, p. 126). The workhouses of the late AD 1830s were to act as a corrective to the personal deficiencies that had led to pauperism. This represented a stark shift in attitude from the Poor Laws in which personal misfortune rather than culpability was preeminent (Hamlin, 1995).

Due to new attitudes and the stigma toward pauperism, the workhouse became widely feared by the working classes and was to be avoided at all costs, which included selling all worldly possessions before applying for aid. This material loss would have made returning to their previous lives and occupations almost impossible (Dickens, 1993). The poor during this time were conceptualized almost as a separate species, and poverty was considered a naturalized form of biological inferiority (similar to race), rather than the result of grinding social subjugation and structural violence (Gowland, 2018).

Materials and Methods

This study utilized existing bioarchaeological and historical records from five postmedieval London cemeteries, as well as the surviving workhouse menus

(Nicholls & Willink, 1898a). The menus were utilized in order to determine and compare the nutritional resources available for workhouse inmates both before and after the AD 1834 Poor Law Amendment Act (New Poor Laws).

Osteological data from the five cemeteries were obtained from the Museum of London's Centre for Human Bioarchaeology's data repository, the Wellcome Osteological Research Database (WORD), as well as unpublished reports from the St. Bride's lower churchyard (Miles & Conheeney, 2005) and Broadgate (Dyson, Malt, Wellman, & White, 1987) cemeteries, provided by the London Archaeological Archive and Research Centre (LAARC). As this was a desk-based study, all individuals that were recorded in the WORD databases for each site were included for pathological analysis.

Osteological Samples

The five cemeteries selected were chosen to include individuals buried both prior to and after the workhouse reforms of AD 1834 (Table 11.1). These cemeteries were associated with the poorest parishes in London and served the lowest social strata, including workhouse inmates (Brickley, Miles, & Stainer, 1999; Carver, 2012; Connell & Miles, 2010; Dyson et al., 1987; Geber & Murphy, 2012; Harding, 2002; Miles & Conheeney, 2005; Newman, 2010; WORD database, 2012a, 2012b, 2012c, 2012d, 2012e). Of the five cemeteries, St. Thomas' Hospital and Broadgate were in use from the 16th to early 18th centuries (WORD database, 2012a, 2012e) and could be associated with the Old Poor Laws. St. Thomas' Hospital is included within this study as it was noted in Stow's survey of London as the place

TABLE 11.1 Postmedieval London cemetery use dates, number of individuals analyzed, and study category.

Cemetery	Dates of cemetery use	Number of analyzed remains	Study category
St. Thomas' Hospital	1540–1714	193	Parish (Old Poor Laws)
Broadgate	1569–1714	147	Parish (Old Poor Laws)
St. Bride's lower churchyard	1770–1849	544	Union (New Poor Laws)
Cross Bones	1800–53	148	Union (New Poor Laws)
City Bunhill	1833–53	239	19th-century independent

that parish officials were sending "the aged, impotent, sick... lame, or blind" applicants for poor relief to St. Thomas' Hospital (Stow, 1842, p. 240). For the purpose of this study, they were identified as "parish burials" (i.e., parish sample). The cemeteries of St. Bride's lower churchyard and Cross Bones (WORD database, 2012c, 2012d) were dated from the late-18th to mid-19th century, with the majority of burials dating to the period after the New Poor Laws were in effect (i.e., union sample). These cemeteries were chosen due to their locations in relation to workhouses and poor relief and their relationships with London's most economically and socially marginalized citizens. The final cemetery is the suburban 19th-century skeletal assemblage from City Bunhill, which was included in order to provide a comparative analysis of an independent (i.e., not reliant on workhouse relief), but still relatively poor population.

In total, 1271 individuals were included in this analysis, and these were subdivided based on the date of burial and subsequent association with either the Old or New Poor Laws. A total of 340 individuals (27% of sample) were classed as "parish burials," while "union burials" comprised a total of 692 individuals (54% of sample). The final 239 individuals (19% of the sample) were those excavated from City Bunhill.

The number of individuals recorded with evidence of infectious disease, joint disease, metabolic conditions, trauma, or "other" (blood-related pathologies like cribra orbitalia, etc.) conditions were identified, along with age and sex distributions from WORD (recorded according to the guidelines outlined in Powers, 2012). Crude prevalence rates (CPRs) for pathological lesions were calculated from the data accessed from WORD. CPR is a less accurate representation of disease prevalence than true prevalence rate, because it may be skewed by differential skeletal preservation; nevertheless, it has value for providing an overall impression of the disease burden within a skeletal sample. Additionally, data regarding trauma and joint disease may provide information regarding the effects of the increased quantity of manual labor on the bodies of the inmates.

This was a desk-based study utilizing the osteological databases provided by the Museum of London for the five cemetery collections (WORD database, 2012a, 2012b, 2012c, 2012d, 2012e), which included a demographic breakdown of the cemeteries including age, sex, and recorded pathologies. Age determination for all cemetery samples was established utilizing established methods, including tooth wear (Brothwell, 1981), phases of the public symphysis (Brooks & Suchey, 1990), the auricular surface (Lovejoy, Meindl, Pryzbeck, & Mensforth, 1985), and finally the costochondral method following Işcan, Loth, and Wright (1984, 1985). Sex determination was established based on the visual assessment of sexually dimorphic skeletal features located on the pelvis and skull as outlined in *Standards* and the Museum of London *Human Osteology Method Statement* (Buikstra & Ubelaker, 1994; Powers, 2012) (Table 11.2).

TABLE 11.2 Age categories (Powers, 2012).

Description	Age group
IU-neonate	Perinatal
Early infant	1–6 months
Later infant	7–11 months
Early childhood	1–5 years
Later childhood	6–11 years
Adolescence	12–17 years
Young adult	18–25 years
Young middle adult	26–35 years
Old middle adult	36–45 years
Elderly	46 years +

Nutritional Materials

A primary aim of this study was to examine the physiological impact of changes to the workhouse diets associated with the New Poor Laws of AD 1834. The workhouse menu provided to the inmates of the parish workhouse of St. John's in Hackney, East London, in AD 1750 was compared to the six diets recommended by the Poor Law commission for the more punitive union workhouses (Nicholls & Willink, 1898a, 1898b).

The daily average caloric intake of the workhouse inmate was calculated by determining the caloric values of all aspects of the menu (e.g., 112 oz. of the specified bread equals 1184 cal/day, etc.). These values were obtained by placing modern caloric values of each item as laid out by historical recipes where possible (Calorie Lab, 2015; Higginbotham, 2008). The caloric compositions of the various diets were then divided by the recommended caloric intake for average adults, based upon the combined caloric value for males and females, to determine the average daily percentage of consumed calories (Clayton & Rowbotham, 2008; Rowbotham & Clayton, 2008).

The overall health of an individual is linked with nutritional status (Sharpe, 2011), including adequate amounts of calories being consumed. A calorie is a measure of energy found within food to fuel the body for breathing, proper circulation, cell repair, and various other bodily functions (Heltberg, 2009). As there was no indication that males and females were served different diets, the caloric values for males (3000–4500 cal/day) and females (2400–3500 cal/day), who undertake labor intensive activities (as would be expected in a workhouse environment), were combined into a generalized average recommended value for caloric intake for active adults

(3350 cal/day) (Rowbotham & Clayton, 2008). Using this combined value is not commonly done, but as there were no large distinctions in the menus by sex it was more parsimonious to discuss this as one value; we acknowledge, however, that this may lead to underestimation of intake in some males and overestimation in some females. The menus given at the Union workhouse were designed to keep inmates from starving, in line with the principle of "less eligibility" discussed earlier (Clarkson & Crawford, 2001, p. 185).

Basal metabolic rate (BMR) is an important factor to consider when investigating past diets; this represents the minimum amount of energy that is required to maintain normal bodily functions (e.g., breathing and keeping the heart beating) (Floud, Fogel, Harris, & Hong, 2011). BMR is typically the largest portion of an individual's total daily caloric expenditure. Since this rate is different for every individual, it was not considered within the context of this study. It is difficult to accurately quantify energy expenditure and activities within the workhouse as these varied between males, females, and children, and likely also between workhouses. Nevertheless, it is an important factor to consider when interpreting the evidence since the increase in physical activity with the New Poor Laws would have increased basic nutritional requirements.

Results

Nutritional Changes

Under the Old Poor Laws, the St. John's Workhouse in AD 1750 was serving a rather monotonous diet consisting of bread, butter, cheese, and beer. The majority of the diet was beer and bread (420 oz. and 112 oz. respectively), while the butter and cheese constituted only a small proportion of the weekly intake (14 oz. and 28 oz. respectively). This would make the average caloric intake of the St. John's inmates 82% ((2758/3350) × 100) of the average daily recommended calories for active adults (i.e., 3350 kcal/day) (Fig. 11.2), which may have been adequate for some females, but not for the average male individual.

Following the Poor Law Amendment, six menus were established. These were regionally varied; workhouses in the City of London would have served the third Poor Law menu (Poor Law Commission, 1836) which afforded the inmates the most calorically sound diet, with 58% (1937.36 kcal/day) of the daily recommended calories. At face value, the union workhouse diets appear more varied in content, but despite this, at least three of the recommended menus would have provided less than 50% of the daily recommended calories (Fig. 11.3). Crucially, when compared to the parish diet, union workhouse inmates would have been consuming between 20% and 40% fewer calories per day, despite the increase in expected physical activity. The first menu provided the least calories, which would have provided

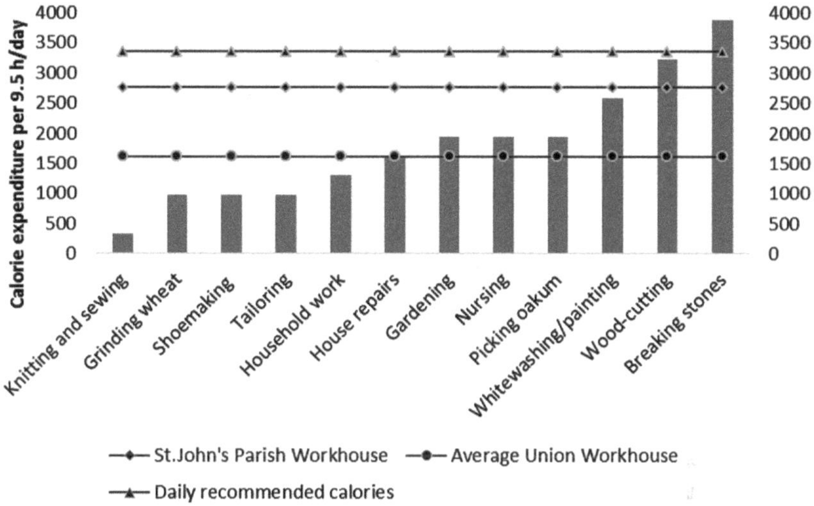

FIGURE 11.2 The average caloric intake of the workhouse diets, along with the daily recommended calories, and overlaid onto the average caloric expenditure of various activities likely to have been utilized within the workhouse.

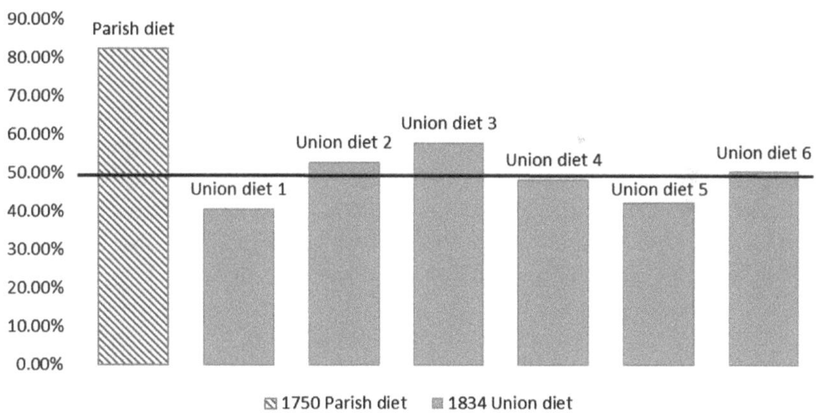

FIGURE 11.3 Average caloric intake provided by workhouse diets with starvation line. The starvation line was determined by Keys et al. (1950) during their study on starvation and the effect it has on living individuals.

inmates 41% (1362.86 kcal/day) of the recommended daily caloric intake (Keys, Brozek, Henschel, Mickelsen, & Taylor, 1950).

The types of strenuous labor required of workhouse inmates would have incurred a large caloric deficit when compared to the value of the menus provided. The primary forms of employment in union workhouses were breaking either stones or bones for an average of 9.5 h a day until a particular quota was reached (Longmate, 1974), resulting in a higher caloric expenditure than the intake supplied by the menus. Modern caloric expenditure values for an individual who continuously lifts objects between 10 and 20 pounds in weight, with limited walking and/or resting, have been estimated to be approximately 1938 kcal/day (Calorie Lab, 2015). This level of activity would have exceeded the daily calorie intake of individuals on the union workhouse menu by about 300 kcal. By contrast, inmates under the Old Poor Laws regimen were more commonly employed manufacturing textiles either by spinning or weaving (Oxley, 1974), but the menu provided would have been sufficient in terms of caloric energy.

Age and Sex Structure of the Cemeteries

The union and independent laborer samples had higher percentages of perinatal infants, infants aged 1–6 months, and most notably children of 1–5 years of age (Fig. 11.4). Perinatal infants are most prevalent in the union sample compared to either the parish or independent laborer samples. In the union and independent laborer samples, children aged 1–5 years were the most prevalent, while adolescents aged 12–17 years were more prevalent in the parish sample. Aging of the nonadult skeletons could have been impacted by nutritional inadequacies related to socioeconomic status (Potter, 2010) as growth would have been arrested.

Young adults (18–25 years) were more frequently recorded in the parish sample when compared with the union and independent laborer samples. The prevalence of old middle adults (36–45 years) is approximately equal in both the parish and union samples, while the independent laborer sample included fewer old middle adults (6%). Elderly adults (46 years +) were the most prevalent of all in the union sample (26%), which was an increase compared to the parish sample (10%). Males were more frequent than females in the parish (23% and 19%, respectively) and the union (30% and 22%,

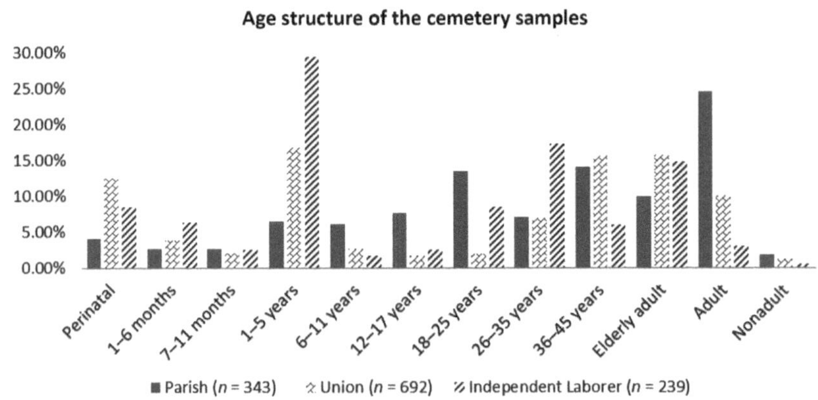

FIGURE 11.4 Age structure of the cemetery samples.

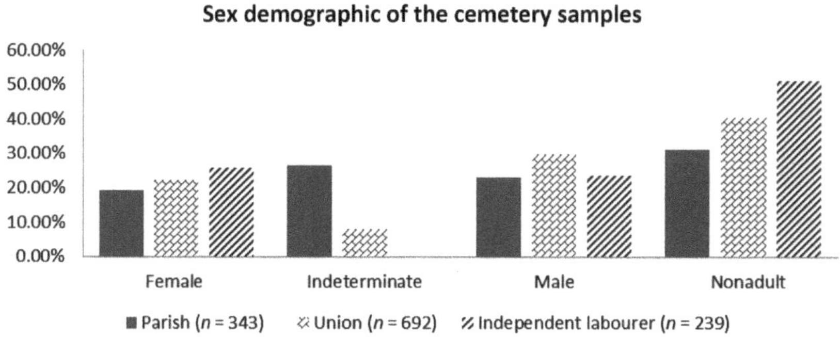

FIGURE 11.5 Sex structure of the cemetery samples.

TABLE 11.3 Percentage of samples with recorded pathological conditions.

Cemetery	Individuals with evidence of pathology *N* (% of total sample)	Total sample
St. Thomas' Hospital	137 (71)	193
Broadgate burial ground	25 (17)	147
St. Bride's lower churchyard	325 (60)	544
Cross Bones burial ground	129 (87)	148
City Bunhill burial ground	64 (27)	239

respectively) samples (Fig. 11.5), while in the independent laborer sample females were slightly more frequent than the males (26% and 23%, respectively). There were, however, a considerable number of individuals within the parish and union samples for whom sex was indeterminate, and this may have a bearing on the actual demographic profile.

Pathological Changes

Some of the recorded pathological conditions are directly influenced by diminished diets (i.e., rickets and scurvy) while the synergistic effect between infectious disease and poor nutrition accounts for others. As displayed in Table 11.3, the Cross Bones cemetery sample had the highest percentage (87%) of individuals with evidence of at least one of the five pathological conditions recorded (infectious, joint, metabolic, trauma, or "other")—many of which were present in the perinatal infants, suggesting very poor maternal health in this parish (Gowland, 2015).

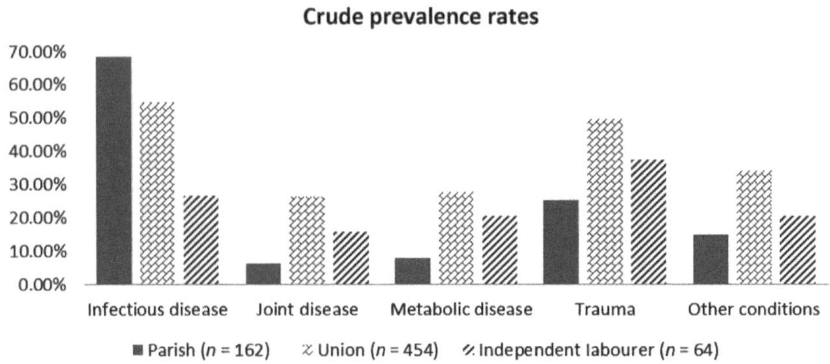

FIGURE 11.6 Crude prevalence of major pathological conditions.

Four of the five categories of pathological lesions increased in prevalence between the parish and union samples (Fig. 11.6). Only skeletal evidence for infectious disease decreased from 69% in the parish sample to 55% in the union sample. There was a notable difference in the prevalence of metabolic conditions between the working-class City Bunhill cemetery, in which only 27% of the sample had evidence of metabolic conditions and the much higher levels within the workhouse cemeteries. The other four pathological categories doubled in frequency amongst the union sample. Joint disease in the two 19th-century samples increased from the earlier parish sample. The parish sample had no evidence of surgical intervention (e.g., autopsy, craniotomy, dissection), which is a contrast to the union sample where 6% of the CPR was from some form of surgical intervention.

Discussion and Conclusion

Humans "have a basic desire for energy and will eat to satisfy this need alone" (Horrell & Oxley, 2012, p. 1359), and health is intimately intertwined with the quantity and quality of food consumed (Clarkson & Crawford, 2001). During the early 19th century the Commission reformed the diets for the workhouse, and believed that it was the quantity of food that was the most important aspect of an individual's diet. When medical practitioners attempted to submit dietary reform examples to the committee (Johnston, 1985), many of the Whig commissioners criticized their attempts as being too vague, and Prime Minister Lord Melbourne went so far as to state that "medical men were only familiar with feeding the sick" and were not qualified to make contributions to the diet of healthy individuals (Miller, 2013, p. 18).

The commissioners of the New Poor Laws implied that the dietary provisions of the Old Poor Laws workhouses had been particularly unrestrained (Miller, 2013). The Old Poor Laws were considered to have encouraged the increasing rate of pauperism, supporting the poor in a life of idleness. Under the "less eligibility" principle, the main function of the nationalized institutions operating under the New Poor Laws was to deter new potential paupers from becoming reliant on the union for aid (Johnston, 1985, p. 5). Therefore established guidelines for the new workhouse diets were designed to be bland and minimal. Furthermore the diets could be subject to further reduction as a means of punishment, or at the discretion of the workhouse master and matron (Anstruther, 1973). When inmates did not consume all of the food served during meal times, most likely due to it being unpalatable, the menus were deemed sufficient (Johnston, 1985).

The menus changed vastly from the parish to the union workhouses (i.e., from the Old and New Poor Laws), superficially going from the simplistic menu of bread, butter, cheese, and beer, to a more diverse one. One of the major changes to menus in AD 1834 was the addition of meat in various forms, including bacon and meat dumplings (Dunkley, 1981). This study demonstrates, however, that despite this increase in the variety of food, the nutritional quality of the menus decreased and inmates of the New Poor Laws institutions would have effectively been consuming a starvation diet. In AD 1839 William Farr recorded 63 starvation deaths and a further 16 deaths from various forms of privation which correlated with the London *Times* labeling the New Poor Law menus as a "starvation diet" (Hamlin, 1995, p. 858). A nutrition-related death involved an individual succumbing to "nutritionally sensitive diseases brought on by impaired immunity, or to poisoning from inferior foods," while an indirect death would be "caused by the disruption of personal life" (Mokyr & O'Grada, 2002, p. 340) from a diet that was not nutritionally sound. Ultimately, diet affects not only the body weight of an individual but also the biological systems that require calories to function, and the promotion of an adequate immune system to protect the host from a multitude of diseases. Those seeking aid under the Poor Laws were vulnerable members of society who, if depending upon parish relief, would have been surviving in a state of semistarvation.

Under the Old Poor Laws regime, female recipients were treated equally to males, and if healthy and able-bodied, they were required to work to maintain themselves (Hollen Lees, 1998). Following the Poor Law Amendment, however, overseers of the poor were more willing to give aid to single mothers or widows than they were to single fathers or widowers (Goose, 2006; Hindle, 2004). This difference in attitude between the different poor law regimes may well explain the change in the sex distribution of the cemetery sites. This provides a contrast with the nonworkhouse cemetery at which females are slightly more prevalent than males. The workhouses under both periods seemed to be dominated by males, or at least those dying within the workhouse were primarily male (Jackson, 2005). Females may have been more transient users of the workhouses during this time, and elderly females were more likely to have been employed as coresidents for their domestic skills (Goose, 2006).

The New Poor Laws contributed to the breakdown of the nuclear family unit of the very poor. Once admitted, families were separated by sex and age into different sections of the workhouse (Picard, 2005). For those who entered the workhouse, this tearing apart of family units was considered "worse than the gruel, the uniform, the regulation haircut, the delousing, the degrading and mind-numbing drudgery" (Hilton, 2006, p. 596). Such conditions were also likely to deter mothers and their children applying to enter the workhouse.

In contrast to metabolic conditions, instances of infectious disease decreased in the 19th-century cemetery samples. While such a decrease appears paradoxical in relation to the lower nutritional status of the inmates, it does align with what we would expect from skeletal data. As discussed, poor nutrition and infectious disease interact synergistically, and it is far less likely that skeletal evidence of infectious disease would manifest in an individual whose immune status has been compromised by poor diet (Wood, Milner, Harpending, & Weiss, 1992). This is referred to as the osteological paradox—most individuals with skeletally manifested evidence of disease would have to be chronic sufferers (that is, those with immune systems healthy enough to mount an opposition to the infectious agent) as opposed to individuals who died prior to the disease affecting the bones. Communicable diseases were rife within the workhouse environment, and it seems very likely that the inmates, with immune systems compromised by inadequate diets, would have succumbed to the more fatal conditions quite rapidly (Boulton, Davenport, & Schwartz, 2013; Tomkins, 2013; Wakefield et al., 1909).

Joint disease also increased in later cemeteries and it is tempting to link this to the more arduous labor undertaken within the union workhouses. This trend is, however, far more likely to be a demographic artefact, given that there were more elderly individuals in the later-period workhouses and the strong correlation between joint disease prevalence and increasing age (Loeser, 2010). The high proportion of elderly individuals within the union workhouses warrants further investigation in relation to the social perceptions of impoverished older people and their care during the 19th century. There was no state pension during this period and when people were too old to work they were reliant upon family members to care for them. If their families were unable or unwilling to provide care then they often had no choice but to enter the workhouse. In his survey of AD 1894, Charles Booth identified that a third of individuals over the age of 70 years were forced to seek poor relief (Glendenning, 1997).

The increase in surgical intervention, either perimortem or potentially postmortem, in the union sample is interesting to note as in AD 1831 the Select Committee on Anatomy successfully passed the Anatomy Bill, which became the Anatomy Act of AD 1832. This new bill allowed for medical schools to legally acquire cadavers for dissection, which would have been more likely than not to have been the unclaimed bodies of workhouse inmates (MacDonald, 2009). Prior to the act only the bodies of criminals were dissected; the act therefore served to conflate paupers and criminals, thus further reinforcing the demonization of the poor so that as well as their worldly goods they also lost the right to determine the postmortem fate of their body (Durbach, 2005). This increasing use of paupers for anatomical dissection is potentially reflected within the union sample.

Overall, this analysis concurs with wider research on London's poor, which identifies the diminished health of those living in poverty in the 19th century (e.g., Fissell, 1989; Pinhasi, Shaw, White, & Ogden, 2006; Roberts & Cox, 2003; Tanner, 1999). It highlights the effects of the New Poor Laws, which compounded and exacerbated the marginalization of the poor and destitute. Paupers were considered a contagion, they were spatially segregated from society, forced to surrender their freedoms, along with their family units, and sacrifice their bodies to hard labor and semistarvation. This punitive regime occurred in a socio-political context in which the poor were vilified and deemed almost subhuman. Even after death, their impoverished state stripped them of any agency over the fate of their own corpse; instead their bodies were dissected and/or buried in unmarked or mass graves. Both of these outcomes reflected a continuation of this marginalization and dehumanization by denying the poor an individual identity, bodily integrity, and self-determination even after death.

References

Anstruther, I. (1973). *The scandal of the Andover workhouse*. Glouster: Alan Sutton Publishing Limited.

Blaug, M. (1963). The myth of the Old Poor Law and the making of the New. *The Journal of Economic History*, *23*(2), 151–184.

Boulton, J., Davenport, R., & Schwartz, L. (2013). "These ANTE-CHAMBERS OF THE GRAVE"? Mortality, medicine, and the workhouse in Georgian London, 1725-1824. In J. Reinarz, & L. Schwartz (Eds.), *Medicine and the workhouse* (pp. 58–85). Rochester: University of Rochester Press.

Boyer, G. R., & Schmidle, T. P. (2009). Poverty among the elderly in late Victorian England. *The Economic History Review*, *62*(2), 249–278.

Brickley, M., Miles, A., & Stainer, H. (1999). *The Cross Bones burial ground, Redcross Way Southwark London*. London: Museum of London Archaeology.

Brooks, S. T., & Suchey, J. M. (1990). Skeletal age determination based on the os pubis: Comparison of the Acsádi-Nemeskéri and Suchey-Brooks methods. *Journal of Human Evolution*, *5*, 227–238.

Brothwell, D. (1981). *Digging up bones: The excavation, treatment and study of human skeletal remains* (3rd ed.). London: Museum of Natural History.

Brown, D. (2016). Supplying London's workhouses in the mid-nineteenth century. *The London Journal*, *41*(1), 36–59.

Buikstra, J. E., & Ubelaker, D. H. (Eds.), (1994). *Standards for data collection from human skeletal remains*. Fayetteville: Arkansas Archaeological Society, Research Series No. 44.

Burton, M., & Kagan, C. (2003). Marginalization. In I. Prilleltensky, & G. Nelson (Eds.), *Community psychology: In pursuit of wellness and liberation* (pp. 293–308). London: Palgrave MacMillan.

Calorie Lab. (2015). *Calorie lab*. Retrieved from <http://calorielab.com/burned/>

Carter, P. (2014). Joseph Bramley of East Stoke, Nottinghamshire: A late victim of crusade against outdoor relief. *Family & Community History*, *17*, 36–46.

Carver, J. (2012). London Crossrail: The New Churchyard AD1569 to AD1714 archaeology investigation and dealing with mass exhumation. In *Proceedings of the 17th international conference on cultural heritage and new technologies 2012*. Retrived from <http://www.chnt.at/wp-content/uploads/eBook_CHNT17_Carver.pdf>

Clarkson, L. A., & Crawford, E. M. (2001). Feast and famine: Food and nutrition in Ireland *1500-1920*. Oxford: Oxford University Press.

Clayton, P., & Rowbotham, J. (2008). An unsuitable and degraded diet? Part One: Public health lessons from the mid-Victorian working class diet. *Journal of the Royal Society of Medicine*, *101*(6), 282–289.

Connell, B., & Miles, A. (2010). *The City Bunhill burial ground, Golden Lane, London: Excavations at South Islington schools* (p. 2006) London: Museum of London Archaeology Service.

Dickens, C. (1993). In F. Kaplan (Ed.), *Oliver Twist, by Charles Dickens: A Norton Critical Edition*. New York: Norton and Company.

Dunkley, P. (1981). Whigs and paupers: The reform of the English Poor Laws, 1830-1834. *The Journal of British Studies*, *20*(2), 124–149.

Durbach, M. (2005). Bodily matters: The anti-vaccination movement in England, *1853–1907*. Durham and London: Duke University Press.

Dyson, L., Malt, D., Wellman, T., & White, B. (1987). *Excavations at Broad Street station: The Broadgate development archive report*. London: Crossrail Archive Report.

Englander, D. (1998). *Poverty and poor law reform in 19th century Britain, 1834-1914*. New York: Addison Wesley Longman Limited.

Fissell, M. E. (1989). The "sick and drooping poor" in eighteenth-century Bristol and its region. *The Society for the Social History of Medicine*, *2*, 35–58.

Floud, R., Fogel, R., Harris, B., & Hong, S. C. (2011). *The changing body: Health, nutrition, and human development in the Western world since 1700*. Cambridge: Cambridge University Press.

Geber, J., & Murphy, E. (2012). Scurvy in the Great Irish Famine: Evidence of vitamin C deficiency from a mid-19th century skeletal population. *American Journal of Physical Anthropology*, *148*, 512–524.

Glendenning, R. (1997). Attitudes to elderly people. In P. Decalmer, & F. Glendenning (Eds.), *The mistreatment of elderly people* (pp. 5–12). London: Sage.

Goose, N. (2006). Poverty, old age and gender in nineteenth-century England: The case of Hertfordshire. *Continuity and Change*, *20*(3), 351–384.

Gowland, R. L. (2015). Entangled lives: Implications of the developmental origins of health and disease hypothesis for bioarchaeology and the life course. *American Journal of Physical Anthropology*, *158*, 530–540.

Gowland, R. L. (2018). 'A mass of crooked alphabets': The construction and othering of working class bodies in industrial England. In P. Stone (Ed.), *Bioarchaeological analysis and bodies*. London: Springer.

Halper, T. (2012). The poor as pawns: The new "deserving poor" and the old. *Polity*, *6*, 71–86.

Hamlin, C. (1995). Could you starve to death in England in 1839? The Chadwick-Farr controversy and the loss of the "social" in public health. *American Journal of Public Health*, *85* (6), 856–866.

Harding, V. (2002). *The dead and the living in Paris and London, 1500-1670*. Cambridge: Cambridge University Press.

Heltberg, R. (2009). Malnutrition, poverty, and economic growth. *Health Economics*, *88*, 77–88.

Higginbotham, P. (2008). *The workhouse cookbook*. Stroud: The History Press.

Hilton, B. (2006). *A mad, bad, and dangerous people? England 1783-1846*. Oxford: Oxford University Press.

Hindle, S. (2004). *On the parish? The micro-politics of poor relief in rural England, c. 1550-1750*. Oxford: Oxford University Press.

Hollen Lees, L. (1998). *The solidarities of strangers*. Cambridge: Cambridge University Press.

Horrell, S., & Oxley, D. (2012). Bringing home the bacon? Regional nutrition, stature, and gender in the industrial revolution. *The Economic History Review*, *4*, 1354–1379.

Humphreys, R. (1995). *Sin, organized charity and the Poor Law in Victorian England*. Hampshire: MacMillan Press Ltd.

Işcan, M. Y., Loth, S. R., & Wright, R. K. (1984). Age estimation from the rib by phase analysis: White males. *Journal of Forensic Science*, *29*, 1094–1104.

Işcan, M. Y., Loth, S. R., & Wright, R. K. (1985). Age estimation from the rib by phase analysis: White females. *Journal of Forensic Science*, *30*, 853–863.

Jackson, D. G. (2005). *The Medway Union workhouse, 1876-1881: A study based on the admission and discharge registers and the census enumerators' books, . Local Population Studies* (75, pp. 11–32).

Johnston, V. J. (1985). *Diet in workhouses and prisons, 1835-1895*. New York: Garland Publishing, Inc.

Keys, A., Brozek, J., Henschel, A., Mickelsen, O., & Taylor, H. L. (1950). *The biology of human starvation Volume 1*. Minneapolis: University of Minnesota Press.

Lee, R. (1980). A historical perspective on economic aspects of the population explosion: The case of preindustrial England. In R. A. Easterlin (Ed.), *Population and economic change in developing countries* (pp. 517–566). Chicago: University of Chicago Press.

Loeser, R. F. (2010). Age-related changes in the musculoskeletal system and the development of osteoarthritis. *Clinics in Geriatric Medicine*, *26*(3), 371–386.

Longmate, N. (1974). *The workhouse*. London: Maurice Temple Smith Ltd.

Lovejoy, C. O., Meindl, R. S., Pryzbeck, T. R., & Mensforth, R. P. (1985). Chronological metamorphosis of the auricular surface of the ilium: A new method for the determination of age at death. *American Journal of Physical Anthropology*, *68*, 15–28.

MacDonald, H. (2009). Procuring corpses: The English anatomy inspectorate, 1842 to 1858. *Medical History*, *53*, 379–396.

Marshall, J. D. (1985). *The Old Poor Law 1795-1834*. London: MacMillian.

Miles, A., & Conheeney, J. (2005). *A post-medieval population from London: Excavations in the St Bride's lower churchyard 75-82 Farringdon Street, City of London*. London: Museum of London Archaeological Studies Series (unpublished).

Miller, I. (2012). The chemistry of famine: Nutritional controversies and the Irish Famine, c.1845-7. *Medical History*, *56*(4), 444–462.

Miller, I. (2013). Feeding in the workhouse: The institutional and the ideological function of food, c. 1834-1870. *Journal of British Studies*, *52*, 940–962.

Mokyr, J., & O'Grada, C. (2002). What do people die of during famines: The Great Irish Famine in comparative perspective. *European Review of Economic History, 4*, 339–363.

Newman, C. (2010). *The place of the pauper: A historical archaeology of West Yorkshire Workhouses 1834-1930*. Unpublished PhD dissertation. University of York, York.

Newman, C. (2013). To punish or protect: The New Poor Law and the English Workhouse. *International Journal of Historical Archaeology, 18*(1), 122–145.

Nicholls, G., & Willink, H. G. (1898a). *History of the English Poor Law, Volume Two, 1714-1853* (2nd ed.). Edinburgh: Morrison and Gibb Limited.

Nicholls, G., & Willink, H. G. (1898b). *A history of the English Poor Law, Volume One, 924-1714* (2nd ed.). Edinburgh: Morrison and Gibb Limited.

Oxley, G. (1974). *Poor relief in England and Wales, 1601-1834*. London: David & Charles Ltd.

Poor Law Commission. (1836). *Second annual report of the Poor Law Commission. Parliamentary Papers 1836*, XXIX.

Picard, L. (2005). *Victorian London: The life of a city, 1840-1870*. London: Orion Publishing Group Ltd.

Pinhasi, R., Shaw, P., White, B., & Ogden, A. R. (2006). Morbidity, rickets and long-bone growth in post-medieval Britain—A cross-population analysis. *Annals of Human Biology, 33*, 372–389.

Potter, W. E. (2010). *Evidence for a change in the rate of aging of osteological indicators in American documented skeletal samples*. Unpublished PhD dissertation. University of New Mexico, Albuquerque.

Pound, J. (1971). *Poverty and vagrancy in Tudor England*. London: Longman Group Limited.

Powers, N. (Ed.), (2012). *Human osteology method statement*. London: Museum of London. Retrieved from <https://www.museumoflondon.org.uk/application/files/4814/5633/5269/osteology-method-statement-revised-2012.pdf>.

Roberts, C., & Cox, M. (2003). *Health & disease in Britain: From prehistory to the present day*. Gloucester: Sutton Publishing.

Rose, M. E. (1971). *The English Poor Law 1780-1930*. Newton Abbot: David and Charles Limited.

Rowbotham, J., & Clayton, P. (2008). An unsuitable and degraded diet? Part Three: Victorian consumption patterns and their health benefits. *Journal of the Royal Society of Medicine, 101*, 454–462.

Sharpe, P. (2011). Explaining the short stature of the poor: Chronic childhood disease and growth in nineteenth-century England. *The Economic History Review, 4*, 1475–1494.

Stow, J. (1842). *The survey of London*. Oxford: Oxford University Press.

Stuckler, D., & Basu, S. (2013). *The body economic: Why austerity kills*. London: Allen Lane.

Tanner, A. (1999). The casual poor and the City of London Poor Law Union, 1837-1869. *The Historical Journal, 42*(1), 183–206.

Tomkins, A. (2013). Workhouse medical care from working-class autobiographies, 1750-1834. In J. Reinarz, & L. Schwarz (Eds.), *Medicine and the workhouse* (pp. 86–102). Rochester: University of Rochester Press.

Wakefield, H. R., Chandler, F., Lansbury, G., & Webb, S. (1909). *Report of the Royal Commission on the Poor Laws and relief of distress, being the minority report*. London: Eyre and Spottiswoode Ltd.

Wood, J. W., Milner, G. R., Harpending, H. C., & Weiss, K. M. (1992). The osteological paradox: Problems of inferring prehistoric health from skeletal samples. *Current Anthropology, 33*, 343–379.

WORD database. (2012a). *Museum of London online database: Broadgate.* Retrieved from <http://archive.museumoflondon.org.uk/Centre-for-Human-Bioarchaeology/Database/Post-medieval + cemeteries/Broadgate.htm>

WORD database. (2012b). *Museum of London online database: City Bunhill Burial ground.* Retrieved from <http://archive.museumoflondon.org.uk/Centre-for-Human-Bioarchaeology/Database/Post-medieval + cemeteries/citybunhillburialground.htm>

WORD database. (2012c). *Museum of London online database: Cross Bones.* Retrieved from <http://archive.museumoflondon.org.uk/Centre-for-Human-Bioarchaeology/Database/Post-medieval + cemeteries/Cross + bones.htm>

WORD database. (2012d). *Museum of London online database: St Bride's Lower.* Retrieved from <http://archive.museumoflondon.org.uk/Centre-for-Human-Bioarchaeology/Database/Post-medieval + cemeteries/St + Brides + lower.htm>

WORD database. (2012e). *Museum of London online database: St Thomas Hospital.* Retrieved from <http://archive.museumoflondon.org.uk/Centre-for-Human-Bioarchaeology/Database/Post-medieval + cemeteries/StThomasHospital.htm>

Chapter 12

Innovation in population health intervention research: a historical perspective

Paul Hackett[1,2], Juanita Bascu[1], Tom McIntosh[1,3], Bonnie Jeffery[1,4] and Nazeem Muhajarine[1,5]

[1]Saskatchewan Population Health and Evaluation Research Unit, [2]Department of Geography and Planning, University of Saskatchewan, Saskatoon, SK, Canada, [3]Department of Politics and International Studies, University of Regina, Regina, SK, Canada, [4]School of Social Work, University of Regina, Prince Albert, SK, Canada, [5]Department of Community Health and Epidemiology, University of Saskatchewan, Saskatoon, SK, Canada

Chapter Outline

Introduction

While population health as a field of research has garnered much attention in the past two decades in Canada, health inequities among marginalized population groups continue to rise. "Marginalized" or "vulnerable" refer to the processes and conditions by which specific populations are impacted by structural, avoidable, and unnecessary inequities which result in disproportionate illness and hardship (Browne et al., 2012). Due to their marginal position in Canadian society in terms of both power and resources, these populations face unequal, unfair, and preventable deficits in their health status. For example, among Indigenous seniors, the incidence of chronic conditions such as hypertension, heart problems, diabetes, and arthritis is

Bioarchaeology of Marginalized People. DOI: https://doi.org/10.1016/B978-0-12-815224-9.00012-9

double or triple the rate of non-Indigenous seniors (First Nations and Inuit Regional Health Survey National Steering Committee, 1999). In addition, significant health inequities have been found for a range of child health and development measures, such as infant mortality, immunization coverage, respiratory illness, school readiness, mental health, and low birth weight (Muhajarine, Vu, & Labonte, 2006; Wright & Muhajarine, 2008). Among rural populations, health inequities manifest as higher mortality rates, as well as higher rates of stroke, certain cancers, diabetes, chronic obstructive pulmonary disease, suicide, infant death, and accidents compared to their urban counterparts (Kenny et al., 2013; Vance, Basta, Bute, & Denham, 2012).

Globally, there has been an increasing call for the development of population health intervention research to address health inequities through action on the social determinants of health (Bärnighausen, 2017; Frankish, 2012; Whitehead, 2008). The World Health Organization held an international conference to share experiences and identify effective strategies to reduce health inequities among vulnerable populations (World Health Organization, 2011). Recently in Canada an international summit was held to foster new knowledge and methodological insight to support health outcomes through the advancement of population health intervention research (Canadian Institutes of Health Research, 2016). In the United States the Centers for Disease Control (CDC) evaluated interventions and provided an overview documenting the "most promising" interventions on their website (Centers for Disease Control, 2005). More recently in the United Kingdom the Medical Research Council provided guidance on the application of natural experiments through the evaluation of population health interventions (Craig et al., 2012).

Despite the current progress to date, there is a growing acknowledgment that significant challenges remain in addressing the underlying origins of health inequities (Hankivskya & Christoffersen, 2008). A historical approach, drawing on data from the past to facilitate observational studies, provides a powerful tool for studying the health of the present (Hackett, 2005). Understanding the historical patterns of illness and the social determinants of health (such as culture, gender, and geography) can provide insights into how present-day interventions may play out with certain populations. Moreover, using a historical analysis enables researchers to explore the ways in which past interventions such as programs and policies impacted different population groups, and identify ways to address current health inequities. In that way, we are able to learn from both the mistakes and the successes of the past.

The purpose of this chapter, then, is to use the work of the Saskatchewan Population Health and Evaluation Research Unit (SPHERU) to present several strategies by which study of the health of marginalized populations of the past can be used to understand the underlying origins of current health inequities. SPHERU serves as a local example of how population health research is being conducted through the use of historical analysis and provides a broad range of examples of how this research can be done. This chapter sets the stage with a brief discussion of the advantages of applying a historical approach to population health intervention research by examining the importance of what are termed natural experiments embedded in the past. Building on this, it identifies methodological innovations and novel applications in using a historical approach to advance the field of population health intervention research. From this, it showcases innovative examples and outcomes exemplified in the authors' research through SPHERU of using a historical approach to support population health intervention research.

Why Use a Historical Approach to Population Health Intervention Research?

There is much value in understanding the role of historical interventions on health equity among vulnerable populations. The past exists as a natural data bank of health information and health outcomes of real world health, social, and economic policy choices that can be used by researchers across disciplines with an interest in contemporary public and population health outcomes—work that can be done with or without the assistance of professional historians (Fee & Brown, 1997). We know that past government policies contribute to the current ill health of certain populations, those we consider to be marginalized. For example, the host of health disparities between Indigenous and non-Indigenous residents of Canada that were noted earlier (Wilson & Rosenberg, 2002) has their roots in the experience of colonization, destruction of culture, loss of language, and forced relocation from traditional lands (Kulmann & Richmond, 2011). As Bayer and Fairchild (2004) assert, historical knowledge can enable policy-makers to design effective interventions in the present, while avoiding the mistakes of the past.

There are several examples that highlight the potential for using a historical perspective to better understand the underlying origins of health inequities (Milton, Moonan, Taylor-Robinson, & Whitehead, 2011). For instance, Bartlett (2003) has observed that the present high degree of stress experienced by Indigenous people in Canada, which contributes greatly to their ongoing poor health, is itself partly a legacy of the cultural changes brought about by the contact processes of the past. Thus she argued that legacy must be used to inform policy in order to generate "the most appropriate design for culturally grounded contemporary life approaches that will increase First Nation, Métis and Inuit health and well-being" (Bartlett, 2003, p. 166).

Another relevant example concerns tuberculosis (TB). Currently, Indigenous Canadians, including the Métis, First Nations and, especially, Inuit, people face far higher rates of TB than Canadian-born, non-Indigenous people. The same was true historically, and although the rates for both have fallen substantially since the mid-20th century, and despite systematic health interventions to correct this inequity, this troubling gap persists into the present. In their consideration of the region-wide outbreak of the disease among the First Nations people of western Canada in the late 19th century, Daschuk, Hackett, and MacNeil (2006) showed that the combined morbidity and mortality impact was not simply a case of the organic spread of a pathogen through a genetically vulnerable population but rather was a consequence of social and economic constraints imposed by the treaty and reserve systems on a marginalized population. In their case study the "positive deviance" of the nontreaty Dakota in relation to the general trend of sickness and death showed that the catastrophic mortality of TB was not an inevitable outcome of European settlement. Their findings also demonstrate that, whatever the genetic relationship with the disease, social and economic changes were required to initiate the epidemic. This is a critical lesson as we deal with current TB outbreaks in First Nations communities (and indeed communities belonging to all three Indigenous peoples).

In a recent study, Gibson, Cave, Doering, Ortiz, and Harm (2005) found that a significant number of people from high-risk groups, including Indigenous and immigrant Canadians, were poorly informed about current TB treatment and transmission. Several of the Indigenous participants referenced past negative interactions with TB sanatoria. This seems to suggest that historical experiences may influence present-day attitudes toward treatment, echoing Jenkins' (1977) findings for First Nations people in British Columbia during the 1970s. Gibson et al. (2005, p. 931) concluded that "accessible and culturally appropriate health education" is necessary for effective treatment of the disease. Given the influence that past experiences have on current knowledge of TB, specifically in the case of Indigenous Canadians, it is imperative for culturally appropriate programs to reference historical inequities in treatment as a starting point for explaining current interventions.

The potential benefits of addressing the origins of health inequity are considerable, and may be divided into two primary approaches that focus on understanding the nature of health inequities in the past (historical context), and evaluating social and public health interventions within a historical perspective. First, at the most basic level, a historical approach can provide valuable context for understanding current health inequities and can inform the research community about "the complexity of the social, cultural, political and financial circumstances that frame each particular case" (Perdiguero, Bernabeu, Huertas, & Rodríguez-Ocaña, 2001, p. 668). If health inequities are historically rooted in, or associated with, processes like colonization and dispossession from the land then the current population-level interventions meant to address those inequities need to be framed with that understanding in mind.

Second the past can also serve as a laboratory providing an opportunity to assess the effects of public health interventions by comparing the earlier health outcomes in otherwise similar jurisdictions that implemented different public health practices (Fee & Brown, 1997; Perdiguero et al., 2001). "Natural experiments" refer to evaluating the impact of interventions across comparable jurisdictions in the past. The interventions used in the natural experiments could include the development of, or any changes to, policies, programs, research, legislation, funding, or any other form of action on the determinants of health to affect the health outcomes of populations. Relevant examples of comparative historical analysis using natural experiments include seat belt legislation or the influence of smoking bans and the improvement of health outcomes that may result from these policies. Natural experiments based in history have shown considerable promise for health research in recent years, particularly in circumstances where there is a lack of evidence for evaluations of current health policies and interventions. Indeed, given the paucity of evaluation with respect to health inequalities (Petticrew, 2011) in general, these historical studies may provide some of the strongest lines of evidence for studying the factors leading to inequalities in health faced by marginalized populations.

Comparative historical analysis using natural experiments is advantageous as it can explore cultural and geographical variations, and the impact that these have on the application of specific policy interventions and health outcomes in different jurisdictions (Diamond & Robinson, 2010; Milton et al., 2011). For instance these natural experiments can be used to assess different population health outcomes of social policies, economic policies, health insurance schemes, or epidemic interventions, such as the supply of clean water in urban areas (Cutler & Miller, 2005). A potential challenge for conducting comparative historical analysis of natural experiments is accounting for jurisdictional differences such as cultural or socio-political differences. Accordingly, it is important for researchers to be well-informed and cognizant of the unique contextual factors that may influence the findings.

It is imperative to note that many historical policy interventions were undertaken with little or no thought to their potential impact on health outcomes. Indeed the tendency was (and often still is) to treat different policy realms as silos where, for example, labor market interventions were evaluated for labor market impacts, but no consideration was given to whether there were positive or negative health impacts related to those labor market policy changes.

In Canada, this has been complicated by the federal division of powers which situates much of the social policy in the hands of the provinces with the federal government providing funds to provincial programs that meet the agreed upon national objectives such as those in the Government of Canada (1985). For instance when the federal government reformed the national Employment Insurance (EI) program in 1995–96 such that fewer workers would be eligible for benefits, it assumed that such workers would be picked up by provincial social assistance programs. But the federal redesign of EI did not take into account that provincial governments had similarly redesigned social assistance programs to make them less generous and more difficult to access. Both orders of government were responding to budgetary concerns over persistent deficits and growing public debt, but in solving those problems they served to exacerbate the precarious position of both the short-term and longer-termed unemployed across the country (McIntosh & Boychuk, 2000).

This highlights the need to be aware of the policy interdependencies that exist when, say in federal states, two orders of government exist that can impact the same populations with policy changes that have unintended negative consequences. In the case earlier, neither order of government thought about the impacts of the policy change in anything except budgetary terms, yet we know there are health consequences when workers' access to social supports in times of unemployment is reduced. These insights drawn from past interventions highlight longstanding challenges and the need for collaboration in the orders of government to effectively address issues of health inequity.

It should be emphasized that these interdependencies grow, decline, and change over time as the result of specific choices made by both orders of government. This highlights another important reason for examining historical policy choices and their interplay, namely the impact of path dependency as a shaper of the choices governments currently have. Each time a government makes a policy choice it chooses one path over another (or over multiple other options) and, over time, that choice will shape and condition the future choices. For example, the choice by governments in the postwar era to assume greater responsibility for the design, delivery, and funding of social services removed a whole set of charitable and religious actors from the provision of those services. Over time, then, the perception changed that such services were part and parcel of "what governments do"—a perception that lasted until the 1980s and 1990s when governments, as the result of other fiscal decisions, began to contract out social service provision to new nongovernmental actors that were decidedly different in nature and scope than those that existed previously. All of this is to say that understanding the choices made historically (and the paths not taken) can give us deeper insights into the choices that governments face in the present. Policy changes tend not only to be incremental and partial but also deeply and profoundly conditioned by the choices made in the past that brought us to our present place on the present path.

Methodological Application: Conducting Population Health Intervention Research Using a Historical Approach

Adopting a historical perspective to assess health interventions requires a markedly different approach to selecting a research methodology compared to contemporary research. In traditional intervention research protocols for data collection can be set by the researcher based on the means of analysis, the nature of the intervention, and the desired results. When studying interventions of the past, control over the selection of data is far more limited. With rare exceptions, the historical researcher is unable to study new data but must instead rely on existing historical records. This may require a greater degree of creativity, in terms of data selection, collection, and methods of analysis.

SPHERU is an emerging leader with respect to the development of innovative population health intervention research from a historical perspective. Using diverse data sources, the SPHERU team is working on one project to explore the health outcomes of past social and economic policy interventions, while on another we seek to assess the historical role played by community-based organizations in population health. In a third, we are working to recreate the changes to the health and nutrition of Indigenous Canadians, with the goal of better understanding the current set of health inequities that they face. In these projects, data are being collected from a wide variety of sources, including those directly related to health and health care, and others that provide critical historical context. Government health reports from the day are supplemented by a vast array of archival records, newspapers, published local histories, statistical accounts, and other textual material.

Beyond the focus on written records, SPHERU researchers are documenting the health of the past through the analysis of contemporary photographs (Fig. 12.1). Such visual approaches have a potentially valuable role to play in health research, including that which seeks to incorporate historical context (Harrison, 2002). Photographs provide a new dimension by, for instance, visually documenting the implementation of past interventions on population groups or providing important evidence of environmental issues. These photos help to document evidence concerning the factors that contributed to health inequities.

For example, the photo in Fig. 12.1, from the early 20th century, shows First Nations children from southern Saskatchewan who have been surgically treated in a shack for the lymphatic form of TB, to be left to recover in a tent hospital. In many cases, First Nations people were denied treatment altogether prior to the 1940s. When compared to the facilities available to the general population, these were substandard. The photo, when compared to others of mainstream health care facilities, provides an illustration of fundamental historical health inequities. Indeed, it demonstrates the poverty of TB

FIGURE 12.1 First Nations children surgically treated in a shack for lymphatic form of tuberculosis, Southern Saskatchewan, 1900. *Courtesy of Peel's Prairie Provinces, http://peel.library.ualberta.ca/index.html.*

care for First Nations people at the time as compared to the broader provincial population. In contrast to the minimal surgical ward depicted in the photograph, the latter people would have received superior care in far more elaborate hospitals and sanatoria. In all likelihood this difference in care would have contributed to the consistent gulf in TB mortality rates then seen between First Nations people and the broader population.

Another innovative method for historical population health intervention research includes the usage of oral histories. Oral histories involve conducting interviews to explore past events and interventions. When properly carried out, they provide rich data and document more comprehensive details that are rarely captured in existing textual records. As Gyde (2006) elaborates, examples of health issues that have been addressed through oral histories range from recollections of hospital patients to the development of new imaging technology. The personal recollections and impressions of people can offer new understandings by capturing suppressed or undocumented data which can provide insight into why, how, or what past interventions occurred. Moreover, oral histories supplement existing records by adding local-level perspectives and new depth. Nowhere is this truer than for those populations who historically have occupied less advantageous positions within society. It is often the case that the administrative records that survive into the present provide a perspective that favors the dominant society and fails to capture the understandings of those who have traditionally been marginalized. Oral history, then, can provide a remedy to this selective viewpoint, and a fuller understanding of the impact of past interventions.

Technology such as Geographic Information Systems (GIS) has the potential to play a key role in conducting leading-edge historical population intervention research. GIS can facilitate the management, cataloging, and analysis of valuable historical data. Ideally, as McLafferty (2003) argues, GIS enables researchers to address the changing spatial organization of health care, examine the health impact of different interventions, and identify how health outcomes can be improved. The classic example is Dr. John Snow's usage of maps in the identification of cholera outbreaks in relation to a water pump in 19th-century Soho, London (Koch & Denike, 2004). Although the advantages of using GIS are well-documented, not all researchers recognize the potential benefits of using GIS to explore the impact of past interventions on health equity. Exploring historical health data through GIS presents a myriad of possibilities, such as identifying historically embedded political and socioeconomic hierarchies that influence current health equity. For instance, layering different indicators through GIS mapping enables researchers to examine historical patterns of disease, mortality, and health care interventions, revealing key disparities in incidence (Gundersen, 2000). Accordingly the growing availability of national and international historical health-related data presents a novel opportunity for researchers to explicitly address the underlying origins of health disparity.

Interdisciplinary teams and community partnerships are important for advancing innovation in historical population health intervention research. By collaborating with diverse partners acting collectively, researchers are better able to identify, assess, and evaluate the health impact of past interventions on current health outcomes. As in Johnson et al. (2008), research teams involving interdisciplinary, interprofessional, multijurisdictional, and community-level input build capacity for collective innovation and shared knowledge to improve health equity. For example, the adoption of new methods and creative approaches to explore health inequity largely depends on the research team. Different disciplines and stakeholders offer unique perspectives, and by combining elements from different theoretical frameworks, researchers are able to develop more robust historical population health intervention research.

Innovative Outcomes: Examples

Novel applications of historical methods, combined with unconventional data sources, can yield innovative outcomes in research. In turn, these research results can contribute to guiding the development of our health interventions. For instance, SPHERU researchers are using residential school records to generate body mass index (BMI) values for First Nations children who entered the school system during the era from the 1930s to the 1950s (Fig. 12.2). These BMI figures suggest that high youth BMI, and obesity, now part of the driving force for the current diabetes crisis in First Nations

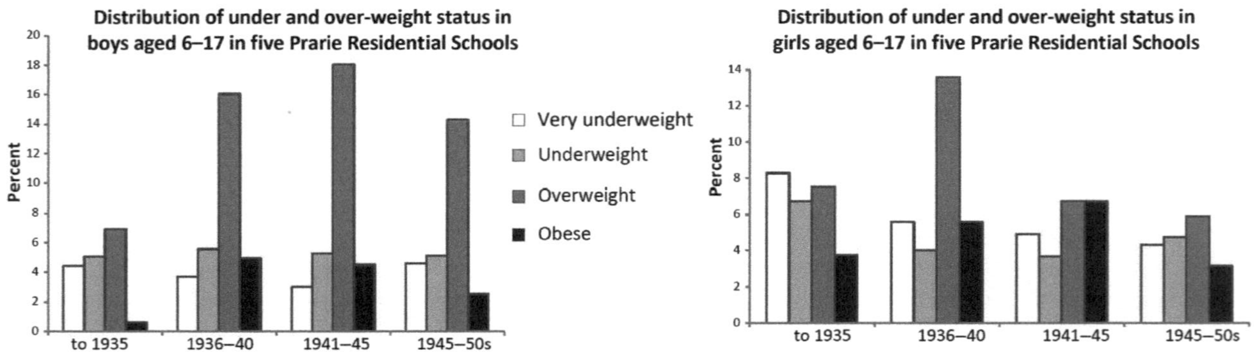

FIGURE 12.2 BMI values of students entering select Manitoba and Saskatchewan Residential Schools, 1930–50s.

communities, were not an inherent problem as recently as the 1950s. This era of rising obesity coincided with a period of abrupt sociocultural and economic change in many of those communities. Seen in this context, the historical data would support the need for Indigenous diabetes interventions that address the issue of cultural and economic change as part of the colonial process, and that successful interventions will therefore need to address those underlying issues.

As noted earlier, the past can provide a laboratory for conducting natural experiments, in order to evaluate health interventions. During the first half of the 20th century provincial TB rates varied considerably, with some provinces, notably Saskatchewan, leading the way in terms of successful treatment and prevention, minimizing mortality rates (Canadian Tuberculosis Association CTA, 1942). Other provinces fared much more poorly. As part of our history project, we are evaluating Saskatchewan's anti-TB efforts at both the health policy level and with regard to specific medical and community health interventions, such as X-ray surveys, sanatoria, and the use of chemotherapy. These are to be compared to the policies and interventions in the neighboring provinces of Alberta and Manitoba, which tended to lag behind in terms of preventing the disease.

This allows us to both understand how the responses differed and why Saskatchewan's past approach was more effective, but it might also give us insight into why that approach failed to forestall the contemporary reemergence of TB as a health threat, especially for Indigenous peoples in the province. Did Saskatchewan change course in some way, did it fail to adapt to changing conditions, did it let its guard down? To what extent are present-day outbreaks and persistence of the disease in certain isolated communities a legacy of those past policies and failures, through the reactivation of old, latent infections, combined with the many challenges that the province's Indigenous communities face today? Only a detailed understanding of historical choices made by past health authorities can answer those questions and, thus, inform today's decisions. SPHERU researchers are using GIS to better understand past spatial variations in health among Saskatchewan communities (Fig. 12.3). For instance by tracking TB rates by rural municipality over the 20th century, we are able to understand how TB mortality varied between rural and urban communities and Indigenous and non-Indigenous rural municipalities. By following these variations over time and examining the change in patterns at key points in time when public health interventions were implemented, we can also assess the varying impact of those interventions as they contributed to the decline of the disease in the province.

It can be argued that understanding the history of health interventions may enable us to recapture lost lessons from the past. One such example concerns strategies for successful aging, a question of increasing importance as Canada's population grows older in the 21st century. Questions we now

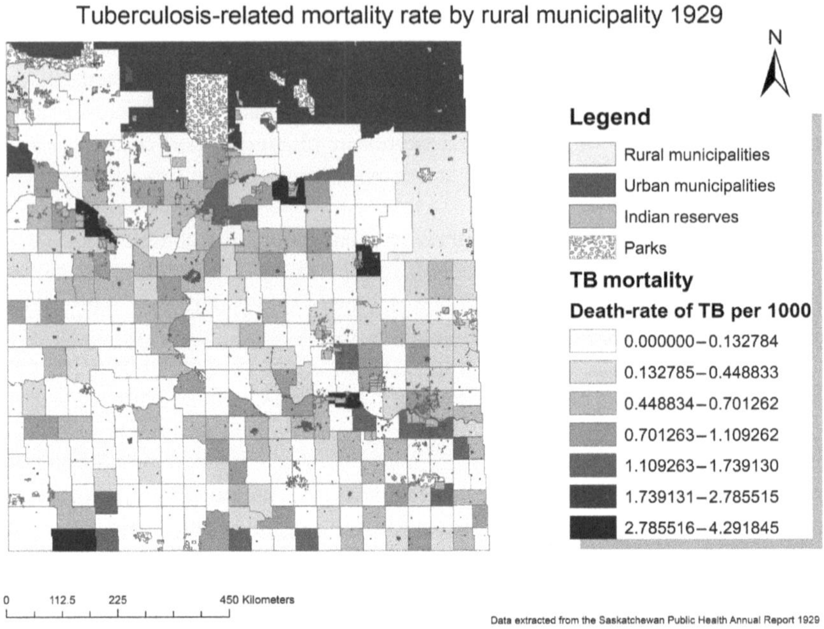

FIGURE 12.3 Saskatchewan tuberculosis mortality by rural municipality, 1929.

face about where and how to accommodate the elderly have been pertinent issues in the past. Overall, aging residents in rural communities face more difficult choices as they may lack local access to important resources, making successful aging in place more difficult for them than those residing in major cities. Nevertheless, this is not a new problem and it is possible that there are lessons to be learned from the past. In the Saskatchewan Health Services Survey Commission Report of 1944, Commissioner, Henry E. Sigerist expounded on the need to build new facilities in rural Saskatchewan, and what form those facilities would take. He noted:

> *There is a great need for additional Old Folks' Homes...It would be inadvisable to consider the construction of some large institution, since the old folks wish to die near the place where they lived, and where they have friends. It would be preferable to establish a larger number of small homes in various localities, which could be operated at little cost, and to pay a subsidy to institutions and individuals that attend to the aged*
>
> Sigerist (1944, p. 6).

The quote from Commissioner Sigerist highlights the debate of the time between those who, unsuccessfully, argued for keeping seniors in their communities, and a provincial government that was moving toward institutionalization, with the latter group's ascendance setting the stage for Saskatchewan's current aging strategy. The quote indicates that the

Commissioner's opinion was firmly grounded in supporting healthy aging in place. The importance of this still resonates today and is highlighted in a recent study that suggests that rural seniors who have the supports and the opportunity to remain in their communities are happier, more socially engaged and able to live healthier lives (Bacsu et al., 2014). Building on Commissioner Sigerist's statement the SPHERU history team will evaluate the changing nature of aging in Saskatchewan, and in particular the concept of aging in place. Further, these lessons from the past will seek to inform policy-makers of the present, in order to affirm the value of a more humane approach that was once the norm.

Exploring the past also enables us to understand the impact of past policies and medical interventions on the current health of Canada's Indigenous people, in keeping with the spirit of the Calls to Action of the Truth and Reconciliation Commission (Truth and Reconciliation Commission of Canada TRC, 2015). SPHERU researchers and their collaborators interviewed First Nations TB patients from the Prairie Provinces to assess the relationship between past contexts of TB and present-day attitudes toward the disease (Komarnisky, Hackett, Abonyi, Courtney Heffernan, & Long, 2016). They found that negative past experiences with the disease on the part of the patients, their families, and their fellow community members persist and, indeed, inform current attitudes toward the disease and TB interventions. In turn, these attitudes may contribute to the failure of public health programs to eliminate the disease from First Nations communities. Future attempts to eliminate the disease must therefore be guided by this historical legacy.

Finally, SPHERU has created the first iteration of a "History of Health Timeline" for the province that can serve as a multifaceted and interactive teaching tool for both secondary and postsecondary students. Entries on the timeline include historical health and social outcome data for different subpopulations, key political and social events relating to both health and social policy, data on the evolution of key economic sectors, legislative changes, and a potential host of other historical data relating to population health interventions. As the timeline is populated with layers of such data, it will allow one to trace the changing health status of different subpopulations relative to the prevailing economic and social conditions over time as well as pinpointing key policy and political interventions on important health issues. Where health data generally focus on the "average" the data in the timeline will allow us to explore the history of the health of populations both in the mainstream and at the margins. We should be able to explore the wide variations in the historical experiences of Indigenous, northern, and rural residents whose health status is generally poorer than "the average" resident such that we can trace where and how those inequities arose, were reinforced, and persisted over time. The goal is to create a means by which students, teachers, and researchers can explore the health of the province by coming to understand how that health has changed across both time and space for different populations in the province. By disaggregating the health of those on the margins we can rethink population-level interventions that are sensitive to and account for how and why those populations were marginalized.

Future Directions

There is much value in applying a historical perspective to population health intervention research. Health inequities among different groups cannot be understood merely by looking at present-day interventions. As Irwin and Scali (2007) have noted, in order to effectively improve health equity, action on the social determinants of health must draw on historical knowledge. Health inequities are complex, intertwined, and rooted within the historical context. They are directly connected to history and the unequal distribution of socioeconomic, political, and environmental resources (Center for Disease Control, 2012). Accordingly, this paper has highlighted the importance of using a historical perspective to better understand the underlying causes of health inequities. To act on the inequities that marginalized populations experience today, researchers and health policy-makers must understand their origins in the past.

Applying a historical perspective to population health intervention research is a relatively new approach that presents both challenges and opportunities. For instance, one key challenge is the absence of existing knowledge on effective strategies for measuring past health inequities. Another challenge is determining how to address the historical gaps and inconsistencies in datasets. For researchers this highlights both a need and an opportunity to develop innovative strategies for understanding the role of historical interventions on health outcomes. More research is needed to explore the theories, methods, and applications that best support historical population health intervention research. Research evidence is essential to providing a solid foundation for understanding how to conduct and engage in historical intervention research. Policy-makers and government leaders can support this research by providing funding opportunities for educational training, research, and syntheses of existing knowledge on historical population health intervention research.

Opportunities exist for innovative historical approaches to reduce health inequities through community and interdisciplinary partnerships. For instance how researchers study the impact of historical interventions depends largely on the team. Community-level input is needed to ensure that the research is inclusive and addresses important barriers of health equity which may not have been documented by historical literature, such as the intergenerational impacts of colonization on Indigenous Peoples (Loppie Reading & Wein, 2009). Oral histories and photographs may provide innovative data to supplementing important gaps in historical records on vulnerable populations. SPHERU researchers with expertise in anthropology and geography, working alongside a clinician and medical researcher, were able to generate valuable insights into the nutritional health of First Nations youth in the middle decades of the 20th century by using historical medical examinations to calculate BMI values (Hackett, Abonyi, & Dyck, 2016). By combining different theoretical frameworks, viewpoints, and disciplines, more robust research is created than could be achieved by a single theory or discipline.

Globally, many countries are looking for ways to improve health outcomes while cutting health expenditures. A historical perspective can guide researchers in identifying lessons learned on what has or has not worked to improve health outcomes (Martin, Cheng, & Stranges, 2017). As noted by the World Health Organization (2007), health systems would be more effective if they had more access to critical information, relevant data, and coordinated knowledge exchange. The importance of synergy and coordination between researchers, health professionals, and policy-makers cannot be overstated. To ensure that historical evidence informs current population health interventions researchers, practitioners, and policy-makers need to work together to share knowledge, research findings, and lessons learned. Accordingly, in working to reduce health inequities, collaboration among researchers, practitioners, and policy-makers is paramount.

Conclusion

This paper has highlighted the advantages, methodological innovations, and outcomes of applying a historical perspective to advance population health intervention research. It adds insight to the relatively new and limited literature using a historical perspective to support population health research (Berridge, 2010; Milton et al., 2011). However, it is important to note that many of the challenges present unique opportunities, such as the need for future research to explore the theories, methods, and applications that best support historical population health intervention research.

References

Bacsu, J., Jeffery, B., Abonyi, S., Johnson, S., Novik, N., Martz, D., & Oosman, S. (2014). Healthy aging in place: Perceptions of rural older adults. *Educational Gerontology*, *40*(5), 327–337.

Bärnighausen, T. (2017). Population health intervention research: Three important advancements. *International Journal of Public Health*, *62*(8), 841–843.

Bartlett, J. (2003). Involuntary cultural change, stress phenomenon and Aboriginal health status. *Canadian Journal of Public Health*, *94*(3), 93–96.

Bayer, R., & Fairchild, A. L. (2004). The genesis of public health ethics. *Bioethics*, *18*, 473–492.

Berridge, V. (2010). Thinking in time: Does health policy need history as evidence? *The Lancet, 375*(9717), 798–799.

Browne, A., Varcoe, C., Wong, S., Smye, V., Lavoie, J., Littlejohn, D., ... Lennox, S. (2012). Closing the health equity gap: Evidence-based strategies for primary health care organizations. *International Journal for Equity in Health, 11*(59), 1–15.

Canadian Institutes of Health Research. (2016). *Sparking population health solutions: Research for a healthier future – An international summit 2016.* Available from <http://www.cihr-irsc.gc.ca/e/49177.html>.

Canadian Tuberculosis Association (CTA). (1942). *Bulletin of the Canadian Tuberculosis Association, 20*(1), September.

Centers for Disease Control. (2005). *The guide to combumunity preventive services: What works to promote health?* New York: Oxford University Press.

Centers for Disease Control. (2012). *Health disparities.* Available from <http://www.cdc.gov/healthyyouth/disparities/>.

Craig, P., Cooper, C., Gunnell, D., Haw, S., Lawson, K., Macintyre, S., ... Thompson, S. (2012). Using natural experiments to evaluate population health interventions: New Medical Research Council guidance. *Journal of Epidemiology and Community Health, 66,* 1182–1186.

Cutler, D., & Miller, G. (2005). The role of public health improvements in health advances: The twentieth-century United States. *Demography, 42*(1), 1–22.

Daschuk, J., Hackett, P., & MacNeil, S. (2006). Treaties and tuberculosis: First Nations people in late 19th-century western Canada, a political and economic transformation. *Canadian Bulletin of Medical History, 23*(2), 307–330.

Diamond, J., & Robinson, J. (2010). *Natural experiments of history.* Cambridge, MA: Belknap Press of Harvard University Press.

Fee, E., & Brown, T. M. (1997). Why history? *American Journal of Public Health, 87*(11), 1763–1764.

First Nations and Inuit Regional Health Survey National Steering Committee. (1999). *First Nations and Inuit regional health survey: National report 1999.* St. Regis, QC: First Nations and Inuit Regional Longitudinal Health Survey National Steering Committee.

Frankish, J. (2012). Population health intervention research: Advancing the field. *Canadian Journal of Public Health, 103*(1), S3–S4.

Gibson, N., Cave, A., Doering, D., Ortiz, L., & Harm, P. (2005). Socio-cultural factors influencing prevention and treatment of tuberculosis in immigrant and Aboriginal communities in Canada. *Social Science and Medicine, 61*(5), 931–942.

Government of Canada. (1985). *Canada Health Act.* Available from Canada Justice Laws website. <http://laws-lois.justice.gc.ca/eng/acts/c-6/>.

Gundersen, L. (2000). Mapping it out: Using atlases to detect patterns of health care, disease, and mortality. *Annals of Internal Medicine, 133*(2), 161–164.

Gyde, H. (2006). Oral history and health informatics: Mutual support. AMIA Annual Symposium Proceedings, p. 938.

Hackett, P. (2005). From past to present: Understanding First Nations health patterns in a historical context. *Canadian Journal of Public Health, 95,* S17–S21.

Hackett, P., Abonyi, S., & Dyck, R. (2016). Anthropometric indices of First Nations children and youth on first entry to Manitoba/Saskatchewan residential schools—1919 to 1953. *International Journal of Circumpolar Health, 75*(1), 1–9.

Hankivskya, O., & Christoffersen, A. (2008). Intersectionality and the determinants of health: A Canadian perspective. *Critical Public Health, 18*(3), 271–283.

Harrison, B. (2002). Seeing health and illness worlds – using visual methodologies in a sociology of health and illness: A methodological review. *Sociology of Health & Illness, 24*(6), 856–872.

Irwin, A., & Scali, E. (2007). Action on the social determinants of health: A historical perspective. *Global Public Health: An International Journal for Research, Policy and Practice, 2* (3), 235–256.

Jenkins, D. (1977). Tuberculosis: The native Indian viewpoint on its prevention, diagnosis, and treatment. *Preventive Medicine, 6*, 545–555.

Johnson, S., Abonyi, S., Jeffery, B., Hackett, P., Hampton, M., McIntosh, T., . . . Sari, N. (2008). Recommendations for action on the social determinants of health: A Canadian perspective. *The Lancet, 372*(9650), 1690–1693.

Kenny, A., Hyett, N., Sawtell, J., Dickson-Swift, V., Farmer, J., & O'Meara, P. (2013). Community participation in rural health: A scoping review. *BMC Health Services Research, 13*(64), 1–8.

Koch, T., & Denike, K. (2004). Medical mapping: The revolution in teaching and using maps for the analysis of medical issues. *Journal of Geography, 103*(2), 76–85.

Komarnisky, S., Hackett, P., Abonyi, S., Courtney Heffernan, C., & Long, R. (2016). "Years ago": Reconciliation and First Nations narratives of tuberculosis in the Canadian Prairie provinces. *Critical Public Health, 26*(4), 381–393.

Kulmann, K., & Richmond, C. (2011). Addressing the persistence of tuberculosis among the Canadian Inuit Population: The need for a social determinants of health framework. *The International Indigenous Policy Journal, 2*(1), 1–16.

Loppie Reading, C., & Wein, F. (2009). *Health inequalities and social determinants of Aboriginal Peoples' health. National Collaborating Centre for Aboriginal Health.* Available from <http://ahrnets.ca/files/2011/02/NCCAH-Loppie-Wien_Report.pdf>.

Martin, J., Cheng, D., & Stranges, S. (2017). Population health intervention research: Myths and misconceptions. *International Journal of Public Health, 62*(8), 845–847.

McIntosh, T., & Boychuk, G. (2000). Discovered: EI, social assistance and the growing gap in income support for unemployed Canadians. In T. McIntosh (Ed.), *Federalism, democracy and labour market policy in Canada* (pp. 65–158). Kingston, ON: SPS/McGill-Queen's University Press.

McLafferty, S. (2003). GIS and health care. *Annual Review of Public Health, 24*, 25–42.

Milton, B., Moonan, M., Taylor-Robinson, D., & Whitehead, M. (2011). *How can the health Equity impact of universal policies be evaluated? Insights into approaches and next steps.* Copenhagen, Denmark: WHO Regional Office for Europe. Available from: <http://www.euro.who.int/__data/assets/pdf_file/0019/155062/E95912.pdf>.

Muhajarine, N., Vu, L., & Labonte, R. (2006). Social contexts and children's health outcomes: Researching across the boundaries. *Critical Public Health, 16*(3), 205–218.

Perdiguero, E., Bernabeu, J., Huertas, R., & Rodríguez-Ocaña, E. (2001). History of health, a valuable tool in public health. *Journal of Epidemiology and Community Health, 55*(9), 667–673.

Petticrew, M. (2011). Commentary: Sinners, preachers and natural experiments. *International Journal of Epidemiology, 40*(2), 454–456.

Sigerist, H. (1944). *Saskatchewan health services survey commission: Report of the commissioner.* Regina, SK: King's Printer.

Truth and Reconciliation Commission of Canada (TRC). (2015). Truth and Reconciliation Commission of Canada: Calls to Action. Available from <www.trc.ca/websites/trcinstitution/File/2015/Findings/Calls_to_Action_English2.pdf>.

Vance, R., Basta, T., Bute, J., & Denham, S. (2012). Identifying the health needs in rural Appalachian Ohio: Outcomes of a rural community-academic partnership. *American Journal of Health Sciences*, *3*(2), 115–124.

Whitehead, M. (2008). Policy intervention research to address social inequalities in health: Opportunities for cross-national research. *Pop News*, *16*(2-3). Available from <http://www.cihr-irsc.gc.ca/e/documents/ipph_issue16_jun08_e.pdf>.

Wilson, K., & Rosenberg, M. (2002). Exploring the determinants of health for First Nations peoples in Canada: Can existing frameworks accommodate traditional activities? *Social Science and Medicine*, *55*(11), 2017–2031.

World Health Organization. (2007). *Everybody's business strengthening health systems to improve health outcomes: WHO's framework for action*. Available from <http://www.who.int/healthsystems/strategy/everybodys_business.pdf>.

World Health Organization. (2011). *All for equity*. Available from <http://www.who.int/sdhconference/resources/Conference_Report.pdf>.

Wright, J., & Muhajarine, N. (2008). Respiratory illness in Saskatoon infants: The impact of housing and neighbourhood characteristics. *Social Indicators Research*, *85*, 81–95.

Chapter 13

Mapping marginalized pasts

Madeleine L. Mant[1] and Alyson Jaagumagi Holland[2]
[1]Department of Archaeology, Memorial University of Newfoundland, St. John's, NL, Canada,
[2]Department of Anthropology, McMaster University, Hamilton, ON, Canada

Chapter Outline

Discussion/Conclusion

This collection of papers forges new paths in understanding the intricacy and ambiguity of marginalization. Turning our attention to the variety of ways which marginalization—understood broadly as peripheralization of individual bodies—is borne out in the archaeological and historical record, provides the opportunity to gain new insights into the physical effects of marginalization. These physical effects are manifested in skeletal markers of stress and disease, which can be read in context within the historical record to develop broader understandings of vulnerability and the social determinants of health in the past. The integration of bioarchaeological, archaeological, and historical datasets starkly illustrates the varied ways in which individuals may be marginalized both during and after their lifespan, and how widespread marginalizing practices were in the past. These chapters bring to light how subtle the marginalizing process can be, including the potential role that contemporary research and curation plays in perpetuating the placement of individuals on the periphery.

This volume aimed to problematize marginalization and consider its multifaceted effects on individuals through time. We suggest the following themes as a foundational reflection for further studies of this important topic.

Bioarchaeology of Marginalized People. DOI: https://doi.org/10.1016/B978-0-12-815224-9.00013-0

Marginalization as a Process of Peripheralization

This theme highlights marginalization as a process of the separation and privileging of certain groups over others. Marginalization as peripheralization is not a new concept and is reflected in the definitions provided by Hall, Stevens, and Meleis (1994), who draw upon clinical contexts, and Tucker (1990), using an anthropological approach. This view of marginalization focuses upon the inherent power structures acting upon individual bodies while they are alive, which may also influence their postmortem treatment.

Contributions to this volume focusing upon the role of social class as a driving factor in marginalization illustrate the ways in which the privileging of certain bodies over others has measurable health impacts. Ludlow and Hackett speak directly to this idea in their investigation of childhood mortality in working-class neighborhoods in Hamilton, ON during a period of industrialization. The complexity of marginalization is demonstrated through the interplay between age, social status, and economic change. Infants have been marginalized in bioarchaeological and historical research due to a paucity of evidence recovered in the archaeological record and the comparative infrequency of historical documentation of children. Children in working-class families have been marginalized through underreporting, but physically they were among the most vulnerable members of industrializing populations. The working-class dealt with precarious employment and fluctuating access to resources, leading to their placement on the periphery of society by a socio-economic system that valued wealth and resource acquisition. As Ludlow and Hackett illustrate, the varying access to safe environments and health care led to clear patterns in morbidity and mortality.

The power of economic status as a marginalizing force can be difficult to tease apart from other determinants of social status, as illustrated by Doubek and Grauer. In their examination of a single individual of unclear provenience they draw attention to the interaction between race/ancestry, social standing, and economic potential and how these multiple factors act together to influence peripheralization of individual bodies. In the case of their featured individual, historic racial tensions combined with the perceived lower status of employment in labor-intensive positions would have exerted marginalizing pressures. These forces also continued postmortem, where his status on the periphery and categorization as an "other" led to curators dismissively labeling his remains with a racist term.

While most of the contributions in this volume discuss the role that marginalizing forces play in shaping individual experience, Shields Wilford and Gowland also draw attention to the way that the peripheralization of individuals becomes self-perpetuating. Nineteenth-century English workhouses were institutions that could marginalize people through reputation alone since the concept of the workhouse was tied to the contemporary notion of nonproductive citizens and entrance to the workhouse required absolute economic destitution. Once within the workhouse, the physical demands combined with inadequate nutrition created a population that was functionally unable to gather enough capital to rejoin the workforce, resulting in indefinite marginalization.

de la Cova's work powerfully emphasizes the effects of structural violence on the bodies of marginalized individuals in the creation of the anatomical collections. The Hamann-Todd and Terry anatomical collections are comprised of vulnerable individuals, whose socially and culturally marginalized bodies were donated and dissected without informed consent. By asking ourselves as academics to consider the power dynamics that created the very collections we use to speak about marginalization, we are reminded to be reflective of the role that scholarship plays in giving and removing these voices. The role of collection curators is examined critically, demonstrating the importance of continued reflexivity as we embrace a more ethically conscious biological anthropology.

Together these chapters demonstrate the mechanism and consequences of marginalization as a peripheralizing force. For individuals who were separated from the majority of society, denied equal access to resources, and treated as "other," we see embedded health disparities. Studying marginalization in this way helps inform our understanding of the role of social forces in determining health outcomes by illustrating the physical effects of poor access to adequate health care, but also as a comparative population against the more privileged individuals whose stories and voices are most prominent in the historical record.

Marginalization as a Loss of Individuality

This theme explores tensions evident in bioarchaeological research: the possibility of losing nuance in interpretation through subsuming individual lives into a collective whole. Population-level research provides useful insights into the past, but broadstroke interpretations of past groups can overlook the independent actors populating the scene. Osteobiographical approaches bring individuals to the fore, revealing the breadth and depth of information it is possible to glean from a single skeleton. Robb (2017) notes that osteobiographies can integrate both analytical and philosophical elements, integrating "deeply layered" osteological and cultural datasets with a broader understanding of the "material and conceptual factors in the creation of human bodies."

Individual stories are well represented in this volume and draw attention to the ways that restoring individuality to past actors expands our understanding of past lives. This is most strikingly shown by Doubek and Grauer in their discussion of the unnamed individual. His marginalized status was obvious not only in life as evidenced by his poor health, but also continued in death as he became a numbered object in a collection with no history aside from the recording of his perceived race. Focusing on his story represents an attempt to counteract the erasure of the individual that occurred when he was added to a collection as a representation of a "Chinaman," rather than as an individual with a unique story.

Similarly the stories told by Lovell and Palichuk, and Nelson are designed to highlight how problematizing marginalization acts to unpack the layers of identity that individuals may gain throughout life and death. Lovell and Palichuk discuss the dental remains of an Egyptian female, revealing her likely role as a professional craftsperson, an occupation not previously attributed to women in Ancient Egypt. Her lived experience is recorded clearly in her remains, revealing an individual life that does not match the broader social perceptions of women in Ancient Egypt.

Nelson's unique approach to the story of Lady Hudson considers how academic inquiry is itself a marginalizing force. He engages with concept that an individual could be "marginal" or separate in terms of how they are viewed archaeologically/historically. Through tracing the journey of Lady Hudson, an Egyptian mummy, after her removal from her tomb, he draws attention to the treatment of human remains in museum collections. This serves as an important reminder of the liminal space that skeletal remains occupy, as both object and individual, and how easily objectification and the resulting loss of individuality can happen. Nelson also reminds us, however, that marginalization is context dependent and one can transition through different degrees of marginalization depending on one's environment. This notion of fluctuating marginalization allows a certain degree of agency for individuals as well as providing access for researchers to influence these spaces of marginalization through returning identities to individuals and placing them within contexts.

Ultimately the individuality of marginalized individuals should inform our work. Klaus reminds us that the marginalized are not passive victims, we should expect "marginalized people...to exercise as much agency as possible" (2012, p. 37).

Marginalization: Positivity Through Difference

Marginalization is relative. The negative connotations generally associated with the term may bias our understandings of the past; the separation, insularity, or uniqueness of a particular group should not be read immediately as deleterious. In bioarchaeology, as discussed by Weiss-Krejci (2008) and Donnelly and Murphy (2008), nonnormative or seemingly "deviant" burials may appear in the archaeological record for a wide variety of reasons. It must not be assumed that an unusual burial necessarily denotes a person repudiated by their wider society. Conversely, individuals who may have suffered social stigma and marginalization during their lives may appear in expected and usual inhumations (Zuckerman, 2017). This invisible marginalization should be considered when examining seemingly "normal" burial samples. Similarly, when consulting historical data, it is important to consider multiple perspectives and to place the individual/population in context. This approach has the potential to recast social separation or deviance from the accepted norm in a positive light, depending on the individual's circumstances.

Martin's contribution on the Kayenta is an excellent example of how consideration of the context in which evidence is found can fundamentally alter our interpretations. The Kayenta were geographically marginalized, living in a harsh environment without monumental architecture or complex material culture. In the archaeological context, more prolific populations with more impressive material culture were viewed as more socially complex. However, Martin challenges the association between simple material culture and decreased social complexity, drawing attention instead to the details of their cultural interactions and framing their marginalized lifestyle as adaptive, rather than a consequence of segregation. In doing so she also calls attention to the historical preference of archaeologists to intentionally avoid further study of marginalized groups with "unimpressive" material culture, in essence furthering their marginalization through scholarly disinterest.

Lovell and Palichuk also raise the idea of marginalization as a positive force. The Egyptian woman they analyze was likely a professional craftsperson, an arena dominated by men. Craft specialization was a respected profession in Ancient Egypt; while her sex would have separated her from her contemporaries, it is likely she would have experienced some positive gains in status through her occupation. The identification of her skeletal changes as related to her profession also allows archaeologists to return to her the status that she had in life, which was not preserved after her death. She serves as a reminder that differences based upon class and sex may act as marginalizing forces, but that consideration of multiple perspectives is needed to understand how marginalization was actually experienced by individuals.

Marginalization as a Divorce From Context or a Process of Forgetting

Postmortem marginalization hinges upon the actions of the living. An individual may appear to have lost their identity or voice due to the fact that modern researchers do not have enough archaeological and/or historical context to place them in the past. This paucity of evidence may be due to excavation bias or a lack of surviving documentary evidence. The cliché states that *history is written by the victors*, and this sentiment must be considered when studying the past. A lack of scholarship on specific groups does not necessarily indicate a lack of interest in these groups or a lack of potentially rich scholastic opportunities.

Battles addresses the importance of considering the relationship between historical authors, their perception of events, and the actual events themselves. The context of the polio epidemic in New Zealand was manipulated by historical authors, who chose to highlight certain events and minimize others, leading to polio being subsumed into wartime fears and prejudices. Polio, and by extension those who survived or were affected by the disease, was marginalized by this collective process of forgetting that slowly removed polio from the public memory. Seeking out the spaces where events have been misremembered, through a careful reading of the historical record, opens the potential for reintroducing these marginalized voices to the collective memory.

Redfern and Hefner approach the issue of collective forgetting from a different perspective, one that includes both historical authors and contemporary bioarchaeologists. The authors reflect on the difficulty of retrospectively identifying specific individuals within past populations. The primary goal of their research was to clarify the presence of individuals with Black African ancestry and to speak to their potential roles in Medieval society since a lack of scholarship exists concerning population diversity in the British Isles during this period. Their analysis suggests that population diversity in Medieval London has likely been underrepresented in primary sources, suggesting that ancestry analysis and intersectionality theory may provide a way forward in better understanding the lives and identities of previously silent historical individuals.

Clark and colleagues discuss the marginalization of Indigenous Canadian voices through settler appropriation of their ancestors' stories. Their contribution describes the successful use of a community-based partnership to bring material culture and the associated interpretation back under the control of Indigenous peoples. This collaborative project fostered a collective remembering that returned material objects and human remains to the spaces and places where they could be contextualized and ideally act to demarginalize these voices. Through recognizing the historical effects of systemic, institutionalized marginalization, archaeology has the potential to contribute to the restoration of Indigenous voices being the authors of Indigenous history.

These chapters cast marginalization as both a process and a product, an embodied force, that is the result of a nexus of political, social, economic, and environmental factors. They remind us that engaging with marginalization demands the asking of difficult questions, most importantly: who are we missing? Recognizing these holes in the tapestry of our history is the first step in creating a more holistic understanding of the past. Hackett and colleagues remind us that the past represents more than a static recording of history; by using the appropriate tools we can gain important information for preventing and managing health issues in the present. The papers presented here illustrate a variety of ways in which anthropological approaches have been used to investigate marginalization and together they present a useful toolkit for future studies. They also remind us that marginalization is not restricted to the past and that contemporary research behaviors play a role in contributing to the marginalization of certain groups through anatomical collection creation, the treatment of skeletal remains as objects first and individuals second, the display and interpretation of history in museums, and the decision-making surrounding who and what events receive commemorative attention.

These four themes are not mutually exclusive, and it is likely that various forms of marginalization—political, social, economic, and environmental—may affect individuals throughout the life course. The complexity of this topic necessitates the interweaving of disparate forms of contextual data in order to begin to approach an understanding of the forces of marginalization on individuals and the populations they comprise. This volume has only scratched the surface of this critical topic for bioarchaeological and historical studies of the past. It is our hope that further applications of intersectionality theory and other synthetic approaches will aid in the untangling of the various threads whose warp and weft create the complicated tapestry of marginalization, representing its embodied and diachronic processes.

References

Donnelly, C. J., & Murphy, E. M. (2008). The origins of *cillini´* in Ireland. In E. M. Murphy (Ed.), *Deviant burial in the archaeological record* (pp. 191–223). Oxford: Oxbow Books.

Hall, J. M., Stevens, P. E., & Meleis, A. I. (1994). Marginalization: A guiding concept for valuing diversity in nursing knowledge development. *Advances in Nursing Science*, *16*(4), 23–41.

Klaus, H. D. (2012). The bioarchaeology of structural violence: A theoretical model and a case study. In D. L. Martin, R. P. Harrod, & V. R. Pérez (Eds.), *The bioarchaeology of violence* (pp. 29–62). Gainesville: University Press of Florida.

Robb, J. (2017). Osteobiography: A conceptual framework. In *Presented at the 81st annual meeting of the society for American Archaeology*, Vancouver, BC. 2017 (tDAR id: 430621).

Tucker, M. (1990). Director's forward. In R. L. Ferguson (Ed.), *Out there: Marginalization and contemporary cultures* (pp. 19–38). Cambridge, MA: MIT Press.

Weiss-Krejci, E. (2008). Unusual life, unusual death and the fate of the corpse: A case study from Dynastic Europe. In E. M. Murphy (Ed.), *Deviant burial in the archaeological record* (pp. 169–190). Oxford: Oxbow Books.

Zuckerman, M. K. (2017). The "poxed" and the "pure": A bioarchaeological investigation of community and marginalization relative to infection with acquired syphilis in post-medieval London. *Archeological Papers of the American Anthropological Association*, *28*(1), 91–103.

Index

Note: Page numbers followed by "*f*" and "*t*" refer to figures and tables, respectively.

G

H

I

J

K

L

M

T

U

V

W

X

Z

FSC
www.fsc.org
MIX
Papier | Fördert gute Waldnutzung
FSC® C083411

Kolibri 360 GmbH
Ferdinand-Jühlke-Straße 7
99095 Erfurt, Deutschland
produktsicherheit@kolibri360.de